CALLIN' OUT AROUND THE WORLD

A Motown Reader

Edited by Kingsley Abbott

foreword by Martha Reeves

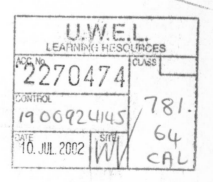

Helter
Skelter
Publishing

This edition published in 2001 by Helter Skelter Publishing
4 Denmark Street, London WC2H 8LL

Design by Bold; typesetting by Caroline Walker

Printed by The Bath Press

Every effort has been made to contact the copyright holders of the articles and photographs in this book, but one or two were unreachable. The publishers would be grateful if the writers concerned would contact Helter Skelter Publishing.

A CIP record for this book is available from the British Library

ISBN 1-900924-14-5

Dedicated to the memory of Roger Heal whose talent and love of music affected everyone he met.

Also to the memories of Blondie and Dusty, both sadly missed

Contents

Part 3

Appendices

Foreword
by Martha Reeves

Martha meets British fans at a fan club reception.

After being drilled and pre-warned that the weather might be cold, damp and foggy, we're headed for the *United Kingdom*, the Mother Country. The land that we had only dreamed of visiting is now suddenly a reality. Rosalind and Betty are here at the airport ahead of time, and as we stood sharing thoughts of anticipation, fear, excitement, the other artists gather.

We prepared for the long airplane ride. Our hearts pounded faster as the countdown began before departure time. British Airways had kindly people dressed in blue, who were very helpful in giving us the proper forms and checking passports. The Miracles – William (Smokey) Robinson, Claudette, Ron White, Bobby Rogers, Pete Moore, Marv Tarplin and their drummer Spike – all arrived together, and eased our tension by being calm and relaxed, as they were always our mentors.

My parents Ruby and Elijah (now deceased) needed to meet with the leaders of the tour, and changed their busy schedules to see me off. I had my package of food, just in case we needed reserves. They were nervous, but tried not to show it. They always encouraged me, and sent me off to do my best. Mrs. Esther Edwards assured them that we would do well in the care of Mrs. Ardena Johnson and Mrs. Evelyn Johnson, our chaperones, and Booker Bradshaw the tour manager. The Temptations – David Ruffin, Eddie Kendricks, Paul Williams, Otis Williams and Melvin Franklin – were busy saying goodbye to their host of loved ones. The Supremes showed up, and there was Berry Gordy with Florence, Diane and Mary in a huddle near the gate. As Stevie Wonder, Clarence Paul and his tutor Ted Hull arrived, we formed a line to get on board. Marvin Gaye, his wife Anna, and Eddie Bongo were there finally. We made a head count, and were all present and accounted for, including all of Earl Van Dyke's 'Cats' – Uriel Jones, Eddie Willis, Robert White, Tony Newton and Thomas 'Beans' Bowles.

I had been honoured to make Dusty Springfield's acquaintance, and what came from a purposed introduction at the Brooklyn Fox Theatre in New York was a genuine friendship and her invitation to join her on her TV Special. It was a kind and generous gesture that certified our mutual admiration. When she and Vicki Wickham staged her broadcast and wrote us all in the script, she featured us and gave us a place in history by introducing the Motown Sound.

We had toured the U.K. with Georgie Fame a year before, and we re-visited small quaint villages, cobblestone roads and roundabouts. We'd see two-laned roads with farmland, and rolling hills always green with farm animals on every side. Then we'd pass through large cities filled with shops, clock towers and magnificent churches. Every once in a while we would see signs of the past war, with blackened walls and crumpled structures, a reminder of past times. The tour bus sailed us to wonderful gatherings of music lovers, fans and friends who welcomed us and our music. London, Dingwalls, Birmingham, the Odeon Theatres, Liverpool, Manchester, Leeds, The Motorway, Fish and Chips (in newspaper), Big Ben at twelve o'clock midnight, The Crown Jewels, The Subway, Trafalgar Square and Hyde Park are all my first recollections. I could go on, but there are far too many to mention.

This arrival at Heathrow Airport was comparable to the greeting received by the Beatles when they toured America. The serious time difference kept me in a dream-like trance, but the cheering and calling of our names was sensational. The flash of cameras was blinding and, before we could touch the ground, we were prompted to "Dance In The Street" with arms full of flowers. The Motown Appreciation Society met us with flowers and banners of welcome. Dave Godin had rounded up all the members, and we knew that the first Motown Revue was on!

Every visit is always one of wonder, and we have witnessed the growth and changes. The biggest thrill however are the audiences that fill to the brim the many venues that have opened their hearts and doors to accommodate our Soul Music. Every time I hear or sing "Forget Me Not", I get sentimental and know that I no longer have to stay "In My Lonely Room". I look forward to seeing England time and time again.

Love and God Bless

Martha Reeves
Detroit, Michigan.
4th October 1999

Editor's Introduction

*The tiny backstage room at London's Marquee Club in Wardour Street. (l-r rear: Clarence Paul,
Virginia's sister (fan/friend), Stevie Wonder, Virginia (fan/friend), Chris Lorimer.
l-r front: Kingsley Abbott, Enid Buckland-Evers, Hamilton Bohannon (road drummer on that tour).*

I sat on the edge of a bed in a room at the Cumberland Hotel overlooking London's
Marble Arch. The room was not large, just a regular hotel room that Stevie could nego-
tiate with ease. He had been staying there for one night, but it was evident that he had
already mentally mapped the whole room. We talked about the tour for a while, but gradually moved on to general teenage boys conversation, comparing notes on schooling and
youth in our differing environments. Any nerves I had dissolved fast, as we laughed
about daft things, and, at his insistence, made what seemed at the time to be outlandish
demands of room service. This was to be one of several visits that I would make to the
hotel, often before accompanying a small entourage to a London or nearby club date. I
was there by dint of the title that I proudly proclaimed to anyone who would listen:
Secretary of The Stevie Wonder Fan Club of Great Britain. This grand title gave me
access to visiting Motown artists, through the good offices of the accompanying tour
managers or local EMI artist liaison staff. It gave access to some wonderful experiences,
concerts, TV shows and laughs with some very, very lovely people.

As a sixteen year old, I was a record collector of some three years standing. My tastes
were wide and varied. Nowadays they would be called eclectic, but school-friends usually called them weird. I was definitely attracted to what I now know to be Doo-Wop, to
vocal harmony groups and to almost anything with saxophones. I loved American music,
and scoured release sheets to identify US based labels, and those UK based ones that
would regularly release American product. Anything suffixed with –ettes, -elles, or –els
would immediately gain my attention. I was quickly aware that most other kids around
me did not share my passion, but a few kindred spirits did emerge to swop information
and to lend records. Through the weekly record magazines, I became aware of, and
joined, the Kent based Tamla Motown Appreciation Society. Here was a small group of
like-minded enthusiasts who had banded together for the love and promotion of a certain
sort of music. They even managed to hold meetings and gatherings to which the artists
themselves would come! This sort of contact was unusual then, and in many quarters

even more unusual now. The Motown artists that I met at the time were genuinely surprised and delighted that they got such a positive reaction from white kids in Britain, and they treated us with openness, interest and kindness. The club was active at a time when people in Britain, partly through the musical repertoires of the new wave of beat groups, were beginning to wake up to the wealth of black American music. British record charts were still broadly reflective of mainstream Tin Pan Alley product, but here and there certain black sounds and influences were breaking through. The club scene led the way, with The Flamingo in London's Wardour Street at the head of the pack. As well as their regular disc nights, these clubs were the only places to see any visiting American or Caribbean acts that ventured to these shores.

The standard and quality of Motown records that reached British ears in the earliest days was already unmistakable, though somewhat rough hewn compared to the product of the mid to late sixties. Initially Motown product appeared on a variety of labels in this country through the various licensing deals that existed at that time. Berry Gordy sought out any avenue for his records at first, and it was only later, as the sales showed potential, that he was able to make deals with EMI. All this release activity was followed avidly by members of the Tamla Motown Appreciation Society. It was quickly evident that the senior members of TMAS were to be revered, as they talked intelligently about records that I had never heard of. I was without doubt at junior clerk level, but enthusiastic enough to take part in as many of the London based events as I could. This was evidently noted by Dave Godin and the upper echelons of TMAS as, when in late 1964 Detroit decreed that they would like separate UK fan clubs for each of the artists, I was offered the job of taking on Stevie Wonder. For would-be fan club heads waiting to see which artists they were allocated, it was, I suppose, akin to potential cabinet ministers waiting to see which departments they would get in a new government. I did not expect to get any of the real glamour outfits, but Stevie was obviously to be a challenge as he was at that time the least known of the main acts, and had released a series of records that had made him difficult to categorise.

The Motown Revue had visited our shores with variable results, but by the '64/5 period the Motown organisation had been convinced that the way forward was with individual artist promotional tours. My real involvement was during this period, and it was on such quick tours that I got to know Stevie better than the other artists, although the delightful Martha and The Vandellas ran a close second. The Tamla Motown label was established as a separate entity by a monolithic EMI, who were hardly known for such radical steps. However, it did give the group of artists and labels a distinctive packaging for the British market, through which the individual acts could be developed. The percentage of hits in Britain was excellent, with The Supremes, The Four Tops and the Miracles leading the way. Whilst early promotion was scarce, the publicity machine now exuded a confidence that reflected the overall growth of Berry Gordy's empire. Hits on both sides of the Atlantic flowed easily, and even those records that missed chart action showed that the company had a real strength and depth.

This book comes about from my abiding love of that early Motown music, and of those early times when such superb artists could be seen in small, sweaty clubs (at that stage around London and the Home Counties) playing to people who simply loved the sounds. Accordingly the book purposefully errs towards a broadly British perspective, and unashamedly concentrates on 'The Golden Era' of the sixties. The book's purpose is to re-visit a wonderful era with a selection of new and previously published pieces from a variety of sources that will be of interest to both the casual and hardcore fan, both British and worldwide. I have placed the pieces within three sections: firstly with overview pieces about the growth of Motown generally and specifically in Britain, secondly with articles on the main sixties artists and musicians, and thirdly with more details about the records and concerts. Lastly I present some appendices which I hope will help to maintain an interest in collecting and listening to the music of Motown. Interspersed amongst the main articles and interviews are germane quotes and individual writers' choices of records from the relevant period. This goes some way to moulding the book into a reference book to be returned to time and time again.

The job of the editor of such a collection is to guide the overall feel of the book by searching out the best people to fulfil the sections as planned. Each main inclusion is given a brief introduction by way of explaining its place in the whole. The book has been gently shaped with ongoing discussions with Sean Body at Helter Skelter Publishing, whose interest has made it all possible. I was aware that I wanted this book to be different from earlier Motown publications to justify a place on collectors' bookshelves, as well as being full enough to earn a purchase from other buyers. Whilst there was a need for a certain amount of basic information, I had to open up some new avenues as well. The aim is to make the content equally accessible and interesting to older Motown fans, wider ranging soul fans, and students of pop music in general. To achieve this, I have tried to balance British and American written pieces to achieve a book that places the development of Motown and its artists in the social and musical context of the sixties. I also hope that even the most assiduous of collectors will find something new. The addition of some photos adds to this, as there are items from my own, and Dave Godin's, collection that have never been seen. As an added bonus, I was delighted when Martha Reeves agreed to write a special foreword to the book with her very personal memories of Motown's early encounters with British shores.

Even when I had whittled down my long list of favourite articles, I had the difficult task of contacting the relevant authors. It took a seemingly endless series of phone calls. Some enquiries come to dead ends, but others produced unexpected extra goodies. To everyone that I have encountered in this way, I give my sincere thanks for their enthusiasm and practical help. My thanks are due to the writers who have allowed us to use their work: Joe McEwan, Jim Miller, Michael Goldberg, Dave Marsh, Brian Ward, Bill Dahl, Carl Lozito, Paul Zollo, David Cole, John Rockwell, Mike Critchley, Nick Brown, Dave Rimmer, Tim Brown, Jim Stewart, Peter Doggett, Steve Towne, and for the permissions that have come through publishers for pieces by Adam White, Bill Millar, Michael Heatley, Max Oates and Gerri Hershey. My thanks also go to all the Motown artists and staff who have spoken to me for the book. Without exception they have been generous with their time and memories. In some cases it was delightful to renew old friendships, and in others it was the making of new friends. Esther Edwards and her staff at The Motown Museum, the late Beans Bowles, Cindy Birdsong and Maxine Powell have all helped specifically.

Fuller support has come from many people in a variety of ways: Adam White for help beyond the call of duty, Timothy White for his top ten and kind words, Derek Everett for a delightful long lunchtime conversation, Sharon Davis for encouragement and reminiscences, Mike Critchley and David Cole for providing a wealth of interesting material, Bill Randle for some great insight-packed interviews, Bill Barran for helping with contacts and advice, John Reed for further contacts and suggestions, Carol Kaye for her enthusiasm, photocopies of her journals and her memories, and Tamsin Heaser for collage and memorabilia photography. There also exists a box of names and miscellaneous hastily scribbled notes representing many other people who I phoned along the way. Thank you one and all.

A separate mention must go to Dave Godin whose part in the whole Motown story on these shores cannot be underestimated. It was Dave in the early sixties who raised my interest from a casual but interested observer to an active participant in the promotion of black music. His interest in this project has been central, and I thank him for all the time he has spent with me helping it to fruition. I also remember fondly my partners in the early visits to London clubs to see American Soul Acts: Chris Scott, Enid Buckland-Evers and Chris Lorimer.

Special thanks must go to Martha Reeves for consenting to write the foreword to this book. Having seen her perform many times from the sixties up to a few months ago, she is a lady that I have the utmost respect for as a performer and as a strong, principled woman. It was a real pleasure to renew my acquaintance with her. I was lucky enough to meet most of the other early Motown stars as they were making their way, and I thank them all for their kindness, endless smiles and enthusiasm. I also salute Berry Gordy and his staff for making a dream into an amazing reality. It seems that it never would have happened in such a cohesive way without his drive, talents and vision.

Finally, thanks go to Sean Body and all at Helter Skelter for publishing the results and enthusing all the way, and to Elaine, Rosie, Ian, Luke and Molly for putting up with the disruption which took so many forms in so many rooms.

Kingsley Abbott
Norfolk, England,
December 2000

PART 1

Dave Godin's trip to Hitsville. (l-r: Harvey Fuqua, Iris Gordy, DG, and The Vandellas.)

1

Motown

by Joe McEwen and Jim Miller

Rolling Stone *magazine has been responsible over the years for some of the best in-depth music journalism that has ever been written. This article, which serves as an excellent introductory piece for this reader, comes from* The Rolling Stone Illustrated History of Rock & Roll *which was published in 1992. Containing fifteen new chapters, rewrites, revisions and additions to the original 1976 edition, this 700 page book should be on everyone's wants list. The writers cover all the expected themes for a history of Motown, and introduce us to the key characters.*

Sandwiched among a row of modest private homes and professional enterprises like Sykes Hernia Control and Your Fair Lady Boutique and Wig Room, the white bungalow at 2648 West Grand Boulevard in Detroit is distinguished only by a large sign proclaiming it HITSVILLE, U.S.A. The two-storey frame structure with the angular jutting picture window, along with a cluster of nearby houses is the home of Berry Gordy's Motown Records, currently the country's hottest hitmakers.

Shortly after 9 a.m. on a warm morning in June 1965, songwriter-producer Lamont Dozier strolls in, ignoring the company time clock that used to govern his paycheck. Company president Gordy rushes from his office to tell Lamont that Motown needs a quick follow-up to the Four Tops' "I Can't Help Myself," the label's second Number One pop hit in less than a month (Dozier had helped write and produce the other as well: The Supremes' "Back In My Arms Again"). The Tops had recorded for Columbia before their Motown association, and Gordy explains that the New York label has just released an old record in an attempt to cash in on the group's current success.

Dozier nods and walks down the corridor, past closet-sized offices where groups and producers rehearse material. Lamont's partners, Brian Holland and Eddie Holland, are already in their cubicle, sketching out a preliminary arrangement that bears more than a passing resemblance to the Four Tops' current smash. Lamont Dozier sits down at the piano and smooths out some rough edges in the melody line; all three contribute to the lyric. By noon the song is complete, and the trio take their finished work into the studio, where the Four Tops run down the lyrics while Earl Van Dyck's band negotiates the changes. Later that afternoon the track will have been recorded and the Tops' vocals added. Within three days the record will be on the streets, the pick hit at local soul station WCHB. The Columbia disc is quickly forgotten and by August "It's The Same Old Song" by the Four Tops hits Number Five on the *Billboard* pop chart.

The success of Motown Records is almost entirely attributable to one man: Berry Gordy. A former boxer and onetime record-store owner, Gordy, through a combination of pugnacious panache, shrewd judgement and good taste, became the mogul of the most profitable black music concern in the world.

It all began in Detroit in the early Fifties. When Gordy's record store specializing in jazz went bankrupt, he decided to redirect his musical money-making interests to the burgeoning field of rhythm and blues. While supporting himself with a series of odd jobs, Gordy began writing songs for local R&B acts. At first his amateur efforts failed miserably; but he soon acquired a local reputation as a songwriter, producer and hustler. In those days Gordy would write songs for a performer, cut a demo tape and then take the finished masters to New York, where he would try to peddle his product for a 5-percent royalty on net sales. Unfortunately, even when somebody purchased his masters, they were never promoted properly and if they did sell, royalties were rarely accounted for.

It was a tough racket, but Gordy persevered. His first break came in 1957 when Brunswick Records bought a song he had written, called "Reet Petite,"' for Jackie Wilson. "Reet Petite" was a pop hit, and though his profit only amounted to $1000, several successful follow-ups for Wilson and Brunswick soon established Berry Gordy as Detroit's leading songwriter. But that was not enough: Gordy was determined to produce and market his own music himself.

The Motown mythology has it that Berry Gordy, fresh off an automobile assembly line, borrowed $800 to start his company. In truth, by 1959 Gordy was a prospering songwriter; he first borrowed money not to start a label, but to go into independent production.

At the time, he had his eye on a local singer named Marv Johnson. Their first joint effort, "Come To Me", was leased to United Artists, and although it was only a modest hit (Number 30 on the pop chart), it gave an indication of where Gordy was headed.

The song itself was slight: simple lyrics set to a stock rock chord progression (compare Gordy's smash hit for Wilson, "Lonely Teardrops"). But to accompany Johnson, who followed in the gospel footsteps of Clyde McPhatter and Wilson, Gordy added a churchy female chorus for some call-and-response trades (shades of Ray Charles) and a bubbling male bassman (shades of Clyde McPhatter's "A Lover's Question" on Atlantic). Instrumentally, the record was anchored by a persistent baritone sax and tambourine, with a flute break in the middle (recalling Bobby Day's "Rockin' Robin"). The result was a clean R&B record that sounded as white as it did black.

Gordy perfected this gospel-pop fusion in the two months that followed, and by 1960 he'd made two similarly styled Top Ten hits with Johnson, "You Got What It Takes" and "I Love The Way You Love". After leasing yet another single, "Money" by Barrett Strong, to Anna, a label owned by one of his sisters, Gordy decided to form his own label, Tammie, soon changed to Tamla Records.

It wasn't surprising that the first Tamla hit of any size belonged to a vocal group called the Miracles. Gordy had discovered the quintet working in Detroit. Although initially attracted by the group's only female member, Claudette – the lead singer's girlfriend – Gordy quickly realised the potential of the Miracles' main songwriter, Smokey Robinson, who also happened to be the lead singer. He leased a few Miracles sides to Chess Records in 1959, but it was with "Way Over There" on Tamla in 1960 that the group (and label) began to sell records: 60,000 on that release. In a few months that would seem like chicken feed.

As a follow-up to "Way Over There," Robinson came up with a song called "'Shop Around". Gordy found the first master too sluggish and called the Miracles back into the studio at three o'clock one morning, to cut a new version at a faster tempo. The result was Tamla's first real hit; by January, "Shop Around" had reached Number Two on the pop chart, and Gordy's company was in the black.

The little bungalow on West Grand was soon teeming with activity as a host of aspiring local singers and songwriters flocked to Gordy's studio. With Robinson and Gordy handling the bulk of composing and producing, Tamla and Gordy's growing family of labels (Motown and Gordy were formed in the next two years, later to be joined by Soul, V.I.P. and Rare Earth) began to log an impressive track record, their hits ranging from Eddie Holland's slick "Jamie" to the Contours' raunchy "Do You Love Me?" By the end of 1962 the Gordy roster included Mary Wells, the Marvelettes and Marvin Gaye.

Although several of these acts, particularly Mary Wells and the Marvelettes, made consistent inroads onto the pop chart, Motown's early productions differed markedly in feel and appeal, depending on who was doing the singing. Mary Wells cooed seductive lyrics, the Marvelettes declaimed the girl-group sound, while Marvin Gaye and the Contours both rasped over rotgut rhythm tracks only one step removed from rural blues and gospel. Motown had hits, all right; but it hadn't quite yet evolved a distinctive sound.

From the beginning Berry Gordy relied on a handful of dependable writers and producers. In late 1961 he began to expand his staff of writer-producers, and among the new additions was Lamont Dozier, a veteran of the local group scene who toiled in relative anonymity at Motown for a couple of years until he began a creative partnership with Motown cohorts Brian and Eddie Holland. Two years later the fledgling trio of writers clicked. Working with Martha and the Vandellas, the Holland-Dozier-Holland team set out to refine and systematise the production techniques Gordy had pioneered with Marv Johnson. "Heat Wave," by Martha and the Vandellas, inaugurated a three year stretch that saw the H-D-H amass twenty-eight Top Twenty pop hits.

As soul producers, they were little short of revolutionary. The trio rarely used standard song forms, opting instead for a simpler, more direct, *ababcc* pattern, anchored by an endless refrain of the song's hook line. The effect of this cyclical structure was cumulative, giving Holland-Dozier-Holland productions a compulsive momentum. Even better, the constant refrains and consistent use of repetition helped make their hits ubiquitous: after you'd heard one, you'd heard them all – and each and every one of them was immediately familiar, subtly distinctive and quite unforgettable.

The trio's lyrics were nothing to write home about. But what mattered was their sense of structure and the musical devices they used to animate that structure. Following Gordy's lead, Holland-Dozier-Holland exploited gospelish vocal gestures in a pop context, now defined by their own streamlined approach. If the vocalists provided the emotion, the band mounted a non-stop percussive assault highlighted by a "hot" mix, with shrill, hissing cymbals and a booming bass – anything to make a song jump out of a car radio. With tambourines rattling to a blistering 4/4 beat, the H-D-H sound, introduced on "Heat Wave" and perfected on records like the Four Tops' "Reach Out, I'll Be There" and the Supremes' "You Can't Hurry Love" (both from 1966), came to epitomise what Motown would call "The Sound of Young America".

"Heat Wave" and the arrival of Holland-Dozier Holland kicked Motown into high gear. By the late Sixties Gordy's company had become one of the biggest black-owned corporations in America, as well as one of the most phenomenally successful independent recording ventures in history. Motown succeeded beyond anyone's wildest expectations, and did so with black people controlling the company at the technical, musical and artistic levels.

The reasons behind Motown's popularity are diverse. Overseeing the whole operation was Berry Gordy, who endorsed the old bromide for predictable success: Keep it simple. Under his tutelage, Motown's musicians took the concept of formula pop to a new level of sophistication and, thanks to the music's gospel-blues roots, visceral intensity.

The formulas might have quickly become tedious, of course, were it not for the ingenuity of Gordy's stable of producer-songwriters. Smokey Robinson, who handled the early Temptations and Mary Wells, in addition to the Miracles, was able to transfigure the most banal romantic motifs with clever lyrics and catchy hook lines; Norman Whitfield, who worked extensively with the Temptations as well as Marvin Gaye and Gladys Knight, was able to go beyond R&B cliches with punchy melodies and arrangements and topical lyrics; such latecomers as Nicholas Ashford and Valerie Simpson, who produced the Marvin Gaye/Tammi Terrell duets as well as Diana Ross' early solo records were able to amplify secularized gospel lyrics with grandiose orchestral settings; and finally, Holland-Dozier-Holland did nothing less than make The Formula a work of art in itself.

And then there was the Motown house band, some of the best R&B musicians in the Sixties. The Motown rhythm section, which included Benny Benjamin on drums, James

Jamerson on bass, Joe Messina on guitar, Earl Van Dyke on keyboards, James Giddons on percussion and Robert White on guitar, developed a unique dexterity, and adaptability. Jamerson left his own mark on the music (the explosive bass line on Marvin Gaye and Tammi Terrell's "Ain't No Mountain High Enough" could have come from no one else) and has influenced scores of bassists since. Their existence was hardly glamorous however. Usually paid a flat salary, the Motown musicians toiled in relative obscurity; where Memphis soulmen Booker T. & The MGs cut instrumental hits, Earl Van Dyke and the Soul Brothers played small lounges near West Grand for a few-dollars, free pizza and the applause of local patrons. In the morning, it was back to the nine-to-five grind.

Indeed, the assembly line atmosphere had something to do with Motown's success. If nothing else, it enabled Berry Gordy to keep tabs on his empire. He called his direction "quality control"; often, second-string Motown acts would have virtually no public exposure for months at a time while their recordings were polished to Gordy's satisfaction.

Even popular performers found themselves restricted, as well as aided, by the Motown hit machine. Gordy's innate caution dictated follow-ups that only slightly altered the elements of the previous hit; a formula was mined until it was commercially exhausted. Thus "Heat Wave" reached Number Four on the pop charts; its sound-alike successor, "Quicksand," got up to Number Eight – and only after the third go-around, when "Live Wire" stalled at Number Forty-two, did Martha and the Vandellas get the opportunity to try something different.

Gordy's cultivation of Motown's image was equally restrictive. As soon as the company domination of Top Forty pop and soul was clear, Gordy hustled his star acts into "class" venues like the Copa, the Latin Casino, Las Vegas or bust. As if to confer respectability upon his artists, he encouraged albums such as *The Four Tops On Broadway* and *The Temptations In A Mellow Mood*. Finally, Gordy's artist management division, International Talent Management Incorporated (I.T.M.), included a kind of finishing school for Motown stars. Here, an artist learned how to sit, walk and talk and even how to smoke a cigarette with grace and elegance. Above all, Motown's flock was taught the good manners any adult member of the white middle class would expect to see exhibited at a swank nightclub.

Motown's roots may have been in gospel and blues, but its image was purely one of upward mobility and clean, wholesome fun (Gordy's vision of "Young America"). Motown's stars were groomed to offend no one; the songs they sang were equipped with romantic lyrics that could appeal to practically anyone; and the music itself was rarely demanding, or even aggressive in the tradition of Southern soul. Martha and the Vandellas' "Dancing In The Street" (1964) may have been interpreted by black activist-poet LeRoi Jones as an evocation of revolutionary times, but the closest thing to an overt political statement released by Motown in the mid-Sixties was Stevie Wonder's "Blowin' In The Wind" (1966). (Of course, ever sensitive to changing fashions, Motown eventually hopped onto the political – and even psychedelic – bandwagon, with such 1970 hits as the Temptations' "Psychedelic Shack" and Edwin Starr's "War," both Norman Whitfield compositions.)

One statistic gives eloquent testimony to Gordy's success in courting the white market. In 1966 Motown's "hit ratio" – the percentage of records released that made the national charts – was nothing less than 75 percent. It was an appropriately awesome achievement for a truly astonishing record company.

Although its hits have occasionally been dismissed on grounds of monotony, the truth of the matter is that Motown, even in its assembly-line prime, released a remarkably diverse lot of records, varying in sound, arrangement and feel. While Berry Gordy dictated the overall direction and the producers and studio musicians stamped the sound, it was the performers themselves who ultimately conveyed the Motown image.

To the outside world, Motown seemed like one big happy family. While a number of

Motown stars have confirmed the accuracy of this picture in the early Sixties, by the middle of the decade serious problems had begun to appear. The autocratic determination that had carried Gordy's company to the top could not help but foster resentment, especially as Gordy's proteges became used to their status in the limelight.

Yet the company continued to control virtually every relevant detail of a performer's career, dictating the songs to be sung, the producers to be used, the singles to be released, the image to be presented to the public. Even Motown's biggest stars remained curiously nondescript; reliable biographical details were few and far between. In financial affairs, Gordy governed his flock with patronising authority: his younger stars were kept on allowance, ostensibly to help them avoid the pitfalls that had left other nouveau riche R&B stars penniless at thirty.

His attitude toward the Supremes was typical. "We had some trouble with them a first," Gordy said in 1966. "You must be very strict with young artists. That instills discipline. But once they get a Number One record, they tend to get more independent. They start spending their money extravagantly … After a year, they saw their mistakes and came to appreciate our handling of their affairs".

Though their yearly income was in the five figures – record royalties were divided equally – they were on an allowance of $500 a week.

In late 1967 the first major crack appeared in the Motown facade. Holland, Dozier and Holland demanded an accounting of their royalties. Shortly after a suit was initiated, the trio left Motown to form their own label and production firm, a move from which neither Motown nor H-D-H ever fully recovered.

But internal dissension was not the only problem plaguing Gordy. By 1968 the industry had begun to catch up with the Motown Sound. Without Holland-Dozier-Holland, neither the Supremes nor the Four Tops were able to maintain their popularity. Even worse, the label's new properties were becoming rare; only Gladys Knight and the Jackson 5 were able to match the style and talent of earlier Motown acts. Gordy himself increasingly retreated from company affairs, choosing instead to lavish his attention on Diana Ross, who was being groomed for a career in Hollywood.

In 1971 both Stevie Wonder and Marvin Gaye negotiated contracts giving them artistic control; the same year, the company moved its headquarters from Detroit to Los Angeles. The old studio system was dissolved, and many of the old stars drifted away. By 1975 Martha Reeves, Gladys Knight, Jackson 5 and the Four Tops had all left.

The company's music, with few exceptions, was no longer particularly distinctive; its quality was increasingly erratic. In the unkindest cut of all, Gamble and Huff's Philadelphia combine finally surpassed Motown as the leading purveyor of top notch assembly-line black pop, using many of the same ingredients that Gordy had parlayed into a corporate empire.

Motown in its heyday, on the other hand, knew no peers. In the end it was a wholly mechanical style and sound that roared and purred like well-tuned Porsche. Contrived yet explosive, the very epitome of mass-produced pop yet drenched in the black tradition, the Motown hits of the Sixties revolutionised American popular music. Never again would black performers be confined to the fabled chitlin circuit; never again would black popular music be dismissed as a minority taste. For more than a decade, Berry Gordy and his many talented cohorts managed, with unerring verve and against all odds, to translate a black idiom into "The Sound of Young America".

Motown Quotes I

"I was basically a dreamer of love songs, and that's what I wanted to write, too.

But wanting to write love songs and also living in the real world – in what is called the ghetto now – and listening to the earthy problems of life, I tried to mix that in with the love and the feeling" *Berry Gordy*

"We started Motown with a record called 'Come To Me' on an artist named Marv Johnson. Berry had this apartment on the west side of Detroit, and we used to go and rehearse with Marv, with the back-up singers and with Berry playing the piano." *Smokey Robinson*

"When we started, we were 17 or 18 years old, just kids really. Being a creative person himself, Berry could understand creative people and – this is important – recognise talent in the raw. Some of the people at Motown had great talent and only needed a chance to grow. Others were just marginal talents that he stuck with." *Eddie Holland*

"Probably Berry Gordy's best talent was that he set fire to people around him and he'd set fire to your ass to where you felt you had to live up to something and if you didn't do it, he'd do it. He'd kick your ass." *George Clinton*

"At the end of the month Berry would bring in the neighbourhood junior-high school and high school kids for soft drinks and sandwiches and play all the tapes. And whatever artist got the strongest reaction, that would be the next release. Nine times out of ten, it would be a hit record." *Joe Billingslea of The Contours*

2
Interview With Dave Godin
by Kingsley Abbott

One of the 'reception committees' at London's Heathrow Airport, obviously post "Stop In The Name Of Love"! (l-r: unknown, Chris Scott, Kingsley Abbott, Greg ?, unknown, Mick Page, Roy ?, Dave Godin, Enid Buckland-Evers, Enid's friend?)

As soon as I began to list the elements that I considered necessary for inclusion in this book, the name of Dave Godin was top of the list. He ran the legendary Tamla Motown Appreciation Society, and as such he was the person who was largely responsible for my own introduction to Motown music back in 1963/4. He prompted me to become more involved when he entrusted me with the running of Stevie Wonder's fan club when TMAS was split up. His role in the developing acceptance and interest in Motown, and indeed black American music in general, was paramount. As well as his own efforts with the Tamla Motown Appreciation Society, he wrote a regular column for Blues And Soul, *helped with radio broadcasts and ran Soul City both as a shop and a record label. His most recent efforts have been incredibly well received with the release of his CD series on Ace Records of Deep Soul Treasures. We discussed at length as to how he might contribute to the book, eventually settling on an interview format. Our conversations often wandered happily off track, but what follows is his response to the questions that seemed to be most germane to a project of this nature. Renewing our acquaintance has been one of the joys of working on the book.*

Kingsley Abbott: *What were the very first Motown artists or records that you were aware of?*
Dave Godin: That's interesting. Well, let me see, it must have been Barrett Strong's "Money" and then The Miracles' "Shop Around". But they were just good R&B records that came out on the London American label here. I didn't realise at the time that they

went together in any way. London was unique in the U.K. then, as it was the conduit through which all good American records seemed to come at that stage. The first one that I remember being really special was The Marvelettes with "Please Mr. Postman'. That was a cracking record, and it had a special little shop display with it that had half featuring The Marvelettes and half with someone else. I begged the shop to give it to me when they were done with it, which they did. The photo of the group had the five original members in it. Much later on, I met Brian Holland and his wife. She told me how excited he had been about that record and how he had come home one day and played the song to her on the piano. She thought that it was a cacophony then with him singing it! She understood it much better when the single came out with the girls. He was sure it was a huge hit, and I reckon that he must have been working on it at the time, even though he was never credited.

Ever since I had begun to buy records in 1953, I had enjoyed female vocals, and I was a particular fan of The Chantels. Smokey Robinson told me that he had also been very influenced by them, which pleased me because I adored them. Some people thought that they weren't real R&B, as they did not have so called ethnic authenticity. But my liking of them led me to immediately pick up on The Marvelettes. After that record, which was the first out here on Fontana, there were three others on that label, including Eddie Holland's "Jamie" which I never particularly cared for, although I did really like his "Leaving Here" which didn't come out here at that time.

Then came the Oriole singles' releases and we got Mary Wells for the first time! And albums! You could hear then that there were links, and you could hear the sound. It was a DETROIT sound. The only real comparison then was with the Chess/Checker group of labels in Chicago. They issued an eclectic mix of records, but without a truly distinctive sound. Perhaps Motown was like that at first, but then they found a winning formula and ran with it.

What were your first contacts with Motown?
The Oriole releases were in full swing in 1963 bringing us more Marvelettes, The Contours with "Do You Love Me?", The Miracles, Mary Wells, as well as obscure things like Mike & The Modifiers and The Valadiers. I found the Detroit address and wrote a really long letter to Berry Gordy. It was about the soul scene in general and the fate of Black records in Britain at the time. Things had been erratic up to then, and I wrote how they really needed to develop a regular release pattern. I had started TMAS as publicity for the music. I didn't get any reply directly to my letter, until one day in 1964 when I got a multi-paged telegram. Well, telegrams in those days were usually bad news, as no one used them unless they really had to. I opened it nervously, and in it was an invitation to visit Detroit all expenses paid. I read it about six times before it sank in! Eventually the visit was set up, with some delay due to a postal strike that delayed the airline ticket they had sent, and I became the first English person to visit Motown. I went in about early summer 1964, and I was met at the airport by The Spinners, Emily Dunne and Fern Bledsoe, who were both secretaries at Motown at the time. Fern later became a member of The Fascinations. Well, don't EVER ride in a car with The Spinners!! It was a frightening experience! I didn't know them then, but Pervis was really nice. It turned out that they had been under Harvey Fuqua's wing for some while, having had a hit as early as 1961. Anyway we went straight back to Hitsville where there was a reception party out on the veranda. Everyone was there: Smokey, Claudette and others, but not The Supremes because they were low down in the hierarchy at that time. It was before they had "Where Did Our Love Go?", but I had really enjoyed two of their previous singles "Let Me Go The Right Way" and "When The Lovelight Starts Shining Thru His Eyes". Later there was a proper reception and I asked where they were. There was some embarrassment and talk about there not being enough space to invite everyone, and someone rung them to get them to come on by. They came later, and it was most interesting! Mary

was great and an up-front confident woman, and Flo was a real sweetie. But as soon as I met Diana, I had her number. It was like monster meets monster! I could see that she was going to get to the top … however she could. Later, in England, I caught her with Berry quite by chance, and it confirmed my diagnosis. I was sworn to secrecy at the time. Some time after, she refused a phone call from me, and I've never spoken to her since. She got what she wanted, but I bet she's lonely now.

What did you talk about on that trip?

They were asking *me* things. I spent some time with Berry, but in some ways it was Esther Edwards who seemed to be very powerful. She was in charge of international operations. I liked the absolute and complete trust that they seemed to show in me. Berry wanted me to help choose the next Martha & The Vandellas single. He said that they had three hot choices. I think it may have been a nice set up for me, but he played acetates of "Dancing In The Street", "Jimmy Mack" and one other that I forget now. I said how I really liked "Dancing" and thought that it could sell strongly in England. It did turn out to be the next one, and a big seller. "Jimmy Mack" of course eventually came out much later, but it was finished in early summer 1964. I took a chance to plug The Supremes to Berry as we were driving somewhere, and he told me to rummage in a pile of demos on the floor of the car to find one marked 'Supremes'. I found it and we put it into a car record player, one of those where you posted the disc like a letter into a slot. Well, the stomp intro of "Where Did Our Love Go?" hit me, and immediately I felt it was the one to break them as a big act. I was in ecstasy!

At one stage on the trip, they took me to The Playboy Club. Anna and Gwen Gordy were there, and it was the first time that I met Harvey Fuqua. I had one of his records at home that I loved, and it only dawned on me that he was the same Harvey! At the club, all I could eat was garlic bread, because I was a vegetarian. I also spent time with Emily and Marvin Gaye. After about an hour with Marvin, he struck me as an extremely lonely person. Not physically, but spiritually I mean. He was very guarded, and I had to break it all down. I don't think that he had met anyone there who had talked to him like I did.

Tell me more about how The Tamla Motown Appreciation Society started. Whilst I was a member I'd like to hear it from your point of view.

It started before the trip. I put ads in the *Record Mirror*, and spoke to all the people I knew. There was a writer at *Record Mirror* called Norman Jopling, who did really good things. He had a column called 'Great Unknowns' where he would write about many great unknown black artists. He wrote a great piece about the trip to Detroit. *Record Mirror* was the first mag later to have an R&B chart.

Anyway TMAS started to pick up members, and we eventually had between 200 and 250. I did a small mag, where I wrote the entire thing myself at first. It wasn't just Motown, because I reviewed other things like Barbara Lynn's "You'll Lose A Good Thing". I felt that the long-term goal was for the music scene to become more accepting of Black music in general, rather than Motown in particular. For instance, as I've said, Chess/Checker never quite got the level of praise that they deserved, as they were too eclectic. In some ways they were even more admirable than Motown. Incidentally, I think it was partly the pirate radio stations that were responsible for breaking Black music in this country. Some of them talked to me, and I suggested that they play things that the BBC wouldn't touch. Then if something started to sell, they could say that they were responsible.

After my visit to Detroit, Motown issued the double-sided 'Greetings' single record especially for the fans in this country. They pressed 1,000 and sent them all over, and even sent documentation to show how all the pressing masters had been destroyed after the run. I felt that it was a very special gesture to all the true fans here. They put music behind the greetings, and even included a bit of "Where Did Our Love Go?" which was at that time still unreleased!

What other TMAS activities were there?

We would try to always meet artists at London Airport. There was a network of people who would ring around as soon as we had the notification about the flights. We tried to make it a surprise for them. I suppose the biggest one was for The Supremes when they came in with Berry Gordy. We had these huge banners organised and lots of photos were taken with them. All the fans could get their photos taken with the group, The network of people were not just Motown fans, as many of them were also involved in other clubs for people like Irma Thomas, Otis Reading, James Brown and the Scepter/Wand group of artists. Once when we were meeting Irma Thomas, it happened that Wilson Pickett was coming in on the same flight. He saw all the banners for Irma, stood back and said to Irma, "It's your show girl!" He took a real back seat in the whole thing even though he was a bigger star. There was a sense of cohesion between us all. I suppose we were bound together because we felt like a beleaguered minority. There was a lot of mutual aid and a genuine liking of each other. [*Ed. As a reasonably regular attendee at such events, I can vouch for this strong bond. On one occasion I can recall being only one of three of us meeting Jimmy Ruffin, who was arriving in Britain for the first time on the strength of his "Brokenhearted" hit. It was midweek and so difficult for many to get there, and he was tremendously touched that we had made the trek out to welcome him. He insisted on spending time with us and having a drink before departing to town. We met up with him again on the trip at TV studios for some of his promo appearances.*] We would also hold some party receptions for some artists when it could be arranged.

However, it was quite soon after this that I decided that TMAS had run its course. I felt we had done what needed to be done. Maybe I started to lose a bit of interest then. With hindsight I feel perhaps that by the time of my trip to Detroit in 1964, Motown had already peaked in some ways. At that point the company was changing from family to being a corporation and that affected everything. Maybe I felt that I needed to look around for other orphans. So we split up TMAS into individual fan clubs for each artist. I looked for willing volunteers, and everyone seemed keen.

Did you stay in good contact with Motown at that point?

I did have a distinct difference of opinion with Berry Gordy about the Motown Revue coming to Britain to tour. I had said to them that I thought that they should wait awhile and get some more hits and the artists better known. I said to them that they didn't need a flop. Well, they all came and did *The Sound Of Motown* TV show, and then toured. The TV show and the London dates were great, partly because we were able to ring people and get lots to come. However, the dates in the provinces were very poorly attended. For instance, it was horrendous in Cardiff where there were more people on stage than in the audience. Berry was very pleased to be in England, even a bit smug. He thought he had the Midas touch, but the country simply wasn't ready for them. Somehow, *Billboard* was reporting that The Revue was doing wonderful business, playing to houses with standing room only. I was amazed at the reporting, because it was just naked lies! It really threw me. Berry was sulking, because he had been proved wrong, and he was blaming every-one but himself. They even added Georgie Fame to the bill to try and boost ticket sales. The tour must have lost a fortune. *Record Mirror* was still really the only paper report-ing on Motown, and they were covering the tour. The following week there was a letter in *RM* from someone saying that the British audiences didn't *have* to go and see them. No, the country really wasn't ready! So, it was then that I thought it was time to take a back seat. I mean, I liked Howlin' Wolf and Ruth Brown as much as I liked Smokey!

I formed The Friends Of American Rhythm And Blues (F.A.R.B.S.) which ran for a couple of years. We put out about three good A5 magazines. After that my next step was the Soul City record shop, which eventually turned into a record label for a while.

What were the elements of the early Motown records that really caught your ear?

[*After a pause for reflection*] The excitement. The innovative quality. The percussion use was so good. There was an equal balance between the backings and the vocals. Previously, with other companies, the vocals were right up at the expense of the backing. Motown's backings were up there cheek by cheek with the vocals. The lyrics were also so good. They broke rules. They really introduced such a strong percussive element. Once I said that it sounded as if someone was flicking chains, and that's what they were doing! Almost anything could and would have been used. One of the main tricks, that was secret at first, to boost the percussive feel was sellotaping a tambourine ring onto the top of the hi-hat. That came from Holland, Dozier and Holland, I think. I met them briefly on my trip. They were working in one of the rooms at Hitsville, and I poked my head in to say a quick hello. They were all sitting and listening to Stravinsky's *The Rite of Spring*. They said that they searched all sorts of music for ideas and inspiration.

All the Motown vocalists were so brilliant too. I had a soft spot for Mary Wells, who had such a distinctive sound. Also the lead vocalist with The Marvelettes. They were all so brilliant. What we got in Britain was the cream of the crop.

Maybe we assumed that all black records were of the same standard, which of course we found out later that they weren't. They had their fair share of duff ones too!

What about the songwriters?

I was aware early on that anything that had Smokey Robinson or Holland, Dozier and Holland on it was going to be interesting. I've always said that it was HDH that were the real sound of Motown. They were the real 'Sound Of Young America'. I think they were the creators of whatever made it special, as writers who also produced and arranged their songs. Smokey was more poetic with wonderful songs like "Tracks Of My Tears" and "Two Lovers". Smokey had more influence from Gospel, where words had more significance. He also wasn't afraid to reflect his female side, which was admirable in a hostile, homophobic world as it was then. Smokey was not ashamed to be Motown's new man. That was not HDH's bag. They were more upfront and aggressive. Smokey's voice also fed into his writing stance as well. I tended to focus on the songwriters, and not pay so much attention then to the production, partly I suppose because we didn't have the knowledge or vocabulary to describe and discuss it then.

What about the contracts that Motown artists were under? Was Berry Gordy running too tight a ship?

Motown offered contracts, they read them, and signed them. That really ends the affair.

Who do you think were the key figures apart from Berry Gordy?

Well, not to minimise others, it was Holland, Dozier, Holland that really had the pulse of young people. Their talent and contribution was so great. Aside from them, there was Smokey whose input with his writing and involvement with career direction was vital; there was Mickey Stevenson with his writing as well; there was Harvey Fuqua who also wrote and produced. He, I think, is undervalued as he really had the experience at the beginning. He'd know which button to press!

What about your notion of Deep Soul? Were there any Motown records that you would consider fell into this category?

No, very little, very, very little. *[Thinks for a bit]* Maybe Hattie Littles on Gordy and some early Miracles. Voice wise, perhaps Brenda Holloway on "Every Little Bit Hurts", Kim Weston, and Hattie Littles, and even some Mary Wells. You see, they were making DANCE records, and always looking at what was selling.

Even a soul ballad doesn't necessarily get DEEP. I think of Deep Soul as when they are not afraid to let go a little. Mind you, I did love the flip of The Marvelettes "Please Mr. Postman", that was called "So Long Baby".

Which acts should have been pushed more?

The Originals, The Velvelettes, The Spinners, The Elgins… With regard to singles, there are some that stand out. All The Velvelettes issues! The Elgins' "Heaven Must Have Sent You" should have been much bigger, and the Eddie Holland track "Leaving Here"…

Wonderful!

Do you have any thoughts about the Ian Levine/Motorcity revival attempt?

Quality will always be the final arbiter. The whole thing always seemed to be about excess, a bit like Elvis impersonators. There was only ever ONE. It all seemed to be a bit sad...pathetic...I thought, leave it out and get a life. You don't create legends by revival.

What about some final reflections on the whole period?

The best period in my eyes was between 1962 and 1967, the HDH years, as it is what Motown represents to me. After that they changed. Other black companies did not change so much. Motown wanted something like Blair's Third Way. They wanted both markets: to break big in the black charts and then everywhere else. They didn't want to alienate the black market, so there was a sort of fusion.

Motown was essentially part of its time, and the opportunities that it presented. Motown took those opportunities, and white people all over the world became aware of how great black American music could be. Berry Gordy was essential in that. I suppose he was a bit of a megalomaniac, but lesser people would have been daunted and intimidated. He had a vision, probably hazy at first, and he followed it. He understood all the aspects of the overall picture. The recording industry is the industry of human happiness!

Dave Godin's Top Ten

Here's my Tamla-Motown Top 10 from the Golden Era between 1961 and 1966. (I suspect *all* "Golden Eras" last just five years if you think about it; after that, self-consciousness sets in, and/or psychological "disorders" start to heal!!).

It was more or less self-selecting, but to me, these sides epitomise all that was great and glorious about "the sound of young America", and that unique Detroit blend and identity that Motown achieved.

I've listed them in strictly alphabetical order since these ten are of such equal quality that they could each merit being Number 1. Hope that's OK. But if, as Sue Lawley demands, I had to take just one, it'd probably be "Please Mr. Postman" which is *so* layered and intense it impacts like *l' amour fou*, but then, I've always been a bit of a surrealist, and they were very taken with *l' amour fou* too!

"Heaven Must Have Sent You" – The Elgins	(V.I.P. 25037, 1966)
"Dancing in the Street" – Martha and the Vandellas	(Gordy 7033, 1964)
"Please Mr. Postman" – The Marvelettes	(Tamla 54046, 1961)
"The Tracks of My Tears" – The Miracles	(Tamla 54118, 1965)
"Where Did Our Love Go" – The Supremes	(Motown 1060, 1964)
"The Way You Do The Things You Do" – The Temptations	(Gordy 7028, 1964)
"These Things Will Keep Me Loving You" – The Velvelettes	(Soul 35025, 1966)
"Two Lovers" – Mary Wells	(Motown 1035, 1962)
"Helpless" – Kim Weston	(Gordy 7050, 1966)
"Do I Love You (Indeed I Do)" – Frank Wilson	(Soul 35020, 1965)

3

Berry Gordy: Motown's founder tells the story of Hitsville, U.S.A.
by Michael Goldberg

Berry Gordy Jnr. was the key figure in the whole story. It was his vision and drive that turned a tiny record company into a multi-million dollar concern. This interview comes from Rolling Stone *Issue No. 585, published on 23rd August 1990, It was a special Sixties issue, and this was Gordy's first in-depth interview for twenty years. In it we get a glimpse of him as a businessman and a boss, and perhaps more importantly as a man who desired to keep a level of involvement in all the aspects of the record company.*

ON A BRIGHT LOS ANGELES DAY, Berry Gordy Jr., the man who founded Motown Records and made stars of Michael Jackson, Marvin Gaye, the Temptations, Stevie Wonder, the Four Tops, Diana Ross and the Supremes, Martha and the Vandellas, Smokey Robinson and many others, removes his shirt. "We'll do the *Playboy* shots now," jokes photographer Norman Seeff, who is shooting a portrait at the wealthy record man's Bel Air estate. Gordy, bearded and looking quite fit at age sixty, demurs: "I've rejected *Playboy* so many times. "Actually," asks Seeff gently, "could I take some without the shirt?" "I'd better not," says Gordy with a grin. "That could start a sexual revolution." It was a *musical* revolution that Gordy launched in Detroit in the late Fifties, when, at age twenty-nine, he borrowed $800 from his family to make "Come to Me," a simple R&B record that reached Number Six on the black-music chart. Five years later, Motown was one of the hottest record companies in the world. Looking back, Gordy would say, "I earned $367 million in sixteen years. I must be doing something right."

Gordy's impact on popular music cannot be overstated. Motown's artists, songwriters and producers have influenced everyone from the Beatles and the Rolling Stones to recent chart toppers like Janet Jackson, Paula Abdul and Madonna. Motown artists were usually black, but the music they made – dubbed the "Sound of Young America" by Gordy – was indeed loved by nearly everyone who was young, or young at heart. Motown crossed over before anyone thought to use that term to describe black records bought by whites. "We were a general-market company," is the way Gordy puts it. "Whether you were black, white, green or blue, you could relate to our music."

Although there were other important record companies during the Sixties, Motown was the greatest, producing an unprecedented body of work. The street poetry of Smokey Robinson, the inventive productions of Holland-Dozier-Holland and the striking vocal performances of the Motown artists themselves were key elements in dozens upon dozens of classic record. Consider that Smokey Robinson and the Miracles scored twenty-five Top Forty hits during the Sixties; Diana Ross and The Supremes had twenty-three.

It is doubtful that anyone should have gambled much on the likelihood that Gordy, previously unsuccessful as a professional boxer, record-store owner and Ford auto worker, would succeed in the record business. Before starting Motown, Gordy had moderate success as a songwriter, co-writing hits like "Reet Petite" and "Lonely Teardrops" for his former boxing buddy Jackie Wilson. Gordy says he just wanted to be a songwriter – but that he couldn't get adequately paid for his efforts. "I didn't want to be a big record mogul and all that stuff, he says. I just wanted to write songs and make people laugh."

But when the royalties trickled in, eighteen-year-old Smokey Robinson encouraged

Gordy to start his own company "Why work for the man?" Robinson told Gordy. "Why not *you* be the man?"

"I didn't know any better," says Gordy. "If somebody told me today, 'Okay, you're gonna go into business, and you've gotta make a profit every year for the first five years or you'll be out of business,' I'd say that's not a good gamble. But that's what we did. Motown was a freak."

In 1988, Gordy sold his company to MCA and the investment group Boston Ventures for $61 million, but he still owns Jobete Music Publishing, the gold mine of a publishing company that holds the copyrights for nearly all the Motown hits. And as head of the Gordy Company, he remains involved in the production of records, movies and other entertainment projects. Gordy lives in a multi-million dollar Tudor-style mansion set amid a ten-acre estate in the hills of Bel Air.

It's been more than two decades since Gordy has spoken at length about the Motown sound. While Gordy has been silent, others – ranging from Gordy lieutenant Smokey Robinson to disillusioned artists like former Supreme Mary Wilson – have offered their memoirs of life inside Hitsville, U.S.A. But Gordy dismisses most of the words that have been written about Motown. "These books are all erroneous," he says brusquely. What follows is his version of the Motown story, a version that at times diverges from those of the people who worked for him. "For thirty years I've just been so goal oriented," he says at the onset of the first of two interview sessions held in his dark, wood-panelled study. "You know, it's like a football player running on the field.. If he stops to try to bother with one of his attackers, somebody's gonna say, 'Let's get him.' He's gotta keep running as fast as he can straight forward. So we had the various stories coming out about us, and I would never comment, because I didn't have time. Consequently, after thirty years, people think that the things that were said were actually true. But now I realise that I *do* have time."

During the Sixties, did you understand how popular and influential Motown was?

No. At the time I had no sense of how big this thing was. All these different factions were fighting each other: the police and the radical groups, the government and the Black Panthers, and the black organisation groups and the bigots. All these people were fighting each other, but they were all listening to Motown music. I read about this one Black Panther leader in Chicago who was shot down in bed, and his favourite song was "Someday We'll Be Together" [which went to Number One in November 1969]. And there was this big, big funeral, and all the blacks from all over came, and "Someday We'll Be Together" was constantly playing.

And in Vietnam. In *Platoon* you see the soldiers going to their deaths dancing to Smokey's music – "The Tracks of My Tears" [Number Sixteen, August 1965]. It gave them confidence; it gave them hope. You know, you've got to get a feeling when you look at that. The music pierced the Iron Curtain. And you know that on The Beatles' second album there were three Motown tunes. The influence that the music had – when the Motown Revue went to England, I went with my father and my kids to meet the Beatles. And we had pictures taken of us with them, and they were so respectful and grateful to me. I'm looking at the Beatles, and I'm saying, "This is *so* incredible." I mean one of the songs they did I *wrote*.

Smokey Robinson was one of your first and most important discoveries. You first met him in 1957.

He had some songs for Jackie Wilson's manager, and he was turned down and I happened to be there that day. He was leaving the office dejected, and I went and caught up with him. 'Cause I thought those songs were not that bad; I mean, they were pretty good songs. I went up to him, and he said, "Who are you?" I said, "I'm Berry Gordy." And he said, "Berry Gordy! You write for Jackie Wilson." He was like a fan. So I said, "Yeah, I heard some of your songs, and you have one there called 'My Mamma Done Told Me.'

That's not a bad song, nice little rhythm." He said, "Well, I got a book of a hundred songs." He was so excited, he sang every song and each one either missed the point or had something wrong with it. And I started telling him, with each one, what was wrong. He kept me there for like an hour, and he went from song to song to song, and I rejected every single one of them – a hundred songs. But instead taking this as a rejection, he was very excited that someone understood his songs and talked to him about them. So anyway, we became friends.

He started writing songs for you.

I gave him advice. I told him to go out and listen to the radio. And at the time the Silhouettes had a Number One record called "Get A Job". So he came to the office one day so excited. He had this song he'd written called "Got A Job". He started singing the song to me, and I liked it right away. I stopped him for a moment right after he got through the first part and told him it was great. He said, "Wait 'til I finish." And he sang the whole song, all eight minutes of it – and I said, "It's much too long. We got to edit it, but it's a hit." So we worked on it, we put it out, and it was a hit ["Got A Job" went to Number One on the R&B charts in 1958.]

But the thing I liked about Smokey was bigger than a song. He had a purity about him, and he had a feeling of great thankfulness. Even as I rejected every song, he got stronger, and that's hard. That's the mark of a real kind of winner.

You called Motown "Hitsville, U.S.A." You hung a big sign up on the outside of the offices. You were pretty confident.

Oh, yes. I also did an ad for *Billboard* or *Cashbox* in '59 or '60, when I was just starting my company. It's even a little more cocky than that. It started off with little letters, and it got bigger and bigger, and it said: From out of the West comes a young man who's gonna revolutionise the record business and do whatever – I forget what I said exactly. And people said, "That is so arrogant." I said, "No, that's what I'm gonna do."

It's been said that when you were developing Motown, you modelled it after the Ford auto plant where you had worked.

Yes, yes. I worked in the Ford factory before I came in the [record] business, and I saw how each person did a different thing. And I said, "Why can't we do that with the creative process?" It was just an idea of coming in one door one day and going out another door and having all these things done. You know, the writing, the producing, the artist development – that's the grooming of the act, how to talk, how to speak, how to walk, choreography, all that stuff. And when you got through and you came out the door, you were like a star, a potential star. It was just that assembly-line approach to things.

Tell me about the legendary Motown studio.

It was a very small studio. We would record everything there at first. We had a two-track machine that I had bought from a local disc jockey. I was doing the engineering. We didn't know anything about having an engineer and an arranger. We just went down and did everything. And we all knew how to work the machines. And everybody came and played at everybody's session. Marvin would play drums on certain people's sessions. The secretaries would sing on the sessions. That's how Martha [Reeves] was discovered, singing on a Marvin Gaye session. When someone didn't show up, she ended up singing the lead on something, and the next thing you know, there's Martha and the Vandellas.

Some of your biggest stars started out as secretaries.

The way that people could get into Motown was to get a job there and do something meaningful, and then they could come every day. I'm not even sure Martha was getting paid at the time she was a secretary. Diana Ross worked for me for a summer. They [the Supremes] had come to us, and they were rejected 'cause they were in the twelfth grade, and I had a responsibility not to have them quit school. Later they came back and they sang background on some Marvin Gaye recordings. And then Diana wanted to get a job at Motown so she could be there, but there was not really a job she could do. But I needed a secretary at the time, so I let her try that out. She worked for me for a summer, but she was so bad as a secretary that I had to let her go. You know, my messages were mixed up and everything.

There were some very unusual sounds on Motown records.

Oh yeah. There was a sound we got on "Reach Out I'll Be There," with Holland-Dozier-Holland. There's a point near the beginning of the song where the music breaks and there's this little drumbeat [he imitates it] – da da da da da da da – and everybody around the world was trying to figure out how that was done, and it was so simple. It was just on a chair, and that was it, you know [demonstrates drumming on coffee tumble with his hands]. And everyone said, "What instrument was that?" And we were doing things with tin cans, we were doing things with cardboard. On the Supremes song "Where Did Our Love Go," [Number One, July 1964] we'd get a piece of cardboard, and that was our drumbeat [demonstrates beat by slapping hands together and sings "*Baby, Baby*"]. We weren't concerned about whether it was right or wrong, we just wanted to know if it sounded good.

Since you were using a two-track machine for the early records, there were no overdubs – you had to record the music and the vocals at the same time.

Oh, yes. On two tracks. And we would never be happy with the sound. I remember when we cut "Way Over There" with the Miracles [in 1959]. It was a great record with feeling and soul. So we put the record out, and it started selling but I was unhappy with it. There was a great studio in Chicago, so I put the Miracles into that studio, and we recut the tune. I got the exact same tracks, the exact same everything, only I had strings on it. We had a beautiful recording. I was so happy and proud of that recording! Now, when we first put it out, without strings – our original version – it sold 60,000 copies, which was incredible for us because we were new. Sixty thousand copies! Then I went and recut it, 'cause I wanted to get a real home run. We switched records and started shipping the one with the strings, and the record stopped selling. It did not sell another copy. And that was such a lesson to me. 'Cause the first version had a certain honesty about it. It wasn't slick. So after that, we continued to produce songs in our own little studio. But we just didn't have respect for the studio. It was a little studio that had real wonderful acoustics and magical sound, but we just never fully recognised that at the time. We took it for granted.

Every week you would hold a meeting with key executives at Motown to listen to the recordings made that week and to decide what you would release.

We had meetings each Friday, and we would evaluate all the records. Five, six, seven, records, you know. A lot of stuff was being cut all week, and the one that would get released was the one that we liked best for the week. We would debate and fight over which ones to release.

What were those meetings like?

Those meetings were taped. I have the tapes. I listened to one the other day; I've got it here. [*Gordy has an aide locate the tape and a machine to play it on.*] This is maybe twenty-six years ago.

[The tape begins just prior to the start of a weekly creative meeting. Gordy is talking.] "I definitely want my A&R to be here. That's $100 [fine] for Mickey [Stevenson, director of A&R]."

[Unidentified voice on the tape] "He's got five minutes."

[Gordy responds.] "Four minutes. Lock the door." [As it turned out, Stevenson showed up and was only docked fifty dollars.]

So we used to lock the door. [Gordy laughs.] There was never a question in my mind – the minute you were late, you were fined. The heads of the office had to be there five minutes before the meeting started. Even though Mickey came in, he was supposed to be there five minutes early. He was three minutes early so he got a fifty-dollar fine instead. See, at Motown, no-one had any questions about the direction we were going in, because I was the leader. I was very firm and very strict. I remember the days Smokey was knocking on the door. He would be a little late, and he couldn't get in. He'd be locked out: "Let me in, let me in! This is Smokey. I'll never be late again!"

You earned a reputation for sending records you were unhappy with back to be reworked, re-recorded.

Yeah. Like "Baby Love" was a sad song. When Holland-Dozier-Holland finished it the first time, I said, "It's great, but it has no life, there's no gimmick here, there's nothing here that makes it sound really good. There's nothing really different about the record." And they looked at me and of course they disagreed with me, because they always did. But they went back in the studio and recut it. And at the beginning, they put in the little thing, *ooh-ooh-ooh* – that little bit. And I said, that's perfect. It gives it something different, yet it's not crazy. And they cut it fast. So it was brighter, and then we put it out that way ["Baby Love" went to Number One in October 1964.] I was known for recutting things that were almost there.

As a songwriter, your best-known composition is "Money (That's What I Want)". Your original version, featuring singer Barrett Strong, reached Number Twenty-three in March 1960. It became known to millions of people around the world when it was recorded by the Beatles a few years later.

Many psychologists have studied that song and studied me and tried to figure out why I wrote it. People have had all kinds of different reasons to explain why I wrote the song. The truth of the matter is that I was broke at the time and I had a couple of girlfriends who said they loved me and so forth. I thought to myself, I'm gonna write a song about this. I don't really want to write about love, because everybody else is writing about love, and I don't remember anyone writing about "I need money." I thought that would be kind of funny. Later, a lot of people said, "Oh, that's the way you feel, you just wanted money." But I thought other people would find the song funny and amusing.

In 1961, Motown scored its first million seller with "Shop Around".

When Smokey came to me with the song, he actually wanted Barrett Strong to sing it. I had just done "Money" with Barrett Strong. So Smokey sang the song for me, and I said "No, Smokey, this is perfect for you." But he said, "No. I didn't write it for myself. It's not for me." Finally he agreed. So he did the song, and we released it. But it didn't quite have the life that I thought it should have. I listened to it and listened to it. You go through these changes where you think that your mind is playing tricks on you. You loved it at one time, and now you don't love it, and you just feel that maybe it's just your mind so maybe you should put it out anyway. And we did. But I couldn't sleep, and finally I made up my mind to recut it. It was two o'clock in the morning when I called Smokey. Of course, he was very sleepy. I wanted him to come down to the studio with the group to recut the song. He was very, very surprised and very confused. But he did get himself together and got the rest of the Miracles, and they were all grumbling like mad. They came into the studio at three o'clock in the morning. The piano player, he didn't get up, so I played piano. And we recorded it again. So we put the new record out, and it went straight to Number Two pop and Number One R&B.

Three Motown songs – "Please Mr. Postman", "Money" and "You Really Got A Hold On Me" – appeared on The Beatles' second album. What did you think when you heard the Beatles were recording Motown songs?

[Long pause] Well, it was a very strange reaction. Brian Epstein's office called for a [discount] rate on the publishing royalty. They wanted to pay a cent and a half instead of two cents per song [for each album sold], I had mixed emotions. I was honored that they wanted to do the songs, but to ask for a lesser rate… We didn't do that unless a person would do a lot of our tunes. But three tunes! We were very arrogant about it. Maybe not arrogant but firm, because I thought that quality songs were quality songs. At that time we felt the songs would help to make their second album a success. We said no until the last minute. So it wasn't until later that I really enjoyed them doing it.

Mavin Gaye was not only one of your biggest stars, he was also your brother-in-law for a time. Tell me about the first time you met him.

We were having a party at Hitsville. Marvin Gaye came with Harvey Fuqua [formerly of the Moonglows] and my two sisters. And I noticed him sitting in the studio, just messing around at the piano. It was a big party going on, but there was this guy at the piano. One of my sisters said, "That's Marvin Gaye. He wants to be a singer. He's a great singer. He used to sing with the Moonglows." They were building him up, and I had no idea that my sister [Anna Gordy] liked him, but anyway, they brought him to my attention. He played some jazzy-type Broadway things, and I could hear the mellowness in his voice, and it was really good. He really wanted to do ballad-type things, and after hearing his voice – the velvetness of his voice – I really wanted to do that kind of an album with him. I thought Motown could branch out into this kind of music. Unfortunately, I was wrong on that one, because his first album, *The Soulful Moods of Marvin Gaye*, didn't sell. Marvin did a rendition of "Mr. Sandman" that was so great. It's still one of my favourite songs

How did you get him to do pop music?

He was a very stubborn man, and he was determined to stick with the semi-jazz stuff he was doing. But one day he needed money or something, and they ended up coming up with a thing, "Stubborn Kind of Fellow" [Number Eight on the R&B charts in August 1962]. And it was a really nice little hit. So then we started really watching him. We said, "Okay, where should this guy be?" And I realised that he was a very handsome man and had sex appeal, and I thought that we should have him work directly to the women. So I said, "Let's write songs with *you*" – you are a wonderful one, you are my pride and joy. We wanted him to be direct. We right away hit with that, and he became the sex symbol – he became everything we wanted and more.

And later, of course, he would get tired of this and go on to his protest things, which turned out to be bigger than everything, even though I personally wasn't for it. I tried to convince him that talking about war and police brutality and all that stuff would hardly make him more popular than the romance stuff.

What was it about Stevie Wonder that impressed you?

When I first saw Stevie, I did not think that he was a great singer.

So why did you sign him?

Because he had other talents. He was ten or eleven years old, and he was not anything that special with his voice, but his talent was great. His harmonica playing was phenomenal. But I was worried that when he got to thirteen or fourteen, his voice would change and we wouldn't even have that. But lucky for us, it changed for the better.

You told me a few years ago that Stevie Wonder played a lot of practical jokes on you.

Oh, yes, he played tricks. His biggest trick was imitating my voice. He used to call my secretary and say, "Give Stevie Wonder $50,000," you know, and "Hurry this is me, this is me." And they would say, "Mr. Gordy?" And he would say, "Don't ask me questions. Give Stevie Wonder a check for $50,000." They'd be very confused, and they might come back and say, "You still want me to do that?" And I'd say "Do what?" Give Stevie $50,000." And I'd say, "Are you crazy? That was Stevie calling you. Can't you tell the difference between my voice and Stevie's voice? Didn't he laugh?" She said "No, he laughed a little bit but just hung the phone up." I said "I never thought you'd fall for that. Call him back and tell him his 50,000's on the way." And when they did, he'd bust out laughing.

Marvin would also imitate me, and they would have imitating-me contests. One day Stevie and Marvin were imitating me, and I walked up behind both of them.

What happened when they saw you?

Well, well, they both looked at me, and of course they both just bust out laughing. They were saying all the stuff I'd say. Like when I didn't like a record I'd always say it was ridiculous and garbage. "It's garbage, it's garbage, it's garbage!" They were a comical version of everything in me. I never thought I talked like that, but everyone in the office said, "They're imitating you perfectly." I said, "Okay, fine."

The Temptations were with you for four years before they had a real hit. Why did you stick with them for so long?

Because they had talent. And I was always a believer that talent will out in the long run. It's not about who gets hits and who doesn't get hits. These guys – the Temptations – could sing a cappella and had the greatest barbershop harmony that you've ever heard. They had this warmth. There was so much love coming from Melvin and artistry from David, who was a superstar in his own right. You had, like, five stars there, and each one could sing lead so the public was getting tremendous benefits for their money.

The Temptations' "Cloud Nine," co-written and produced by Norman Whitfield, was probably the most controversial record Motown released.

"Cloud Nine" was an interesting situation. 'Cause I hated that record. Not because it was bad. I loved the record's sound, but I felt that it was talking about drugs. That was our biggest argument. I felt that Norman was promoting drugs with that record. And I said "Norman, I have this company, Motown, that stands for something. We can't say, 'I'm doing fine on cloud nine,' referring to drugs." He said, "This is art, and it's not about drugs. It's talking about something else"

But it was about drugs, wasn't it?

I know, but Norman convinced me that it was something other than that.

He convinced you it wasn't about drugs?

Well, you want to believe it. Especially since I thought it was such a great record. That record was very painful for me – until it went Top Ten [*laughs*]. ["Cloud Nine" reached Number Six, December 1968.]

The Supremes were with Motown for at least four years before they had a major hit.

I cut stuff with them, but it wasn't until Mary Wells left that we had a chance to really devote ourselves to the Supremes.

Why did Mary Wells leave?

I made a major mistake with Mary. I made a lot of mistakes, and one of them was that shortly before her twenty-first birthday, I put out a smash-hit record on her, "My Guy" [Number One, April 1964], not ever thinking or knowing that at twenty-one, she would be able to disaffirm all contracts – which she did. I mean, the record was Number One, you understand and all of the sudden she's out of the pocket – she's not talking to anybody. And I'm going, "What is this?"

That's when you really pushed the Supremes?

I had talked to Mary's attorney and convinced him that I was the best place for her, and then I understood that she fired him and got another attorney and left anyway. I was trying to cover up any hurt that I might have had and said, "To hell with her. Let's deal with these new girls here who I like anyway." I'd always wanted a female star, and Mary was like the first one. And when she left we were down, but we weren't out. I always had this desire to have an artist who I could really mold, and Diana happened to be that. And it wasn't until Michael Jackson came on later that I had that same kind of thing again.

Why did the Supremes break up?

It had gotten to the point, as it does in many groups, when there's total miscommunication between the two factions. The ones in the background were having conflicts with the one in the front. Diana never wanted to leave the girls, particularly. She was more or less pushed out, but that's what happens when a person is up front and people are telling the background singers that she's stealing the show. They would complain to me, and I would say, "Wait a minute. She does roll her eyes and she does have a flirty look, but that's *helping* the group not hurting the group." It was always a problem for me having to take the responsibility for the choices. I made the choices of who sung lead, and my opinion was always that Diana had the magic and Mary [Wilson] didn't. But Mary felt that she should be the one, and I said no and then, of course, favouritism was charged. And it was perhaps favouritism, because Diana *was* a favourite of mine. But she had the talent to justify the favouritism. But it wasn't a favouritism in terms of their personalities as much as it was the fact that we had a commercial venture here and the lead singer had to be a person that would best move the group forward. Now, the breakup of that group was very sad for all of us, but we tried very hard to make the group remain successful. We brought in Jean Terrell to replace Diana, and the group had a couple of big hits. As Mike [Roshkind a former Motown vice-chairman now employed as a consultant to Berry Gordy] put it, we had a two-for-one split. And actually, the Supremes had a better shot than Diana. Because the Supremes were a much, much bigger name than Diana Ross

Over the years people have written some nasty things about Motown.

It used to hurt me a lot when those kinds of things were written. Stuff that was totally without foundation. Some people who used to be at Motown would be unhappy about a decision I had made. All the major decisions, I made them personally, and so unfortunately for me, Motown was synonymous with Berry Gordy. At other record companies, when an artist would leave, or they wouldn't make money, or they weren't a success, there was no individual singled out. But when one of our artists didn't make it, it was Berry Gordy's fault. I'd say, 'Wait a minute. It's the company, it's the business. Everybody's not going to be successful." I've had people come to me and say, "I would love to sign with you, but I heard you ripped off several artists." And I'd say, 'Well, what artists did I rip off?" And they'd say, "Well, you ripped off Diana Ross, Marvin Gaye, Stevie Wonder, Michael Jackson and Smokey Robinson." And I'd say, "Well, every artist you named is a superstar. Wouldn't you like to be ripped off like that?" And they'd say, "You know, I never thought of that."

What effect did the civil rights movement have on Motown?

I was very conscious of human suffering and freedom. I don't like bigotry in any sense of the word. And so I was indebted to the civil-rights leaders at that time, as everyone was, black or white. I was a very, very close friend of Dr. King's. To have a hero, your hero, as your friend was incredible [*He gets up and brings over a photo*] That's Dr. King and Lena Horne and myself. I was so inspired by the "I Have a Dream" speech that we released it on an album. We started the Black Forum label, where I put out various albums of people like Elaine Brown and Stokeley Carmichael. But as far as the civil-rights movement, I was not so much affected by it as I was appreciative that they were moving in that direction, and I liked Dr. King's approach, the nonviolent approach. I admired his courage. When you say the civil-rights movement, what did it do? It did a lot for me as a human being, to know that other people were fighting and dying, black and white, who just believed in people having equal rights. It was a great part of my life. I mean, it's a great part of the lives of all of us who lived through that. You know, the Sixties is an era not to be believed in terms of what was happening in our culture and society.

Do you think you could have had the success you had with Motown if there hadn't been a civil-rights movement?

It's hard for me to say. I don't see the connection to success and failure based on any one thing. It was not a visible factor as to whether a person had a hit record or didn't have a hit record. When we went on tours to the South, we were attacked in our motorcades like everybody else.

But both sides were playing Motown music. So, you know, the whites and the blacks, the liberals and the conservatives were playing Motown music. People are people. That was the whole basis for our whole kind of musical thing. To realise that white people are people, too [*laughs*]. That's a joke. That's a joke. That all people have the same wants and likes and dislikes. That's always been my thing – trying to get the thread between all people. We were just trying to create the type of music that would move us into a wider audience.

If rap had been happening in the Sixties, would Motown have been a rap label?

I like rap. But if rap was in when I was in, I wouldn't be where I am today, because I would have done all my records myself. Because I had no voice quality, so if rap had been in I would have been doing all my own songs because I wouldn't have needed the voice quality. I would have been talking many of my songs. There wouldn't have been any need for me to have artists.

[*Michael Roshkind, who arranged this interview, interrupts.*] "Uh, Berry, I think we've got to cut this off now."

[*Gordy says to Roshkind*] "You've already gone over [the time allotted]. It's your responsibility. So that's a fine for you!" [*Laughs.*]

The famous Berry Gordy family loan document.

4
Tamla Motown Top Ten Singles
by Dave Marsh

Dave Marsh is a native Detroiter whose reputation as a rock writer rightly puts him in the highest echelons. These selections are extracted with his permission from his book The Heart Of Rock And Soul – The 1001 Greatest Singles Ever Made. *Published in 1989, it has I believe remained in print ever since. Along with Dave's selection of his ten favourite Motown Records, and his thoughts on each record, are the numbers where they were placed within his whole Top 1001. We have used this piece as a trigger for a collection of other people's Top Ten choices, which you will find spread throughout the book.*

1 I HEARD IT THROUGH THE GRAPEVINE
Marvin Gaye
Produced by Norman Whitfield: Written by Norman Whitfield and Barrett Strong
Tamla 54176 1968 *Billboard* #1 (7 weeks) [Marsh's Top 1001 singles position, #1]

"I Heard it Through the Grapevine" isn't a plea to save a love affair; it's Marvin Gaye's essay on salvaging the human spirit. The record distills four hundred years of paranoia and talking drum gossip into three minutes and fifteen seconds of anguished soul-searching. The proof's as readily accessible as your next unexpected encounter on the radio with the fretful, self-absorbed vocal that makes the record a lost continent of music and emotion.

How does something so familiar remain surprising for twenty years? To begin with, Gaye plays out the singing with his characteristic amalgam of power and elegance, sophistication and instinct: now hoarse, now soaring, sometimes spitting out imprecations with frightening clarity, sometimes almost chanting in pure street slang, sometimes pleading at the edge of incoherence, twisting, shortening, and elongating syllables to capture emotions words can't define. And Gaye does this not just in a line or two or three but continuously. As a result, a record that's of absolutely stereotypical length creates a world that seems to last forever.

"Grapevine" is also a triumph for producer Norman Whitfield. The music begins with an obsessively reiterated electric piano figure. Its churchy chords are followed with a plain backbeat off the drum kit and a rattlesnake tambourine, then a chopping guitar and soaring strings. So Whitfield creates a masterpiece before Gaye ever strangles a note. That ultra-percussive beat on the tambourine is the sound of the rumour reaching home; the rest of the record is about the consequences.

The welter of voices – horns, female choruses, echo, bass-drum breakdowns over string arpeggios – serves as a community of gossip, with the singer isolated but engulfed within it. Though he rails against the facts, he knows they have him trapped. What makes "Grapevine"'s most anguished lines – "Losin' you would end my life, you see / Because you mean that much to me" – so harrowing is that they come from the mouth of a man raised to believe in the literal fires of hell who now worships love. For Gaye being cheated out of his lover is a sign of heavenly condemnation. So he lets his voice make a gospel leap for that first "you", then immediately brings it back into control, as if he's still struggling with how much she does mean to him.

The lyric as Gaye sings it is also an internal dialogue. In the first half of the record, as the singer grabs at the truth, it seems less likely that he's actually staging a confrontation than that he's imagining one, weighing the story he's heard against seemingly meaningless events that now assume the status of clues. By the middle verses, the shame and humiliation have overwhelmed him, and all that's left is "you coulda told me yo'self," a claim on the past that's meaningful only because of what isn't being delivered in the present. Then, we find out that his lover's not only left him, but that she sneaked off with "the other guy [she] loved before." From this moment through to the end, a good forty-five seconds (which is an epoch in the time scale of a three-minute single), Gaye accepts the truth and enters into mourning.

Even if that's how Whitfield and Strong conceived the lyric, it is the measure of the importance of records over songs that Gaye is the only singer who really gets to its heart. Gladys Knight, who had a hit with Grapevine" in 1967, gave a journeyman rendition in which neither gossip nor grief seemed so significant. And the extended rock band workout Creedence Clearwater Revival gave the song in 1970, after Gaye's interpretation was already famous (and therefore seemed inevitable), is just overwrought; partly because it never catches a groove but mostly because it takes too seriously the implied voodoo rhythms, as if Detroit were New Orleans. Nevertheless, John Fogerty understood that "I Heard It Through the Grapevine" was a work of art. And there's no shame in not improving on it. Neither could anybody else.

2 REACH OUT I'LL BE THERE
The Four Tops
Produced by Brian Holland and Lamont Dozier; written by Brian Holland, Lamont Dozier and Eddie Holland
Motown 1098 1966 *Billboard*: #1 (2 weeks) [Marsh's Top 1001 singles position, #4]

The shibboleth is that pop music – from jazz to soul to punk – is better off as a purely expressive vehicle in which feeling overwhelms thinking. But that's a dangerously sentimental delusion. The fact is, working in a strictly defined, even formulaic context, Holland-Dozier-Holland and Levi Stubbs came up with a record that is a match for anything in the history of rock and roll. It was in part the restrictions of Motown and Top 40 pop made it possible, by establishing the tension that the producers and performers worked against.

"Reach Out" is perhaps the truest single of all: Motown has released "Reach Out" dozens of times, on every medium from singles to CDs, but not one of the remasterings comes close to the sheer sonic crunch of the seven-inch 45. (Not just the Motown "map label" original; even reissued singles will put away any LP track or even the digitalized CD.)

Unfortunately, in the squinched-up versions most often available, most of the things that make this the greatest Holland-Dozier-Holland record are missing. The sheer size of the sound, its physical impact; the wild echo that makes the countermelody carried by the flute exotic and eerie; equalisation that polarises voice and drums; the producers' use of what must have been about half of the Detroit Symphony as an adjunct rhythm section; whatever the hell it is that establishes the clip-clop rhythm in the intro.

Even Stubbs fans understand why his style can be too declamatory, but here he's undeniable, a man lost in a welter of misery, his shouts emerging from an abyss. The music is dizzying, the drums collide against every phrase he sings, but Levi soldiers onward, riding out a maelstrom.

There are only a couple of hints of spontaneity in what Stubbs does, and even those may be part of the plan: a "hah!" at the end of the first verse seems just a nervous tic until its reiterated more forcefully at the end of the second. But like a great preacher who can make merely reading the gospel a creative act, Stubbs masterfully interacts with his text – one of the great things about the single is hearing him start to sing a (probably, or at least possibly, unplanned) "Don't worry!" just before the needle lifts off.

3 NOWHERE TO RUN
Martha and the Vandellas
Produced by Brian Holland and Lamont Dozier; Written by Brian Holland, Lamont Dozier, and Eddie Holland
Gordy 7036 1965 *Billboard*: #8 [Marsh's Top 1001 singles position, #10]

Holland-Dozier-Holland's greatest triumph? Extracting legendary music from a singer as distinctive as Levi Stubbs is one thing; pulling it out of a singer as moderately gifted as Martha Reeves is another. And "Nowhere to Run" is one of the definitive Motown 45s: huge drums and popping bass propel a riffing horn section, while the frantic lead vocal recites straight pop verses with a gospel bridge. HDH's deployment of echo and EQ enables the record to begin at the height of excitement and sustain it all the way through

Some elements of this arrangement – the baritone sax undertow, particularly – have almost the same feel as the lighter records being made in New Orleans in the mid-sixties. But what adds weight and power to "Nowhere to Run"'s shrieking paranoia – what makes it Motown – is the rhythm section. Bassist James Jamerson is justly celebrated today as one of the two or three most creative players on that instrument ever, and there's as much to be said for drummer Benny Benjamin, another of the remarkably distinctive session players Motown never credited. On "Nowhere to Run" Benjamin simply explodes all over his tom-toms. Thanks to them this relentlessly rhythmic record ranks with the most fearsome of all time.

4 DO YOU LOVE ME
The Contours
Written and produced by Berry Gordy Jr.
Gordy 7005 1962 *Billboard*: #3 [Marsh's Top 1001 singles position, #19]

Next time somebody tells you Motown's too slick, slap this on the box and accept their apology gracefully. Benny Benjamin's drums are the lead instrument, and he's every bit as biting as anyone else's lead guitar. The drums overwhelm even Billy Gordon's hoarse lead vocal, which sounds like Frogman Henry after a shot of pure adrenaline. Breaking the beat down and putting it back together again, Benjamin dominates a record that has everything, from the best spoken introduction ever ("You broke my heart because I couldn't dance …,") to an artful false ending (it fakes me out every time).*

Berry Gordy's business genius sometimes makes him seem like nothing more than the Henry Ford of pop music. In fact, he was a superb musician, songwriter, arranger, and producer – closer to Thomas Edison than Ford. Presuming he plays piano here (as he often did in Motown's early days), every one of those skills is put to use on "Do You Love Me" and the result is not only classic rock and roll but a tribute to his stature as the greatest backstage talent in rock history.

5 WHAT'S GOING ON
Marvin Gaye
Produced by Mavin Gaye: written by Al Cleveland, Marvin Gaye, and Renaldo Benson
Tamla 54201 1967 *Billboard*: #2 [Marsh's Top 1001 singles position, #25]

---

* The glory of "Do You Love Me", it must be noted, has now been bowdlerised and traduced by contemporary hit radio stations, which play an edited version made for the soundtrack of *Dirty Dancing*, that omits, among other things, the fake ending. That's an abomination, of course, because the song's so short to begin with, only 2:49, and because omitting anything from such a seamless disc disrupts the greatness of the whole. Future generations may grow up thinking there is no other version of "Do You Love Me", which would be tragic and infuriating.

"What's Going On" wasn't the same kind or breakthrough as "Papa's Got a Brand New Bag" or Sly and the Family Stone's "Dance to the Music". But it did establish a new kind of adult black pop by bathing Gaye's voice in an almost weightless atmosphere of post-psychedelic rhythm and harmony. "What's Going On" is the matrix from which was created the spectrum of ambitious black pop of the seventies: everything from the blaxploitation soundtracks of Curtis Mayfield to Giorgio Moroder's pop-disco. Not bad for a record whose backing vocalists include a pair of pro football players.

But neither its influence nor its role in breaking the grip of the Motown machine is what makes "What's Going On" great. It's great because it's every bit as gorgeous as it is ambitious. After making it, "I felt like I'd finally learned how to sing," Gaye told biographer David Ritz. Gaye taught himself to "relax, just relax," which resulted in a vocal that moves through a dreamscape in which facts and wishes are equally terrible. The song is most famous for attacking war and poverty but it's also an affirmation of love. And that's why, for all its references to long hair and Vietnam, "What's Going on" will never sound dated.

At its best "What's Going On" amalgamates soul and Latin jazz, but at times it's so laid-back that it approaches Hollywood schmaltz. What saves it then is the unmistakable Motown underpinning that comes from James Jamerson's liquid bass and what might be castanets but could just as easily be fingers popping. All the label's session stalwarts are there and they never played better, maybe because they'd never been so stringently challenged. You don't make music like this unless you're surrounded by loved ones.

6 MY GIRL
The Temptations
Written and produced by Smokey Robinson and Ronald White
Gordy 7038 1965 *Billboard*: #1 (1 week) [Marsh's Top 1001 singles position, #27]

Sometimes it's at least as much the song as the singer, and "My Girl", one of the most memorable melodies of the rock era, is a fine example. But even here, the meaning of the music is just as much in the atmospheric productions which has the same ozone-intoxicated feeling as the air just after a summer thunder shower, and in the exquisite playing, particularly the bass and guitar. David Ruffin sings as if Smokey Robinson derived his great metaphors through a direct pipeline to the singer's soul, but the moment that makes the record is the soaring bridge, strings and guitar shimmering against the Tempts' repeated "Hey hey hey," out of which Ruffin comes with a swooping but understated "Oooah yeah." It's done offhandedly, which is just what gives the lyric's saccharine romanticism credibility.

7 BERNADETTE
The Four Tops
Produced by Brian Holland and Lamont Dozier. Written by Brian Holland, Lamont Dozier, and Eddie Holland
Motown 1104 1967 *Billboard*: #4 [Marsh's Top 1001 singles position, #37]

Phil Spector called "Bernadette" "a black man singing Bob Dylan," and indeed, when Levi Stubbs sings "They *pre-tend* to be *my friend*," his cadence is as unmistakeably Dylanesque as anything that ever came from the mouths of the Byrds or Manfred Mann.

As the final leg of Holland-Dozier-Holland's great Four Tops trilogy, "Bernadette" is wreathed in the same dark, foreboding atmosphere as "Reach Out I'll Be There" and "Standing in the Shadows of Love". Levi Stubbs struggles his way out of a similar sea of contrasting melodies, pushed and prodded by the bass, provoked into near panic by sharp, keening flute and organ. All the while, he fights to tell one of the most scarifying tales in the history of rock and romance.

Bernadette is not only Levi's lover, she's a mystical symbol of what men spend their lives battling to discover. Stubbs sings from within a tumultuous emotional whirlpool, boasting of Bernadette's charms and bitterly mocking other men's attempts to win her. Telling this part of the story, Stubbs becomes virtually paranoiac, claiming not only that everyone else is looking for what this charmed couple has found (and that most of them never will locate it), but that every friend he has really only wants to steal her away: "They'd give the world and all they own / For just one moment we have known."

The source of his paranoia comes clear soon enough. He's not a healthy Love Man (like Otis Redding) but a desperate Love Addict. And Bernadette is not his lover but a definition of self, their relationship not nurturing but perpetually inflammatory. Even his praise for Bernadette smacks of a junkie's self-justification. And so, when his voice breaks close to a sob as he implores his beloved to "keep on lovin' me," Stubbs speaks as nothing more than a guy craving a fix. Other men just want Bernadette; Stubbs needs her "to live".

Engulfed and trapped by the power of his own passions, needing what even Bernadette cannot ultimately provide (the very peace of mind he claims to have found yet sings as if he would never recognize if it showed up), Levi Stubbs becomes a symbol of every guy who tried to find outside himself what can only grow internally. If the potency of his embroilment at first seems seductive, what echoes is the final line, the truth he can't keep from expressing: "And Bernadette, you mean more to me / Than a woman was ever meant to mean." The man reaching out just two hits before has now succumbed to the dark side of what lurks in the shadows of love.

8 THE TRACKS OF MY TEARS
The Miracles
Produced by Smokey Robinson; Written by Smokey Robinson, Warren Moore and Marvin Tarplin
Tamla 54118 1965 *Billboard*: #16 [Marsh's Top 1001 singles position, #46]

Though he was black and indubitably one of the enduring performers of his era, Smokey Robinson wasn't really a soul singer. His singing was informed by Doo-wop and R&B, but there was little gospel in it; he always remained smoother, more controlled, an unruffled ballad singer, Motown's answer to Bing Crosby.

Robinson's talents as songwriter, arranger, and producer far surpass his vocal ability anyway. Typically, it's the things that set up the singing that make his records memorable. With its crying lead and doo-wopping vocal background, "The Tracks of My Tears" is a throw back to the days of R&B smoothies like Clyde McPhatter. What brings it up to date are the details: huge drums, a lovely guitar line by co-writer Marv Tarplin, sharp horns, hi-fi dynamics. The lyrics might be flimsy if their rhyme scheme weren't so intricate. "My smile is my make-up I wear since my breakup with you" is tremendous not for what it says but because it *sings*. If you're going to be the coolest crooner around, it helps to know how to craft such material. Only one guy did.

9 HEAT WAVE,
Martha and the Vandellas
Produced by Brian Holland and Lamont Dozier; written by Brian Holland, Lamont Dozier, and Eddie Holland
Gordy 7022 1963 *Billboard*: #4 [Marsh's Top 1001 singles position, #50]

"Heat Wave" revolves around a basic question: "Has high blood pressure got a hold on me or is this the way love's supposed to be?" By the end, Martha knows that there is no answer: "Can't explain it, don't understand it, ain't never felt like this before." But her description of the symptoms and Holland-Dozier-Holland's use of the Motown house band as an enactment of the fever defined this particular contagion for a generation. Personally, I'd be willing to endure hospitalization for a few weeks just to feel the way the baritone saxophone sounds."

10 SINCE I LOST MY BABY
The Temptations
Produced by Smokey Robinson; written by Warren Moore and Smokey Robinson
Gordy 7043 1965 *Billboard* #17 [Marsh's Top 1001 singles position, #53]

A neglected Motown masterwork. Smokey Robinson's lyric conveys everything, including the weather. But if only Smokey could have forged such forlorn wordplay ("But fun is a bore / And with money I'm poor") into a pop song, only David Ruffin could have rendered those lines with so much gritty conviction. The effortless way that Ruffin swings from the last line of the bridge ("I really really care") back to the far different rhythm of the verse by slipping in a quick "Ooh," is something no other soul singer could have pulled off so smoothly while still sounding so tough.

"Since I Lost My Baby" is perhaps Smokey Robinson's greatest production, certainly his most massive. The constant reiteration of the melody by the strings, the vibrant bass, the timing of the Temptations' backing vocals, and the brilliant commentary from the piano all lend a sense of groove, drama, and majesty.

5
Just My Soul Responding
by Brian Ward

Any examination of the rise of Motown during the Sixties has to include a look at the economic and sociological contexts for a black-owned company aiming for a good slice of the white entertainment market in the midst of the struggle for black civil rights. Berry Gordy had to decide early on what his approach was to be as a businessman, aside from any artistic considerations. As the following piece shows, while Gordy was determined to keep a very tight rein on everything within Motown's sphere, he took an essentially pragmatic approach to both economic strategies and racial politics.

This text has been assembled especially for this reader from Brian Ward's Just My Soul Responding *which was published by UCL Press in 1998. This wonderful book examines the relationships between Rhythm and Blues and Soul music and the struggle for black freedom and equality in the '50s, '60s and '70s. In 1999 it won an American Book Award, the Organization of American Historians' James A. Rawley Prize for the best book on the history of US race relations, and the 2000 European Association of American Studies' Network First Book Prize for the best first book on an American Studies topic*

Brian Ward is an Associate Professor of American History at the University of Florida, Gainesville. His major publications include The Making Of Martin Luther King And The Civil Rights Movement *(ed., with Tony Badger). He is currently completing a book on the links between radio and the African American freedom struggle.*

Money – That's What I Want
Black Capitalism, Motown and The Movement

The Motown miracle

The basic history of the Motown Corporation has been recounted many times, by insiders, outsiders, mud-slingers and tribute-bringers. Yet, that remarkable story warrants brief rehearsal here since it illuminates both the nature and dilemmas of black entrepreneurial capitalism and the routine misrepresentation of the label's achievements and racial credentials in much of the existing literature.

In 1929, Berry Gordy was born into an ambitious middle-class black family with roots in Georgia farming and retail, which had relocated to Detroit during the 1920s. There, in addition to running a painting and construction firm, his father, Berry Sr., opened the Booker T. Washington Grocery Store, and instilled in his children the virtues of frugality, discipline, family unity and hard work so dear to the "Wizard of Tuskegee". Less committed than some of his siblings to the formal education which Booker T. Washington had also advocated, Gordy left school at the 11th grade to become a professional boxer. In 1953, he indulged his love of modern jazz by opening the 3-D Record Mart. Unfortunately, the masses of black Detroit cared little for the music and in 1955 the venture failed, forcing Gordy into a much-vaunted, but relatively brief, sojourn on the production line at Ford. The failure of 3-D had a profound impact on Gordy: rarely again would he put aesthetic, artistic or, for that matter, racial, considerations ahead of a simple concern for whether and how widely his products would sell.

Gordy's breakthrough in the music business came as a songwriter when he co-authored "To Be Loved" and "Reet Petite" for Jackie Wilson. In early 1958 he produced "Got A Job" for the Miracles, with whom he also had a management deal. As the Miracles' career took off, Gordy apparently managed to retain control over their contract only by persuading black deejays to threaten a boycott of several white labels who were trying to poach the group with more generous terms, Apocryphal though this story may be, it illustrates a recurring pattern in Gordy's business dealings whereby he appealed to black solidarity and pride to secure whatever protection and preferential treatment the few blacks with power in the industry could offer. Throughout the 1960s, Gordy would shrewdly use race, so often an impediment to black economic advance, as one of the tools of his entrepreneurial ambitions.

Using family money, Gordy had formed Tamla – his first label – in January 1959, releasing a blues-tinged black pop number called "Come To Me" by husky-voiced Marv Johnson. When that disc began to pick up extensive regional airplay on WJLB-Detroit and the black-owned WCHB-Inkster, Tamla simply could not cope with the demands of mass production and national distribution and leased the master to United Artists. UA had both the financial resources to pay for the pressing of tens of thousands of copies before it had recouped any monies from sales, and the distribution network to place those disks on record racks and radio playlists around the nation. Gordy learned more about distribution in 1960 when Tamla acted in that capacity for Barrett Strong's highly successful, and aptly titled, "Money": a song co-written and produced by Gordy and released on the eponymous Anna label run by his sister and her husband, the ex-Moonglow Harvey Fuqua.

By this time Gordy had established various fiefdoms within the Motown empire: the Motown Record Corporation, Hitsville USA, and Berry Gordy Jr. Enterprises. He also set up his own publishing firm, Jobete Music, and a management agency, International Talent Management Inc. (ITMI). Around the turn of the decade he supplemented Tamla with a list of subsidiary labels like Motown itself, Miracle (which was renamed Gordy in 1962), Mel-O-Dy, VIP and a gospel experiment, Divinity. This strategy was primarily designed to protect against the possible failure of individual labels, but it proved unnecessary as Gordy began to rack up an impressive run of crossover hits with artists like the Marvelettes, Contours, Marvin Gaye and Mary Wells.

Aside from the astonishing quality of so much of Motown's music, what differentiated the label from most of its rivals was Gordy's extraordinary business acumen and ingenuity, and the single mindedness, many would later claim ruthlessness, with which he set about realising his dreams. At the heart of Motown's economics were the classic business strategies of vertical integration and cross-collateralisation. Gordy controlled and profited from every aspect of the careers of his artists, writers and musicians, and every dimension of record production and promotion. Put simply, Gordy developed a structure which enabled Motown to offset losses on any unprofitable projects with income from another branch of the total operation. For example, all Motown performer-writers were required to sign with Gordy's Jobete Music publishing company, which not only claimed its own share of the songwriter's income, but also ensured that Gordy could recoup any costs incurred in the preparation of recordings by making deductions from the relevant artist's songwriting royalties.

Similarly, all Motown acts and creative personnel were managed by ITMI, which did relatively little to protect their financial or artistic interests, but made money for the corporation by arranging notoriously mean and restrictive contracts for the young black hopefuls who joined the label. ITMI routinely took a cut of the weekly salaries paid to all the corporations creative staff, whether they had been productive that week or not.

Gordy considered paying non-productive staff a gesture of great generosity, but it has to be measured against the fact that all weekly payments were later reclaimed by the company against the artist's royalties from any recordings. ITMI also controlled the income from live performances, organising gruelling Motown tours on which the artists were given a daily allowance, again deductible from any future royalties. In return, artists and writers were allowed only periodic access to Motown's accounts, which Gordy refused to allow the Recording Industry Association of America to audit until the 1970s, and had few rights concerning when, what and with whom they recorded.

Motown royalties were usually fixed at a meagre rate of 8 per cent of 90 per cent of the wholesale price of albums and singles. By 1968, bitter disputes over those royalties led the brilliant songwriting and production team of Lamont, Dozier and the brothers Eddie and Brian Holland to leave the label, eventually winning a court settlement worth several hundred thousand dollars. Others, like Eddie Kendricks of the Temptations, also began to question if Motown's much vaunted family ethos was really just a front for an exploitative mode of black paternalism, not very different from exploitative white paternalism. Martha Reeves was torn between gratitude and disillusionment with the way Motown treated its artists. "Motown had signed us to ironclad contracts and turned us into international stars. Yet after several years of million-selling records and sold-out concerts, in 1969 I realised that my personal income was but a fraction of what it should have been". When Reeves began to ask questions about her earnings, she "suddenly experienced a lack of personal and professional attention".

There is some evidence that Motown's studio musicians were treated more generously than its name artists and writers, but this was all relative. The going rate for a Motown session in 1962 was $7.50 a side and until 1965 the label routinely paid musicians below union scale. Although by the second half of the decade musicians like pianist Earl Van Dyke, leader of the Funk Brothers studio band, could earn five-figure sums annually, there was still resentment about the lack of artistic credit and adequate financial recompense for musicians who had virtually co-written songs which later earned millions of dollars. Although Gordy later protested that Motown writers and musicians were paid exactly what they were owed according to the letter of their contracts, Motown was in fact perpetrating precisely the kind of exploitation of its artists which had prompted Harold Battiste to form AFO. (All For One, Battiste's own label formed to promote black musical endeavour). James Jamerson, one of Motown's finest bassists, recalled: "There is sometimes a tear because I see how I was treated and cheated. We were doing more than we thought and we didn't get any songwriting credit".

The Motown sound and the myth of authenticity

Consummate musicians like James Jamerson, Earl Van Dyke (piano), Benny Benjamin (drums) and James Messina (guitar) were crucial in the development of what has become instantly recognisable, if analytically elusive, as the "Motown sound". Yet, given the oceans of print devoted to this "sound', one of the most striking features of Motown's early output was not its homogeneity, but its diversity.

Bluesy performers like Mabel John, Barrett Strong and Marv Johnson were initially balanced by coy girl groups like the Marvelettes and soloists like Mary Wells. Long-forgotten white acts like the Valadiers coexisted with the Four Tops, who at first found themselves on Gordy's Jazz Workshop subsidiary where they experimented with big band arrangements of Tin Pan Alley standards. The Supremes recorded everything from Rodgers and Hart tunes to country and western, and from a Sam Cooke tribute album to a collection of Beatles songs, hoping to find a winning formula. Meanwhile Marvin Gaye was encouraged to indulge his considerable talent for crooning on albums like

Hello Broadway and *A Tribute to the Great Nat King Cole.* With such an eclectic mixture of styles, and Gordy's keen eye for any potentially lucrative market niche, it was
easy to credit the 1962 *Detroit Free Press* article which announced that Motown was
about to launch a line of polka records.

Eventually, however, Motown did more than just produce a diverse range of records,
any one of which might appeal predominantly to a different market. It forged a flexible
house style which appealed across regional, racial and even generational boundaries.
"We were a general-market company. Whether you were black, white, green or blue, you
could relate to our music', Gordy rightly boasted. From the maelstrom of early experimentation, it was Martha Reeves who blazed the gospel-paved, string-lined trail to the
label's mid-1960s crossover triumph. In the summer of 1963, Holland-Dozier-Holland
furnished Reeves with "Heatwave" and then "Quicksand" on which they enlivened the
slightly mannered basics of the girl group sound with a driving gospel beat, tambourine
frenzy and soaring strings. Above it all, Reeves, who was comfortably the finest female
vocalist on Motown's books until Gladys Knight joined and ran her close in the late
1960s, unleashed her rapt soul vocals.

Following the Top Ten pop success of these recordings, this basic formula was refined
and adapted to fit the peculiar talents of individual Motown acts. The leonine roar of lead
singer Levi Stubbs meant that the Four Tops retained the melodrama of the Vandellas'
recordings on songs like "Reach Out, I'll Be There" and "Bernadette'. By contrast, the
Temptations harked back to their doo-wopping origins as the Primes to feature rich harmonies and a generally sweeter sound on Smokey Robinson-penned and produced songs
like "Its Growing" and "My Girl". The most successful of all the Motown acts to work
within this basic framework was the Supremes, for whom Holland-Dozier-Holland soft-
ened the hard-driving gospel beat with more prominent strings and muted brass. The mix
was topped with vocals by Diana Ross which were much lighter and breathier than
Martha's on chart-topping songs like "Where Did Our Love Go?" and "Baby Love". The
Supremes proved to be the perfect black crossover act. Between 1964 and Ross's departure from the group in 1969, they secured 25 pop hits, including 12 number ones – only
the Beatles could claim more.

If there was a classic "Motown Sound", neither its ubiquity nor its rigidity should be
exaggerated; not even for the period between 1964 and 1967 when it was at its zenith. In
1965, Motown released the Miracles' soulful post-doowop lament "Ooo Baby Baby", Jr
Walker's saxophone-led blues stomp "Shotgun", Stevie Wonder's grinding rock'n'soul
remake of Tommy Tucker's "Hi Heel Sneakers", and Marvin Gaye's gospel shout, "Ain't
That Peculiar". All were highly successful, yet all somehow circumvented, or greatly
extended, the basic formula.

Even those artists who stuck tight as a Benny Benjamin backbeat to the classic
Motown Sound, could, just like that precocious skinsman, actually produce a broad range
of moods and shadings within its confines. Thus, 1965 also saw the release of the
Temptations' melancholic "Since I Lost My Baby", the Contours' barnstorming "Can
You Jerk Like Me", the Four Tops' distraught "Ask The Lonely', and the Vandellas' dis-
turbing, claustrophobic masterpiece "Nowhere To Run".

Despite this constrained diversity, however, the idea of a single Motown Sound, clin-
ically designed by a team of songwriters and producers led by Gordy, Robinson,
Holland-Dozier-Holland, William Stevenson and Ivy Hunter, and mechanically riveted
onto the label's recordings by musical artisans, pervades the literature. Not only is this
view inaccurate, but it betrays an insidious form of racial stereotyping, and has become,
in Jon Fitzgerald's phrase, a "major impediment to general acknowledgement of
Motown's role as a major *innovative* force in 1960s popular music.

The signs adorning the offices of Motown and Stax respectively – "Hitsville, USA"
and "Soulsville, USA" – have frequently been taken to symbolise a completely different

musical ethos, a different commercial agenda, and even a different degree of artistic and racial integrity between the two labels. Critics have regularly made unfavourable comparisons between the slick Motown soul production line and the more relaxed, spontaneous, atmosphere of southern labels like Stax, with their rootsier feel and country-fried licks. Paradoxically, Southern soul, largely recorded on white-owned labels by integrated groups of musicians who drew on black and white musical influences, has been reified as more authentically black than the secularised gospel recordings of black musicians on a black-owned label with virtually no white creative input – at least not until English woman Pam Sawyer made a name for herself as a staff writer in the late 1960s with songs like the Supremes' "Love Child".

Even the usually sensible Arnold Shaw fell headlong into this trap (in "The World of Soul", 1970) describing Motown in terms which made it sound like a pale imitation of something blacker, something more real, more substantial, lurking in the southlands. Motown songs, Shaw claimed, "are light and fluffy. It is hardly soul food, but rather a dish for which white listeners have acquired a taste". In a similar vein, Mike Jahn (in "The Story of Rock from Elvis to The Rolling Stones", 1975) derided Motown as "a black-owned version of popular schmaltz", thereby recycling conventional stereotypes about the nature of "real" black music. Tony Cummings did the same (in "Black Music", 1976) when he casually dismissed Marvin Gaye's crooning as "appalling ...ill-conceived mushmallow". Cummings was apparently unable to countenance even the possibility that a black American singer could be a magnificent interpreter of Tin Pan Alley Americana.

Bidding for the mainstream

While there is no evidence that any black-oriented label or Rhythm and Blues artist ever sought anything less than the widest possible commercial success, it is nonetheless true that Berry Gordy went to extraordinary, often hugely creative, lengths to give his performers the opportunity to make it with white audiences. This was a matter of presentation as well as sound. Motown acts were formally schooled by Maxine Powell, the owner of a Detroit finishing and modelling school, in matters of etiquette, deportment, cosmetics and elocution. Gordy felt this might make them more acceptable to white America and an expanding black middle-class for whom mainstream notions of respectability remained important.

Veteran dancer Cholly Atkins was hired to supervise the sophisticated stagecraft and slick choreography which was designed to equip Motown acts for the "transition from the chitlin' circuit to Vegas". Touring London in the autumn of 1964, Mary Wilson made no secret of Gordy's and the Supremes' crossover ambitions, and their willingness to adjust to white expectations to achieve them. "We want to get into the night-club field and we know we're going to have to change our style a good bit to get there. We're working on that kind of singing now ... I know there's a lot of work ahead of us but we really hope to play the Copa some day". The following July, the Supremes became the first of many Motown acts to play that New York shrine of middle American wealth and respectability: in 1967 they were the first Motown artists to play the even ritzier Las Vegas Copa.

Music critics, far more than fans, have frequently struggled with the idea that showmanship, artifice and spectacle can sometimes be the vehicles, as well as adornments – or, worse, replacements – for genuine creativity, expression and artistic endeavour. Certainly, most accounts which focus on Motown's unapologetic pursuit of the mainstream market assume that it was simply impossible to produce a music which was artistically potent, truly expressive of aspects of contemporary mass black consciousness. and at the same time an ambitious showbiz phenomenon hugely popular with a biracial audience. For example, in a particularly pompous and insensitive 1967 article in *Rolling Stone*, rock critic Ralph Gleason used the fact that the Supremes and Four Tops were choreographed to support his claim that black soul performers were "almost totally style with very little sub-stance". Gleason denounced them for being "on an Ed Sullivan trip, striving as hard as they can to get on that stage and become part of the American success story". In fact, as Simon Frith has recognised, "if some of Motown's marketing strategies have touched depths of cynicism that just makes its continued musical inspiration even more humbling".

Motown's unparalleled popularity among black consumers suggests that the black masses shared little of the critics' sense of fakery and fraud. The corporation enjoyed 174 black Top Ten entries during the 1960s. Apparently unable to recognise "real" black music without the guidance of critics like Gleason, blacks even bought huge numbers of records by the Supremes, the bewigged flagship of Gordy's race treachery and integra-tionist aspirations, giving them 23 black hits and 5 number ones between the restoration of a separate black chart in 1965 and 1969. These black consumers were not unthinking, malleable sponges, who, racial loyalties notwithstanding, bought Motown products they did not really much like simply because Berry Gordy told them to, or because they were force-fed them on the radio. They bought Motown records because they could dance to them and relate to their timeless, witty, erudite and passionate messages of love, loss, loneliness, joy and belonging.

Moreover, black acts at Motown and elsewhere had always worn their sharp mohair suits and silk gowns with, as Marvin Gaye might have said, much pride and joy, seeing them as symbols of how far they had come from humble beginnings. Certainly, the span-gled pursuit of success carried no stigma among black fans who had routinely been denied equal opportunity to compete for the financial rewards of the mainstream, but who in the 1960s glimpsed the prospect of a real change in their fortunes. While Gleason and other critics may have preferred their black artists poor and marginalised, Motown made the earnest bid for mainstream success and respect a matter of black pride.

Singer Kim Weston believed that it was the voracious black appetite for such con-spicuous images of material success which explained much of Motown's extra-musical appeal and cultural resonance. "When I was coming up in Detroit I had no one to look up to who had made it. Through Motown's help and guidance, today's kids have all the Motown stars to emulate. We were from all sorts of backgrounds and we found success right here in our hometown." Fortunately, this fitted perfectly with Gordy's personal ambitions and his own conception of the role and responsibilities of black capitalists. For Gordy, the creation of personal wealth and the spirited pursuit of mainstream success was in itself a form of political, black economic and cultural leadership."

What Motown offered in its 1960s pomp, then, was less a dilution of some authentic black soul than a brash new urbane synthesis of pop, R&B and gospel, derived from, and perfectly fitted for, a particular moment in black and American history. Stylistically, Motown resolved some of the earlier musical and personal dilemmas of the black pop era, when a Jackie Wilson, or even a Sam Cooke, had sometimes struggled to reconcile roused black pride with the enduring dream of making it, the bigger the better, in the mainstream of American entertainment.

Realising that dream was a large part of what the Movement was all about in the 1960s, and Berry Gordy succeeded better than any black man of his day. Between 1960 and 1969, Motown released 535 singles, of which 357 made either the Rhythm and Blues and/or pop charts. Of those records, 21 reached number one on both the pop and Rhythm and Blues listings; 6 made the top slot in the pop charts alone; 29 reached number one in the Rhythm and Blues charts only. By 1965, Motown had a gross income of around $8 million and was the nation's leading seller of singles. Five years later it was the rich-est enterprise in African-American history. All this was achieved with a music which was fuelled by gospel and much closer to the "black" end of a notional black-white musical spectrum than any popular style which had previously enjoyed such sustained and mas-sive white appeal."

Recording the Movement

With Berry Gordy viewing his own economic success as a form of progressive racial politics, it was perhaps not surprising that he did not wish to jeopardise his position by becoming too closely associated with a still controversial black movement for civil and voting rights. Certainly, there is little evidence of any direct financial support for the Movement from Motown until 1966, when CORE (Congress of Racial Equality) received a donation of $3,000 for its Scholarship, Education and Defense Fund. The previous summer, however, the Hitsville Merchandising branch of the Motown Corporation did assist with the production and distribution of the *Americans in Harmony* souvenir book associated with a benefit concert of the same name. The book raised around $4,000, distributed in unequal amounts among the major national civil rights organisations, the United Negro College Fund (the biggest single beneficiary), and various Detroit community projects.'

The "Americans in Harmony" concert, and a show organised in March 1965 by WDAS-Philadelphia deejay and local NAACP (National Association for the Advancement of Colored People) Freedom Fund Committee treasurer, Georgie Woods, to raise funds for the Selma campaign, marked the tentative beginnings of a much greater presence for Motown at Movement-related events. In the early years of the Movement, however, Motown artists performed at relatively few such benefit concerts. This was hardly usual. Junius Griffin – a Pulitzer Prize-nominated black journalist who worked as director of the SCLC's (Southern Christian Leadership Conference) publicity department in the mid-1960s before moving to Motown's public relations' office in early 1967 – could not "recall black or white entertainers playing a major visible role in the Movement … until the Selma March".

An exception was Stevie Wonder's appearance at a 23 August 1963 Apollo benefit sponsored by the Negro American Labor Council (NALC), which raised $30,000 for the March on Washington. Without wishing to impugn Gordy's motives, allowing Wonder to appear alongside jazz luminaries like Art Blakey, Carman McCrae and Herbie Niann and, especially, white celebrities like Patti Newman, Joanne Woodward and Tony Bennett in a show where ticket prices ran as high as $100 certainly did nothing to thrill Motown's bid for recognition as an emerging power in the wider American entertainment business. At the same time, of course, it safely aligned the company with what was to be the Movement's greatest symbolic expression of biracial brotherhood and faith in the ultimate inclusiveness of the American Dream.

This, however, was not Motown's only connection with the March on Washington. In late 1963, the company put out an album featuring Martin Luther King's "I have a dream" oration and other key speeches from the March – although not until King had obtained a court injunction against the label and taken steps to sue it for infringement of copyright.

Not surprisingly, the most sought-after and potentially lucrative movement recording star was Martin Luther King Jr. Almost from the beginning of his public career some of the same independent labels which cut the bulk of Rhythm and Blues music saw in King an opportunity to make money and earn some kind of progressive image among the audiences most likely to invest in King on disc. King, meanwhile, saw recordings as yet another useful means to raise funds and spread the Word…

Berry Gordy's sister and Motown vice-president Esther Edwards took the first step towards offering just such a deal. In September 1962, Edwards wrote to King about the "possibility of recording some of your literary works, sermons and speeches". After negotiations, King agreed to let Motown record and release his speech at Detroit's Cobo Hall, which followed a major rally in the city on 23 June 1963. All royalties from the recording were to be assigned to the SCLC, a decision which clearly left its mark on Berry Gordy.

It says something about Gordy's priorities that 30 years later, when he wrote his autobiography and tried to explain the depths of his personal admiration for King, he could think of no better testament to the civil rights leader's true, almost otherworldly greatness than the fact that he had rejected Gordy's suggestion that "since it was his artist and his performance, it was only fair that half the royalties go to him and his family".

By late August 1963, no recording of the Detroit oration had been released. Then suddenly, in the wake of the enormous publicity surrounding the 28 August March on Washington for Jobs and Freedom, the Detroit speech appeared on an album cleverly entitled *The Great March to Freedom*. Gordy had also christened a portion of King's untitled Detroit address "I have a dream". According to King, it was only after Motown "saw the widespread public reception accorded said words when used in the text of my address to the March on Washington", that it retrospectively bestowed this title on part of his earlier Detroit speech.

King was clearly piqued at the way Gordy's name games exploited his success at the Washington march to promote Motown's Cobo Hall album. But the real crux of the suit he brought against Motown and two other labels – Mr Maestro and 20th Century Fox – in the fall of 1963 was their intention to use the "real" Washington "I have a dream" speech on albums which were produced in direct competition to the "official" March on Washington record, as sanctioned by the leaders of the Council for United Civil Rights Leadership (CUCRL). King and his lawyer (Clarence Jones) claimed that the CUCRL – a sort of multi-partisan clearinghouse which divided the income from major joint projects among the different civil rights groups – held exclusive rights to King's Washington speech and non-exclusive rights to those by other participants in the March. Moreover, the CUCRI had already arranged for WRVR, the radio station of New York's Riverside Church, to produce the official record of the events, with all the profits going to the Movement.

Not surprisingly, in addition to VRVR and the three labels which had simply gone ahead and issued records of the event without permission and with no arrangement to pay anything to the CUCRL, there were several other companies which had submitted more courteous formal bids for the contract to record the March. Bobby Robinson's black-owned Enjoy label was one, offering CUCRL a highly respectable 50 percent share of the anticipated $1.40 per album profits. Another was the non-profit-making Pacifica Foundation's WBAI-New York radio outlet, whose proposal would have netted the CUCRL around $3.00 per disk, assuming they were sold at $4.98 each. In the end, Maele Daniele Dufty, longtime manager of Billie Holiday and wife of William Dufty, the ghostwriter for Holiday's autobiography *Lady Sings The Blues,* worked with Jack Summerfield of WRVR to put out the unambiguously titled *The Official March on Washington Album* for a bargain $2.98. Although they hoped to attract more sales by keeping the price at rock-bottom, this arrangement still yielded more than $1.80 per sale to the CUCRL.

There was a curious conclusion to Motown's involvement in this episode. On 3 October 1963, New York federal judge James Bryan granted King a temporary injunction which prevented Motown, 20th Century Fox and Mr Maestro from selling recordings which featured the "I have a dream" speech until further hearings on the matter could be held in November. Shortly after this preliminary decision, King suddenly dropped the suit against Motown while continuing to press those against the other two companies. Clarence Jones claimed that this was because Motown had only intended to use excerpts from King's Washington speech, but by the end of the year the company was promoting its snappily titled *Great March to Washington* album, featuring "I have a dream" in its entirety. It may never be clear precisely what prompted King to relent in his suit against Motown while pursuing the other companies into the courtroom. But it is not too fanciful to suggest that there may simply have been a sense that it was impolitic to assail a black-owned company of increasing financial power and prestige in this way.

Motown on air

Berry Gordy also experienced difficulties finding suitable black professionals to help him run Motown efficiently and so filled many of Motown's key executive positions with experienced whites. Alan Abrams, who headed the publicity department, was one of his first appointments, while in 1962 Gordy hired Sidney Noveck as the chief accountant for Jobete and Motown. Noveck's brother Harold expertly handled the company's tax affairs for years. Liberal New York attorney, George Schiffer, who was also one of CORE's retinue of volunteer lawyers, was Motown's chief copyright lawyer. Schiffer was instrumental in successfully internationalising the operation in the mid-1960s. Barney Ales ran the distribution department, along with Phil Jones and Irving Biegel. Legal advisor Ralph Seltzer became Gordy's special assistant and later head of the A&R department. Along with other whites, Michael Roshkind – who succeeded Abrams at the helm of the public relations department – and Ales, Seltzer eventually became a vice-president of the company.

Gordy's attitude towards the hiring of these white executives again illustrated that, for all his appeals to black brotherhood when it came to selling records, or placing them on black playlists and record racks, and for all the Corporation's much vaunted personal links to the black community in Detroit, which supplied artists, staff and even impromptu panels to audition material for possible release, his priorities were essentially those of a hard-nosed entrepreneurial capitalist who just happened to be black. Gordy simply hired the best help he could afford, regardless of colour or sentiment.

And this was probably critical, rather than incidental, to his phenomenal success in a world where myriad obstacles to successful black businesses persisted.

One of the main consequences of the strong white presence among Motown's promotional and distribution staff was that the label enjoyed much better access to white-controlled retail outlets and radio playlists than most other black-owned companies. "Black radio was everything to people like me," Berry Gordy admitted, "and Motown's success was inextricably bound up with developments in radio during the 1960s."

In the 1960s, however, no company was more adept than Motown at courting black-oriented radio both as the conduit to a black community which had some $27,000 million of spending power by 1966, and as a stepping-stone to the even more lucrative white market. Initially without the financial resources or promotional and distribution networks to compete with even the bigger black-oriented independents like Vee Jay or Atlantic, let alone with the resurgent Majors of the early 1960s, Berry Gordy made personal, race-based appeals to black deejays for preferential treatment, and sent out his promotional staff to badger those in key markets to play Motown records. He even offered the free services of some of his acts when deejays put on live shows to persuade them to give Motown products a sympathetic hearing.

The appointment of esteemed veteran "Jockey" Jack Gibson to the label's promotional department in 1962 strengthened the links with black deejays until, as Nelson George (in his 1988 book, *The Death of Rhythm and Blues*) explained, "it got to the point that Motown began, not totally unreasonably, to take black radio for granted, since these deejays were committed to Motown's success by economics and by race". This strategy was a conspicuous success. Long before the Supremes enjoyed their first hit record, Mary Wilson recalled tours on which she heard the group's songs, and those of other Motown artists, already on black-oriented stations throughout the nation. Meanwhile, the presence of white executives in sales and distribution helped ease the path of Motown product onto black-oriented stations which still had white programme directors and owners, and did no harm at all when dealing with Top Forty stations either.

Racial solidarity and Gordy's keen eye for the main chance apart, however, it was the quality of Motown's recordings that ultimately accounted for the company's extraordinary access to both the pop and soul airwaves. Until the late 1960s and the advent of stereo FM radio and improved hi-fi, Motown records were carefully geared to the audio limitations of the humble transistor radio, particularly the car radio, and the portable record player. Mike McClain, the technical wizard of the Motown Studios, even rigged up a radio speaker in the label's quality control office so that Gordy and his advisors could hear newly recorded songs as the potential customer might over the airwaves. For much the same reason Gordy insisted on hearing cut discs, rather than pristine tapes or acetates, when selecting material for release.

Not only did Gordy take exceptional care to ensure that his records were mixed just right for radio, he also catered for the mechanics of Top Forty playlist selection. Top Forty station manager Bill Drake reckoned he routinely reviewed a hundred records for possible airplay in a 30-minute session, rejecting those which did not immediately grab his attention. Thus, it was no accident that many Motown singles should have particularly startling or seductive intros: the gunshot which opened Jr. Walker's "Shotgun", or the beguiling flute and galloping drum beat which launched the Four Tops' "Reach Out, I'll Be There". Motown records, with their riveting openings and customised sound, impressed programmers and frequently got onto Top Forty stations, where, because of the concern with balanced playlists, the number of soul records scheduled for any week was strictly limited.

Motown Matures and joins the movement

The configuration of economic and managerial power within the recording and broadcasting industries of the early-to-mid 1960s consistently worked against the likelihood that Rhythm and Blues would become a major source of artistic comment on American racism or of public support for black insurgency. The whites and the handful of blacks in positions of real power within the music business usually proved more concerned with market penetration than political mobilisation, As SNCC (Student Non-violent Co-ordinating Committee) organiser Stanley Wise recalled, "Marvin Gaye had attempted for a number of years to just do something with us... And I know Stevie Wonder was just trying really hard. They were the two I remember specifically who indicated over and over again they wanted to do something with us, they wanted to help us somehow'. Before Selma, however, despite repeated attempts to enlist their services, Motown's support was usually, at best, covert and fleeting. "I think it was primarily because ... they just weren't sure how the population would accept that. Because they were trying to get to their main market and ... they didn't want to be viewed as militants or belligerents, or that sort of stuff."

However, as the '60s progressed. Motown's music was changing subtly. Real and imagined musical echoes both of Africa and of a more recent, spiritual and physical black homeland, the American South, also became more prominent in the soul of the period. As many labels successfully turned to southern studios and musicians to produce an earthier, gutbucket soul sound, even Motown experimented with a more raw-boned approach to some of its recordings. This was most evident in the field-holler soul of Edwin Start, who said it all in the hard-driving screech of "Funky music sho' nuff turns me on".

In the mid 1960s, Berry Gordy had reactivated an old gospel label, fortuitously entitled Soul, where songwriter-producer Norman Whitfield cut a number of highly successful tracks with Gladys Knight and the Pips. "Take Me In Your Arms and Love Me" and the original version of "I Heard It Through The Grapevine" glittered with as much southern grit as Detroit polish. When Whitfield took over writing and production duties for the Temptations from Smokey Robinson in 1966, he began experimenting with tom-toms and elaborate Africanesque cross-rhythms. For a while almost all Whitfield's productions for the group, including the classic soul ballad "Ain't Too Proud To Beg" and the string-driven "You're My Everything", were laced with these percussive "ethnic" trimmings. It was as if Whitfield was trying to sound an ever blacker note within the context of the basic Motown formula and Gordy's congenital caution about addressing racial matters in Motown lyrics. Only in 1968, however, did Whitfield begin to merge these Africanesque flourishes with psychedelic rock and solid R&B grooves on records which also had explicitly social messages, like the Temptations' "Ball Of Confusion" and Edwin Starr's "War".

As white liberal support and financial help for an increasingly militant movement dwindled, there was a growing dependency on black funding, which in turn encouraged a more vigorous courtship of black stars who could help tap that meagre resource.

Soul appeared to offer an excellent route to black cash and publicity. Moreover, with political alignment clearly not sounding a commercial death-knell, many more soul stars and black music entrepreneurs seemed willing to donate time, energy and money to the Movement, "It was", Junius Griffin recalled wryly, "a match made for justice – both sides appreciated huge audiences".

Griffin himself was partly responsible for the steady increase in Motown's level of public engagement in Movement-related activities during the decade after Selma. In the summer of 1966, while still the SCLC's director of publicity, Griffin had successfully pestered Motown into allowing Stevie Wonder to join B.B. King and the Red Sanders Orchestra for a benefit concert at Soldier Field in support of the Chicago movement. As a consequence of his work of this show, Griffin came to the attention of Esther Gordy, who eventually persuaded her brother to hire him in May 1967. Berry Gordy later described Griffin as "passionate, deeply committed to the civil rights movement. Junius was our link to the black community and theirs to us". According to Gordy, Griffin, lawyer George Schiffer and Ewan Abner, who joined Motown as director of ITMI after the demise of Vee Jay, were the "most outspoken at Motown when it came to social causes". Together, they helped to ease the label in the direction of more conspicuous Movement-related activities.

Shortly after Martin Luther King's death, it was Griffin who, with Gordy's blessing, hastily arranged for leading Motown acts to play a major benefit for the SCLC and the Poor People's Campaign in Atlanta. Griffin also ensured that Motown outpaced the competition to be first in the stores with a posthumous compilation of King's greatest speeches, *Free At Last*. Griffin assured Levison that Gordy was "not concerned with how the proceeds should be handled", or with "the programmatical part of it but with SCLC getting as much money out of the thing" as possible. According to Griffin, Gordy had already assured Ralph Abernathy, King's successor as president of the SCLC, that "if he needs money a cheque will be forthcoming. He can advance him as much money as he wants to keep going". Griffin was even "getting some funds to be sure [Abernathy] has the right kind of clothes."

Even amid this genuine altruism and concern to preserve and extend King's legacy, Gordy's entrepreneurial instincts remained unimpaired. All he wanted out of the arrangement with the SCLC for *Free At Last* was an assurance that Motown had exclusive rights to produce the official memorial album. "One thing has to be made clear right away to the public and everyone else", Griffin explained to Levison: "that one recording company is going to handle this thing". In terms of enhancing Motown's reputation as an engaged, socially responsible black enterprise, there were obvious advantages in seeking this exclusive sanction from the SCLC and King's heirs, not least from Coretta Scott King, who was in the process of being canonised for her choice of husband. Yet the arrangement also suited Levison and others who were understandably concerned about controlling the rash of memorabilia which King's death generated, or, as Levison said, making sure that his widow and the SCLC got "at least something out of them".

Motown songwriting and production stalwart Mickey Stevenson claimed that,

"Motown was a very strong backer of Martin Luther King's total program" and the King connection certainly endured after the civil rights leader's death. Having missed out on the 1963 March on Washington, in June 1968 Gordy joined other celebrities, including Sammy Davis, Sidney Poitier, Jerry Butler, Marlon Brando and Paul Newman, for a Solidarity Day as part of the Poor People's Campaign in Washington. On the first anniversary of King's assassination, he had his acts play benefit concerts around the country and, perhaps even more astonishing given Gordy's notoriously strict business acumen, gave all other Motown employees a day's paid leave.

In 1969, Gordy also allowed Diana Ross and the Supremes to join Sammy Davis, Nancy Wilson, Bill Cosby, Dick Gregory and Diahann Carroll in publicly endorsing a bill presented by black Michigan congressman John Conyers, calling for King's birthday to be made a public holiday. When the King holiday was finally secured in 1983, Motown – and especially Stevie Wonder – was again at the forefront of the campaign. By that time Gordy had also contributed funds to the founding of the Martin Luther King Jr. Center for Non-violent Social Change in Atlanta, while in the 1990s, Gordy has been one of the sponsors of the Martin Luther King papers project based at Stanford University.

Throughout the late 1960s and early 1970s, Berry Gordy's personal ambitions and business priorities often danced an awkward sort of dance with his wider concerns for black justice, power and opportunity in America. For a while he devoted considerable energy to trying to keep the demands of capitalism, conscience and community in some kind of step, never letting the one tread all over the needs of the other. When push came to shove however, there was seldom any doubt where his priorities lay.

Gordy, the most successful black entrepreneur of his generation and a living embodiment of black integrationist aspirations, was always reluctant to allow his artists to embrace potentially controversial subjects or publicly espouse causes which might jeopardise their white audience. This basic conservatism and caution persisted even in Motown's most activist phase during the black power era. When the Jackson Five emerged as the hottest property in the late 1960s and 1970s with massive crossover hits like "I Want You Back" and "ABC", Gordy was paranoid that the young group might somehow appear too black or too militant and alienate their white audience. After one interviewer asked the brothers if their impressive afro hairdos "had something to do with Black Power", Gordy promptly banned discussion of any political matters – and drugs – in all future press conferences.

Typically, Gordy had accepted more social commentary in Motown recordings, alongside more progressive sounds and a new attitude towards making albums, only when he was convinced that they would increase sales and street credibility. Moreover, it is important to recognise that the musical and lyrical innovations of the Temptations, Stevie Wonder and Marvin Gaye were sanctioned at a time when the classic Motown sound was losing its pre-eminence in the market place to white rock, southern soul, and the new black funk-rock-soul fusions. In other words, Motown's politicisation was always a commercial as well as a political and racial decision, with Gordy following, rather than leading, broader social and cultural trends.

Another vinyl initiative which bespoke Gordy's new, public social conscience was the creation of the Black Forum subsidiary, which opened in October 1970 with a collection of Martin Luther King's anti-Vietnam speeches, *Why I Oppose the War.* The label subsequently became an outlet for recordings by both black political nationalists, including the Black Panthers' Deputy Minister of information and subsequent chair, Elaine Brown, and cultural nationalists like Larry Neal and Imamu Amiri Baraka. At a time when the Panthers and Ron Karenga's US were exchanging bullets as well as verbal insults on the west coast in their debates over the proper strategies for black liberation, at least political and cultural nationalists could co-exist peacefully on Black Forum, which survived a couple of years before poor sales prompted Gordy to close it.

As part of the general expansion of Gordy's financial support for certain individuals, organisations and causes through corporate and private donations, benefit concerts and public endorsements, some of the proceeds from Black Forum releases went directly to the Martin Luther King Jr. Memorial Fund Foundation and the SCLC. Given the distinctly ambivalent attitude to the non-violent tactics and integrationist goals of the SCLC expressed by many of the contributors to the Black Forum releases, this disbursement of royalties was not without its irony. It did, however, suit Motown's purposes rather well, allowing the label to flirt with black radicalism and acquire a patina of militancy, while actually offering much more formal and tangible – which is to say financial – support to what were perceived as more moderate civil rights groups and black initiatives.

Certainly, Motown contributed to the mayoralty campaigns which ushered in a new era of black electoral politics in the North during the late 1960s and early 1970s. It supported Richard Hatcher in Gary, Indiana, the home town of the Jackson Five, who performed with Gladys Knight and the Pips, Shorty Long and Motown's Canadian soul band, Bobby Taylor and the Vancouvers, in a benefit concert at Gary's Gilroy Stadium. In Newark, Stevie Wonder, the Supremes and recent Motown acquisition Chuck Jackson, joined other black celebrities – and even some of the dwindling band of white celebrity activists, like Dustin Hoffman – in the campaign Imainu Amiri Baraka organised to raise money and support for Kenneth Gibson. After Gibson's triumph, the Supremes returned in December 1971 and performed another benefit concert, swaddled in African costumes and spouting the odd phrase of Swahili much to the delight of an audience rejoicing in its new Afrocentric identity.

Apart from providing promotional and financial support for the SCLC and black politicians, other recipients of Gordy's largesse included the NAACP and its Legal Defense and Education Fund, the United Negro College Fund, the National Association for Sickle Cell Diseases, the Afro-American Heritage Association, the Urban League, Howard University, and boxer Sugar Ray Robinson's Youth Foundation. These grants were usually administered in amounts of less than $1,000 and rarely more than $10,000 through the Gordy Foundation Inc., although they were reputedly supplemented on occasions by much larger personal contributions. Again, it is striking that almost all of this money went to decidedly respectable, moderate groups and organisations. Gordy made no secret of his essential conservatism when it came to strategies for black protest. He even defended the unfashionable workhorse of the black struggle, the legalistic NAACP, from radicals who complained that it "had done too little". Gordy insisted that "if it hadn't been for them we wouldn't have come this far".

As befitted a corporation suffused with an integrationist ethic, not all the recipients of Motown's generosity were black. Detroit's East Catholic High School, the National Jewish Hospital in Denver, the Detroit Symphony Orchestra and the Los Angeles International Film Exposition were among the beneficiaries. The label also supported liberal white Democratic Party candidates and endorsed coalition, rather than separatist, politics. As early as June 1965, the Supremes had contributed to a CBS television special promoting Lyndon Johnson and his War on Poverty. Again, this was a shrewd choice of political allegiance, since by endorsing a presidential social welfare programme which just happened to greatly benefit blacks, the label demonstrated its social concerns, but avoided rigid identification with exclusively black issues.

A year later, the same group graced a presidential fundraiser in Las Vegas for Lyndon Johnson and Hubert Humphrey, who the label eventually endorsed for the presidency in 1968 after the murder of Robert Kennedy. The company also contributed to both the Humphrey Institute in St Paul, Minnesota and the Robert F. Kennedy Memorial in Washington, while proceeds from a $1,000-a-plate fundraising concert by Diana Ross and the Supremes in April 1969 were used to defray some of Kennedy's outstanding political debts. The Kennedy connection continued when Edward attended a June 1969 benefit concert by the Temptations on behalf of Michigan's white Democratic senator Philip Hart.

This all amounted to a significant contribution to the financing and promotion of the mainstream civil rights movement and what remained of its liberal allies during the late 1960s and early 1970s. Yet Gordy never allowed these new racial and political concerns to compromise his spirited quest for an ever larger share of the white market. There was no retreat to the ghetto for Gordy: no real ideological connection with the growing parochialism and insularity of much black cultural, economic and political nationalism. Indeed, if at one level Gordy's mission was to promote an unmistakably black American music in the mainstream, on another level it was just to compete in that mainstream successfully, irrespective of the product – and that was a far more radical gesture within the context of America's continued racial compartmentalisation. In the heart of the black pride and consciousness era, Motown signed and recorded a succession of white artists, including Kiki Dee, Chris Clark and Crystal Mansion. Gordy also established the rock-oriented Rare Earth and MoWest labels, and the highly successful country subsidiary, Melodyland, all of which were conceived initially to produce white acts for a primarily white audience.

At the same time, Gordy continued to push his established stars away from the black theatres and clubs, towards the showbusiness mainstream. Between the Supremes' breakthrough appearance at the Las Vegas Copacabana Club in May 1965 and Stevie Wonder's date at the New York Copa in March 1970, eight Motown artists had headlined at these shrines of middle-American wealth and blue-rinse respectability. Motown acts also became more visible to a national audience via television. While many black artists struggled for exposure, there were regular spots for Motown performers on prestigious network shows hosted by Ed Sullivan, Dinah Shore and Mike Douglas. Gordy cultivated an especially close relationship with NBC. In January 1968, the network even broadcast an episode of *Tarzan* – the most watched in the series' history – in which the Supremes played three nuns. The following April, NBC provided Diana Ross with her first solo appearance on the *Dinah Shore Show*. Marvin Gaye's duet with *Tammi Terrell* on a July 1967 television commercial for Coke represented another breakthrough into a previously white-dominated field. That same month, Gordy signed a lucrative distribution deal with the mail-order Columbia Record Club, expressly for the purpose of reaching the white market even more efficiently.

At a time when the relationship between corporate capitalism, racism and systemic inequalities in American society was the subject of intense scrutiny among many black power activists, the cosy relationship between Gordy, Motown and major white corporations like Coca-Cola and NBC was sometimes viewed suspiciously. When, in July 1967, the Four Tops and Supremes were scheduled to play Central Park under contract to the Schaefer Beer Company, death threats from black militants led to a major security operation. That same month, the worst of all the 1960s racial uprisings forced the temporary closure of Motown's offices on Detroit's West Grand Boulevard. Allegedly following an anonymous phone call threatening that "Motown will burn by Halloween", the company decided to move, first to a more salubrious part of Detroit and then, in 1972, to Los Angeles, where Gordy had spent increasingly long periods since the mid 1960s.

The move westwards was perfectly justified in terms of Motown's new interest in film and television as manifested in the motion pictures *Lady Sings the Blues* and *Mahogany,* a succession of Motown television specials, and the Jackson Five's animated television series. Gordy was head of an ambitious, rapidly diversifying entertainment corporation and naturally wanted to be nearer the main levers of media power and showbusiness influence. Nevertheless, Motown's abandonment of its neighbourhood roots in pursuit of profit simply intensified black radical and white critical resentment of a company whose major sin was to pursue the American Dream with relentless enthusiasm, verve and extraordinary success.

Gordy was undaunted by accusations that he was selling out black America and traducing its culture. He took comfort from the fact that blacks continued to buy Motown records in huge numbers throughout the black power era. Indeed, they seemed considerably more impressed by his conspicuous material success and relative power in a white-controlled industry than bothered about his refusal to pay lip service to voguish ideas of racial, political, cultural economic correctness. Like James Brown and most black capitalists and professionals, Gordy firmly believed that the creation of personal wealth and attainment of mainstream success *was* a form of progressive racial politics, and of black economic and cultural leadership. Paradoxically, however, this sometimes required a ruthless disregard, or subordination, of racial loyalties and ultimately helped to legitimise a socio-economic system in which racism flourished and exploitation was deeply embedded.

Certainly, Gordy did not hesitate to terminate his dealings with black booking agencies like Henry Wynne's Supersonic Attractions in favour of white tour operators like International Creative Management and the William Morris Agency who were better placed to book Motown artists into plush white venues, Moreover, at a time when NATRA and other black media and civil rights groups were campaigning for greater black managerial opportunities within the recording and related industries, he continued to hire white executives and professionals to key strategic positions, simply because they would help secure better access to the white market. By 1970 four of Motown's eight executive vice-presidents were white. When in 1974 another white, Rob Cohen, was appointed creative vice-president of the newly consolidated Motown Industries, his brief was to find "fresh new approaches with the broadest possible appeal to the largest potential audience".

For Gordy, then, black power was a worthy goal, but one which he felt must necessarily be pursued pragmatically, within the context of superior white economic, political, legal and police power. Some of these beliefs brought him close to Jesse Jackson, who also had little time for fanciful notions of black economic and political separatism. Instead, Jackson sought better black opportunities and power within the established political and corporate structure, and more investment from existing corporations in the development of black-owned businesses and financial institutions. In October 1969, Motown supplied the Four Tops, Originals, Marvin Gaye, and Martha and the Vandellas to perform in support of the first Black Business and Cultural Exposition in Chicago, a celebration of black capitalism with a conscience organised under the auspices of Operation Breadbasket. Jackson warmly thanked Gordy, who also sent a "galaxy of Motown stars" to subsequent expositions, for his support. "Motown's presence here establishes beyond a doubt that you are personally committed to the struggle for social justice and that Motown, an economic corporate giant, also has a corporate social conscience", said Jackson.

In September 1971, Gordy also supported the launch of Jackson's new organisation, People United to Save Humanity (PUSH). As part of PUSH's inaugural sessions in Chicago, Gordy delivered an address to the annual National Businessmen's Breakfast which sounded the unmistakable note of self-interest at the heart of his brand of black capitalism. "I have been fortunate to be able to provide opportunities for young people", he explained. "Opportunities are supposed to knock once in a lifetime, but too often we have to knock for an opportunity. The first obligation we (as black businessmen) have is to ourselves and our own employees, the second is to create opportunities for others". It was a sense of priorities Gordy shared with most entrepreneurial capitalists.

Motown 1960s Top Ten – Brian Ward

1 "Heatwave" – Martha and the Vandellas
An impossibly joyous rush of sound, which in many ways ushered in the 'classic' Motown sound of the 1960s. Above it all, Martha's vocal hits you like a, well, like a heatwave...

2. "Ask The Lonely" – Four Tops,
A vastly underrated ballad boasting one of Motown's very best melody lines. The great angst-ridden vocal by Levi Stubbs, coupled with the soaring background harmonies, give it an epic feel, but without the histrionics which marred some Four Tops productions.

3. "Ooh, Baby Baby" – The Miracles
There is an utterly transcendent moment on this track when Smokey Robinson pauses an extra nanosecond between one 'baby' and the next. It still sends shivers up and down my aging spine.

4. "The Way You Do The Things You Do" – The Temptations
This marvellous up-beat lyric and infectious tune provided a perfect vehicle for the closest Motown ever came to an old-fashioned vocal group. The Tempts' harmonies never sounded smoother.

5. "Determination" – The Contours
I always liked the Contours' no-holds barred, party animal approach to filling dance floors. "Do You Love Me", "Can You Do It" and the wry "First I Look At The Purse" might all have made the list, but "Determination" – like the Vandellas' "Dancing In The Street" – is one of those Motown songs in which African Americans found a little extra meaning at the height of the civil rights struggle.

6. "Needle In A Haystack" – The Velvelettes
On another day I might have had the Marvelettes' "Please Mr. Postman", or even Mary Wells' "My Guy", but this is just as good an example of Motown's mastery of the girl group sound.

7. "Nothing's Too Good For My Baby" – Stevie Wonder
As a big fan of Stevie Wonder's early 1970s work, it's easy to forget just how good he was at these sorts of witty, high energy dance stomps.

8. "I Heard It through The Grapevine" – Marvin Gaye
Immaculate blend of vocal, instrumentation and material – and probably the first Motown record I owned.

9. "Way Over There" – The Miracles
Given that Smokey Robinson has my favourite Motown voice, this is him working at some remove from his usual sweet coo. A passionate, rough-edged rhythm and blues shout guaranteed to stir the blood.

10. "It Takes Two" – Marvin Gaye & Kim Weston
Touch and go as to whether I prefer Marvin with Tami Terrell or Kim Weston, but this just about gets the nod. A classic love song of timeless charm.

Motown Quotes II

"During the sixties, there was a struggle for black music acceptance among whites. Before Berry Gordy, it was thought of as not particularly chic to have black record collections in your home if you were white. Motown did a great deal to alleviate that." *Marvin Gaye*

"In the South you'd have to do one show for the blacks and one show for the whites, and you'd go in there and some of them would yock it up and really have a good time with you. Then you'd go back out and wonder who's going to have to pull the gun first because of getting the bus overturned or something like that." *Katherine Anderson of The Marvelettes*

"The long bus rides were a drag, especially in the Deep South, where hotels willing to accept blacks were scarce, and often the only place to wash up would be a bus terminal. Finding a restaurant could also be tough; many meals had to be carried out the back door and eaten in the bus." *Don Waller in* The Motown Story

6

Motown Style – The Charm School and Miss Powell
by Kingsley Abbott

Being a member of the Tamla Motown Appreciation Society in the early sixties could be pretty exciting for someone in their mid-teens. Living in easy reach of central London, I was able to visit most of the places and venues that I heard about through the Society. Even more importantly, it meant being part of the network that got to hear about the visiting artists and their itinerary of London club dates and TV shows. In those days it was usually pretty easy to talk your way into TV studios, and visits after school in Hampstead to the Ready Steady Go *studio at Wembley Park were an easy and fun way to spend an afternoon. The airport authorities were also tolerant of banner waving groups arriving to greet visitors to our shores. Numbers never got so great that there was ever any crowd problems, indeed, more often than not, it was no more than a handful of us who were able to make the trip.*

The Motown artists were genuinely appreciative of the greetings, and were always happy to hold up the impatient limo drivers hired by EMI to whisk them off to hotels or receptions. The artists, their musicians and tour managers (some of these roles were often doubled up), appeared touched that people were there to welcome them, especially for singers who were yet to have British hits. Those of us who made the trips were rewarded with chats, autographs and photo opportunities with artists who behaved in every way as stars. They looked good with great clothes and hair, they carried themselves well, and they talked to us in such a way that we felt valued. They were well groomed, and very, very good looking. By any standpoint, both the boys and the girls would have turned heads in any room. These gods would not only talk to us, but also suggest further contact through visits to clubs and hotels. They were often happy to leave names on doors for gigs, or to make arrangements for us to contact key personnel to give us access to them. In the early stages, Motowners would usually stay at the Cumberland Hotel opposite Marble Arch, where we fans would frequently visit and be welcomed into their rooms to share teas or coffees whilst they questioned us about Britain and the music scenes. Even off duty like this, Martha & the Vandellas especially, would maintain a poise that particularly impressed me.

Not until much later did I realise that I was experiencing first hand the results of Motown's Charm School. Early on in 1962, wise advisers like Beans Bowles had counselled Berry Gordy of the desirability of proper artist presentation. The advice was taken up and led to the involvement in the Motown story of Miss Maxine Powell. Miss Powell was the director of a successful black modelling school – the US's first such organisation (at which two of Berry's sisters, Anna and Gwen, had modelled) as well as running a black Finishing School.

When speaking to Martha Reeves in preparation for this book, it was obvious that she still held Miss Powell in the highest esteem and she was most insistent that I should call her. When I rung the lady for a chat, I quickly found her to be a fascinating interviewee. The following thoughts and memories are excerpts from our conversation:

Miss Powell: "I grew up with actresses and models. When I came to Detroit, I thought that it was like a pumpkin that I could awake. I thought of it as my mission. I developed my building, and many people would come to me. It was a huge building that could hold hundreds of people. That was my school, for modelling and finishing. We would put on a production show once a year, and in the Fifties I remember paying $285 just for the lighting. That was indeed a lot of money in those days. We would need over 175 yards of material just to do the drapes! The floor of my ballroom was like a bowling alley, and we had a brand new grand piano in there.

I knew the Gordys before there was Motown. Their printing shop printed one of my booklets. They did the best offset printing work. Through this I met Esther Edwards, and her husband George Edwards who was a local politician. He came to one of my shows and gave out the prizes. I donated some space for his campaign headquarters. The Gordys were a very close knit family. They helped each other out a good deal. Gwen became one of my models, and she became the first black model to be on the back page of *The Free Press*. In the Fifties that was a very good thing to get.

Berry Gordy came to me about the artists. We had the first finishing school in the record business, although I do not recall any official contract during the period. I ran it for four years, and the artists had to work at their tasks for two hours a day. They would get their itinerary of things to do, even when they were on the road. When they first came, I would have them all in a circle, and I would teach by example. I would always teach things by example, in a positive way. Some of the artists were rude and crude when they came to me; some were from very humble beginnings. I would say to them that my department would make them able to appear before kings and queens, and so I treated *them* like kings and queens. I offered *class*. Class will turn heads, so in that way I was teaching them self-growth. I taught them about who they were and what made them tick.

I would make them look at their clothes, and together we would find what was right for each individual. Certain colours make people glow. I fitted the clothes to each person, depending on things like neck length and waist size. I would go with them sometimes for big occasions or visits, and I would do their make-up, buy clothes, and I would carry different items of jewellery in my purse. I would put them into suits that we could dress up or down. Good taste and looks is an *art*. It is not to do with money. As well as this, Motown artists learned how to treat people. There was never any day when you got out of the wrong side of the bed. If they were insecure, we worked on that, and then they felt beautiful. They had to realise that *everyone* has something to offer, but they had to develop self-discipline and not to wear their feelings on their sleeve. I always teach to be a *winner*. They were my flowers. There were some weeds, some diamonds in the rough, but you cultivate them. They also had experienced people like Harvey Fuqua and Maurice King to help them on the road. Maurice would help them as music and vocal coach.

I don't believe that I had any favourites, but some occasions do stay in my mind. I loved Marvin Gaye. He had been a ballad singer with Harvey's group The Moonglows before Motown. He said that he didn't need any charm or finishing school. I told him that he sang with his eyes closed and looked asleep, and that his posture was poor, so he said OK. When Diana Ross first came to me, she held the microphone too close to her mouth. She looked as if she was trying to eat it, so we worked on microphone technique. The Supremes once visited me to show me a new dance that they had for a record. It was what I called a 'naughty' dance. It was most unsuitable, so I showed them how to change it to be much classier. Instead of shaking their whole bodies, I showed them how to do a roll of their buttocks *with class*. I also taught them how to sit properly at different heights. Soon after, they were to do a television show where they sat on high stools.

In their act, The Temptations could sweat a good deal, which was problematic in a performance if they were raised above the audience. So we worked on ways of keeping them cooler. Stevie Wonder had his own tutors, so I didn't really work with him. Gladys Knight came to Motown as an already polished and poised performer, and Tammi Terrell was a delight as she had what I would call a natural poise on stage. Another class lady was Martha Reeves. I spent a good deal of time with both Kim Weston and Brenda Holloway helping to develop them. I recall I came to England with Kim Weston during the Sixties, and I believe we stayed in the President Hotel.

All the Motown artists treated me with respect, as I did with them. I believe that I brought class to Motown."

Miss Powell went to work at the Wayne County Community College in 1971 as an instructor in Personal Development. She wrote a book on the subject, which is still a set text at the college. Whilst speaking to her, I recognised a teacher who remains eager to spread her personal philosophy wherever possible. Her beliefs centre upon excellence, positive attitudes and self-belief, which certainly came out through her brief spell with Motown. Perhaps more importantly, she is still eager to impress these deeply held beliefs on anyone who is lucky enough to come into her orbit. Looking back on my own early contacts with Motown artists, I can understand more fully where their impeccable behaviour originated from. Miss Powell did a very good job.

With special thanks to Mike Critchley.

7

Launching The Tamla Motown Label:
Reminiscences with Derek Everett
by Kingsley Abbott

Initial Motown releases in the U.K. appeared on a variety of labels. There were eleven on London American, four on Fontana and nineteen on Oriole before Motown settled with EMI and their Stateside label. Derek Everett was largely responsible for the Stateside releases and the time that ran up to the launch of Motown's own label in the U.K. We met for a lengthy Soho lunch just round the corner from Ronnie Scott's where Derek now runs that club's Jazz record company.

KA: *How did you come to be at EMI?*
DE: I joined them in 1954 as a young lad in their sales promotion department. I was desperate to get into the music business somewhere, and EMI always answered letters. The director L. G. Wood interviewed me and gave me a test on the business. I think it was because I knew Bonnie Lou was at number 29 that week that I got the job! It was a very, very straight-laced traditional English company. Not a hair or trouser crease out of place! In fact, they had a very strict dress code. Once someone had been to a morning wedding and he was smartly but slightly casually dressed, and he was told to go back home and change into proper working clothes! It was a very strict atmosphere for my introduction to the music business, and I pretty well started at the bottom.
What were their American links like then?
I think that around about 1956 they lost RCA to Decca and CBS to Philips, so they were very keen to acquire more U.S. product. They had MGM, Capitol and Verve, but these did not yield the most exciting records. Decca's London American outlet had most of the good independent stuff. In the early Sixties, we were looking at Motown. At least we were aware of them, but it seemed that no one really wanted to know at that stage. There had been a handful of odd releases before Oriole started to pick some up for here. Oriole was a small independent then, and they only picked up a few which couldn't have been too good for Motown. Oriole was bought by CBS. At that point, Motown started to approach EMI, but the top brass knew nothing about them or the music. Around the same time Top Rank, which had been putting out several odd American releases, was offered to EMI when someone wanted to get shot of it. Top Rank was set up big at one point with big Oxford Street offices. They got U.S. stuff, but they really only got the leftovers. Freddy Cannon and B. Bumble & The Stingers were about as big as they got around '62/3. I think that it had lost about £1m then. Anyway, I was given the job to look after it. "Sort it out" they said to me. The offices had been wrecked and stripped bare! The best part was that it gave some small U.S. label distribution to EMI which was to later to prove important when they were trying to break the Beatles in the U.S. The odd reciprocal deals is why the early Beatles product was on odd labels like Vee Jay and Swan, which I believe both came to us as part of the Top Rank deal. We also got Laurie and Scepter. They were all standard low cost deals, with the aim of giving us routes to selling in the U.S. I went over with Ronnie Scott to investigate selling Cliff there, but they had millions of Cliffs there! They didn't need it; until the Beatles that is! Even then, Capitol turned them down at first, which is why we turned to the smaller set-ups that we had deals with for the first issues. They were very suspicious at first, but then they sud-

denly realised there were people screaming for Beatles records. Then they were *very* happy!

Tell me about Stateside, which was about my favourite label as a young record collector when it appeared.

Stateside was set up by EMI with the very specific aim of trying to destroy London American because they realised it was the market leader for exciting U.S. product. Most U.S. independent labels did not understand the European market, so they needed a decent outlet. We used to scour the U.S. Hot 100 to try to make quick deals for what were the newer types of records that were selling. I guess that we went mostly for pop and early soul mostly, whereas London ranged a bit wider and included things like Country. It was at this time that the interest in Motown grew quickly, as it was then that their records were really taking off in The States. Motown were building up, and they sent a delegation to London. Barney Ales, Phil Jones and Esther Edwards came with the brief of putting international business together. Barney was a tough guy. He could turn off one minute, and then be all "We want this and we want that" the next. Esther was at some of the meetings, but she was also interested in the shopping opportunities!

There was a lot of resistance to Motown at first, with all sorts of "It's all the same" press comments. Reviewers then were mostly dumb, and generally life and attitudes were different. For future releases, EMI had scheduling meetings on Friday afternoons. Ron White would chair them, and it was all quite old school tie. We'd play things we had and try to justify why they should be released. I used to try Vee-Jay Blues stuff like John Lee Hooker and Jimmy Reed. Once L. G. Wood asked me "Did we get offered 'The Locomotion' and the Carole King woman?" I told him that we had, but that we had turned it down. "Oh, well," he replied "We can't win them all. It's yet another American dance." [*At this point I show Derek a list of the Motown Stateside releases.*] "Good grief, I didn't realise that we had issued as many as that!"

Tell me how the relationship with Motown developed.

In many ways it was a magic era. Suddenly, there was a key factor in the equation, and that was the emergence of Black Power in the States. Black people were emerging *in their own right* for really the first time. Before that time it had been back of the bus time all over. Having said this though, it's interesting to remember that Berry put out a *white* sales team. There was a great mix at Atlantic, but many other companies weren't reaching black audiences. Chess was always the worst in some ways. They never issued royalty statements to their artists, and this caused problems. Berry Gordy saw how *not* to do it. There were of course two sides to it all: the business side which needed profits, and the artists side which needed looking after. To do it properly, Motown *had* to be tight. Anyway, we did not have too much contact with Berry, except there was a time when he asked me to send him a translation of Eric Burdon's lyrics from "House Of The Rising Sun". He couldn't make them out at all! Most of the business contact was with Barney and Phil. All the artists who came over were simply delightful.

Basically we started to put out all the Top 100 hits, all the hot items. We gave them good publicity, and used our own mag *Record Mail* to help break them. This was a mag in record shops priced at one penny, as a sort of loss leader. We had Stevie Wonder on the cover when he came on the scene. It all helped to give us a quicker turnover. I suppose that we didn't look upon it as a 'sound' then, but as an *image*. [*Ed.: Indeed, the Stateside era covered the time when the releases where more varied in sound – when Stevie's releases were harmonica instrumentals and groups like The Contours still had a good rough edge.*]

How about when the Tamla Motown label began in its own right?

Well in 1964 it had really started to break in a big way in Britain. On the *Light Programme* we had Sam Costa and Alan Freeman who were always interested in playing something a bit different. There were hits for Mary Wells, Martha & The Vandellas and

The Supremes, and quite a lot of interest in the other acts. The Beatles had covered Motown material, and had Mary Wells on a tour, and in general the British public were becoming aware that all these acts were coming from the same place; Dave Godin had been over to Detroit that summer, and partly through that Motown was keen to get a really identifiable image over here. So the TM label was set up. There were basically three of us involved at first: Rex Oldfield, Colin Hadley on Sales and Marketing and me as A&R. EMI gave us the go ahead, and once we had it up and running they didn't interfere. Communication with Motown was good. We wanted hits – they gave us them. There were no specific pushes on any particular artists. We saw Martha and Stevie as the future at that point, and we saw Marvin as having a harder sound. We began in March 1965, and we had the perfect launch pad for the label with "The Sound Of Motown" TV special which was done at about the same time when Berry, all the artists and everyone came of for that and a big tour. The 'Image' was in place!

PART 2

Stevie coped incredibly well on stage, moving confidently from drums to mike.

8
Smokey Robinson and the Miracles: Ooh Baby Baby
by Bill Dahl

Smokey and Claudette Robinson meet two fans

Smokey Robinson and The Miracles were one of the very first successes for Motown, with sales of their early records part funding further company development. They also turned out to be one of the best loved acts in the U.K. after they eventually broke through with records like "Tracks Of My Tears" and "The Tears Of A Clown". This extensive article comes from the U.S. magazine Goldmine, *dated 10th December 1993. It contains various interviews with members of The Miracles, and traces their career from their early Doo Wop days. Bill Dahl is a respected Chicago based writer whose work has graced many magazine articles and CD liner notes. Later in the book you will find further examples of his work with the pieces on Marvin Gaye and Junior Walker.*

In a celebrated, often-cited quote, no less a tunesmith that Bob Dylan once humbly cited Smokey Robinson as "America's greatest living poet". But even an unchallenged master of insightful metaphors like Robinson couldn't do it entirely by himself, not, at least, for the first 14 years of his gold record-earning recording career.

Without the Miracles – Claudette Robinson (then his wife), tenor Bobby Rogers, baritone Ronnie White, bass Warren "Pete" Moore, and invaluable Robinson writing partner and ace guitarist Marv Tarplin – backing Robinson's heartrending sky-high tenor, the richly textured "You've Really Got A Hold on Me," "Ooo Baby Baby" and

"The Tears Of A Clown" might have cast very different sorts of Motown moods.

Not only did Robinson write songs like no one else, his floating vocal delivery sounded like no other R&B singer either. The public responded favorably: from 1959 to 1972, Robinson and the Miracles consistently rated as one of the country's premier R&B acts. They charted an impressive 42 times on *Billboard*'s pop charts, scoring another four hits as a group after Robinson's 1972 departure.

As a solo artist, Robinson kept on recording smashes for Motown until 1987, although the Miracle's trademark harmonies no longer cushioned his recorded output. With new front man Billy Griffin, the Miracles had quite a few hits left in them: "Do It Baby," and "Don't Cha Love Me" were huge R&B hits in 1974, and "Love Machine (Part I)" topped the pop charts the following year. As Motown prepares to release a comprehensive multi-disc boxed set retrospective of Robinson's seminal work, it's time to re-examine the contribution of all six principal members of the Miracles.

William "Smokey" Robinson Jr. was born in Detroit on February 19, 1940. From the get-go, the lad loved cowboy movies, and when he was six or seven, his uncle Claude bestowed him with the dusty old Western moniker "Smokey Joe". The frivolous nickname would, in slightly truncated form, stand the test of time.

Surrounded by music as a child ("I've been writing songs since I was six years old," he says), Robinson's playmates included the Motor City's first family of gospel singers, the Franklins – sisters Aretha, Carolyn and Erma among them. His mother, Flossie, cued up 78s on her Victrola that deeply shaped Robinson's musical tastes, ranging from jazzy Billie Holiday to rafter-raising spirituals.

"My mom and my two sisters played a lot of Sarah Vaughan," says Robinson. "I heard all kinds of music in my house. Mostly Sarah Vaughan, Billy Eckstine, Ella Fitzgerald, Count Basie, people like that. Sarah Vaughan, I think, was probably my favourite vocalist out of all of them. She used to cry her songs. She was like an instrument to me. She just did things with her voice that only her and Ella could do."

By the time he was in fifth grade, Robinson was writing songs and singing regularly, forming a vocal quartet in junior high school that included Aretha's brother, Cecil Franklin. In Smokey's early 1950s social circle, doo-wop ruled.

When I got to be about 11 or 12, I became interested in what they termed then as the R&B music and the rock 'n' roll kind of sound," says Robinson. "Billy Ward was the leader of a group called the Dominoes, in which Clyde McPhatter sang the lead vocals. The first record I ever heard by them was a record called "Have Mercy Baby". I mean, I thought it was a woman singing the song! And I had one of those real high voices when I used to sing.

"Then I went to this theater in Detroit called the Broadway Capitol, and they were playing there. And I saw that it was Clyde McPhatter singing, man, and that was really inspirational to me, because I had a high voice, and the girls were going crazy over him. So Clyde McPhatter was probably like my first male idol as a singer. Then of course, Nolan Strong in Detroit with a group, the Diablos. So he was a Detroiter, and he had that same voice, and when we'd go to see them in person, he'd sing a lot of Clyde McPhatter songs.

"Then along came Frankie Lymon and the Teenagers," he says. "I had five idols. They were Clyde McPhatter, Nolan Strong, Frankie Lymon, Sam Cooke and Jackie Wilson. Jackie Wilson turned out to be probably my greatest idol that I ever had, as far as an entertainer. Because, to me, he had everything. Jackie was just a complete package. The other guys could sing, but Jackie could sing and dance and entertain. He was really just great. So I think I admired him more than all the other guys."

While attending Detroit's Northern High School in 1955, Robinson assembled his own group, the Five Chimes, who would eventually evolve into the Miracles. "Ronnie White and Pete Moore and I had been singing since we were about 11, says Robinson. "I met those guys when I was just about to graduate from elementary school. In fact, I knew Ron before then, because Ron used to be our paper boy. So I had known them for a while.

"Then we had a neighborhood group. There were so many groups in our neighborhood. Every other person was in a group. When we got to be about 14 or so, we met Emerson Rogers, who was Claudette's brother. And we had some other guys singing with us – James Grice, a guy named Clarence Dawson. It was Ron, Pete, Clarence, James and me. We called ourselves the Chimes.

Clarence Dawson quit, and Emerson Rogers took his place, and we changed our name to the Matadors. And then James had gotten his girlfriend pregnant when we were about 16, so he quit the group. He got married, and Bobby Rogers, who was Claudette's cousin, took his place. We were still the Matadors."

Smokey had been infatuated with Claudette Rogers, sister of Emerson "Sonny" Rogers since the first time he laid eyes on her in 1954. They dated, but not exclusively, throughout Smokey's high school years. Was it love at first sight? "For me it was. Not for her," says Robinson with a laugh. "I had to work on that one, man."

In August 1957, the group landed a prized audition for the same folks who handled Jackie Wilson, then generally regarded as a deity on the Detroit R&B scene. But the Matadors suddenly found themselves short one member.

"After we graduated from high school, Emerson wanted to go into the Army, so that's what he did," says Robinson. "He had his parents sign for him to go into the Army. And then shortly after he had left to go to the Army, we got a chance to go for this audition. So we were used to singing with five voices, and Claudette was in a sister group to our group called the Matadorettes. So we asked her is she would go down with us to the audition, and she did. And that was how it all started."

The quintet strutted its stuff nervously for a triumvirate of fast-rising music moguls: Wilson's manager, Nat Tarnapol; Alonzo Tucker, who would go on to co-write several of Wilson's bigger hits (including "Baby Workout") and a quiet guy who stayed off to one side. Tucker made no bones about it – he just didn't dig the group's approach.

"When he saw us, he didn't like is because of the fact that Claudette was with us," says Bobby Rogers. "He said we were a similar group to the Platters, and (there) can't be two groups in America like that with a woman in the group."

"He really wanted more of a Mickey and Sylvia-type duo, with the three guys singing in the background and Smokey and I singing dual leads,' says Claudette Robinson. "I wanted to sing, but I didn't really want to do the lead. I wanted to do the background."

Fortunately, the pensive man in the corner hears something in the group's delivery that Tucker overlooked. "It just so happened that Berry Gordy was writing songs for Jackie at the time we went for that first audition," says Robinson. "And he just happened to be there that day that we were to audition for Jackie's managers."

Gordy was especially intrigued by Robinson's prolific songwriting talent. "That was what made him interested in us, because he heard a couple of songs that he liked," says Robinson. "He met us outside, and we started talking about where we had gotten the songs from. He introduced himself as Berry Gordy. I had all of Jackie Wilson's records. I couldn't believe he was Berry Gordy, because he looked so young. He looked like he was about our age at the time.

"He introduced himself, and we struck up a conversation about where the songs had come from, and I had written them and so forth. So he said to me, 'Well, do you sing anyone else's songs?' I said, 'Yeah.' So he said, 'What's a current song that you know that you can sing write now for me?' I said, 'Well, how about 'I'm Not A Know It All'?' Frankie Lymon had a song out at the time called 'I'm Not A Know It All.' And so I said, 'I'll sing that for you.'

"So he played the piano and I sang it. And he told me, 'Man, I really, really like your voice. You've got a different sound. Nobody sounds like you, or you don't sound like anybody. I really, really like your voice. I want to work with you guys.' So that was great for me."

"Smokey had a song book of about 100 songs that he had composed, over a period of time." Says Claudette. "So Berry started talking to him. Smokey was aware of who Berry Gordy was. I was not; I mean, I had not heard of him. But Smokey, I guess, would look on the record labels – one of the few people at that time who actually knew the writers of the songs. I only knew the artists."

One of the originals unveiled at the audition was "My Mama Done Told Me," an alluring Latin-beat rocker that was the first of a string of Robinson numbers built around sound advice from a maternal figure. It would admirably fill one side of their debut 45, but what would grace the flip? Smokey, a fast man with a pen, provided the answer in short order, inspired by an *American Bandstand* broadcast. "The number one record at the time was by a group called the Silhouettes, and it was called "Get A Job," says Robinson. "I heard their record all day long, every day. It was the international anthem."

So Robinson sat down and penned the savvy sequel "Got A Job," his youthful tenor vividly relaying a comical sense of frustration over toiling every day in a grocery store. ("Get A Job" inspired more than one answer number, incidentally – in New York the Heartbeats boasted "I Found A Job" on Roulette.)

With Gordy at the production helm, the group cut the two songs at Detroit's United Sound studio in November 1957 (writer's credits were expanded to include Gordy and his writing partner Tyran Carlo, later known as Billy Davis). But a name change for the quintet was clearly in order.

"We needed a name that would suit us," says Robinson. "We couldn't very well be the Matadors, because there was a girl in the group now. So we needed a name that would suit a group of guys that had a girl with the group. And it just so happened that the name that I picked, which was the Miracles, was the one we pulled out of there."

"I think the name that came out was the 'Miracletones' or something, but we took the "Tones" off," says Rogers. "We had names like the Clouds, and stuff like that."

The first bricks in Gordy's corporate empire had yet to be laid, so he sold the Miracles' masters to George Goldner's End Records in New York. Although it didn't chart nationally, "Got A Job" did well enough for End to issue a followup, "Money"/"I Cry". "Money" was another amusing rhumba-tinged item with Claudette's voice very recognizable in the backing mix, while "I Cry" showcased Robinson's soaring delivery on a delicious doo-wop ballad.

The resultant royalty check from End for both singles – a whopping $3.19, according to the 1989 autobiography that Robinson wrote with David Ritz, *Smokey: Inside My Life* – helped strengthen Gordy's resolve to take matters into his own hands. In the winter of 1958, Gordy released the first single to wear his own Tamla logo: Marv Johnson's 'Come To Me'.

"That was the turning point in all our lives, no question about it," says Robinson. "That's what made Detroit different, as far as I'm concerned, because there are talented people everywhere in the world, in every small township; every big city has talented people. But we had Berry Gordy, and that was what gave us the outlet.

"He had met this guy, Marv Johnson. And he was going to record this song on Marv Johnson, which was the very first Motown record ever. It was a song called "Come To Me.' He decided he was going to do it on his own label, but it was going to be a local label. So he did that, and the record broke so big locally until Marv Johnson, he had to go to New York and make a deal for Marv Johnson with United Artists Records."

Johnson may have been lost to United Artists for a while (Gordy continued to write and produce many of Johnson's hits for UA before the singer returned to the corporate fold in the mid-'60s), but the fledgling Motown machine had other projects to work on, such as the Miracles.

Robinson wrote "Bad Girl," the Miracles' third single, while driving around the streets of Detroit. The dreamy doo-wop balled sported trilling flute flourishes that became an early Gordy production staple. Initially issued on the brand-new Motown logo, "Bad Girl" (backed with "I Love Your Baby," an upbeat item with a baritone sax break and Moore's bass cutting in on the bridge a la Coasters) broke nationally, forcing Gordy to sell the distribution rights to Chicago-based Chess Records. In October 1959, "Bad Girl" dented the #93 slot on *Billboard*'s pop list, but Ronnie White believes the song should have done even better.

"It didn't get played because the phrase "bad girl" had a negative context at the time that had nothing to do with the record," White says. "The white stations wouldn't play it, because of the negative connotations that they put with the song. 'Bad girl' at that time meant a girl who had gone out and gotten pregnant, out of wedlock. But that had absolutely nothing to do with the song."

Chess also released the group's next 45, coupling the atmospheric Latin-beat "I Need A Change" with the forceful ballad "All I Want Is You," to considerably less commercial response. Another 1959 release, this one leased to the Chess subsidiary Argo after seeing the light of day locally on Tamla, was a one-time-only duet departure. "It," sung by Ron (White) and Bill (Robinson), was a cute novelty ditty about an out-of-this-world space creature that somehow failed to soar heavenward on the charts. "As a matter of fact, Smokey coerced me into doing this Ron and Bill thing," says White.

With a handful of single releases under their belt, the Miracles hit the road. They got a booking at Harlem's fabled Apollo Theatre – and promptly bombed. "I don't know how we got there, but Berry coerced Bobby Schiffman into signing us, booking us for the week, " says White. "It was horrible. We were ridiculous.

"A guy named Honi Coles who used to work with Cholly Atkins as a tap dance duo, came to see us and said, 'Look, why don't you go and see this guy? He can help you out with the choreography.' We followed his advice and we went to Cholly. And Cholly groomed us, and created the choreographed act for us.

"Because of the work he did with us, and because of the improvement that the people at the company could see in us, they hired Cholly to come and work with other acts. Cholly is in great measure responsible for many of the acts' choreography – the Temptations, he worked with the Tops, the Velvelettes, the Marvelettes, anyone who was anyone."

Shortly after the Apollo debacle, Robinson hooked up with the guitarist of his dreams. "Marv Tarplin was actually playing for Diana Ross and the Primettes," says Robinson. "I've known her since she was about eight. She grew up down the street from me. And when I started to make records and stuff like that, she used to always tell me, 'Smokey, I want to make some records,' and all that. She was still in high school.

"So I had them come along and sing for us one night, and Marv Tarplin was their guitar player. So we were getting ready to go out and do some dates, and I said, 'Hey, baby, I want to use your guitar player to go out and do some dates.' So she said, 'Fine.' And I never gave him back! And then shortly after that, they graduated from high school, and I recorded some stuff on them. 'Cause Berry wouldn't let me record them until they graduated from high school." Tarplin was a perfect writing foil. His fluid licks inspired some of Robinson's most enduring compositions, and Smokey shares the stage with the guitarist even now.

Not only did Robinson connect with his ultimate accompanist, he tied the knot with his longtime sweetheart Claudette in 1959. Although Robinson recalls in his bio that he popped the question while driving back home form a gig in Philly with the entire group egging him on from the back seat, Claudette remembers the big moment a little differently.

"Actually, it was in Detroit," she says. "I guess we had gone together for a while, and he kept saying that he thought we should get married. Of course, with us being so young and my mother having extremely high aspirations of her daughter getting her college degree before doing anything, I wasn't sure if this was gonna go over too well.

"My recollection of it is that he came over to my house, and he got down on his knee and proposed. I didn't dare tell her that he was only making, at that point from Motown,

$5 a week, which was increased to $8 when we got married."

The Miracles leapt head-first into the soul era in 1960 with the gospel-drenched "Way Over There". Doo-wop influence on the track was virtually nil, Robinson strongly emoting over an exciting violin-enriched groove that was a modern departure from the standard R&B fare previously cut by the group. This time, Gordy's own Tamla label would reap the financial reward.

"I had written a song called 'Way Over There' for the Miracles," says Robinson. "I recorded it on us, and it broke really, really, really, really big locally, 'cause we only had a two-record deal with Chess Records.

"So Berry took us to Chicago and re-recorded it. Because the Drifters had come out then, and they were using violins on all their records, everybody started jumping on the violin bandwagon. So Berry took us to Chicago and recorded this song with violins.

"Before that happened, he was saying, 'I don't know who I'm going to put this with nationally.' And I said, 'Hey, man, why don't you just do it nationally yourself? Because nobody's paying us anyway, so you might as well go national with the record and do it yourself.' So he said, 'Well, man, if you've got that much faith in me, that's exactly what I'm gonna do.'"

"Way Over There" and its spine-chilling flip "You Can Depend On Me" failed to chart ("You Can Depend On Me" was also slated for release under the same Tamla 54028 number with "The Feeling Is So Fine" on the other side. Gordy apparently often had second thoughts about his early 45s and retooled them accordingly), but the single helped to establish Tamla on a national scale.

Robinson reverted to the mother's wisdom formula to write his next single, although "Shop Around" was originally intended for Barrett Strong as a follow-up to his smash "Money (That's What I Want)". Gordy thought it would work better as a vehicle for its co-writer (like everything the Miracles had released to this point, the song listed both Robinson and Gordy as authors).

"There were two different versions of 'Shop Around,'" says Robinson. "The first one was slower and bluesy. I had recorded it myself. Berry called me at three o'clock in the morning one morning. He said, 'Hey, man, what's happening?' I said, 'What's happening?!? Are you kidding? I'm asleep!'

"And so he said, 'I want you to call everybody in the group and come over to the studio, because I'm going to re-record "Shop Around". I can't sleep.' I said, 'I can see that you can't sleep, man.' But he had us come over to the studio about three o'clock in the morning, and he had called all the musicians, and everybody showed up except the piano player, so Berry played the piano himself. And we re-recorded 'Shop Around.' That was the one that went to number one."

Not only did the second version of "Shop Around" top the R&B charts for eight weeks in late 1960, it went #2 pop. Robinson recalls the tenor saxist on the rocker as being Gordy's brother-in-law, Ron Wakefield. Its flip was equally memorable. "Who's Lovin' You" was a breathtaking ballad with stunning vocal harmonies and a killer ending spotlighting each member.

"When we did the song 'Who's Lovin' You,' on the end of the song when I just do my 'who's lovin' you' part, in a live performance, people would just wait for that part," says Claudette.

"We were doing an album at the time, because the record company was going and stuff like that, and we were going to do an album, says Robinson. "So 'Who's Lovin' You' just happened to be one of those songs that I had written for it. I was always writing."

The Miracles were now a national draw. The notes to their first album relate "a well publicized incident in St. Louis, where their appearance at a local show caused a near riot when our wonderful fans learned that all seats had been sold out. The crowd was of such proportion that the police had to summon additional police with dogs to quiet them."

That rabid following didn't bite with such vigor at the group's next offering, the solid Robinson-penned rocker "Ain't It, Baby". Gordy would have probably been thrilled with a #15 R&B and #49 pop showing on some of his other fledgling artists, but it must have been a disappointment for the Miracles coming off the smash success of "Shop Around". On the B-side was a tender ballad, "The Only One I Love," Robinson playfully unleashing his magic carpet tenor with charming innocence.

"We came off of 'Shop Around' and went straight to 'Ain't It Baby,'" says Claudette. "And 'Ain't It Baby' was not anywhere near a hit. I think that what they were looking for was a sound similar to 'Shop Around.' Smokey, at that time he wanted to have something entirely different, and that's what we did. So it wouldn't be like a lot of artists at that time who had one song, and then the only things that was different was the name of the song but the same melody line and everything else was almost exactly the same. He had thought, 'Well, no, no, no, we're not gonna do that. We're gonna have it different, so they'll know we can be diverse in our thinking and in our singing.' I don't think the public really went for that. In fact, I'm sure they didn't, because it was not a hit. Nowhere near it."

In June 1961, the group released its first Tamla LP, *Hi... We're The Miracles*, with seven tracks not available as singles. They included the blues-soaked "Your Love", firmly rooted in a "There's Something On Your Mind" grinding groove: "Won't You Take Me Back," spiced by a rippling piano; covers of Marv Johnson's "Don't Leave Me" and Barrett Strong's "Money," and "After All," a doo-woppish ballad that marked Claudette's debut on wax as a lead singer. It was a task she seldom assumed.

"I was quite shy, even with the group, when it came to leads," she says. "What I would do was I'd ask them to turn the lights really low and sort of turn my back on them so I wouldn't have to see their faces peering down at me. 'Cause I thought being outnumbered as the lone female, I was feeling that they were expecting more out of me that I could give. However, Smokey kept saying, 'You can do it. You can do it.'

"On the other hand, I felt as though while we were recording in the studio, that the guys were basically given – let's say if they were to make a mistake while we were recording, the reaction would be, 'Okay, let's do that over again. All right, Ronnie, Pete, Bobby, whoever it may be, let's do that again.' And since Smokey was basically the one who did most of the producing of our records, if I were the one making an error, it was, 'Boo Boo, you were not paying attention!' And it was, 'Okay, now I'm not going to pay attention!' I think you know how husbands and wives can be."

Neither of the group's next two Tamla waxings made it past the middle reaches of the charts. While R&B buyers stuck with the crisply executed uptempo "Mighty Good Lovin'" in the summer of 1961, pushing it to a #21 showing, both sides of the 45 charted pop: "Mighty Good Lovin'" at #51, the violin-cushioned "Broken Hearted" barely creeping up to #97 for a week.

Chicago's Riley Hampton arranged the swirling strings on the more ambitious "Everybody's Gotta Pay Some Dues," penned by Robinson and Ronnie White; it did quite a bit better on the R&B charts, peaking at #11. Its flip, a very mellow "I Can't Believe," was Smokey at his most devotional. *Cookin' With The Miracles*, the group's encore album (and an exceedingly rare commodity now), emerged somewhere through here as well.

Health problems dogged the Miracles throughout 1961–62, a period when Pete Moore was stuck in the Army and away from the group. First, Smokey took sick while the group was playing the Howard Theater in Washington, D.C.

"By the group being so new and having not traveled all over the country, Smokey came down with what we know as the first case of Hong Kong flu," says Claudette. "He was really, really ill. His temperature was up to about 106. I flew him back to Detroit, where he stayed for a month while we went on tour.

"At that time, it was the Motor Town revue. The Miracles were headliners of the show, with Mary Wells co-starring. Mary Wells had a node on her vocal cords, so she had been advised by her doctors not to perform. With her not performing, and the Miracles with their lead singer gone, something had to be done. So we all just sort of filled in."

Early tours were rough on the group. "They were hectic, man." says Robinson. "Hectic and grinding. Fifty one-nighters, that kind of stuff. Driving, you know. Very seldom did we have a bus. We had a bus sometimes, but most of the time, it was a car or caravan."

Robinson was progressing by leaps and bounds as a songwriter, employing clever, insightful metaphorical twists that were light years removed from formulaic R&B fare. "I always tried to do that, 'cause there are no new words," he says. "There are no new notes, or any of that. So I always try to say things differently than how they've been said. Because they're all the same ideas that have been around for eons. So you just have to try to say it that's going to be ear-catching to people."

The dramatic "What's So Good About Goodbye," with its ironic story line and a stirring arrangement sparked by twangy low-end guitar and a violin line seemingly straight out of *Bonanza*, was a prime example of Robinson's blossoming songwriting genius. Released in December 1961, the bittersweet ode was a #16 R&B hit, topping out at #35 pop.

"I was looking at TV one night, and this woman and this man were talking," Robinson says. "They were saying goodbye. They were lovers, you know, and she was asking him, "What's good about that?' That was where it came from."

"I've Been Good To You," the single's flip, deserved hit status on its own, though none was forthcoming. With an aching quiver haunting his falsetto, Robinson delivers the tune's recriminatory message over muted saxes, powerful vocal harmonies, and a strong slow-grind beat.

For "I'll Try Something New," the last Miracles hit to sport Gordy's name as Robinson's co-producer in mid-1962, Hampton fashioned a particularly lush chart, violins and a harp providing pop-styled support that was a far cry indeed for the prototypical Detroit soul sound. Record buyers heartily approved, sending the sacharine ballad to the #11 R&B and #39 pop slots.

I'll Try Something New, their third album, was something of a departure. Instead of featuring Robinson as familiar front man exclusively, the set included lead turns by White on "A Love That Can Never Be" ("That's probably something that I wanted to forget," White says) and Claudette's "He Don't Care About Me" (with its charmingly innocent teenybopper feel, the latter veered into girl group territory).

Either material was in short supply, or Gordy was already grooming his young charges for sedate supper club engagements with modern harmony renditions of "On The Street Where You Live" and Cole Porter's "I've Got You Under My Skin" that were dragged down by overwrought big band arrangements. The album blurb on the back promised more of the same schlock on an upcoming *The Miracles Sing Modern*, but the project was mercifully scrapped.

Berry Gordy tried to pull a fast one in August 1962, resurrecting "Way Over There" as the Miracles' next single. He barely got away with it, eking out a #94 pop showing (more than the now-classic number managed the first time around). At least it was coupled with a new flip side, another mellifluous string-drenched Gordy production, "If Your Mother Only Knew".

The members of the Miracles didn't spend all of their time in the studio and on the road. Almost against his will, Ronnie White stumbled across a kinetic 10-year-old lad named Steveland Morris whose multi-instrumental prowess was amazing.

"My brother talked to me about this guy," says White. "He talked to me, and I had put him off. And I don't know how much time had passed, maybe a year even. But he caught me and trapped me one time, and he said, 'Look, the guy's over there. Why don't you come on over right now?' So I said, 'Okay, all right, all right.' So I went over, and this little blind kid had his drums set up in my mother's living room. And he was playing drums, bongos, rather, and blowing harmonica and singing. And it just blew my mind.

"So I took him over to the studio and introduced him to Berry, and to Brian and Eddie Holland and Lamont Dozier. They signed him, and put him to work with Clarence Paul, who was one of the persons who was very influential in Stevie's development."

Although his first two Tamla albums, *The Jazz Soul of Little Stevie and Tribute to Uncle Ray*, were rather underwhelming, Little Stevie Wonder was already on his way to superstardom.

The pinnacle of R&B chart success blessed the Miracles for the second time in December 1962 with their impassioned "You've Really Got A Hold On Me". Pop fans were almost as impressed, pushing the tune to the #8 position. Robinson took his writing inspiration from Sam Cooke's then-current hit, "Bring It Home On Me".

"Sam had that record out at the time," says Robinson. "I was in New York. I was actually there because I was a vice-president at the time. So I was in New York taking care of some business for Berry for the company with another publisher. And I wanted to write something like 'Bring It On Home To Me.' I was in my hotel room with nothing to do, so that's what I did, 'You've Really Got A Hold On Me.'"

Careful listening to "You've Really Got A Hold On Me" reveals that Robinson is singing in tandem with tenor Bobby Rogers for much of the number. "We had like a double lead vocal there," says Robinson. "He was singing the other lead part."

How "Happy Landing," the gospel-infused scorcher (penned by Robinson and White) that inhabited the other side of the chart-topper, was overlooked is anyone's guess. This time, Robinson's bent on revenge for a broken romance, his vocal atypically rough-edged and uninhibited over a torridly driving groove, and he emits a confident little grunt coming off the sax break that is reminiscent of his main man, Jackie Wilson.

Robinson described "A Love She Can Count On" convincingly for the group's next single in early 1963. Despite its relaxed groove and attractive sing-along quality, the track didn't fare nearly as well as its predecessor, only climbing to #21 R&B and #31 pop. "I Can Take A Hint" was a very classy flip, gliding over a vaguely Latin feel as Robinson sounds vexed over lost love.

The *Fabulous Miracles*, the group's fourth long-play offering, was an extremely solid collection comprised of hits, B-sides and two cuts, "Won't You Take Me Back" and "Your Love," that were leftovers from their first LP. Pete Moore is missing from the attractive group portrait on the cover; he was stationed in Germany at the time but would soon return.

Nineteen sixty-three was a big year for the Miracles on microgroove. Tamla issued no less than four albums by the group in that one year, including their first concert set, *Recorded Live On Stage*. Unlike their relatively polished studio output, the album, timing out at less than 30 minutes in length, captures the Miracles at their sweat-stained rowdiest (Robinson doesn't recall the venue where it was cut).

Tarplin's axe is prominent and bluesy (he quotes from Freddy King's "San-Ho-Zay" to kick off "Mighty Good Lovin'"), sparking supercharged readings of "Happy Landing" and "Way Over There," while "You've Really Got A Hold On Me" logically segues into its inspiration, Cooke's "Bring It On Home To Me" (the Miracles ably impersonating Lou Rawls in the call-and-response department). Robinson even makes the achingly sung ballad "I've Been Good To You" sounds sweat-drenched and the segue into Barbara Lynn's recent hit, "You'll Lose A Good Thing," is inspired.

The group had come a long way with its choreography since its admittedly stiff Apollo debut. Robinson hit the dance floor with both feet rapidly moving in the summer of 1963, and the move paid off big: "Mickey's Monkey," Holland-Dozier-Holland's snazzy update of the Bo Diddley beat, zipped up to #3 pop and #8 R&B. "Whatever Makes You Happy," a mid-tempo Robinson/White collaboration, made a pleasant if not exceptional flip side.

The group's elaborate visual workout while performing "Mickey's Monkey" developed into a centerpiece of its live show (for convincing proof, check out the group's sizzling performance in *The T.A.M.I. Show*; Robinson and his energetic cohorts more than hold their own on the same bill with the legendarily loose-limbed James Brown and Chuck Berry, although Robinson sounds a little hoarse as he tries to out-project the constantly screaming teenage throng).

Bobby Rogers was easily the group's most agile stepper. "Bobby was a great dancer," says Robinson. "In the early days, he made up a great deal of our routines.

"Our choreographer at Motown, Cholly Atkins," says Robinson, "he used to always tell me when we went to artist's development, he always used to say, 'Smoke, I am so glad you're the lead singer.' Because I couldn't dance at all! So he'd say, 'I'm so glad you're the lead singer, so I don't have to be bothered by you! I don't have to show you these steps!'"

Holland-Dozier-Holland also penned the Miracles' exceptional follow-up single, "I Gotta Dance To Keep From Crying," another eminently danceable effort despite its downbeat title. The soulful tune deserved a better fate that its #35 pop and #17 R&B showing. The trilling flute made a brief comeback on the easy-going B-side, the philosophical "Such Is Love, Such Is Life".

Brian Holland and Lamont Dozier stuck around long enough to produce *The Miracles Doin' Mickey's Monkey*, a dance spectacular containing a well-chosen array of retreads. Robinson and his fleet-footed crew deftly covered the Orlons (Claudette leads "The Wah-Watusi"), the Olympics, Major Lance, the Isley Brothers, Chris Kenner and their stablemates, the Contours. Robinson wrote and produced one original for the LP, a lightweight "The Groovey Thing".

Gordy realized the perennial value of stocking his LP catalog with Yuletide product. By the end of the decade, most of his major artists would be represented by at least one collection of holiday chestnuts. The Miracles were the first Motown act to enjoy the honor, releasing *Christmas With The Miracles* in October 1963 with Ronnie White credited as producer and Robinson as assistant producer.

Although Robinson contributed only one track, the chunky "Christmas Everyday," the entire album was unmistakably a Motown project. Standouts include a hip, percussion-packed "Santa Claus Is Coming To Town" and tender renditions of "Noel," "O Holy Night" and Mel Torme's "The Christmas Song," all led by Robinson (although other members also took their turns up front).

"(You Can't Let The Boy Overpower) The Man In You," the Miracles' first 1964 single, was yet another of Robinson's advice numbers, but this time, Dad was dishing up the homilies. Despite its imaginative key changes and ambitious violin arrangement, the tune only made #59 on *Billboard*'s pop chart. The *Cash Box* R&B chart (the only one in existence in 1964) had the song at a hefty #12. The catchy and more conventional "Heartbreak Road," a Robinson/White collaboration that was also produced by White, would have made a better nomination for pop airplay. Four years later, "The Man In You" was chosen as Chuck Jackson's first single at Motown, and despite his booming baritone and a crisp, funky chart, his revival barely even made the charts.

Robinson locked into a happy party groove for the group's next two releases, and he was rewarded with a pair of very solid sellers. "I Like It Like That," a #27 pop and #10 R&B seller, and "That's What Love Is Made Of" (#35 pop, #9 R&B) were bright and breezy upbeat R&B, constructed around Tarplin's rhythmic, fluid riffs (he co-wrote "I Like It Like That") and a studio-generated party feel that wasn't far removed from what Gary U.S. Bonds had pioneered a few years before, or what saxman Junior Walker would soon cook up in the very same unassuming edifice on Grand Boulevard.

In addition to his front man role with the Miracles, Robinson was fast becoming a star behind-the-scenes player at Motown. Not only did Robinson produce the two above hits for the Miracles by himself, he was busy writing material for and producing Mary Wells, the Temptations, and the Supremes. "I always had people in mind, and I tried to tailor the songs to what I thought they would sound like, and all that," he says. "I used to even pick words that they would sing well."

Wells was his first major project, and he tailored an airy, calypso-influenced groove for her productions. "Harry Belafonte was very big at the time, but nobody in our end of music was doing his feel on records," says Robinson. "So that's why I went sort of for a Latin, islandy kind of feeling on her, 'The One Who Really Loves You.' That 1962 smash was closely followed by more Wells winners produced and penned by Robinson: "You Beat Me To The Punch," "Two Lovers," "Laughing Boy," "What's Easy For Two Is So Hard For One," and their penultimate chart-topping collaboration, "My Guy," in 1964.

Robinson also brought out the best in the Temptations. He wrote (with Bobby Rogers) and produced the metaphor-filled "The Way You Do The Things That You Do" for the quintet. With Eddie Kendricks giving Robinson a run for his money in the floating falsetto department, the infectious number proved the Temps' first major hit in early 1964. Many of the Temps' succeeding smashes were written or co-written and produced by Robinson as well: "I'll Be In Trouble," "It's Growing," "Get Ready" and "Since I Lost My Baby" all prominent among them.

But the biggest of all was the anthemic "My Girl," penned by Robinson and White and presented to the Temptations backstage at the Apollo Theatre. With David Ruffin's magnificent baritone in clear charge, the tune topped both charts in January 1965 and became an instant standard.

"Smokey would come to us with various ideas, because he didn't want to get locked into a pattern of writing," says White. "It's very easy to get locked into a pattern of writing, and you can destroy your creativity. He had the resource of coming to us and getting a different point of view. So that's one of the reasons he did it, close proximity. Anyway, it was my turn, and he said, 'Okay, Ron, look, I want you to help me with this song. I've got this idea I've got for the Temptations.' He came to me, and he begged me for about a month or so. He said, 'Look, we gotta do this song.' So we sat down one day and we started writing it, and eventually finished it."

Robinson harbors no regrets about not keeping the classic theme for the Miracles. "Not at all," he says. "Not one iota, because I always loved being involved in something positive in the other artists' careers. That song was written specifically with David Ruffin in mind to sing it. Because I had recorded them, and the first hit they had was 'The Way You Do The Things You Do,' and that was with Eddie Kendricks' voice. So all the producers and writers at Motown jumped on the Eddie Kendricks bandwagon. And whenever we recorded the Temps, everybody was using Eddie Kendricks's voice, because he had had the first hit with them."

"But I knew that David was in there, man. He was like a sleeping giant. So if I could get a hit on him, man, they would be multi-faceted. I had also used Paul Williams's voice on a few things. In fact, the first record I ever recorded on them was a thing called 'I Want A Love I Can See,' and I used Paul Williams' voice. But 'My Girl' was written specifically with David Ruffin in mind."

Robinson also produced and co-penned (with various members of the Miracles) a trio of major hits – "I'll Be Doggone," "Ain't That Peculiar" and "One More Heartache" – for Marvin Gaye in 1965-66, as well as writing and producing three huge sellers for the Marvelettes: "Don't Mess With Bill," "The Hunter Gets Captured By The Game," and the extremely alluring "My Baby Must Be A Magician".

Claudette retired from the road in 1964, hoping the relaxed pace would improve her chances of having a healthy baby after suffering a series of miscarriages. "Becoming a mother was very, very important in my life," she says. "I had gotten to the point after so many miscarriages that I didn't think that I would ever have any children of my own."

Although she continued to contribute her trademark vocals to all of the group's recordings until Smokey left in 1972, Claudette's days of traveling the nation's highways with a busful of musicians were over. "I always missed the singing and the camaraderie," she says, "I missed being with the guys, like, all the time. Because even though I would travel on the road, there is a difference when people are working together, or if you're just there as more or less a spectator, or whatever. Because they don't really have the time to take the time to really talk.

"I did miss that a lot in those first couple of years after I had left," she says. "The first decision to really stop performing was not my original idea. Actually, Smokey and Berry Gordy were the ones who really felt first and foremost that my health was suffering and that I should come off the road. Because I had these miscarriages, and otherwise, I seemed to be very healthy, they thought, 'Well, maybe it's the road.'"

Although it deserved a better fate with its brass-powered chart and crackling groove, the Miracles' next 45 release, "Come On Do The Jerk," was a commercial disappointment in late 1964, only struggling to #50 on the pop lists and #22 on the R&B charts.

"Some guys in Chicago had 'The Jerk' out," says Rogers. "We wrote that in California, I think. Some of the ladies like Brenda Hollaway was singing on the background on that song with us. We were in Los Angeles."

"I've had a lot of records in my life that suffered because of the previous record," says Robinson. "At the time 'Come On Do The Jerk' came out, it was the followup record to 'Mickey's Monkey.' And 'Mickey's Monkey' was one of those records that just would not die. So 'Come On Do The Jerk' didn't have a chance.

"It was the same thing, a record that I really, really loved, that I thought was one of the best records I've ever made, was a thing called 'I Don't Blame You At All.' But it followed 'Tears Of A Clown,' which would not die. So it didn't have a chance."

"Ooo Baby Baby" inaugurated an incredible run of Miracles hits throughout 1965, cracking the #4 R&B and #16 pop slots. The spine-chilling song, co-written with Pete Moore, may well rank as the ultimate Miracles ballad, Robinson's ethereal tenor dripping aching, tender vulnerability.

"'Ooo Baby Baby' started, actually, on stage," says Robinson. "We used to sing a medley of love songs. It was some of the songs that we had done, some songs that other artists had done. There was a song called 'Please Say You Want Me Too,' which was a song by a group called the Schoolboys. That was like the last song in the medley – (sings) 'Please Say You Want Me Too.'

"We had that there, and right after we sang 'Please Say You Want Me Too,' we were on stage, and spontaneously we started to sing, 'Ooh baby baby,' even though people had never heard that, they loved it. So we said, 'Hey, we're going to write a song like that.' And we did."

A liquid guitar lick from co-writer Tarplin (with Robinson and Moore) kicked off "The Tracks Of My Tears," a moving mid-tempo epic that matched its predecessor's showing on the pop charts and bettered it on the R&B lists at #2. Robinson is quick to cite "Marv Tarplin's music. I had it for about two weeks, and the first thing that I was thinking about on it was the music, which is the chorus.

"Finally, I came up with this thing one day, 'Take a good look at my face, you'll see a smile looks out of place, if you look closer it's easy to trace', and then I didn't know what trace was! It took me about two more days to think about somebody crying enough so that their tears had left tracks in their face – if you look close enough to them, you can see these little ridges, these little tracks that have been left by these tears."

The year was capped by another huge R&B (#3) and pop (#14) seller, "My Girl Has Gone," which listed Robinson, White, Moore and Tarplin as co-authors. The Motown hit-making combine was now operating at peak capacity, its band a seamlessly grooving assemblage. ("The Funk Brothers were the band of life," says Robinson).

It was a fact not lost on British audiences (the Beatles had recently lovingly covered "You've Really Got A Hold On Me"), which welcomed a contingent of the label's finest, including the Miracles, over to their shores. The revue's memorable appearance on the popular *Ready, Steady, Go* TV program, available on home video, climaxes with everyone chiming in on an extended version of "Mickey's Monkey," and the group reprising "Ooo Baby Baby" and "Shop Around" prior to the show's grand finale.

"To me, the early English tours were just incredible, because I was very interested in English history, especially the medieval times," says White, "And the first thing we had an opportunity to do was visit the Tower of London. It blew my mind, because it was everything that I had ever read about it in the history books."

As if his yeomen duties with the Miracles and as a staff producer at Motown weren't enough of a backbreaking workload, Gordy gave Robinson another impressive title: vice president of the firm. But Robinson was already accustomed to undertaking a wide variety of tasks at the bustling record company.

"It was part of my life," he says. "In the beginning of Motown, when he very first started Motown, there were only five people there. And we did everything, man. We packaged records, we called disc jockeys, we took records to record stores, to radio stations. We did everything."

Not long before the close of 1985, the group had unleashed the relentlessly rocking "Going To A Go-Go," yet another smash (#2 R&B, #11 pop) that was tailor-made for the nation's sweaty dance floors. "We did a lot of go-gos," says Rogers. "You had a go-go in Chicago, and there was the Whisky-a-Go-Go in California. And we used to work these two spots. That's how we wrote that song."

The *Going To A Go-Go* album was particularly strong, boasting Robinson-produced LP-only items such as the metaphorical "In Case You Need Love," the buoyant, utterly catchy "From Head To Toe" and "Let Me Have Some," riding atop a rumbling piano figure lifted from Fiestas' "So Fine". Also aboard were three gems that were tucked away on the flip sides of the group's recent hits: "All That's Good," the dreamy "A Fork In The Road" and "Since You Won My Heart," and another, "Choosey Beggar," that managed to dent the R&B charts in its own right as the B-side of "Going To A Go-Go".

"I always felt like there was some things that could have been hits," Robinson. "I felt like that about a lot of things that were on albums that did come out that were never released as singles."

Although it was a comparative disappointment from a sales standpoint (only #20 R&B and #46 pop) in mid-1966, the group's "Whole Lot Of Shakin' In My Heart (Since I Met You)" was another overlooked goodie, with a pumping rhythm track and surging horns in the finest Motown tradition. In a major departure from the norm, Frank Wilson penned and produced the song instead of Robinson. Its flip, "Oh Be My Love," was a string-drenched concoction written and produced by Robinson and Moore.

Far more successful in the sales ledgers was the Miracles' next offering, "(Come Round Here) I'm The One That You Need," which reunited the group with producers Brian Holland and Lamont Dozier. The dramatic ditty, penned by Holland-Dozier-Holland, sounds more like a Four Tops production, with classically influenced strings and woodwinds and a breathless vocal from Robinson. The tune jumped to the #4 R&B position, backed by the gentle, melodic "Save Me".

Penned and produced by Robinson, Moore and Rogers, "Save Me" marked Rogers' first shot in the producer's booth. "That was my first effort," says Rogers. "Smokey has just been a great person in saying, 'Hey, man, come on, let's do this.' We were young, and by him being married to Claudette, he was always home. The other guys, we were running around Detroit, trying to hang out, stuff like that.

"He was instrumental in saying, 'Hey, let's get together and write some songs!' That's how I was able to co-produce, I think, because I had written the background for 'Save

Me' for the group. I sat in the control room and directed the guys, directed him on what to sing."

As a follow-up album to *Going To A Go-Go, Away We Go-Go*, issued in November 1966, was something of an artistic letdown. Cranking out so much product seems to have exacted its artistic toll: Robinson only had a hand in producing four tracks, notably the relaxed "Swept For You Baby" and a pounding, dynamic "More, More, More Of Your Love" that would have made a solid single.

Producer Mickey Gentile chose to employ overwrought sound-alike arrangements of Dusty Springfield's "You Don't Have To Say You Love Me" and Dionne Warwick's "Walk On By" on the group's cover versions, resulting in subpar performances that sounded like the customary Motown sound. Far better were the aching Ivy Jo Hunter/Stevie Wonder composition "Can You Love A Poor Boy" and a Norman Whitfield-produced cover of the Temptations' "Beauty Is Only Skin Deep".

Robinson's penchant for imaginative metaphors was at its zenith on the group's first 1967 hit, "The Love I Saw In You Was Just A Mirage," which just dented the R&B Top and hit #20 pop (and was the first single to be credited to Smokey Robinson and the Miracles instead of the group name alone). Once again, co-writer Tarplin's twisting guitar runs were integral to the song's reflexive feel as Robinson weaved his touching tale of heartbreak.

"See, Marv Tarplin, who is my guitarist still today, his music has always inspired me to write," says Robinson. "He always used to give me tapes of his music, and I would fool around with 'em til I got an idea on 'em. So that just was the idea that came on that song." The flip side of the Robinson/Moore production, "Come Spy With Me," was apparently the theme song for a long-forgotten secret agent movie starring Troy Donahue and has yet to be reissued domestically.

"More Love," an emotionally charged statement of eternal devotion, was written by the singer for his wife, whose determination to have a baby repeatedly met with tragic disappointment. "We had many miscarriages," says Robinson. "Every time I went to the hospital after a miscarriage, Claudette was in there, and she was apologizing to me, 'Oh, I'm so sorry, baby, I let you down.' And all that stuff like that.

"And I'd always tell her, 'You didn't let me down, because even though I wanted those babies, and it would have been a great thing, I know you. I didn't know those babies, but I know you. You're the person who's been in my life since I was 14 years old. I love you. You're okay – I'm fine! We'll try again on another baby.' And I wrote 'More Love' because I wanted her to know that was how I felt. Like I said, it would have been great to have the babies, but we didn't. But we had each other, so that was what was important to me."

Although "Mirage" and "More Love" graced Robinson's *Make It Happen* album, the top seller on the LP wouldn't even be issued on 45 rpm until 1970. "The Tears Of A Clown" was a brilliant collaboration between Robinson, Stevie Wonder and veteran Motown producer Henry Cosby (who co-produced).

"'Tears Of A Clown' was a track that Stevie had," says Robinson. "And he came to me one day – we were having like a Christmas party at Motown. And he came to me, because at that time we were doing a lot of collaboration. Guys who did great music who didn't necessarily write songs would give their music to someone who did. Guys who wrote lyrics who didn't do music would give their music to guys who did music. So he came to me, and he said he had this track he wanted me to hear, and he wanted me to write a song to it.

"So he gave it to me, and I listened to it. And the little thing (sings opening riff) that's a circus thing. So I just wanted to write something that would be profound about the circus and touch people's hearts, I guess. And the only thing I could think of was Pagliacci, who was the clown who made everybody else happy while he was sad because he had nobody to love him. So that's what 'Tears Of A Clown' was about."

Somehow, the normally astute Gordy had failed to take note of the song's obvious potential. "It was on an album in 1967," says Robinson. "In 1970, a young lady who worked for Motown in England was listening to the album. And she said, 'Hey, we should release this song over here.' And they did, and it was number one. So Berry said, 'Hey, it's number one over there. It's the first number one record we've ever had over there. It's starting to be a number one everywhere over in Europe.' So we released it over here." Nevertheless, it belatedly topped both the R&B and pop charts domestically in late 1970.

Make It Happen, eventually retitled *The Tears Of A Clown* in the Tamla catalog, had quite a few other treasures buried within its grooves. "The Souful Shack" and "Dancing's Alright," the latter penned by Smokey, Moore, White, Rogers and Tarplin, were light-hearted workouts with sizzling rhythm beds. Wonder was in on the writing of two other standouts, the elegantly harmonized "After You Put Back The Pieces (I'll Still Have A Broken Heart)" and a driving "My Love Is Your Love (Forever)," while the Holland-Dozier-Holland rocker "It's A Good Feeling" could easily have earned hit status if Gordy had granted it single status. Robinson found Little Anthony and the Imperials' "I'm On The Outside (Looking In)" an inviting cover item with its fragile falsetto feel, while the richly textured ballad "You Must Be Love" served as the flip of the group's next R&B chart-topper.

"I Second That Emotion" was more than just a clever slice of inspired wordplay, Tarplin's elastic licks once again perfectly framing Robinson's soul-drenched lead vocal. "I Second That Emotion" was written because of the fact the guy who wrote it with me, Al Cleveland, and I were very good friends, and we were Christmas shopping one day in a department store," says Robinson. "You know, there's an old saying, 'I second the motion.' So we were talking to this girl behind the counter about something, and Al says, 'Yeah, I second that emotion!' And we stated laughing because he had made that grammatical error."

Able to do no wrong, the Miracles came right back in early 1968 with a #3 R&B/#11 pop seller, "If You Can Want," that sported an irresistible groove heavily laden with percussion and a snappy horn chart. It was coupled with "When The Words Get Caught Up In Your Throat," its impossibly lengthy title probably enough to doom it to eternal flip-side status.

Although the Miracles had by then guested on countless TV music shows, they finally managed a booking on the country's premier variety program, *The Ed Sullivan Show*, in March 1968. "The only show that stood apart from all other shows was Ed Sullivan," says Robinson. "It was the class show of shows. But the others were all the same. They were teenyboppers dancing, jerking, girls-in-the-cage shows."

Of course, the class quotient was dependent on whether its stone-visaged host could recall the name of his next scheduled act. Sullivan really botched the Miracles' introduction; in front of millions of viewers nationwide, Sullivan solemnly solicited a warm round of applause for "Smokey and the Little Smokeys!"

As the group gamely broke into a medley of "I Second The Emotion," "If You Can Want" and "Going To A Go-Go," Robinson's smile momentarily froze on his face. What was going through his mind? "This guy is really ridiculous," he laughs. "It was embarrassing to me, because that's not who the guys were. They were the Miracles." Fortunately, their other Sullivan segment, a beautifully staged rendition of the Beatles' 'Yesterday,' came off without a hitch.

"The Beatles wrote some wonderful songs, and we used to sing a few of their songs," says Robinson. "That was one of them. The rendition of that song was put together by Maurice King, who was our vocal director at artist development at Motown at the time."

"Yesterday" was aboard the group's *Special Occasion* album, along with spirited covers of two Gladys Knight and the Pips hits ("I Heard It Through The Grapevine," in an electric piano-driven version closer to Marvin Gaye's than Knight's and "Everybody

Needs Love"), the highly attractive "You Only Build Me Up To Tear Me Down," and the solid flip sides "Your Mother's Only Daughter," "Give Her Up" and "Much Better Off".

The hits continued unabated throughout 1968 and '69. "Yester Love" (#9 R&B); the chunky "Special Occasion" (#4 R&B); a sumptuous "Baby, Baby, Don't Cry" (# 3 R&B, #8 pop); the sinuous "Doggone Right" (#7 R&B) and its flip, the dreamy "Here I Go Again" (#15 R&B); "Point It Out" (#4 R&B), even a refreshingly upbeat treatment of the maudlin Dion hit "Abraham, Martin and John" (#15 R&B), perpetuated the seemingly infinite string of smashes.

Time Out For Smokey Robinson And The Miracles, a 1969 microgroove offering, was an uneven affair that included four chart items as well as fairly uninspired readings of "For Once In My Life" and "Wichita Lineman" and a vastly reworked treatment of the song that had catapulted the Temptations to superstardom, "My Girl". Tarplin's mellow chording and tasty group harmonies memorably introduced the upbeat "I'll Take You Any Way That You Come," definitely one of the LP's highlights, along with Robinson's reading of "The Composer," a tune he penned for the Supremes, and the originals "The Hurt Is Over" and "Once I Got To Know You (Couldn't Help But Love You)".

Other producers were now working regularly with the group. George Gordy handled production duties on "Darling Dear," the flip side of "Point It Out," while the prolific team of Nickolas Ashford and Valerie Simpson took over as the writer/producer team of "Who's Gonna Take The Blame," a #9 R&B hit in mid-1970.

Miracles albums were popping up fast and furious on the racks, but they contained fewer hits. Nothing on *Four In Blue* was released on 45, although "You Send Me (With Your Good Lovin')" and "Dreams, Dreams," both boasted cooking uptempo grooves from the vaunted Motown house band, and in retrospect seem strong candidates for hit status. The album also found the group tackling the Beatles' "Hey Jude" and the Righteous Brothers' "You've Lost That Lovin' Feelin'" with effective results, though a lethargic run-through of the Supremes' "My World Is Empty Without You" won't make anyone forget the Supremes' hit version.

Worst of the lot was the downright boring *What Love Has Joined Together*, an album virtually devoid of energy or legitimate hit possibilities. Fortunately, the group rebounded in a hurry with *Pocket Full of Miracles*, which included three hits as well as a powerful revival of "Get Ready," which Robinson had written for the Temptations, and the frantic "Backfire" (penned by Robinson, Al Cleveland and Johnny Bristol). The disc housed one very bad idea: an awkward medley of Chris Kenner's New Orleans R&B standard "Something You Got" and the Beatles' "Something".

Although "Tears Of A Clown" proved the Miracles' final number one R&B smash later that year, its immediate follow-up, the extraordinarily catchy "I Don't Blame You At All," topped out at #7 R&B and #18 pop. The Miracles' other two 1971 offerings climbed to identical #20 R&B showings. "Crazy About the La La La" rode atop a driving beat, its playful Robinson-penned lyrics sparked by a scratchy, vaguely psychedelic guitar solo and prominent electric piano toward the fade. "Satisfaction" wasn't the defiant Rolling Stones oldie that Otis Redding had earlier injected with a healthy dose of southern soul: this Robinson-penned ballad was resolutely smooth.

Taking no chances, Gordy brought back "Tears of A Clown" one more time on the group's 1971 *One Dozen Roses* album, which was truly a team effort (six producers and a half-dozen arrangers are credited with working on its contents). Along with housing three then-current hits, the LP takes a relatively relaxed route with "No Wonder Love's A Wonder," "I Love You Dear" and the comparatively uptempo "Oh Baby Baby I Love You". Claudette's pipes ring true behind her hubby on a slightly bizarre cover of Paul Simon's "Cecilia," and Robinson ventured into his own back catalog with an ambitious arrangement of "The Hunter Gets Captured By The Game".

The Miracles' last two singles to feature Smokey Robinson as lead in 1972 were produced and co-written by Johnny Bristol, a veteran Detroit soul figure whose early credentials included a handful of duets with Jackie Beavers (as Johnny and Jackie) for Tri-Phi in 1961. Bristol's Motown track record included co-writing Junior Walker's "What Does It Take (To Win Your Love)" and the Supremes' "Someday We'll Be Together". The Miracles' Bristol-produced "We've Come Too Far To End It Now," a #9 R&B hit, and the #21 seller "I Can't Stand To See You Cry" both featured lush string-heavy arrangements presaging Bristol's own 1974 smash for MGM, "Hang On In There Baby".

Although Robinson had initially decided to leave the Miracles in 1969 after the birth of his first son, he didn't actually pull the plug until 1972. "What really started those wheels to turning was Berry's birth," he says. "He was born in 1968, and I was so in love with him. I was so attached to him. I would put him in a baby seat and sit him on the table while I ate. Watch him, and just look at him, everything he did when he moved his hand, I'd say, 'Oh, baby, he just moved his hand!' And then when he started to grow up, I just hated leaving him. I got to the point where I hated leaving him more and more.

"Then Tamla (his daughter) was born, and then there were some things that were going on with the group. We were always gone, man. We were gone 90 percent of the time. In fact, we were gone so much at one point, by me being the vice-president – see I never really had a rest, 'cause I was always working with some other artists. When I came home, I had to go to the office. And then I was on the road 90 percent of the time. So at one point, I had gotten those guys some jobs at Motown. And when we were off, they could work at Motown, because the road, basically, and semi-annual record royalties were their only source of income.

"So I had gotten them some jobs at Motown, but of course, they didn't like that, 'cause they made as much money in one night as they'd make for two weeks at Motown. Just so they could have some money coming in when we weren't working. But none of that worked, so it just got to the point where …

"Then, at that time, Berry was starting to move Motown out to Los Angeles. There was just a lot of things going on that made me know I had to leave, because I wasn't contributing 100 percent any more. It was better for them and for me if I left."

According to Rogers, the group was well-prepared for its longtime leader's departure. "We knew it,' he says. "We talked about it two years before. The reason he went on solo is because of the fact that Motown was moving to California, and he and Claudette had been trying to have children for a long time. She had about three or four miscarriages, traveling all the time. She decided she just wanted to take some time off. He was vice-president of artists relations at Motown, and a lot of the artists were moving to California. So he just kept that position, and he went to Los Angeles, and he was able to, at that time, have a family, spend some time and stay at home for about five years."

"I looked at (the split) from an optimistic viewpoint," says White. "It gave us an opportunity to go out and explore and see what we could do on our own. It was a fantastic challenge."

The official end for Smokey Robinson's tenure with the Miracles came on the stage of the Carter Barron Amphitheater in Washington, D.C., in early summer of 1972. "It was just a sad event, because I had been with those guys all my life, man," says Robinson. "It wasn't that I regretted leaving. I've never regretted leaving."

Replacement Billy Griffin had plenty of time to assimilate himself. "On our last tour in '72," says Rogers, "we carried Bill Griffin with us for a year so he could get inducted into the group and find out exactly what's happening, what was expected of him."

"Bill was introduced to us by, I believe somebody in the Temptations," says White. "Bill sang in a group, and one of the guys who sang with Bill auditioned for the Temptations, and so did Bill. And they told us about Bill. It so happened that Bill lived in Baltimore. He auditioned for us, and he was perfect." Although no one could ever fully supplant Robinson's magnificent pipes and songwriting genius within the Miracles,

Griffin's high, lilting tenor was well-suited to the group's reconstituted vocal blend, if somewhat less distinctive.

His batteries recharged, Robinson plunged into a very successful solo recording career on Tamla the following year, scoring 38 R&B hits for the Motown empire over the next decade-and-a-half with the likes of "Baby Come Close" (1973), the R&B chart-topping "Baby That's Backatcha" (1975), "Cruisin'" (1979) and "Being With You," a 1981 smash that leapt to #1 R&B and #2 pop. It took quite a while longer for Robinson to step back on stage, however – he debuted his solo act in 1975.

The new line-up of Miracles debuted on Tamla in 1973 with "Don't Let It End ('Til You Let It Begin)," which managed a respectable #26 R&B showing. The followup, the atmospheric Leon Ware-penned "Give Me Just Another Day," was less popular, only creeping up to the #47 R&B slot and unable even to crack the Top 100 on the pop side (an unthinkable insult during Robinson's tenure). *Renaissance*, the group's first album without Robinson, also emerged the same year.

Full public acceptance of Griffin finally came in 1974, with the quartet's third Tamla offering. "Do It Baby" was produced, co-written, and co-arranged by Freddie Perren, one quarter of "The Corporation" that had masterminded the Jackson 5's "I Want You Back" and "The Love You Save". With its #4 R&B and #13 pop rankings, the Miracles had proven once and for all that they no longer required the direct participation of Smokey Robinson to scale the charts.

"There was some gratification, no question about it," says White. "But I don't think it was … not that kind of direct gratification, that is to say, to do it without old Smokey. It was just achieving some success, that supplied more gratification than anything else."

A host of familiar names participated in the control booth during the recording of the *Do It Baby* album in Los Angeles. Motown vet Hal Davis, versatile guitarist Willie Hutch, even ex-Rick Nelson musical director Jimmie Haskell called the shots over the course of cutting the super-slick set.

Although Marv Tarplin initially remained with the group, the guitarist soon rejoined Robinson and remains his invaluable accompanist to the present day. "He stayed there for about a year after I left," says Robinson. "And then he called me and said, 'Hey, man, I'm coming to be with you.' 'Cause I wasn't doing any road work, or even recording at the time. He said, 'I'm coming to be with you, man. We can just write some songs, 'cause I don't like it with you not being here.' He came out to Los Angeles."

Before the year was through, the Miracles came right back with another smash, "Don't Cha Love It," which equalled the R&B popularity of their previous release but did considerably less pop business. Nevertheless, it inspired an album of the same name. "Gemini," the group's first single of 1975, didn't set any of the charts on fire, slithering up to #43 R&B.

Clearly, a change in musical direction was in order. So the Miracles took matters into their own hands, and *City of Angels* was the dubious result. Incorporating the group's star on the Hollywood Walk of Fame into its snazzy fold-out jacket, the Freddie Perren-produced concept album was written in its entirety by Pete Moore and Billy Griffin, and Griffin is also credited as one of four guitarists.

The title track, a spacey ode that frets about L.A. falling into the sea, and the weirdly ahead-of-its-time gay anthem "Ain't Nobody Straight In L.A.," were hardly prime fodder for airplay. There's also a glowing tribute to the city's *Free Press* that should have guaranteed the album a rave review within the paper.

But the set also included the smash disco opus "Love Machine". Part one of the lengthy, supercharged workout proved the Miracles' last giant hit, improbably sailing all the way up to the pinnacle of the pop charts in October 1975 (curiously, it only hit #5 R&B).

Amazingly, "Tears Of A Clown" was the only Miracles single to better its pop performance. But it was a short-lived renaissance; a second single from the same set, "Night

Life," failed to come anywhere near its predecessor's monumental success, failing to turn up on the pop charts at all.

Pete Moore produced *The Power of Music*, the Miracles' final album for Tamla. It was a slim (seven songs and one "overture") Hollywood-cut collection that eloquently reflects its sexually charged disco era (the photo caption adjoining the song title "Love To Make Love" reads "What can be more beautiful than a perfect physical union between man and woman, woman and woman, man and man, or group sex if that's your choice"). Apparently Berry Gordy remained unconvinced of the album's cliched contents, once again written by Moore and Griffin – Tamla never even bothered to press up a single from the set.

In 1977, the Miracles brought their association of nearly two full decades with Motown to an ignominious end, signing for big bucks with Columbia Records. Why? "Because we got a better deal," says White. "It was purely money."

Bobby Rogers is somewhat less sure of the motives involved. "I don't know to this day," he says. "I think it was a ridiculous thing – not ridiculous, but it had something to do with money. Columbia was offering us a lot of money. But it wasn't offering us the support. We didn't know that at the time."

They soon found out, the hard way. Even with Griffin enjoying featured billing on the label, "Spy For Brotherhood" only made it to #37 R&B and #104 pop in January 1977. Nearly a year-and-a-half later, "Mean Machine" crept up to #55 R&B. Two albums were also issued on Columbia, but neither party can have been too pleased with the situation.

Sadly the turn of the decade brought the demise of one of the greatest vocal groups of the soul era. "Everyone just wanted to go their separate ways," says Rogers. "Bill Griffin wanted to try to be a solo artist. Pete was going to start a record company, Ronnie was into real estate, I was doing interior design, which I had been doing for a long time. We just came home and didn't go back out."

"I think everybody was tired," says White. "I know I was. I think the underlying reason was everybody was just tired. After so much traveling, it just really wears you down."

Why were the Miracles so incredibly successful for so long? "There's a lot of luck involved," says White. "I think we had a good support system in the company, and I think that Smokey's drive in the things that we were involved in helped us. I think that we were fortunate in as much as we were able to produce things that the public accepted."

"We were kinda clean-cut," says Rogers. "We didn't get into trouble, we didn't do a lot of hanging out and stuff. We were kinda good guys, I guess you could say. We didn't create trouble."

Perhaps not. But Smokey Robinson and the Miracles created plenty of enduring Motown magic.

Motown Quotes III

"Some people write songs from experience. Not me. I write songs no matter what mood I'm in – it's my work, dig?" *Smokey Robinson*

"Originally, there was another verse before the last chorus of 'I Second That Emotion'. Mr Berry cut it out. Broke Smokey's heart, because he wrote it and that was his baby, but it was just too long." *Billie Jean Brown*

"You don't find guys like Smokey Robinson." *Berry Gordy*

9

Sons of the Snakepit
by Carl Lozito

*There were many elements and individuals who combined to make Motown great, and
there were none more so than the backing musicians. Together they were the rock on
which the empire was built. To find out who they were, and where they came from, we
turn to a native of Detroit. Carl Lozito has always had an interest in the slightly disrep-
utable areas of rock history, as is evidenced in his occasional contributions to Britain's*
Record Collector *magazine. He is also proud to have once held the bowling record at
Detroit's Orbit Room. This piece has been written especially for this book.*

There were a lot of guys and gals around keeping the SS *Hitsville* afloat when it began
sailing the world. Captain Gordy began doing everything with a small crew, but when his
craft grew, he spent much more time on the bridge where he could see further and wider.
He knew early on where he was heading, and he knew he'd better pick the right crew.
Sure he had some smart front people, running around the deck, looking oh-so-pretty. His
radio operators knew what they were about too, and the Captain took care of all the early
navigation. He got a few old sea-dogs in quickly with Harvey Fuqua and Maurice King
who knew where the rocks were. He guessed that all the passengers would take real well
to smartly turned out entertainment staff who could show a neat heel and move around
as if they weren't just out of diapers. He covered all the angles on all the parts of the ship
you could see, but the guy's real genius was down there in the engine room. It was there
that he put, and kept, the finest and most experienced guys. By looking after them like a
Wall Street investment, Capt. Gordy made his craft sail real sweet, and reach previously
unimagined speeds. He added to the downstairs crew when he could and when he needed to, and he never forgot their worth.

Maybe it's a little odd to begin writing about Detroit musicians with a sea-going anal-
ogy, but when so many people have said how tight a ship Berry Gordy controlled, it
seems apt. Anyone who was here in Detroit in the 1950s, will tell you that musically it
was a jazz town. All the best scenes were based around small clubs with smoky house
bands. There were musicians like Hank Jones, Kenny Burrell and Yusef Lateef who
would help out all the young guys. Earl Van Dyke learnt from Barry Harris who learnt
from Burrell. If you went to clubs like The Calumet Lounge or The Apex in 1958, you
could have seen James Jamerson playing with his first band Washboard Willie and The
Supersuds Of Rhythm. When Berry Gordy and his guys started to look for session players, it was to the jazz clubs they went. At first they would use small band leaders who
already had a pool of players they used, like Ivy Hunter or Popcorn Wylie. One of the
first things that Berry Gordy had Mickey Stevenson do when he joined the business as
A&R man was to trawl round the clubs to find hot musicians. I guess he did a pretty good
job! So, Motown was pulling in already experienced players, who maybe played in three
or four different units all over town. At first, Motown was just one of dozens of small
record companies trying to grab a share of what hadn't been covered by the big boys
from New York or Chicago. Fortune, Northern and Tri-Phi were some of the independ-
ents that were in what would be Berry's territory. The musicians that eventually became
Berry's boys mostly started out on this small club and company circuit, and that was how
they got known. Jazz playing was also a great grounding for the guys to learn to listen

to each other and to work up simpatico relationships. A lot of them couldn't read music, at least not in its usual notation, but they developed all manner of scribbled shorthand.

Nobody seems to be able to say for sure just who played on the earliest Motown sessions, but it wasn't the guys that became known as The Funk Brothers. Some of them did get on board quite early, like the drummer Benny Benjamin and Earl Van Dyke, who was an early studio organiser. He'd work with Brian Holland, whose first job at Motown was a studio engineer, working on what had been set up by Mike McLean, who was the man Berry had to join all the wires together. That guy loved his studio set-up and made sure everyone used it properly. The player who was to become the main bassist, the player who everybody wanted on their sessions was James Jamerson. He hitched up with Berry Gordy quite early because he had already got himself a good reputation. The link could have been through Berry's sister Gwen, who had a label called Anna Records. James had worked on sessions for Johnnie Mae Matthews who ran Northern Records. She used him a lot with her artists who included Betty LaVette and Timmy Shaw. She saw how good he was, and it was largely through his work for her that he got known by the others, including Gwen.

James Jamerson played sometimes with The Ivy Hunter Band, and most of that band were starting to work at Motown. He went down there sometime late in 1958, and they were real impressed with his bass playing because he could use his jazz playing and put some of that feel into the R&B tunes Berry was developing. About that time, Joe Hunter, who was a piano player, and Hank Cosby who was his saxophonist were already pretty regular there. There were a lot of other bassists and guitar players in and out. The first song that we are sure that James played on was The Miracles' "Way Over There" in 1959. So, at that point Berry Gordy already had the guys that were to become the nucleus of The Funk Brothers, although they weren't known as that then. That came in the Sixties, and it was their term for themselves, because they always saw themselves as their own little unit, somehow separate and in sonic ways above the rest of the staff. Fact was, they knew early on that they were good, and they realised that they would be worth a lot as the company grew.

Another key player in the set-up was Robert White. He was a great guitar player who was a steady member of the studio group, but not fully until around 1962. He played on "Come To Me" by Marv Johnson as early as 1959. In those early times all these players were selling their talents wherever they could. They would play live most nights in the regular clubs, and pick up whatever they could with sessions. They would also go on the road if people paid them enough to take them away from their bread and butter work. I'd guess they were pulling in the range of $10–$20 for sessions then. Most of The Ivy Hunter Band – Ivy, James, the guitarist Larry Veeder and a baritone sax player called Mike Terry – went on the road with Jackie Wilson in 1961. He was the big, big star in the area, so he would have wanted the best. They were paid $25 a show, which was good until they found that they had to find their own hotel bills and other bills out of it! At that time, it is said that Berry Gordy wasn't paying very good money for the sessions. Earl Van Dyke wrote that he was once paid with a bowl of soup! Well, I hope it was good, hot and plentiful! Berry paid only $5–$10 at first, but it went up over the years, maybe when he knew he had to. Earl used to say that they were mostly older, more settled guys compared to many of Motown's artists. They mostly had families to support, which does explain how, even when they were really hot with Motown in the mid-sixties, they would still try to moonlight.

The hard core of The Funk Brothers, as we said, was Earl on keyboards, James on bass, Robert White on guitar and Benny Benjamin on drums. There were of course lots of others. Guitarists included Eddie Wills and Joe Messina, and percussionists were Jack Ashford (aka 'Black Jack'), Jack Brokensha (aka 'White Jack') and Eddie 'Bongo' Brown. James Gittens was another keyboard player, but he died in a car wreck in 1965 and was replaced by Johnny Griffith. Ivy Hunter was an original keyboard player for sessions, but he got much more involved in the production side of things, allowing Earl to become the father figure of the main session guys. They called him 'Chunk Of Funk' in those days, as he was a big person. Benny was 'Papa Zita', another drummer Richard Allen was 'Pistol' owing to his snare style, and they took to calling the basement studio 'The Snakepit'. This really made it their territory, and a lot of the time that they were cutting tracks, they did not like other people around. In fact, most of the time they would cut tracks and have no idea who they would be for, because Motown would let the producer cut and then try out various artists to see who it fitted the best. It wasn't really until The Supremes started to hit that Holland, Dozier, Holland were really cutting specifically for them. Perhaps the only exception to this was Smokey, who would cut particularly for his voice and The Miracles, and he would use some of his own people like Marv Tarplin on guitar.

As well as all these fine musicians, there were plenty of horn players around. Mike Terry and Hank Cosby were main sax men, Bob Cousar was on trombone, John Trudell was on trumpet, and one of the main organisers was reed man Beans Bowles. Later, when Motown really hit the big time, there were many more musicians, including string players.

At first, there was a mixture of people who went out on the road with the shows. The first Motown Revue, organised by Beans Bowles and Esther Edwards, went out in October 1962 in an old bus and five cars. They played nearly 40 venues, from a week in Washington D.C. to dates in the Carolinas, Georgia, Alabama, Florida and Tennessee, before finishing up just prior to Christmas for a week at The Apollo and a last date in Pittsburgh. Most of the studio guys went on this tour, but pretty soon after Berry started to insist that some of the key players stayed home to keep the sessions running. Probably other reasons were in his mind, because Benny, who did some live work with Mary Wells, wasn't so good on tour. He could disappear sometimes, and come back late after some booze, and even talk to himself on stage. I guess Berry wanted to keep him reined in tight! He was also the very best and fastest drummer they had, so he was genuinely needed. Berry would also keep James and Earl at home usually, although Earl would go on some of the European gigs with Robert White. A bandleader called Choker Campbell would lead the Motown road orchestra on big tours from the early Sixties, taking over from Popcorn Wylie, Ivy Hunter or Earl from the earlier tours. [*Ed. It is interesting to recall who came to Britain on 'The Sound Of Motown' tour in 1965. It was a sextet led by Earl Van Dyke, and included Robert White on guitar, Bob Cousar on trombone, Eli Fountain on sax and Jack Ashford on percussion. The last of the six is uncertain, but may have been Tony Newton*]. James Jamerson had been tempted out onto the road in 1964 with Smokey Robinson, but on his return Berry convinced him to stay doing studio work from that point on, matching his road money to make sure. This allowed James to make a definite $250 a week, and still make a bit more when he could away from Hitsville.

When all the Funk Brothers were working in Motown's Studio A, 'The Snakepit', they were the best Berry could have wished for. They would cut in three-hour blocks, and in that time would usually cut four tracks if things went well with the producer. They would check out the tune for a few minutes, playing it reasonably straight in whatever form that it was presented to them. They would then add in their own flavourings and interpretations to develop their own take on the song. After this they would go straight to the takes, and usually they would not need more than three or four. Later on, when the songs got more sophisticated, and Motown began using arrangers more, the sessions took longer, but in the early times, when The Brothers were cooking, they could cut four or five hits in a day! How well it all worked depended on how they worked with the producers. These guys were their own men, and they knew whom they liked to work with. This basically came down to the producers who would respect their knowledge the most, and let them use their talents most naturally. They liked Clarence Paul, who did much of the Stevie Wonder material, because he would give them room to develop his ideas, which came without any previous notation. He'd hum what he wanted, which was enough for The Brothers. Norman Whitfield spent some time watching and learning from them before he began producing, but then he wanted to exercise a higher level of control. There were also one or two well-known names that they were not so keen on!

In the sessions The Brothers knew each other's abilities well enough that they developed their own roles and styles within the unit. Earl would tend to use the lower keyboard end for medium and faster tempo material, reverting to higher up for ballads and fills. Robert White could double Earl's part so well that sometimes you couldn't tell them apart, and other guitarists like Joe Messina and David Hamilton would fulfil different roles that complemented each other. They would all leave space for James Jamerson to flow freely where he chose. The bassist's earlier playing had been more hidden in the mixes, but as they hit the middle of the sixties it is easier to pick him out. He had supreme abilities with the speed that he could pick up ideas from a single glance at a lead sheet or being told the chord progressions. His jazz background influenced his playing a good deal with his abilities with chromatic passing tones and syncopated 8ths. He would use 7ths and 11ths in his bass lines.

Later extensions to The Snakepit, partly planned and executed by Pops Gordy, allowed for an eight track machine to be put in. This usually gave James his own track and allowed producers the ability to feature him specifically. These musicians' experience and unique abilities to cut so fast and so well put them under tremendous pressure as the producers always wanted the same guys. The studio would be in use constantly, around the clock, and they would cut at least two blocks of three hours, and often three or four. Once Clarence Paul dug them all out of a club where they had been hanging and drinking, and took them for a session in the depths of night. There is no way that they would have done this for anyone, and there are a few name Motowners who would never have got this privilege. There were even some that they would disappear from and hide. Such was their power and talent that they knew that they could get away with this on occasion.

What they didn't get away with, at least not all the time, was their moonlighting with other local Detroit recording companies like Ric-Tic, where they reproduced their delicate blend for Edwin Starr's "Agent 00 Soul" amongst others. Berry was furious when they were caught, and fined them $1,000 each. However the boss of Ric-Tic, Ed Wingate, paid the fines on their behalf. This must have made Berry's later take over of Ric-Tic and Golden World even sweeter. Berry's disciplinarianism didn't stop them living their lives to the full, as they would still somehow manage to play live dates in the clubs and sneak off to other sessions. The only thing that eventually broke The Brothers apart was when Berry Gordy moved the operation out of Detroit to the West Coast. At this point, some players like James Jamerson made the move and followed Berry, doubtlessly with some solid financial incentives. Others like Earl Van Dyke chose to stay in their native Detroit and return to their first love of jazz. They had progressed from the meagre early $5 a session days, through to union scale figures, and eventually to retainers that gave them up to $50,000 a year at the peak. They had moved from the fresh vibrant feel of Motown gut R&B to the smooth and deliberate orchestrated days of the later Sixties. They had partied much, much more than they ever should have, and some, like Benny Benjamin, had already paid the price before the end of the decade. They had probably worked harder than any recording musicians before or since.

They were 'The Sons Of The Snakepit', The Funk Brothers, and the supremely talented engine room that powered SS *Hitsville*. Berry Gordy and every Motown fan should never forget them.

Top Ten Sixties Motown by Carl Lozito

Like everyone else around the world, I love all the great hits made by The Tops, The Miracles, The Temps and Martha. The Supremes were always too poppy for my tastes, so I have chosen some of the looser sounds. Many of these have particular memories from Detroit for me, but those are other stories...

1. "Shotgun" – Jnr. Walker
If you ever saw this guy on stage, you'd have to have him right up there with the best of them. Motown's hard side that they forgot along the way through a surfeit of Miss Ross.

2. "Goodbye Cruel World" – Linda Griner
Early stuff from the time when the sounds were still evolving. Love her voice!

3. "Sweet Thing" – The Spinners
The Spinners were a fave group of mine. They never got the breaks until much later. They were one of the great outfits that ended up getting overlooked at Hitsville. This great song came out during Supremes mania. I'd scream at everyone to listen to it, but they just wanted the girls then.

4. "Come Into My Palace" – Lee & The Leopards
Total Doo-Wop throwback time, written by Smokey and Warren as a possibility for The Miracles who had come from those days. Not a well produced song, but it has the fun that got lost somewhere along the way. Wouldn't all you guys like to know who actually sings on it?

5. "Soul Stomp" – Earl Van Dyke & The Soul Brothers
My boys! Berry Gordy should have given them some more freedom to stretch out on their own album. Not to just cover things, or release the backing tracks, but to really stretch. It wouldn't have killed him, and it might have saved a few heartaches later!

6. "Fingertips" – Little Stevie Wonder.
OK, there was a lot of hype around him to boost him up, but just listen to this thing that he cut when he was 12 or something. The kid didn't need the hype! See him on stage playing drums, singing, and everything else. He was amazing.

7. "Finders Keepers, Losers Weepers" – The Marvelettes.
A lesser-known HDH song that maybe no-one else wanted. I often didn't like the girl records so much, but this one does it for me probably because it has a loose stompy feel with the piano coming through.

8. "Leaving Here" – Eddie Holland.
This is the ultimate piano led early Motown record. Such a groove! Try keeping still to this one!

9. "The Only One I Love" – The Miracles
A real personal one that I grooved to with a special first love in the summer of '61. When Detroit had pride.

10. "My Candy Girl" – The Spinners
May not have been the proper title, and never released that I know of. Given to me on a demo by one of the group after a local concert in '64 I think. They took pity on my youthful enthusiasm. They didn't seem to like the song, but I love it.

Motown Quotes IV

"I started to play. Benny started the beat. We'd look at each other and know whether we needed a triplet, quarter triplet, double time or whatever. We didn't need sheet music. We could feel the groove together." *James Jamerson*

"Man, he (drummer Benny Benjamin) was one of the major forces in the Motown Sound. He could've very well been the baddest; you wouldn't even need a bass, that's how bad he was." *Stevie Wonder*

"We had in-house everything: in-house engineers, in-house studio, in-house arrangers and in-house musicians. Everybody was there seven days a week around the clock." *Henry Cosby, producer*

"Jamerson's bass playing made a certain fabric of my life visual." *Stevie Wonder*

Editor's Note

It is interesting to view Carl Lozito's piece in a wider context. Like many writers before him, he has rooted The Motown Sound firmly in Detroit with The Funk Brothers. Fair enough in general terms, but as is often the case, there is more to the story than meets the eye. There are some fans and writers around, even today, who see the golden period of Sixties Motown as purely a product of Detroit, without even a nod to what was happening out on the West Coast. Everyone knows about Berry Gordy's later decision to up roots and move the operation to LA, but a much smaller number realise just how far back the West Coast recording links go. It can be justifiably suggested that there were in fact two Motown Sounds. From as early as 1963, regular track recordings were being made in LA, using many of the well-known session players who played on Beach Boys and Spector Girl Group records. West Coast session bass player Carol Kaye spoke to me for this book, and she remembers many early '60s LA Motown sessions which is verified by photocopies of her daily log book of her recording activity:

When you listen closely to early to mid-Sixties period Motown, there are indeed distinct differences between Detroit and LA product. Much of the focus of discussion has been on the bass playing, and here there is one obvious difference: Carol Kaye always used a pick, and James Jamerson was always a finger player. Carol Kaye and many of the surviving LA session players understandably don't want their part of the story to be hidden or brushed under the carpet, and over the last few years there have been various letters written to support their claims of work on early product. In 1989 Lester Sill, on behalf of Jobete Music Co. Inc. wrote:

> 'To whom it may concern,
> Carol Kaye has played bass on several Motown hits that were cut between the years 1963 through 1969.'

Lester Sill's son now apparently estimates that some 60 percent of Motown product was LA based. Carol Kaye herself puts the amount at more like 33 percent. Either way, Motown itself has been somewhat coy over the years about what was done on the West Coast, and about the reasons for such early farming out. An easy and obvious explanation would be because Detroit's Snakepit was very simply overloaded. Another reason could have been to do with things that Carl hinted at in his piece, in that there was evidence of unreliability by some of the Detroit musicians when they got over tempted by drink or other drugs. For instance, Martha Reeves would often call in Marvin Gaye for a drum session. She was Mickey Stevenson's secretary, if Benny Benjamin was incapacitated or could not be found. It is claimed by Carol Kaye that the LA musicians smoked a great deal and drank copious amounts of coffee, but indulged in little else. Los Angeles was first and foremost a business town. Using such musicians regularly would therefore prove an attractive option.

Later tracks such as "I Was Made To Love Her", "Someday We'll Be Together" and "Ain't No Mountain High Enough' are all well acknowledged as being as being LA cut hits. Many other earlier ones can also be added: many of The Supremes hits from "Baby Love" onwards, The Temptations' "Get Ready", The Four Tops' "I Can't Help Myself' and "Bernadette", Mary Wells' "My Guy" and many, many more. In all probability, vocals would have been added back in Detroit, and some of the LA sessions could have been sweetening sessions to existing Detroit sessions. However, the idea that The Motown Sound was purely a Detroit phenomenon, as is still being defended in some quarters, is not the case.

10
Interview with Carol Kaye
by Kingsley Abbott

KA: Could you tell us how your first Motown sessions came about?
CK: Jessie Sailes (drummer) recommended me for my first Motown work. He and I had worked together on just a few dates before I was called for Motown work. I knew Jessie as he was playing with Teddy Buckner's great Dixie band on the weekends at the same club I was working at with Teddy Edwards (one of the jazz groups I played with. Jessie was then recording for Motown (about end of 1962) and he said, knowing about Motown being back in Detroit, it was just "demos" being cut out here and would I like to do a cash date for them – cash "demo" on guitar. Sure I said, and then I met Arthur Wright who was the bassist on that date at Armin Steiner's top-of-the 3-car garage studio at his nice home in LA, south of Hollywood. It was a great custom-made small studio. Armin was a sound-genius; who holds an Academy award now for his prestigious work out at Fox studios for many years, but was just getting started back then.

I remember meeting Armin, Arthur Wright, and I believe that Rene Hall, another guitarist, was on the date too. I forget who else was on that first date, but I do remember the pattern I came up with on guitar on a soul type tune. All I can remember was "C'mon Do The Jerk". Having played on a lot of soul records around that time, this was easy to do. It wasn't jazz, but had picked up a lot of gospel type licks and chordal types of riffs that I was good at. Rhythm has always been my strong point being born from professional musicians, and hearing music most of my early life. I'm not sure, but I think it was both Hal Davis and Marc Gordon at that time, later on they had Frank Wilson in the booth too.

Everything was pleasant, and I liked that kind of music. I was getting all kinds of calls, more and more of that surf-rock stuff which I wasn't too fond of, but by 1964 I was divorced and the sole supporter of my kids (well almost – I got $75 a month support for 3 children). I took "everything" I could in the studio work. Everyone was doing cash dates here and there back then anyway, but most of our work was Union. When we took cash dates, when the tune would "hit" out there on the charts, we'd insist that that "new" company go UNION then, and get their Union Recording License. We got a lot of new companies legit that way, insisting that they only hire us for dates going Unionised. They all did. But we kept working for Motown on their "demo" dates. For me, it was the music, but others said, "We're making history here".

The only studio involved for a long time was Steiner's home-studio on Formosa Ave. Later on he built the present KHJ studios on Yucca and Argyle which became the "main" studios that Motown used, but they recorded at quite a few studios.
Who were the other main players on these dates?
At first, it was Jessie Sailes on drums, Arthur Wright on bass, etc. then it was Joe Sample on keyboards, Earl Palmer on drums, still Arthur Wright and Rene Hall. Soon many, many others of our busy group of studio musicians began working for them too. After about 3-4 dates working for Motown, they wanted me to play bass, switching our roles – Arthur on guitar and myself on bass…. It didn't matter to us at all…it was a business. I quickly became No. 1 call on Fender Bass around LA. Ray Pohlman had been the No. 1 recording bassist since 1955. He was playing mainly simple but fine good groove lines with his thumb, and getting a great sound. In 1964 he quit recording as a sideman to take

the musical conductor job on the Shindig TV show for a while. This left a big hole coin-
cidentally about the time I was getting going playing bass. I liked bass better than playing guitar on rock dates. Guitar was holy to me, my jazz box, and it felt better composing lines, I could play anything I wanted on the bass. So I was getting mostly all the calls
Ray left, and I was getting popular for my invented funky lines, and even some busy 16th
note lines. Motown wanted me to play those kinds of things on bass, and I could get a
deep bass sound while playing with a pick. I use a heavy pick and my low-wrist action,
of playing *hard* on the bass, cut through and recorded great whether they wanted a
"picky" sound or a fingers-sounding line. I used always the Fender Precision bass with
medium-gauge Fender Flatwound strings, and had the strings very *high* off the neck as I
picked *hard*. I liked to play hard and the system I used to pick with is the greatest: down
on the down-beats and up on the up-beats. It makes it very smooth and the notes very
even, and you can play all day and night hard that way without much exertion. Triplets,
even fast ones, are down-up-up. On some double-time boogaloo (funky) things, it's 8
beats to the bar and you simply double up your pick action on the faster 16th note things.

Other main players (and even Ray Pohlman said he did a few Motown dates) were:
Guitar: Rene Hall, Arthur Wright, Bud Coleman, John Gray, Tommy Tedesco, Mike
Deasy, Don Peake, Lou Morrell, and even Al Casey and James Burton did a few. A few
others think Al Vescovo was one too. Drums: Jessie Sailes to start with, and then Earl
Palmer did the bulk of the work. Even Hal Blaine claims some, and of course Paul
Humphrey. Keyboards: Joe Sample, Jerry Long, Gene Page, Ray Johnson, Gene Garf, to
name a few. Much later, Don Randi and Don Abney. Saxes: Plas Johnson, Bill Green,
Jim Horn, Jackie Kelso. Trumpets: Ollie Mitchell, Roy Caton, Paul Humbonen (who
even had his teeth shaped more in a "vee" he said as it helped him play those terrifically
high notes for those Motown dates), Steve Hufstter, Chuck Findley (I believe – not sure)
and Bill Peterson. About three or four years ago, Bill Peterson and I spoke about how the
"Lewis Sisters'" mike wasn't plugged in (for the Supremes tracking dates). He played
trumpet on some too, and went on later to be president of our Local 47 Union. And he
helped dummy up the Union contract for "My Girl", which I always thought was a total
Detroit product, but the Hollywood horns evidently did overdub on that one. So the
Detroit rhythm section, along with the Hollywood horns, got some good re-use monies
from that made-up contract around 1990.... Then "all of a sudden", after the "My Girl"
dummied contract started paying royalties, some other contracts were accidentally
"found". Percussion: Gary Coleman (also on vibes, Gary was a very fine jazz vibist and
we used to work private jazz gigs together in the late '50s), Gene Estes, Emil Richards
later on, Jerry Steinholtz much later on. Even Victor Feldman I think did a few Motown,
but it was mostly Gary and then Jerry. Laudir (played on "Feelin' Alright" with us) also
did quite a few Motown dates there in the middle part.

The string section was led by Johnny Vidor. Others were George Poole, Bobby Bruce,
Jimmy Getzoff, Lenny Malarsky, and some others I don't really remember for sure. They
usually waited in the outer room to record on top of what we'd do – the rhythm section
and usually the horns along with us at that time. My little baby was very tiny and, until
I found a good live-in, I'd take her with me and the string section would baby-sit her in
that little waiting room until I got done recording.

What was the format for Motown dates? Did you get guide recordings, charts or what?
At first, we had only skeleton charts (just chord charts with maybe an idea-rhythmic
thing written for one bar), but the horns sometimes were written out. Unlike later horn
sections, our early '60s horns could make up "head-arranged" parts very quickly if they
had chord charts and kind of knew how the song went. They did this all the time at Gold
Star and other places we'd record where there wasn't much music written. Everyone
loved coming to Armin Steiner's recording studio where sometimes other things were cut
too (non-Motown things – like we recorded the very first Dick and DeeDee things

there…just saw Dick and he confirmed this).

Later as it went along, there were more and more arranged parts. At first I remember Jerry Long bringing in charts, then there was Rev. James Carmichael, then Gene Page. At first we didn't have any other recordings to listen to for ideas. They told us what they wanted, we played and they loved it. Later on, they started to have "demo" recordings that sounded very good to us, just to get the "style" of what they wanted.

In what ways did Motown dates differ from your usual West Coast work? Did you have to consciously change your style in any way to fit Motown?

They didn't differ at first. There were many, many soul records cut in Hollywood. I thought that they just were out there to get the fine musicianship. Everyone was getting the word that the studio musicians in Hollywood were creating great lines on recordings, that we were easy to work with, took direction well, and could play *any style* of music. Hollywood took over the No. 1 spot for creating hit records from NYC early in the '60s, maybe around 1961, so it was no surprise when people would fly in from the UK, from Australia, and from all parts of the USA. Motown was just another company who was using us, although we quickly surmised those recordings were very good and probably were getting on the market as hits, but none of us listened to the radio; we didn't care, as we were making pretty good cash.

It would take us an hour to do two tunes and do them up great. Normal time to do 4-5 tunes was three hours (Union dates were 3-hour dates) and they took their time with those. We got big hits out of that; we could bat them right out. If you record hit recordings every day and night of the week, in 1-2 years you get good at it! Our group of musicians was the *best* by 1962-63. Motown simply used us not only for our fine musicianship, savvy recording gear and styles, but also our creativeness.

We would work for cash, and it was 2 tunes for $25 at first (this was when scale was around $45 per 3-hour session and we paid taxes and work-dues out of that), then Tommy Tedesco insisted that we all get paid 2 tunes for $35. We could do about 10 tunes in 4 hours, so it did add up, though I think we only did that a couple of times that I know of. It was usually about 2-3 tunes a session. Sometimes they'd call us for just one tune.

Which main Motown songs did you play on? Which famous bass lines were yours?

I first played bass on Motown things in 1964 sometime. To begin with they would indicate what type of line they wanted verbally. More and more, they had charts with one bar of bass line as kind of an idea. The "I Was Made To Love Her" had the first riff line written out, and only the 1st bar of the piece. Then the Db and Eb triads were written in that one bar, but I played them slightly different as I inched up the neck for the final riff in F – I was fairly new to the bass and don't remember playing up that high on it a lot before that.

I particularly remember one, as it was the first time that I was asked to play a lot of notes especially…. And they had a demo there for me to listen to for the style that they wanted. This was the track for "I Was Made To Love Her".

With "I Can't Help Myself" – we knew this was for the Four Tops, the very 1st bar was written out, and the rest was up to me. I just more of less invented along the lines of that first bar and what they indicated they wanted from me – a certain stop-time riff at the "break" – if you will notice the bass part is slightly different to the horn part. I think the horns were added later.

"Bernadette" was much later on, and it was a Gene Page arrangement.

Gene wasn't in on the very first two years of Motown recordings. While he had a great reputation for writing "bass lines", he wasn't that great of a bassline writer for a lot of the years. He'd write two parts: one easy in case they couldn't book me, which would be for a different bassist. It was written in the key of Gb, not really hard to read, but I noticed right away it didn't "swing" at all (typical of pianist-arrangers who write from their left-hand on the piano), and so I did the usual. I added to the part, and created a lot of up-beat things where there were none, making it go from march-like corniness to bet-ter bounce. You had to be careful not to step in the way of the written horns. Motown, as a rule, usually cut with horns live with the rhythm section for the back-and-forth live feel in the room. But to mix up the good feel and frame it well (on the bassline) for the writ-ten horn parts – they weren't going to change, so in one or two rundowns it became easy and apparent what to do – so that one was half written and half improvised on.

And I can remember on that take of Bernadette, blowing the 1st break but playing something that was close, and then reading the 2nd and 3rd ones perfectly. That always stuck with me, the first mistake I made in that record on that particular take. The record still has my mistakes on it.

At one point on one tune, I forget which now, Gene Page later said "Carol, for once just play the part the way it is written" which I did. It fell flat on its face which I knew it would. He then whispered to me, "Go back and do what you were doing" with a wink and a smile. OK, I got it…he wanted the booth to think he "had written it that way". Not to take away from Gene Page – he was a gifted arranger. He just couldn't write the great bass lines he needed – close, but not it. I did ask him where he was getting his ideas from as it was evident he was getting better and better at writing better bass parts. He told me "some from you and some from Jamerson back in Detroit". He said he'd write down bass lines in a separate book, just the idea lines and then would use them later. I did recog-nise some of my lines he later wrote in his arrangements, and had to read them.

One such line was the driving line of "Reach Out". That is my line – the double-time rhythm guitar skip line. I've always preached to bass players not to lean on the drummer, but learn to DRIVE the whole band, something I've always done. Drummers love it too, as it takes the heat off them to do it, and playing with a driving bass player not only feels good but has a lot more combined bass-drum power for the hit record. It makes the track move better, giving big energy to the band and thereby hiding the flaws in any of the singers.

They were using all kinds of studios there for awhile while Armin got his regular new studio finished with the building. They used Gold Star, Harmony House (the old shack where I also cut my 1965 multi-guitar LP using the same Motown LA studio musicians: Earl Palmer on drums, Gary Coleman on percussion & vibes, Rene Hall on bass on most etc.), Sunset Sound and Columbia to name a few.

I do remember Armin Steiner telling me that he LOVED the sound he got on my bass on our "I Can't Help Myself". He always miked my amp, but added compression in the booth, the ONLY engineer ever to do that to me. Everywhere else I was cut "flat", no added compression nor EQ, as my amp sound was so great, they miked me for record-ing everywhere until the late '60s where some started to go half miked and half direct box, yet the movies and TV shows always miked me. When I asked Armin why he was putting compression on me, he said it was to make it "match the bass sounds they got in Detroit"; well that made sense to me.

By this time we were catching on that the "demos" we were cuttingnwere really big tracks, still…. We carried on with the demos for various reasons. For me, it was still the music and playing bass the way I wanted to, plus the prices they paid were close enough to Union scales or more, so it was worth it. That was our fault for doing that, and we've paid the price for not insisting they went "Union".

There's other things that happened. I never listen to the Motown at all anymore, but did for awhile there…. Someday I'll listen to it all again. I used to listen to the cuts a lot awhile back but not now….

Did you just cut tracks, or were the singers ever present?

It was all tracking dates. From time to time the singers were there just to try out (or make believe they were really singing it on the later Union-Ben Barrett-contracted dates, late '60s). We all met the Four Tops, my kids included (I sometimes took them down to the dates).

Some of the Miracles, or who I thought were the Miracles, were there too, and Little

Stevie Wonder, at about 14-15 years old. We had known he had a hit record or two out. My kids met him and I played a big show at the Shrine with Stevie at about that same time. I just saw him twice actually. It was wonderful to see him again at the 1998 NAMM winter trade show, and I mentioned "I Was Made To Love Her" and he said "Yes, you cut that and quite a few others I did also." I only remembered that one and perhaps one other one personally. It wasn't much for Stevie, but I do remember meeting him, my kids do too, and I remember this track very well and I re-recorded it...it syncs right up with the original. It was good to see him again, and he was really surprised that we bumped into each other, as it had been so many years. He tells his band I played on that cut too.

I remember one particular time when you saw two white girls (The Lewis Sisters) come in and "do" record dates singing in the room with us. They were terrible singers...nice girls, but couldn't sing through their nose. Bill Peterson (who was president of our Union in the '90s), trumpet player and I recalled together on the phone later on how bad they sounded and what a scam was being run with their mikes never plugged in, as if we'd never notice!

It was rumoured back then that they were the "Supremes" tracks, and I remember when the Supremes came out, we knew those were our tracks. We had done a lot of their tracks without the Lewis Sisters too, before they came along. We said something about it amongst ourselves, and were proud of those tracks even though we noticed the Supremes were not that good as a vocal group. It was a visual act mainly, we surmised.

I got to talk with one of the Four Tops a lot, and the bass singer of the Temptations too. I liked them as people when they sometimes came to Steiner's studio to sing along with the tracks (just to check vocal keys etc., not recording).

I never saw Smokey Robinson until a little later in the '60s at Western, and I remember feeling very uncomfortable with his strange glances at me, although he was friendly. We had cut one arrangement with a lot of quarter note triplets in it with Earl on drums. It was a big hit. It was good, but the rest of the tunes really were terrible. I think he caught me looking at him like "you can't sing" (yes, I feel that way – he's not a good singer in my opinion). Very sensitive guy, and though he was pleasant and I was pleasant, I think that's the only time I recorded with him present.

Were you aware of any feelings back in Detroit about tracks being cut in L.A.?
Just don't remember much about if there was any feedback from Detroit. I think the talk was that the Detroit musicians were sometimes on the road touring with the groups, and that's why we were recording a lot in LA. Since then, I've done some research from many books, and think it's much deeper than that. Earl offered the fact that he had heard that the rhythm section was so high all the time back in Detroit, and another bassist from Detroit verified this. They'd get into fights with Gordy etc., but strangely they started recording out here in LA quite a bit about the time that Gordy's second wife split up with him. She was a pianist and the one who started the corporation papers for Motown, rehearsed the groups in Detroit, and arranged for them. To this date she has little idea of our involvement with early recordings of Motown things in LA. I also personally think that, because Gordy laid down the law (after getting the corporation "rights" away from that ex-wife) to the writers, they HAD to have hit tracks in the "Top 20" or they'd never have another chance to produce again. I personally don't think they knew as much about producing as Hal Davis, Marc Gordon (who later did the 5th Dimension) and Frank Wilson did. I think they farmed out things to LA, but didn't want Gordy to know about that. They all got involved with litigation later on and I think it has a LOT to do with that, and they'll deny everything that was done out here. For sure, it's about money.

It seems to me that the LA Motown bunch loved our musicians, our sounds, and our expertise. We were used by everyone, so why shouldn't Motown use us too? That kind of thinking, not as snobs – not in that way at all, but that we were responsible for many hits out there and were used in "adjunct" to the original Detroit people. Don't forget, this was early on, from '62 on, when Motown was not only recording out here, but had 2 floors of suites of offices out here in the new skyscraper Sunset-Vine Towers. This was a very prestigious address, so evidently they had gotten some money rather quickly after starting their Detroit string of hits, and then our hits too; and they were saving a lot too I'm sure, by hiring us for very reasonable prices.

Still, I'd say we were not aware of what anyone back in Detroit were thinking about at all.

Did any of the main Detroit executives, musicians or producers ever come out for the sessions or was it purely California based?

Not at first. But one by one, they were out there. It was mostly producers Hal Davis, Marc Gordon, and Frank Wilson, usually two of them working together for about 1-2 years (Hal with Marc, Hal with Frank etc.). But I did work with Detroit drummer Benny Benjamin who had flown out to LA. specially to record out here he said. I can't remember the year. We saw the groups sometimes, about a quarter of the time the groups themselves were present there.

I know, being a songwriter, I took my songs up to the Motown offices (as a couple others of our group of musicians did too as I recall) to "sell" them my songs to record if possible. I saw one of the star groups rehearsing in one of the many rooms, and other things like dance lessons going on in another room, etc. There were many rooms on their two near-the-top floors in that building. When I first started recording for them, a few men would sometimes come into the Steiner studio to stop by and listen, and I have no idea who they were and didn't care. More and more you saw others popping in too. You see dozens of people around dates all the time and just don't pay any attention to them, 2-3-4 dates a day. That adds up.

In the later part of the '60s, there were bigger and bigger dates. Then they were using strings along with the horns live sometimes, but always horns with the rhythm section for sure. This was in the new studio that Steiner built, corner of Argyle and Yucca, International Sound Studios, and other bigger-room studios too (like Columbia, RCA etc.). You would see Berry Gordy, others too, in the booth by then. This was after someone snitched to the Union (about 1967) about our dates, and the Union came down hard on Motown.

Shortly before that time Earl Palmer called me up and said "Carol, listen to 'Love Child' and 'Bernadette', those hits of Motown are our tracks". So I made it a special point to try to catch those recordings on the air. Sure enough those recordings were our tracks. You always can tell your playing, like hearing your voice, and I recognised Earl on there too. I called him back and said so. And in about 1-2 months from then someone snitched to the Union about the non-Union dates we were all doing for Motown. Ben Barrett, a popular record date contractor in town, stepped in. He was always eager to get a "new account" – he was like an attorney chasing an ambulance. He offered his recording license to loan to Motown to record Union dates with, since I had heard they couldn't get a recording license on their own from our Musicians Union. This was in exchange for them to hire him to be "their" sole contractor. All of a sudden, we got 1,000s of dollars of "back-pay" checks at the Union with Ben Barrett's name at the top of the check, with "Motown" account marked on the checks and Motown marked on all the ID of the checks.

Shortly after that, there was an "announcement" in the papers that "Motown was moving out to LA". We all got a good laugh out of that one.

I believe that you helped James Jamerson when he came to LA. Can you tell us about that?

I was aware of James Jamerson fairly early on; the talk was he was really great and helped start the original Motown sound in Detroit. So when he called me out of the blue the start of the '70s, we talked a little on the phone. I promised him that I'd certainly love to recommend him for record dates and what-have-you, and that we all thought the world of him. I kept my promise, giving his name and phone number to everyone I could, contractors, arrangers, producers, etc. However the word started coming back that he had some 'problems' on the dates I referred him for, and was not doing a good enough job. Some tunes were having to be re-cut. One contractor called me up personally to say, "You're not going to work in this town again if you recommend him – he was late, was drunk or high, couldn't play or read, had the wrong gear, etc.etc." and went on and on. It astounded and worried me – not for myself, but that it was a sad thing to happen to this bassist. It was talked about a little bit among our group of musicians and we all felt terrible about Jamerson. What a great talent, and for it to be so bad. I know everyone was truly sorry for him. I stopped recommending him, hoping somehow that other players from Detroit (many had moved out here from there) would give him work then. I was into my publishing business by then and working even harder the start of the '70s than I had in the sleepless '60s. I was also still raising two children at home, although one had left to go on to college, so it was horrendous as for lack of time. I just lost touch about Jamerson. I never heard about him until my ex came home from a Baldwin Hills party, and said that Jamerson had taken too much of something and had rolled his car in a bad accident, and broken his pelvis, but that he was going to be alright. That was about 1976.

Which are your favourite Motown tracks that you played on?

To tell you the truth, I used to like "Love Child", and "You're All I Need to Get By", both by the Supremes, and the duet by Marvin Gaye and Tammi Terrell "If I Could Build My Whole World Around You".

There has been a good amount of discussion recently about the extent and timing of Motown's involvement in LA. Do you have any thoughts about this?

As you can tell from my other answers, there are plenty of reasons why our involvement with recording Motown in '60s LA was kept quiet. Most of the dates were non-union, and there was our own reluctance to talk about it for various reasons. Some just out and out hate Motown, and there was confusion due to ill-kept records, shifting of whom did what tracks back and forth, and other reasons. I have some personal reasons of my own. Basically I made up my mind while recording "Ain't No Mountain High Enough" (Diana Ross) to *not* record for Motown anymore, but accidentally got called for a couple of dates by Ben Barrett a couple of years later. I informed him I'd finish the one date, but to get someone else for the second one booked. He understood.

This hidden agenda on Motown just opens the door for shifty people to "rewrite" or assume so many wrong things, which is just exactly what happened. People had reasons to keep our dates quiet, and it's quite evident about the pride in Motown recordings, which are natural and a good thing in itself....

What I recorded for Motown does not diminish what Jamerson did at all. However, due to the many secrets involved with Motown for many unspoken reasons behind the corporate scenes (and probably the song-writing scenes too), and for some of the many reasons why our group of musicians stopped recording for Motown too (including myself), probably an injustice was done. I don't know, but I do know that we were used to recording hits with no thought of "credits". We had to raise our families with a comfortable living, and needed to count on work in the future. At that point, if you turned down work, you might not have a career the following year. It's not a "cold" business, but it is a business. It's up to you to keep yourself in good shape both mentally and physically. Yet, it's amazing to look at the sad track record of people involved with Motown....

It's only lately that most of the public have found out who really recorded the Beach Boys' music, let alone most of the rest of the hit groups of the '60s. This is coming out more and more as we all are writing our books. Earl Palmer's is only the tip of the iceberg [*Backbeat – Earl Palmer's Story* – Smithsonian Press]. Whose tunes were really given to the West Coast office? I do mean *office*, as they've been out here in LA since

1962. Did they really write them or buy them? Was it to ensure that the writers got the *necessary* top 20 hits, so they could be able to "produce" the next ones? It was well known out here in LA to "keep writers out of the studios, as they had strange ways of producing and couldn't usually produce any hits".... So it was of no surprise that no writers were present when we cut songs for Motown.

The star-singers (I'm sure), as a group, were under certain impressions too. I bet they had no idea where each hit track really came from although they'll say what they've been told over the years – they have reasons to be reticent about all this too...

Thank God I kept my log as did a few others, and of course, the studio, contractor's name (or producer's/arranger's name), hours worked and dates. Also in my appointment books, some of which I still have, is marked more information and data, and the name of the artist/group I recorded for. But, the tune title was written very rarely simply because that was not important to get *paid by*. I have 149 sessions in my log for Motown....

Earl Palmer said he doesn't remember 90 percent (estimation) of the tunes he recorded. We'd cut 1-2 albums a day! That was fairly normal, and others say the same thing. Most of those tunes started sounding the same; we were so tired, recording 8-12-16 hours every day of the week sometimes....

There's so much more to add, but I think you get the general idea. Due to hearing about many lawsuits later brought by the writers against Motown, I believe it's easier to keep quiet about things than to give credit where credit is due. I'd think, by others involved with Motown – a sort of "don't rock the boat" attitude. Our bunch of studio musicians is resigned to never getting any of their Motown credits, ...

So you see there is a lot of history that probably will never unfold – and it's OK with me – I simply don't care anymore. God knows what I did, and most of my peers too; we know the hits of Motown we cut.... And the truth is stronger than the past lies. What goes 'round, comes 'round as they say. We honestly played and invented hard, and did an honest day's work in recording. That's something we can always be proud of. Who else can say that?

11
Thomas 'Beans' Bowles: A Short Interview
by Kingsley Abbott

'Beans' Bowles was a very well-known figure around Motown from the earliest days. He was a musician (sax & flute) who became part of Motown's management division, International Talent Management Inc. When out on the road as tour manager for the first major Motown Revue in 1962, he suffered several broken bones in a crash that killed his assistant Eddie McFarland. 'Beans' recovered to become one of the major forces pushing Berry Gordy towards better musicianship and better artist presentation. When I spoke to him late in 1999, he was still living in Detroit as a gentleman of advanced years and some ill health. It was with great sadness that I learnt of his death in January 2000. These memories, given especially for this book, are therefore quite probably the last time that he spoke about Motown on the record.

'Beans': "Early on, our musicians were good, very good, but the first writing was not too good at all. They were not very good songs, from a musical point of view. They tried to do arrangements, but they really didn't do it very well. People would try to transpose the music for publication by listening back to the records. It was pretty awful. Later on, when proper arrangers came along, like David Van dePitte and Gil Askey, things got much better.

"The musicians, who were all very experienced players, had to sort it all out for themselves at first. Maybe there would be just a piano copy in some sort of form, and they would work thing out just from that. Other times, someone would just come along and [*Beans hums a snatch of a tune at this point*] they would work it just from that. But they could do it. They had to, because there was no other written stuff. The Funk Brothers would often to their own thing anyway, but it was very difficult in the early days, very difficult. Later on, it was better, and I preferred it then. We got in arrangers who made it all more professional. It quit being just *basic* music. Before that, The Funk Brothers had no real guidelines. They didn't give a damn though about what they played. They didn't realise at the time how important those tracks were going to be.

"I had been in management and I had also been a musician. I had known Mickey Stevenson's mum when she was a singer at the Flame Showbar. Mickey and other experienced people would look round the clubs to find musicians. A lot of the good guys had left town to go and find work in places like New York, but the guys we had were excellent.

"The first tours were just little affairs. We would take people out for a couple of days, and then bring them back. Berry Gordy was a record man, and I was a show business man. I had to prove to him that his artists would do better if they were exposed. He just wanted to make records. Therefore I got him to tour and the sales went up in each of the towns we visited. They went up even more after the publicity from the crash. I was in hospital for months, and then on crutches. That was the tour in the fall of 1962 that I organised with Esther Edwards. I spent six months preparing for it! The Marvelettes were our biggest act then. But the tour was too much and too long…

"I think that perhaps Motown peaked in the mid- to late-Sixties. It had passed its peak when the Jackson Five came along. It was best when Marvin Gaye, The Temptations and The Four Tops were at their height. I worked a lot with those guys. I was often the road conductor for them. I came to England with the Temptations when we did the Dusty

Springfield TV show – for BBC I think. I guess that it was The Temptations and the Miracles who helped me the most. I gave The Temptations their first road lessons. All those groups reflected my musical and presentational philosophies in some way or another. Maxine Powell also really developed those kids. We made a few mistakes along the way, but we always learnt from them. There were always enough hit records to override the mistakes!"

12
Marvin Gaye: Trouble Man
by Bill Dahl

In one of the Hitsville offices, checking out a British itinerary.
(l-r: Emily Dunne, Dave Godin, Marvin Gaye.)

Bill Dahl's Goldmine *piece from 16th June 1989, just five years after Gaye's death, gives a comprehensive introduction to the career of the ill-fated Motown Legend. The piece concentrates on Gaye's musical output; those who seek to know more about Gaye's life are directed to David Ritz's* Divided Soul *[name checked in the piece] and Steve Turner's more recent* Trouble Man.

Throughout his career, Gaye never stopped creating vital, innovative music – from his doo-wop beginnings in Washington, D.C., through the '60s as one of the principal cogs in the vast Motown hitmaking machine, and into the '70s, when Gaye's creativity at last reached full fruition as he assumed total control of his recorded output and cut some of his most enduring work.

Born Marvin Pentz Gay, Jr. on April 2, 1939 in Washington, D.C., Gaye's problems on the home front surfaced early in his troubled life. His father was a self-styled minister with an obscure sect called the House of God, an exceptionally strict religious movement, and the youngest was raised as a member of the church, singing hymns such as "Precious Lord" and "Journey To The Sky" from the time he was three years of age.

According to David Ritz's excellent 1985 Gaye biography, *Divided Soul*, the younger Gaye often suffered beatings at the hands of his father. The abuse left the youth introverted and unsure of himself, especially around members of the opposite sex. But young Marvin soon discovered a way to escape such an oppressive atmosphere.

He became infatuated with the silky doo-wop harmonies of well-established East Coast vocal groups such as the Orioles, Capris and Lee Andrews and the Hearts, many of whom would play Washington's Howard Theatre. Despite his strong religious background, Gaye embraced the doo-wop craze while in high school, joining a group called the D.C. Tones that also included boyhood buddy Reese Palmer and a lead singer named Sondra Lattisaw, whose daughter Stacy would score her first major R&B hit in 1980 at the age of 13.

After a brief and unhappy hitch in the Air Force that ended with an honorable discharge despite numerous conflicts with various authority figures, Gaye hooked up with a D.C. quartet called the Marquis in the summer of 1957. The group also included Gaye's pal Palmer as lead vocalist, baritone James Nolan and bass Chester Simmons.

During a short layover in the nation's capital, Chicago blues rock pioneer Bo Diddley took an interest in the Marquis. He brought them to New York in September 1957 and produced their only single, "Hey Little Schoolgirl" / "Wyatt Earp" for OKeh Records. The same session also produced a 45 by Diddley's distinctive pianist, D.C. native Billy Stewart, "Baby, You're My Only Love," also for Okeh, with the Marquis providing spirited background support. Unfortunately, the Marquis' only single proved to be a stiff commercially, and the group drifted on for a time, with Simmons signing on as Diddley's driver.

When Harvey Fuqua rolled into D.C. in early 1959 with his renowned Moonglows for an engagement at the Howard, he was looking to inject some new blood into his group. Fuqua had formed the original Moonglows in Louisville, Ky. with Bobby Lester, Alexander Graves, Prentiss Barnes and guitarist Billy Johnson, and with the help of DJ Alan Freed, they debuted on the Champagne label in 1952. Perfecting their highly advanced harmonies during a brief stint on the Chicago-based Chance label with dreamy ballads such as "Baby Please" and "I Was Wrong," the group really hit the big time with their first release for Chess in 1954.

With a brilliant lead effort by Lester and breathtaking background harmonies, "Sincerely" made #1 on the R&B charts in December of '54, and follow-ups "Most Of All," "We Go Together" and the jumping "See Saw" all cracked the R&B Top 10. The Moonglows also appeared in the early rock films *Rock, Rock, Rock* and *Mr. Rock & Roll* (Fuqua soloed in another flick, *Go, Johnny, Go*) before scoring their last major smash in late '58 with the dramatic "Ten Commandments Of Love," which featured Fuqua up front. The same personnel also briefly recorded for the Checker subsidiary as the Moonlighters during the mid-50s.

Despite all the past successes, Fuqua was ready to implement wholesale personnel changes by 1959. At the end of the Howard booking, he sacked the old Moonglows en masse and replaced them with the Marquis, augmented by bass vocalist Chuck Barksdale, who was on momentary hiatus from the Dells. The more worldly Fuqua immediately became the impressionable Gaye's first professional mentor and role model.

Rechristened as Harvey and the Moonglows, they hit the highway to Chicago, waxing a date for Leonard Chess that included Gaye's first appearance as a lead singer on the upbeat "Mama Loocie," co-written by Fuqua and Gaye. The stately ballad side, "Twelve Months Of The Year," showcased Fuqua as lead. The group stuck around the Chess studio long enough to lend vocal backing to a couple of Chuck Berry classics, "Almost Grown" and "Back in the USA."

After nine tough months largely spent riding the chitlin' circuit, the new edition of the Moonglows broke up, this time for good, and Gaye accompanied Fuqua to Detroit. The Motor City was just beginning to develop its fabled recording scene; Berry Gordy's empire was still in its primordial phase, although its roster already boasted names like Mary Wells, the Miracles and Barrett Strong, who registered the firm's first major hit with "Money (That's What I Want)" in early 1960. Gordy's sister Gwen, meanwhile, headed Anna Records, with artists like Joe Tex, New Orleans pianist Paul Gayten, and Strong, when "Money" proved too much for Gordy's fledgling operation to handle.

So Fuqua jumped in to the fray and inaugurated his own companies, Harvey and Tri-Phi, cutting sides by future Motown sax hero Junior Walker and the All-Stars, Shorty

Long and local bluesman Eddie Burns. Gaye made himself useful around Fuqua's operation, playing the drums behind the Spinners' Tri-Phi hit, "That's What Girls Are Made For," but he never made a single of his own for either label.

However it came down, whether Fuqua sold Gaye's contract to Berry Gordy or Gordy recognized the young singer's potential while he was still a Moonglow and signed him on the spot – the exact details remain unclear – Gaye ended up on Motown's Tamla subsidiary in early 1961. With the move, Gordy replaced Fuqua as the surrogate father figure in Gaye's life, kicking off an often stormy relationship that led to much frustration on both sides.

Gaye debuted on Tamla in May '61 with the plaintive ballad "Let Your Conscience Be Your Guide," paired with the driving stop-time rocker, "Never Let You Go". The 45, which bombed, also marked the official addition of the 'e' to Gaye's surname, in order to deflect the obvious wisecracks that otherwise would have surely followed.

Gaye's first album for Tamla, *The Soulful Moods of Marvin Gaye*, emerged the following month and proved thoroughly atypical of what would soon follow. The jazzy set was comprised largely of mellow pop standards with an after-hours trio feel better suited to saloon crooners like Tony Bennett or Frank Sinatra than a soul legend in the making. But Gaye was drawn to this sort of material, and he would regularly return to "legitimate" pop fare over the course of his career.

Gaye steadily established himself on the highly competitive Motown scene, working as a drummer on various early productions, notably the Marvelettes' million-selling "Please Mr. Postman". He also found himself in a serious relationship with another of Gordy's sisters. Anna Gordy, for whom Gwen's record label was named, was 17 years older than Gaye and very influential within the Motown hierarchy, and one might surmise that the ongoing affair didn't hurt the young singer's standing at the label one bit. They were married in 1963.

But Gaye's career as an R&B star was somewhat slow to take flight. His second single coupled the uptempo "I'm Yours, You're Mine" with a lilting revival of the Chordettes' "Mr. Sandman". It was followed by the dismal "Soldier's Plea" (rather ironic, considering Gaye's earlier problems with the military, backed with the lighter-than-air "Taking My Time". Neither of these offerings charted.

Finally, in the summer of 1962, Gaye hit on the correct formula. He toughened his vocal approach considerably on the mid-tempo "Stubborn Kind Of Fellow," drawing on those early days in church, and the track became Gaye's first major R&B hit, climbing to #8. The song, which he co-wrote with producer Mickey Stevenson (with an assist from Gordy himself), was also enlivened by Thomas "Beans" Bowles' playful flute break (a staple of Gaye's early work) and the snappy harmonies of Martha Reeves and the Vandellas, who would grace many of Gaye's initial hits. "It Hurts Me Too," the chunky flip side, also found Gaye gaining more vocal assurances.

Still none too confident of his solo stage persona, Gaye nevertheless hit the road with the barnstorming Motortown Revue, forced to polish his act on the fly. But he still found time to help compose an occasional hit for other Motown artists, including "Beechwood 4-5789" for the Marvelettes (and later, "Dancing In The Street" for Martha and the Vandellas).

That instantly identifiable "Motown Sound" was rapidly coming together by 1963, when Gaye began to hit his stride as an acknowledged soul attraction. Keyboardist Earl Van Dyke headed up a peerless combo that also included guitarists Robert White and Joe Messina, incomparable bassist James Jamerson and drummer Benny Benjamin. Dubbed the Funk Brothers, the crew pushed Gaye relentlessly on the upbeat dance workouts that proved to be the young vocalist's early specialty.

Co-written by Gaye, Clarence Paul and producer Stevenson, "Hitch Hike" inspired its very own set of dance steps. Released in December '62, the track shot up to #12 R&B and #30 pop, its insistent beat inspiring another gutsy vocal effort from Gaye. The flip "Hello There Angel," was a tuneful ballad with obvious doo-wop overtones.

Despite the considerable success of "Hitch Hike," Gaye considered himself something else than adequate as a dancer. "Dick Clark started having me on his show," he told Ritz in *Divided Soul*. "He saw that I'd started this Hitch Hike craze, and he got a kick out of watching me stumble about the stage."

However, anyone who has viewed Gaye's electrifying 1964 performance in director Steve Binder's The T.A.M.I. Show knows differently. Decked out for the movie's filming in a blinding white tuxedo, Gaye's spirited high-stepping throughout his segment is every bit the equal of his incendiary vocal histrionics (or at least what you can hear over the screams of the frenzied crowd).

Stevenson remained at the helm for Gaye's next release, the exultant "Pride And Joy". Supposedly inspired by Gaye's new bride, writer's credit was split between singer, producer and a very young Norman Whitfield. With bassist Jamerson laying down a driving walking groove behind Gaye's joyous message of undying devotion, "Pride And Joy" proved to be Gaye's first Top 10 hit, topping out at #2 R&B. "One Of These Days" made a solid mid-tempo flip side.

Two more early sides, "Get My Hands On Some Lovin'" and "Wherever I Lay My Hat," made their first appearances on Gaye's initial all-R&B album, *That Stubborn Kinda Fellow*, which was issued on the last day of January 1963. The Artistics, a Chicago vocal group, waxed a nice cover of "Get My Hands On Some Lovin'" a year later, and put it on the R&B charts.

Tamla released Gaye's first live album in September '63 and although the set suffered from thin sound quality, injudicious editing and the overblown Las Vegas-drenched big band charts of saxist Choker Campbell's orchestra, it nevertheless offered a realistic indication of the sort of adulation Gaye could inspire among his female followers. Besides the expected hits, the live LP featured the bluesy "Mo Jo Hanna" and a heavily Ray Charles-inspired "You Are My Sunshine".

Motown's seemingly infallible composing triumvirate of Eddie and Brian Holland and Lamont Dozier assumed production responsibility for Gaye at the tail end of '63, contributing a pair of very similar gospel-infused rockers, "Can I Get A Witness" and "You're A Wonderful One," that both utilized a variation on Chuck Berry's familiar rhythmic feel.

With it's emotionally charged call-and-response structure, "Witness" harked back once again to Gaye's early gospel training, the Supremes supplanting the Vandellas in the vocal backup role, and made it to #15 R&B and #22 pop. The single also featured a particularly strong B-side, "I'm Crazy 'Bout My Baby," that employed the same steady walking groove as "Pride And Joy" and could just as easily have hit in its own right.

"You're A Wonderful One" was a great soundalike sequel and fared even better on the charts, hitting #15 pop. "When I'm Alone I Cry," which graced the reverse side, was the title track of Gaye's next concerted effort to reach the easy listening crowd, and although Gaye was certainly versatile enough to handle the sort of material (and from all accounts, he genuinely enjoyed performing a wide variety of Tin Pan Alley standards), the lush, string-drenched arrangements often tended to stifle the vocalist's remarkable vocal gifts instead of enhancing them.

Gaye began his long-standing practice of boy-girl duets in May 1964, teaming with the first queen of Motown, Mary Wells, for a double-sided hit single "Once Upon A Time" (#19 pop) / "What's The Matter With You Baby" (#17 pop), produced by Clarence Paul. Gordy rushed out an album, *Together*, to capitalize on the brief partnership.

By June 1964 Gordy seldom produced any of his artists himself. But he made an exception for Gaye's "Try It Baby," a relaxed rocker that Gordy also wrote. The song, which hit #15 pop, was coupled with another easy listening item, "If My Heart Could Sing". The label followed much the same format with Gaye's next offering, "Baby Don't You Do It" / "Walk On The Wild Side". The hit side, penned by Holland-Dozier-Holland and produced by Brian Holland and Dozier, achieved its #27 pop rating on the strength of its slicker Motownized adaptation of Bo Diddley's shave-and-a-haircut beat, while the mellow flip side definitely bore no connection whatsoever to Lou Reed.

Producer Mickey Stevenson stoked the home fires in October 1964, choosing his own wife, the statuesque Kim Weston, to replace Mary Wells as Gaye's new duet partner. Weston had dented the R&B charts a little over a year earlier with "Love Me All The Way," which peaked at #24 R&B but her biggest smash was still a year away when she teamed with Gaye to cut "What Good Am I Without You". Their sultry chemistry resulted in a #61 pop showing, but a proposed album, *Side By Side*, was strangely scrubbed after receiving a release number.

The prolific Holland, Dozier and Holland supplied Gaye with his biggest pop seller yet at the close of 1964. The sensuous "How Sweet It Is" vaulted to #6 pop and #4 R&B, with producers Brian Holland and Dozier assembling a gently rocking rhythm track perfectly tailored to Gaye's enraptured vocal.

"'How Sweet It Is" is my favorite number from that era," Gaye told Tony Cummings in a 1976 feature in *Black Music* magazine. "When they (Holland-Dozier-Holland) first played it to me I said "Whew! That's a smash for anyone!" Sax wailer Junior Walker's rougher cover version of "How Sweet It Is" was similarly successful on Motown's Soul subsidiary only a year later, fulfilling Gaye's prophecy . "Forever," the flip side represented a haunting Gaye throwback to the doo-wop era.

With the sustained success of "How Sweet It Is," Gaye embarked on his first tour of England in November '64, where he lip-synched his latest hit and "Can I Get A Witness" on the English equivalent of *American Bandstand, Ready Steady Go*.

Tamla went on a veritable Marvin Gaye album binge during the early months of 1965, issuing three Gaye LPs virtually overnight. *How Sweet It Is* was a straight R&B compilation, combining four recent hits with rarities such as "No Good Without You," "Need Somebody," "Stepping Closer To Your Heart" (a Gaye-Fuqua collaboration) and "Me And My Lonely Room," which was rescued from undeserved obscurity five years later as the flip side of Gaye's "The Other End Of Our Road".

The other pair of albums fell into the easy listening genre. *Hello Broadway* and *A Tribute To The Great Nat King Cole* were self-explanatory, Gaye's dramatic renditions backed by a plethora of violins and other sweeteners. Even on uptempo Cole classics such as "Straighten Up And Fly Right" and "Send For Me," there was no hint whatsoever of the trademark Motown sound. A further attempt at mainstream respectability, a gig at New York's famed Copacabana nightclub, was also less then successful.

Smokey Robinson fortuitously stepped into Gaye's musical existence in 1965, presenting him with the brilliant "I'll Be Doggone," which proved to be Gaye's first R&B chart-topper. Full of the clever lyrical twists and melodic turns synonymous with Robinson's genius, the song was a prime example of the Motown sound in all its glory. "You've Been A Long Time Coming" marked a welcome return to R&B oriented flip sides.

The follow-up, "Pretty Little Baby," wasn't nearly as strong, although Gaye was one of its writers, and it only made it to a disappointing #16 R&B slot. The other side, the Robinson composition "Now That You've Won Me," was much more impressive, with its cool straight-forward R&B ballad structure.

But "Ain't That Peculiar" was another surefire winner, with its memorable descending bass figure and typically metaphorical lyrics from the masterful Robinson, who also produced. The pulsating number returned Gaye to the #R&B spot, and like "I'll Be Doggone," it hit #8 pop. Miracles' guitarist Marv Tarplin's subtle licks were a major ingredient in most of Robinson's productions with Gaye. "She's Got To Be Real," the memorably raw B-side, was a gritty soul number.

"One More Heartache," Gaye's first hit of 1966 (#14 R&B) contained an appealing bluesy guitar riff that emphasized its doomy minor-key feel (Tarplin was listed as co-writer, along with Robinson and other members of the Miracles). Another contribution from Smokey's camp, "When I Had Your Love," held down the flip side with a vaguely Far Eastern motif.

Robinson and his cohorts also penned and produced the #16 R&B hit "Take This Heart Of Mine," which deserved an even warmer reception, thanks to its pounding instrumental backing and an especially hot vocal from Gaye. Its flip, the grinding "Need Your Lovin'," was a leftover from the *How Sweet It Is* LP.

Moods Of Marvin Gaye (Gordy was already recycling titles), issued in May '66, combined current hit singles with another helping of big band schmaltz, including a foray into Sinatra territory on "One For My Baby," with a heavily echo-laden vocal that sounded downright eerie and a cover of Willie Nelson's "Night Life" that found Gaye struggling to overcome an oppressively ornate horn chart. The album also included an obscure Stevie Wonder ballad, "You're The One For Me".

Holland-Dozier-Holland came back long enough to supply the bouncy "Little Darling, I Need You," a #10 R&B hit with a punchy groove very typical of their usual approach, backed with one of Gaye's own songs, the playful "Hey Diddle Diddle". But it was Gaye's charming duet with Kim Weston, "It Takes Two," that constituted his biggest hit in some time, jumping to #14 pop and #4 R&B in January '67. Penned by Mickey Stevenson and Sylvia Moy, the track hinted at future duet successes in store for Gaye. Tamla finally issued a Gaye/Weston album, *Take Two*, which was split between fresh material and hoary oldies such as "Till There Was You" and "Secret Love".

Those duet successes wouldn't come with Kim Weston, however. Stevenson received an offer he couldn't refuse – to head a new R&B label for MGM called Venture Records – and took his wife with him when he left. Their exit paved the way for Gaye's magical pairing with lovely former James Brown protégé Tammi Terrell, who had debuted on vinyl in 1961 on Wand as Tammy Montgomery. Two years later, she cut "I Believe You Love Me" and "Come On And See Me," both respectable R&B hits, in 1966.

The star-crossed combination of Gaye and Terrell immediately clicked, and their first duet, the inspiring "Ain't No Mountain High Enough," captured the public's collective heart, racing to #3 R&B and #19 pop. Like much of their material, the song was penned by another soulful duo new to the Motown scene, Nick Ashford and Valerie Simpson, who had themselves recorded as a duet for the New York-based Glover label before penning, with Joshie Jo Armstead, "Let's Go Get Stoned," a #1 R&B hit for Ray Charles in 1966.

"Ain't No Mountain High Enough" was produced by Gaye's old mentor, Harvey Fuqua, and Johnny Bristol, who had started his career as half of Johnny and Jackie (Beavers) for Fuqua's Tri-Phi label. One of those old Johnny and Jackie duets, "Someday (We'll Be Together)," later became a #1 hit for Diana Ross and the Supremes, and it was Bristol's voice echoing throughout the remake. Later, Bristol hit himself with "Hang On In There Baby" in 1974 for MGM.

From mid-1967 through early 1970, Marvin and Tammi could do nothing wrong. "Your Precious Love," penned by Ashford and Simpson, and Fuqua and Bristol's "If I Could Build My Whole World Around You" both occupied the #2 R&B slot during the latter stages of 1967, with the relaxed "Your Precious Love" also making #5 pop. "If This World Were Mine," Gaye's own composition, made it to #27 R&B as the flip of "If I Could Build My Whole World".

Gaye and Terrell scored two #1 R&B hits in a row in 1968, "Ain't Nothing Like The Real Thing" (#8 pop) and "You're All That I Need To Get By" (#7 pop). Both tracks were once again written by Ashford and Simpson. Despite their very convincing public pose of endless devotion, however, the pair were never romantically linked. Terrell's beau was David Ruffin, lead singer with the Temptations. Marvin and Tammi's final '68 offering, "Keep On Loving Me Baby," was a #11 R&B seller.

But tragedy struck during a 1967 concert at Virginia's Hampden-Sydney College. As the pair finished a rendition of "Your Precious Love," Terrell collapsed into Gaye's arms, stricken with some sort of mystery ailment. She was diagnosed as suffering from a brain tumor, and despite eight operations over a period of 18 months, Tammi Terrell passed away on March 16, 1970. She was only 24 years old.

Ritz's *Divided Soul* reveals that Valerie Simpson actually subbed for Terrell on much of *Easy*, the third and last Gaye/Terrell album, in 1969. "At first I refused to go along with the plan," he told Ritz. " I saw it as another money-making scheme on BG's (Berry Gordy's) part. I said it was cynical and wrong. I didn't want to deceive the public like that. Then Motown convinced me that it'd be a way for Tammi's family to have additional income. Valerie had sung many of the demo tapes to teach Tammi her songs, so she was a natural choice."

Whoever was handling the female role, the public remained satisfied. "Good Lovin' Ain't Easy To Come By," "What You Gave Me" and "The Onion Song," all from that last album and all penned by Ashford and Simpson, each enjoyed decent runs on the soul charts, with "What You Gave Me" peaking at #6.

By comparison with that string of best-selling duets, Gaye's solo career suffered a bit of a lull during the same period. 'Your Unchanging Love," with its irresistible "How Sweet It Is" bass line takeoff, registered a solid #7 R&B showing but only managed to make #33 pop. It was backed by a weak Holland-Dozier-Holland ballad, "I'll Take Care Of You," that was never heard from again.

"You," Gaye's first 1968 solo smash, reflected the soul idiom's increasing emphasis on funky rhythm patterns at the expense of intricate melodic lines, and hit #7 R&B. Its flip, "Change What You Can," which listed Gaye and Fuqua among its writers, was an early attempt at a message song that retained the familiar Motown beat. Another funk-oriented tune, "Chained," traveled much the same route to #8 R&B, while its infectious flip, the driving "At Last (I Found A Love)," deserved hit status itself, built around an emotionally charged gospel groove that seemed a most welcome throwback to Gaye's earlier work.

None of these singles managed to set the pop charts ablaze. But Gaye's momentous remake of a Norman Whitfield/Barrett Strong composition that labelmates Gladys Knight and the Pips had already taken to the highest reaches of the charts only a year before instantly reversed that brief trend. Gaye's brooding minor-key revival of "I Heard It Through The Grapevine" returned the song to the very peak of both charts once more, the first time that Gaye had ever topped the pop and R&B lists simultaneously.

Divided Soul claims that Gaye's "Grapevine" was actually recorded prior to Knight's sanctified raveup reading. But Gaye told writer Tony Cummings in *Black Music* that, "I wasn't keen on recording the song, like Gladys Knight and the Pips had already had a number one song. But Norman had this whole new arrangement worked out. And it came out pretty good."

Whatever the confusing chronology, Whitfield's seamless production surrounded the singer with a palpable sense of ominous tension, and Gaye's elastic vocal invested the tune with an entirely fresh perspective. As good as Knight's original was – and it still stands as one of her finest performances to date – Gaye's adaptation made "I Heard It Through The Grapevine" all his own.

The resulting album, *In The Groove*, was quickly retitled *I Heard It Through The Grapevine* to hype the song's phenomenal success. It contained some especially impressive filler, including a pair of sublime Drifters covers, "Some Kind Of Wonderful" and "There Goes My Baby," that showcased Gaye's enduring doo-wop roots, and a nod to the Four Tops with "Loving You Is Sweeter Than Ever". Ashford and Simpson contributed "Tear It On Down," and "It's Love I Need," "Every Now And Then" and "You're What's Happening" (the flip of "Grapevine"), all highly enjoyable.

Since "Grapevine" proved to be such a sensation on its second time around, it was therefore only logical to dig into the voluminous Jobete Music copyright files for Gaye's follow-up release. Whitfield dusted off "Too Busy Thinking About My Baby," which the

Temptations had included on their 1966 *Getting' Ready* album. Gaye's remake evoked some of the same atmosphere as "Grapevine," but the track's mood was considerably more upbeat, as Gaye waxed rhapsodic about his lover on the Whitfield/Strong/Janie Bradford tune. The formula paid all over again: "Too Busy" restored Gaye to the top R&B position, although it only noted a #4 pop showing.

Gaye's final 1969 smash, "That's The Way Love Is," was even more musically similar to "Grapevine," its resonating minor-key arrangement enhancing the overall mood of encompassing despair. Whitfield's skillful productions brought out the meaner side of Gaye, relegating the more familiar silky smooth style of the singer to the background. "That's The Way Love Is" nearly matched the success of its immediate predecessors, peaking at #2 R&B and #7 pop.

M.P.G. rivalled *In The Groove* as Gaye's best album of the 1960s. He was no longer dishing up goodtime dance music, but thoroughly adult contemporary soul that show-cased the anger and frustration that the vocalist was reportedly experiencing in own marriage at the same time. Many of Motown's top songsmiths were represented on *M.P.G.* Smokey Robinson was in on "It's A Bitter Pill To Swallow" and "More Than A Heart Can Stand," Holland-Dozier-Holland contributed "It Don't Take Much To Keep Me," Mickey Stevenson and Ivy Jo Hunter in with "Seek And You Shall Find," and Stevie Wonder and Hank Cosby came up with "Try My True Love". There was also another sweet Drifters homage with "This Magic Moment".

If *M.P.G.* contained more fresh material than ever before, *That's The Way Love Is*, Gaye's final conventional Motown album, held the least. The title track was gracing its second LP in a row, and much of the rest of the set was cover material culled from a wide variety of sources, albeit expertly tailored to fit Gaye's style. Of course, there were the predictable Motown retreads, which constituted many of the highlights: remakes of Jimmy Ruffin's "Gonna Give Her All The Love I've Got," which managed to slap onto the R&B charts as the other side of "How Can I Forget You," and the breakneck "Don't You Miss Me A Little Bit Baby". There were a couple of Temptations remakes – a condensed "Cloud Nine" and tougher "I Wish It Would Rain" – and a churning revival of the Motown perennial "Gonna Keep On Tryin' Till I Win Your Love" that came close to rivalling Edwin Starr's peerless version.

Less successful were covers of the Young Rascals' "Groovin'" and the Beatles' "Yesterday," while "Abraham, Martin and John" remained a shameless tearjerker even in Gaye's sensitive hands. All three of the originals were solid, though: "How Can I Forget" was a #18 R&B seller, and "No Time For Tears" and "So Long," a cooking slice of prototypical Motown R&B penned by Whitfield, Eddie Holland and R. Dean Taylor of "Indiana Wants Me" fame, were also memorable.

After the disappointing commercial reaction to "How Can I Forget," the #7 R&B showing for Gaye's reworking of "The End Of Our Road" was a distinctive improvement. Once again borrowing a hit from labelmates Gladys Knight and the Pips, who had done even better with it a couple of years before, the song would prove to be Gaye's last hurrah as a formulaic Motown artist.

Thoroughly devastated by the tragic death of Tammi Terrell, Gaye drew totally disenchanted with the world of show business at the dawn of the 1970s and dropped out of sight completely for a time, turning down all requests for live appearances and Berry Gordy's repeated pleas for new product. He fell in with hometown football heroes Lem Barney and Mel Farr, pursuing a bizarre fantasy of joining the Detroit Lions as a wide receiver. But Lions head coach Joe Schmidt showed little interest in a 31-year-old rookie end, and the dream was eventually shelved.

Gaye's escalating desire to exercise total control over his musical output finally manifested itself around the same time. Despite Gordy's reluctance to allow his artists to become involved in the production end of the industry, Gaye had gotten his feet wet behind the scenes the previous year, writing and producing a #1 R&B smash for a previously obscure Motown act called the Originals.

The soft, dreamy sound of "Baby, I'm For Real" was an accurate indication of Gaye's future direction, with lead vocalist Freddy Gorman caressing each syllable of the love ballad. The Originals had haunted the Motown complex for years, supplying uncredited backing vocals and laying down Motownized versions of chestnuts such as "Goodnight Irene" and "Red Sails In The Sunset," but Gaye was the only producer to coax a major hit from the quartet. Two other tracks Gaye co-wrote and produced for the group, "The Bells" and "We Can Make It Baby," also hit in 1970, "The Bells" going as far as #4 R&B.

Although Gordy kept up the pressure to deliver more hits in the standard Motown fashion, Gaye was sick of all the demands from his surrogate father figure, and remained determined to forge his own musical statement without all the corporate influence. When Gaye finally presented his long overdue *What's Going On* to Gordy, the big boss man and his staff initially expressed serious reservations about its commercial potential. But the massive critical and popular raves that followed its release quickly changed his mind.

What's Going On marked Gaye's emergence as a serious social commentator. Inspired by his brother Frankie's harrowing experiences in Vietnam and his own increasing disillusionment toward the volatile state of affairs around the world, Gaye responded with a groundbreaking suite that represented a tortured plea for peace and understanding.

Gaye had help with the project. The title track was written by Motown staff writer Al Cleveland and Renaldo "Obie" Benson, one of the Four Tops. And Cleveland recalled in Nelson George's Motown retrospective *Where Did Our Love Go?*, that Gaye was initially in no hurry to record "What's Going On". "We begged him for about a month to do the tune," Cleveland told George. "He hadn't had a record out in a year and a half, and he wasn't doing too good financially. As a result he was not in a good frame of mind."

The resulting success of the album may have altered Gaye's mood for the better. "What's Going On," "Mercy, Mercy Me (The Ecology)" and "Inner City Blues" all took their respective turns at the pinnacle of the R&B charts, and all broke the pop Top 10 with "What's Going On" climbing the highest at #2. But the album was intended to deliver its powerful statement on the war, the environment and world hunger in its entirety, and its unprecedented success (reportedly the top-selling album in the label's history at the time) surely erased any doubts Gordy may have harbored about Gaye's abilities as a producer.

Strangely, Gaye's first post-*What's Going On* single, "You're The Man," was by comparison a major disappointment. It was a #7 R&B seller, but only crept up to #50 pop in May '72, and an album planned around the concept was permanently shelved.

Gaye had no time to lament the song's lack of success. He threw himself into composing the score to director Ivan Dixon's black exploitation film *Trouble Man*. The flick starred Robert Hooks and Paul Winfield in a standard private eye plot, and Gaye performed much of the bluesy background keyboard work himself, along with producing the LP. The title cut proved to be a #4 R&B hit. Later in 1972, Gaye would grace the silver screen himself as one of the featured artists in Save The Children, the filmed documentary of a charity concert sponsored by Rev. Jesse Jackson's Operation PUSH in Chicago. Gaye performed the film's title number.

Although he adamantly resisted the move for four years. Gaye finally pulled up stakes and followed the Motown empire to Los Angeles in 1973, leaving his adopted hometown of Detroit behind. He immersed himself in his next project, which once again was well past due when Gaye finally delivered it to Gordy.

Two years in the making, *Let's Get It On* proved a worthy sequel to *What's Going On*, although Gaye this time concentrated solely on personal relationships instead of international conflicts. "Yes, *Let's Get It On* was about sex," Gaye told Cummings in the Black Music piece. "I wanted to do a record which looked at physical love in a much more open and honest way than I'd been given an opportunity to when I was recording with other producers and songwriters."

The seductive title cut, which shot to #1 ratings on both the pop and R&B lists, and steamy themes such as "Come Get To This" (#2 R&B) and "You Sure Love To Ball" (#13 R&B) left precious little to the imagination. Gaye took on another new collaborator during the project, and Ed Townsend credited as composer of "Let's Get It On," was no stranger to the charts himself. His rich baritone was showcased on the dreamy 1958 balled "For Your Love," which sold well for the Capitol label on both the pop (#13) and R&B (#7) lists.

Gaye also welcomed a new duet partner in 1973, although this one was hardly a newcomer in search of a little career boost. But Gaye's anxiously awaited pairing with Diana Ross was widely perceived as less than a triumph on all fronts and for Gaye it was a surprising throwback to the very sort of slickly conceived formula package he had struggled so long to avoid. "You're A Special Part Of Me," which cracked #4 R&B and #12 pop, was the biggest seller from an album seemingly conceived in capital gains heaven. A cover of Wilson Pickett's "Don't Knock My Love" didn't fare nearly as well.

Gaye's heralded concert at the Oakland Coliseum on January 4, 1974, was the source for *Marvin Gaye Live!*, his first in-person vinyl offering in 11 years. The show also represented the vocalist's return to the spotlight after an absence of more than a year. He was back on the road full-time shortly thereafter.

But things hadn't improved on the home front, and in 1975, Anna, his wife of 12 years, filed for a divorce. The painfully drawn-out proceedings would eventually inspire *Here, My Dear*, Gaye's most personal work on vinyl.

I Want You, Gaye's 1975 studio release, found him working with yet another new musical collaborator. Leon Ware had been on the Motown scene intermittently since the late 1960s, when he helped write "Got To Have You Back" for the Isley Brothers, and he also co-wrote "I Wanna Be Where You Are" for Michael Jackson with Thomas "T-Boy" Ross, the brother of Diana. More recently, he had worked with Quincy Jones on his very successful *Body Heat* album. When Gordy noticed similarities between the musical styles of Ware and Gaye, he brought them together, and they hit it off well.

The upshot was another R&B chart topper with "I Want You," which delved deeply into Gaye's consuming passion for erotica, fuelled by his ongoing marital woes and an intense fixation for his new girlfriend and future second wife, Janis Hunter. Some of the set was recorded at Gaye's own studio in Los Angeles.

It was followed by another live effort, *Live At The London Palladium*. But there was a bit of a problem: the live material only occupied the first three sides of the proposed two-disc package. So, with an entire side of an LP to fill and the dreaded disco craze at its zenith, Gaye and studio engineer Art Stewart assembled a mammoth disco opus, "Got To Give It Up," that held down the final side of the set all by itself.

Although Gaye's vocal contributions to the marathon piece were minimal, an abridged version of "Got To Give It Up" burned the charts, topping both the pop and R&B listings in the spring of 1977. The song would prove to be Gaye's last major smash for Tamla.

Gaye went public with his bitter reaction to the divorce proceedings on the two-disc *Here, My Dear*. Decidedly uncommercial in its personal and complex tone, the set's anticipated royalties figured heavily into the monetary end of the 1977 settlement, to the tune of $600,000.

Vilified by the critics, the work chronicled the pair's stormy relationship from beginning to end through its diverse musical collage, even harking back to Gaye's doo-wop beginnings with "I Met A Little Girl". But the lone single pulled from the album, the cosmically comic "A Funky Space Reincarnation," never even broke the pop Hot 100.

Another pair of singles also bore Gaye's name in 1979. "Ego Tripping Out," a #17 R&B seller that never even made the pop lists, was apparently pulled from general release shortly after it appeared, while "Pops, We Love You," Motown's musical salute to

Berry Gordy's beloved father on his 90th birthday, found Gaye in the company of fellow Motown superstars Smokey Robinson, Stevie Wonder and Diana Ross.

While Gaye's recordings remained mired in the lower reaches of the charts, the singer himself dropped off the scene entirely for a prolonged stretch in the winter on 1979, deeply in debt to the Internal Revenue Service and other creditors. He turned into a virtual recluse for nine months, living on the balmy beaches of Hawaii. From there, he exiled himself to London, where he had previously enjoyed warm receptions in 1965 and 1976.

During his unexplained and perplexing absence, Motown finally decided to jump the gun in 1981, and issued *In Our Lifetime*, an album Gaye considered far from complete. Two singles from the set, "Praise" and "Heavy Love Affair," failed once again to crack the Hot 100. Incensed by the album's premature appearance, Gaye swore that he would never record for Berry Gordy again, and he proved true to his word. The rocky relationship between Gaye and Gordy was at an end.

The singer finally touched down in a Belgian town called Ostend in the spring of 1981 and began work on his next album. He signed a lucrative contract with CBS records the following year after negotiating his official release from Motown, and cut *Midnight Love*, Gaye's only LP issued by CBS during his lifetime.

Reunited with his first mentor in the music business, Harvey Fuqua, Gaye staged a very impressive comeback with *Midnight Love*, highlighted by the tranquil rhythms of its first single, "Sexual Healing". The track captured the #1 R&B post for an amazing 10-week run, peaking at #3 pop; "Til Tomorrow" and "Joy," never even broke into the Hot 100.

With his beloved mother, who had acted for so long as mediator between the vocalist and his father, seriously ill, Gaye was finally forced to end his exile and returned to Los Angeles in November 1982, where he was confronted anew by all the marital and monetary woes that he had sought to avoid by leaving.

In desperate need of money to placate the IRS, Gaye embarked on what would be his final tour of the U.S. during the spring of 1983. From all accounts, it was Gaye's strangest show yet: at the climax Gaye would strip down to his bikini briefs, confronting his insecurities toward the opposite sex head on.

His long-standing drug problems rapidly accelerating, Gaye moved back into the home that he had purchased for his parents when they first moved to Los Angeles. On April 1, 1984, a violent quarrel between father and son ensued in the home, and the elder Gay fatally shot his son twice with a .38 caliber revolver. Gaye was one day short of his 45th-birthday. After taking note of Gaye's drug addiction and the accused's brain tumor, Gay eventually received five years probation on a reduced charge of voluntary manslaughter.

Since Gaye's death, Columbia has released a pair of previously unissued albums. *Dream Of A Lifetime*, issued in June '85, was an unfinished project that Gaye was working on at the time of his death, while *Romantically Yours*, released from some more mellow pop standards seemingly culled from the Motown vaults, with production credits by Norman Whitfield, house vets Hal Davis and Marc Gordon, jazzman Bobby Scott and Gaye himself.

As for Motown, the label seemed to be on the right track back in 1979, when their compilation *From The Vaults* included a previously unissued side from 1966, "Sweeter As The Days Go By," with classy production by Frank Wilson.

But in 1986, Motown assembled an invaluable collection of previously unissued tracks dating from 1963–72 and then inexplicably desecrated the priceless performances with crunching contemporary rhythm tracks and layers of overdubbed synthesizers in a horribly misguided attempt to update their timeless sound.

Hopefully, MCA, which recently purchased the entire Motown catalog, will eventually see fit to correct this travesty and release the sides as they were originally conceived. For all he meant to the development of the vast Motown empire, Marvin Gaye deserves a better salute than that.

13

Motown Doo-Wop: The Satintones
by Steve Towne

Early on in Motown's development, Berry Gordy needed singers and musicians who were also local and accessible. Amongst these were The Satintones who developed a very particular role at the company at the start of the sixties. Whilst some of their contemporaries went on to great things, their star was to wane. Steve Towne told their story for Goldmine *in April 1982, well before they became one of the many acts re-assembled by Ian Levine for his Motorcity project. You will see that there are several early links to the Originals story.*

Motown Records has been since the early '60s, one of the most influential forces in music. But few remember that Berry Gordy tried his hand at production during the late '50s. As Motown was coming together, the most important musical happening in the black inner city was rhythm and blues and doo wop. Some of the first acts contracted to the struggling Motown organisation were rhythm and blues singers Barrett Strong, Sammy Ward and the then doo wop group, the Miracles, featuring a young Smokey Robinson. At about the same time, 1960 or so, a quartet of young men from the East side of Detroit showed up at Motown's door calling themselves the Satintones. James Ellis, Sonny Sanders, Robert Bateman and Chico Leverette came up in the streets of Detroit like so many others, passing the time singing in a network of vocal groups so common to the '50s. Sonny Sanders tells the story.

"Freddie Gorman was in a group called the Quailtones. This was about 1954 and Freddie and myself were in junior high school together. The Quailtones were already in existence but they needed a tenor. Freddie heard me singing with the radio or something and asked me to join."

The Quailtones consisted of Freddie Gorman, Sonny Sanders, Johnny Franklin, James Martin and Ted Scruggs. They made one obscure record for Josie Records in New York which was arranged through a local record store owner and part time saxophone player, Sax Kari. Sax Kari and the Qualitones, "Roxanna" / "Tears Of Love", came and went without a trace, and soon after, the group disbanded. Sanders took up trumpet for a while at Eastern High and Cass Technical, but disillusioned with singing, he steered clear of vocal groups.

James Ellis recalls a similar experience while growing up on the East side of Detroit. "I was with a group called the Five Sounds. In fact we even had a record out, but I can't remember the names of the sides. The group consisted of Pete Bologna, my brother Albert Ellis, Homer Glover, Gerald Buzzy Smith, and myself. We had won a talent contest at a movie house at 4th Street and Cadillac in Detroit. All the East side groups used to sing in their talent contests. Robert Bateman had a group that sang there. We were singing what was on the radio then, but Jackie Wilson was our major influence. We won the show by singing Jackie's version of "Danny Boy" three weeks in a row. This was about 1958. After the Five Sounds won the talent contest, so many people were coming up to us saying, 'Look guys, I want you to sign with us' and we didn't know what to do. So Larry Dean, the disc jockey that gave the show, became our manager. He took us to Chicago and Chess Records to meet Phil and Leonard Chess. Nothing came of it, so we came back to Detroit pretty disillusioned and shortly after that the group broke up."

In the meantime Sanders was persuaded to return to group singing by long-time friend Freddie Gorman. Freddie had met Eddie Holland, who wanted to form a group, and Gorman remembered Sanders from the Quailtone days. Adding a bass singer, remembered only by the nickname "Bosco", the Fidelitones were formed. Two sides were recorded for Berry Gordy, who hadn't yet formed Motown Records. Gordy hustled the tapes to another company, but they remained unreleased. The Fidelitones broke up, but all except Bosco stayed with Berry Gordy. Sanders recalls, "I was singing background on Berry's demos ("You Got What It Takes" with Marv Johnson) before he formed Motown. I sang background on "Money" by Barrett Strong and I think I did one or two things with Marvin Gaye and a couple of things with Mary Wells – "Bye Bye Baby" and a few others.

Following the break-up of James Ellis and the Five Sounds, it wasn't long before Ellis was back singing with a new group. Says Ellis, "The night our group broke up I happened to run into Robert Bateman at the theatre and he said he had something going and to give him a call. I called Robert the next day and he got hold of Sonny Sanders and Charles Chico Leverette and we formed the Satintones. We began rehearsing at Chico's house."

Besides Sanders' connection with Berry Gordy, Sanders remembers "Chico was a songwriter who was related to Ronnie White of the Miracles."

Probably at about this same time that the Satinones were forming, Chico Leverette had a landmark release. Not a landmark musically, but "Solid Sender" by one Chico Leverette (Tamla 54024) is the first known release on Tamla's 54000 series, or probably Berry Gordy's first commercial pressing on his own label. Gordy had a few earlier releases, very rare three digit and one digit reissues on Tamla and Motown, but this uptempo "Solid Sender" was probably his first original release.

Following on the heels of "Solid Sender" was the first record by the Satintones, "Motor City" / "Goin' To The Hop (In My Raggedy Jalop)". The uptempo "Motor City" is fairly primitive but has become a very rare and sought-after record to Motown collectors.

James Ellis sang lead on "Motor City" as well as this Satintones second release, "My Beloved". "My Beloved" was the first commercial release on the new Motown label (disregarding reissues). Ellis remembers, "Berry Gordy used to say we were his second best group, but he only had two groups at the time, us and the Miracles [*laughs*]. We were the second group at Motown. The first Motown artist was Marv Johnson, but he was a single artist."

"My Beloved" is a hypnotic ballad sung with a smooth high tenor lead while the background bubbled "my beloved, don't go." A true street group sound, it was released in two versions, one with an organ background and one with strings in the background, but neither made the *Billboard* charts. The flip-side, "Sugar Daddy," was sung by the whole group in sort of a Coasters style, but smoother and without the satirical bite.

In early 1961 the Satintones answered the Shirelles smash hit, "Will You Still Love Tomorrow" with their "Tomorrow And Always". This is probably their best recording. The heavily echoed background and heartfelt James Ellis lead helps make it one of the more appealing answer records of the period.

Also at this time, the Satintones got their biggest exposure, touring the Midwest and doing a show at the Regal Theatre with, appropriately enough, the Shirelles. But all was not to stay bright for the Satintones. Says Ellis, "We added a couple of other guys, Vernon Williams and Sammy Mack, and began recording. We had enough material for three albums in the can. I was working during the day, so I would go to the studio at night and Robert Bateman would engineer the sessions. We would go over so many tunes now that I can't remember, but we would record until about midnight. We were scheduled to play at the Apollo Theatre in New York. We had the record out ("Tomorrow And Always"). Then we got sued because of the song being the one by the Shirelles. Right about that time, I left. Everybody had different things going on. Robert was getting more into writing and I was getting kind of disgusted because we weren't making any money. I wrote a couple of songs and one was recorded by a group who stole it. Back in those days, you would do a show and you wouldn't get paid, you know, so I just told the music business goodbye."

Growing up might have had a hand in Ellis quitting the music business; "I had recently gotten married," says Ellis, "so I went to work with my dad in his body shop and this gave me more of a steady income." Four sides out of the marathon recording sessions were released after Ellis left. The releases were "I Know How It Feels" / "My Kind of Love" (Motown 1010) and "Zing Went The Strings Of My Heart" / "Faded Letter" (Motown 1020). Both releases are very rare and all four leads are taken by Vernon Willams. James Ellis is in the background on all four sides, but he had already left the group.

About mid-1961 the Satintones called it quits, but unlike James Ellis, some of the group went on to contribute greatly to the field of rhythm and blues as it grew into its most successful period, soul.

Sanders remembers: "Robert Bateman became sort of a salaried writer and producer for Motown. He worked with the Marvelettes and co-wrote their biggest hit, 'Please Mr Postman'. Berry Gordy had noticed that I never could stand to hear a wrong note. I was always correcting somebody in the studio so he asked me if I could do lead sheets. I had never written any music before, but that's how I got started, doing lead sheets. I worked quite a bit with Richard Popcorn Wylie at the time and learned a lot doing his charts. In the beginning, Motown was a real tight family thing. We all helped each other. Robert Bateman was busy bringing acts to Motown, like the Primettes, who later became the Supremes, and I was writing charts. Chico Leverette also did some writing and we all sang background. It was one big happy family.

Sanders learned his lessons well, and by 1964 he was doing arranging for Golden World Records. He arranged the smash hits "Just Like Romeo And Juliet" for the Reflections and "Agent Double-O-Soul" for Edwin Starr, before moving to Chicago. In Chicago, Sanders arranged most of Brunswick Records' biggest soul hits for Carl Davis. Among these are the classics, "Whispers" and "Higher And Higher" by Jackie Wilson, "Love Makes A Woman" by Barbara Acklin and Sanders' favorite, "Soulful Strut" by the Young-Holt Unlimited. Quite a track record! Sanders was later employed as an arranger and music director for Carl Davis at Chi-Sound Records in Chicago. For a more thorough look at Sanders' contributions to soul music see Robert Pruter's fine articles, "Sonny Sanders", in *Goldmine*'s May 1980 issue.

As mentioned, being in a recording group in the '50s and '60s wasn't always as financially rewarding as maybe it should have been, however sometimes memories are not measured in dollars and cents. James Ellis recalls, "A lot of the guys actually lived at the Hitsville building on the boulevard and I was there like every night. We'd go out partying and come back with the girls, you know we'd say, 'Hey, let's go to the studio,' you know. People were always dropping in, like I remember one night singing my heart out with my eyes closed, and when I opened my eyes and looked up, Jackie Wilson was in the control room! He was my main idol. I was like 19 or 20 years old. I had stars in my eyes [*laughs*] in fact, I remember we were at a little place called Kelly's, a little grill near the studio, and Mary Wells was hanging around. We all knew her, but I didn't know she could sing. One day I walked into the studio and heard "Bye Bye Baby" and I asked who it was because it was so good, and they said it was Mary Wells. The last time I left the Hitsville building Sonny and I walked out of there together and sitting on the steps was a secretary named Diana Ross. But she was just Diane then."

One era ends and another begins.

14
The Four Tops' Quarter-century Of Quality Soul
by Michael Heatley

Mirroring their long build-up to success in the States, the Four Tops took a while to gain a foothold in Britain, but, when they eventually did, we took them to our hearts. They became, with The Supremes, the most successful of Motown's acts, their classic singles sometimes becoming even bigger hits in the UK than in the US. Since this piece was written their longevity has been further proved with their "Loco In Acapulco" hit and further classic reissues. After Laurence Payton's sad death, Abdul Fakir's heart by-pass and Levi Stubbs' poor health, it looked for a time like the group would fold, but as this book goes to press the group still exists. It is a testament, first and foremost, to their wonderful friendship.

"Standing In The Shadows of Love", "Reach Out I'll Be There", "Baby I Need Your Loving" – like a sheaf of yellowing love letters, the greatest moments of the Four Tops' long career retain the ability to touch the emotions. Two decades after Motown's golden age, when the combination of writers-producers Holland, Dozier and Holland and the Four Tops produced music of energy and warmth, the group's recordings still offer an open invitation to the dance floor.

The fact that the Four Tops remain a chart act and a major force in music in the Eighties may be ascribed, in large part, to that rare virtue, loyalty. Unlike most of their contemporaries in the first great wave of Motown groups, the Tops' line-up never changed. Similarly, there has been no star billing for lead vocalist Levi Stubbs, which might have presaged a solo career and a dilution of the group's hit formula. The Tops stand four-square, a team that stuck together. "We still enjoy singing together," said Levi Stubbs in 1982, "but we're friends first".

Their apprenticeship began when, as the Four Aims, they made their stage debut in 1954 in the Detroit neighbourhood in which they were born and raised. Levi Stubbs, Abdul "Duke" Fakir, Lawrence Payton and Renaldo "Obie" Benson refined their performing technique through a mixture of graduation balls, garden parties, socials and talent contests before themselves graduating to the club circuit. The group made a healthy living by playing one-nighters from Canada to Las Vegas. Their developing style, relied heavily on gospel: said Levi, "We were raised in the church, that's all we ever knew".

An important figure in the early days was Lawrence Payton's cousin, Billy Davis. Active in the Detroit music scene, he encouraged the group to go on the road and eventually helped them to a contract with Chess Records in 1956. The Four Aims – so-called because they were "aiming for the top" – had by now become the Four Tops. Despite both this optimistic change of name and the Chess label's success with local blues artists, sales of the group's Chess release disappointed and they were not retained. Subsequent liaisons with the Red Top, Columbia and Riverside labels also proved fruitless, and it seemed that the group might never break out of the club circuit, on which they enjoyed continuing success.

At this point, Billy Davis again took a hand. As the pseudonymous Tyran Carlo, Davis had penned hits for the fast-rising Jackie Wilson whom Levi Stubbs had briefly partnered in the Royals some years before. Davis' co-writer, Berry Gordy, was in the process of expanding his small-scale Motown record company. On a tip from Billy the group contacted Gordy, who signed them up. Their first (and tentative) recording, *Breaking*

Through, appeared on Motown's Workshop label and was a jazz album in the vein of the Hi-Los. They were then brought down to earth by a year-long stint with Billy Eckstine's Revue: Gordy felt that there was still room for improvement. This experience provided the finishing touch to their stage education and was to place them well ahead of their less experienced label-mates, whose sudden success often found them unprepared for the glare of the spotlight.

On their return from the road, the Tops were rushed into the studio – not as star performers, but as backing vocalists for Motown's first hit recordings. As Lawrence Payton commented: "For a couple of years, we sang on practically every Motown record that was put out – you name it, we were on it." Nevertheless Berry Gordy had not forgotten the Tops, and they were chosen to work with the producer-songwriting team of Eddie and Brian Holland and Lamont Dozier, a relationship that Payton later described as "the perfect marriage".

Lamont Dozier had been a friend of the group from early days and his knowledge of the Tops' vocal abilities was a major factor in the choice of "Baby I Need Your Loving" as their Motown label debut. The song set the pattern for so many subsequent smashes: a harmonised intro followed by Levi Stubbs' pleading tones, the harmonies chiming in again on the chorus with renewed effect. Released in the summer of 1964, "Baby I Need Your Loving" peaked at Number 11 in *Billboard*'s Hot Hundred; it was their first hit.

Holland, Dozier and Holland had other commitments within the Motown organisation, notably with the Supremes, but they managed to produce three more records for the Four Tops in the next nine months. It was the third of these, "I Can't Help Myself", which hit the top in mid-1965. Curiously, its mid-paced tempo tambourines and lush orchestration were reminiscent in many ways of the Supremes, whose position as Motown's hottest act was then under threat. Unlike their rivals, however, the Tops made only occasional appearances in the UK charts: "Baby I Need Your Loving" had lost out to a typical Merseybeat cover by the Fourmost and subsequent releases had also failed.

Stateside success continued unabated, however. "It's The Same Old Song" hit Number 5 and "Ain't That Love", a genuine Four Tops oldie and one of Columbia's previously unsuccessful releases entered the Hot Hundred, if only for a solitary week. From then on, the chart entries became as predictable as the sounds were rewarding. Even the group's lesser hits, like Stevie Wonder's "Loving You Is Sweeter Than Ever", were subsequently covered by artists from Alan Price to Elton John. But the UK breakthrough was not to come until late 1966, with what was possibly the Tops' – and Holland-Dozier-Holland's – finest record.

From the haunting flute-and-oboe intro over an insistent drumbeat through the tambourine-laden verse to the chorus harmonies, "Reach Out I'll Be There" had class stamped right through it. It was a deserved Number 1 on both sides of the Atlantic and established Levi Stubbs as "the voice of Motown" for UK fans. From that point onwards, the Four Tops' releases rarely failed to make the UK Top Twenty, and the group began a rewarding relationship with British audiences, touring regularly.

The Four Tops and their producers had found a winning formula. Take a mid to uptempo backing track of typical Motown style, let the instrumentation fall away to highlight the emotive, desperate tones of Levi Stubbs tackling a lyric of heartbreak and desertion – then the hook, a tidal wave of sound, would engulf the listener with harmony as the backing continued relentlessly. A trio of splendid hits in 1967 – "Standing in The Shadows of Love", "Bernadette" and "Seven Rooms of Gloom" – continued the Tops' Top Twenty touch, although "Bernadette", a hymn of devotion with an epic Motown bass-line, departed from the group's usual type of lyric.

As one of the first internationally-famous Motown acts, the Tops had the chance to test out their stage act in front of many different audiences. Not that it was to change much over the years. As the backing band brought their instrumental warm-up to a close, the group (in matching suits) would bound up to the mike and hit the opening note as one. The first signs of sweat would see jackets discarded: Stubbs might remove his mike from its stand and move into a ballad, ad-libbing soulfully as Obie, Duke and Lawrence crooned stage right. Then – bang! up tempo again with the twinkling feet and sure routines born of countless club and cabaret dates. Like each of their songs, the Tops would build their act to a series of crescendos before quitting the stage with much hand-shaking and smiles.

Despite the group's consistency in the charts, later Holland-Dozier-Holland productions occasionally varied the ingredients of the hit recipe, but only by a little at a time. "If I Were A Carpenter", a UK Number 7 and US Number 20 in early 1968, combined a contemporary folk-pop number (written by Tim Hardin) with a harpsichord-style backing, but the vocal quartet put the Four Tops' stamp on an ambitiously "clean" sound. Albums came at the rate of two a year, but were for dedicated fans only, the obligatory brace of hit singles being accompanied by such unashamed fillers as the Monkees' "Last Train To Clarksville".

The departure from Motown of the Holland-Dozier-Holland team in 1968 was traumatic for the label as a whole; but the Four Tops eventually found an able replacement producer in Motown stalwart Frank Wilson, although the days of innovation were over. Unlike label-mates and contemporaries the Temptations, the Tops steered clear of psychedelia and social comment, restricting themselves to the emotion-filled numbers in which Stubbs' voice excelled. By the turn of the decade, however, the importance to the group of their former producers was evident from the Tops' decline to the lower reaches of the US Hot Hundred, although British fans remained comparatively loyal. Their recipe for success turned into a straitjacket.

The time was ripe for experiment, and one of the more interesting options taken up was a recording made with the Moody Blues in the early Seventies. The Tops had just come offstage after a one-nighter on a British tour when they were approached by Moodies' producer Tony Clarke with a demo of Mike Pinder's "Simple Game" in hand. As Lawrence Payton remembers it, "We didn't even know who he was.... We thought it was a good song, so the next day we went in, rehearsed and recorded it." With the Moody Blues uncredited among the backing musicians and Payton sharing lead with Stubbs, the record was released in 1971 and made the UK Number 3 position. It was not merely nostalgic reasons that placed it at the end of the Four Tops' set on their 1982 UK tour a decade later.

The Tops rang the changes in the production sphere, too, with Ivy Hunter, Johnny Bristol and Smokey Robinson among those recruited – with varying success. It was widely felt that the group had passed their peak. Certainly, collaboration with the Diana-less Supremes yielded only insipid fare. An album released in 1972 showed both groups wearing cowboy gear and uncomfortable expressions on the cover; the record itself was hardly aural *Dynamite*, either.

The departure of the Four Tops from Motown shortly afterwards coincided with the company's move from Detroit to the West Coast. The label had embraced new sounds but the Tops had remained the same – and Motown no longer saw the group as a long-term money-spinner.

A parting of the ways was inevitable, but the choice of new label was surprising: Dunhill Records had made most of its money out of of Sixties folk. The combination of the Tops and producers Brian Potter and Dennis Lambert achieved initial success with "Keeper of The Castle" – the title track of a popular album – and "Ain't No Woman (Like The One I Got)", the only song of this period featured live in the Eighties; but this burst of popularity soon faded. The production team's subsequent success with Tavares in a similar field suggests that the group was unable to get out of the rut, but such projects as the soundtrack to *Shaft In Africa* (1974) seemed wholly ill-advised.

The group had clocked up nearly a quarter-century in the business, and the gruelling round of touring and recording was one from which they wanted to escape for domestic and professional reasons. Writers Obie Benson and Lawrence Payton took time out to write for Marvin Gaye and Aretha Franklin respectively; Benson co-wrote the influential "What's Going On". Live appearances, when they happened, tended to be cabaret seasons rather than the one-nighters that had formed the schedule in the Fifties and Sixties. It wasn't so much a case of selling out as going back to their roots in the Detroit days, even if it meant reliving former glories night after night.

During their exile from the charts, the Four Tops had watched and listened to the groups who were changing the face of black music. When they signed with Casablanca Records in 1980 it seemed as if they might have tied themselves to the disco bandwagon with a label best-known for promoting such acts as Donna Summer and Lipps Inc. But the Tops were taking positive steps to put the hitless years behind them. "With disco, we found ourselves a little disoriented," recalled Payton, "but Casablanca wanted to go with a different thing." The label paired them with producer David Wolfert and provided a nucleus of musicians previously known as sidemen for West Coast "white-soul" artists. Accepting that they were no longer dictators of style, the Tops decided on a more sophisticated feel.

Released in late 1981, "When She Was My Girl" deserved its success in the UK and US charts. Obie Benson's acappella bass was especially attractive and the use of a melodica as solo instrument was both unusual and effective. The follow-up, "Don't Walk Away", boasted a "popping" octave bass-line worthy of Earth, Wind and Fire, while the album *Tonight* (1982) bore witness to the fact that, whatever the musical changes, the Tops were still in fine and distinctive vocal form. And during their 27-date tour of the UK in 1982 the group showed a renewed relish for live performance. The sound they produced was undeniably of the Sixties, yet it continues to exert a strong appeal despite the many vagaries of fashion.

15
Junior Walker: Motown's Screaming Sax Star
by Bill Dahl

Many of Motown's commercial hits were perfectly formed and finished examples of black pop. However, Motown's beginnings had been rawer, grittier and often ragged around the edges. Junior Walker and His All Stars were the one hit act who continued to plough their own furrow through the golden commercial era. Here was Motown showing they could still get "down and dirty"! Walker's comparative anarchy was then, and is now, a joy to listen to. Bill Dahl's short article, from Goldmine *of 16th November 1990, explains how he found and kept his unique sound.*

The noble gutbucket wail of the tenor saxophone had largely been relegated to the relative anonymity of the horn section when Junior Walker single-handedly revived the instrument's role within the R&B idiom in 1965 with his grinding workout, "Shotgun". Long gone were the days when horn wildmen such as Sil Austin, Red Prysock, Lee Allen and Sam "The Man" Taylor galvanized the early rock scene with their blasting solos and crazy gyrations; only King Curtis was in a similar position of keeping the classic sax flame ablaze at the time, and his crossover-minded Atlantic producers often insisted on saddling him with such unfortunate middle-of-the-road drivel as "Theme From The Valley Of The Dolls" and "The Look Of Love." Walker's early albums for Motown's Soul subsidiary smoked like old-fashioned hickory barbecue from beginning to end, and his instantly identifiable screaming high notes remained a principal influence of the countless ultra-slick studio reedmen of the 1970s that followed in his wake.

Born Autry DeWalt Jr. in Blythesville, Arkansas in 1942, Walker had moved to South Bend, Indiana by the time he began blowing the sax in the late 1950s. "I came out of high school like any other kid, and we started trying to put a little band together, that's all," says Walker. "At first we called ourselves, the Jumpin' Jacks, and then we played little clubs for two or three dollars, five dollars, whatever we could pick up. We played for little school proms and stuff like that.

"(Guitarist) Willie Woods was from South Bend, I was from South Bend for a while. I moved to Battle Creek, Michigan. And Victor Thomas, who played the organ, he was from South Bend. Jimmy Graves was from Cleveland, Ohio. He played the drums. We didn't have a bass player. He played the bass on the organ. That's the way we run it down then. It was pretty strong." Rechristened the All Stars, this line-up would remain constant into the late 1960s.

Walker cites some pretty disparate influences on his distinctive sax style. "There's quite a few guys that were blowin' saxophone when I picked up. Boots Randolph, Stan Getz and there was Charlie Parker, I used to listen to him a lot," says Walker, also naming jazz giants Lester Young and Gene Ammons. "I used to listen to all those different guys – Illinois Jacquet; all those great horn players really influenced me and gave me a big start."

Buoyed by frequent club gigs across the Midwest, Walker strolled into the Detroit offices of ex-Moonglow lead singer Harvey Fuqua in 1962 in search of a recording contract, and although Fuqua was reportedly a bit intimidated at first by the saxist's unsophisticated manner, one quick listen to his energetic wailing resulted in a contract with Fuqua's Harvey label. Harvey and its parent Tri-Phi logo already boasted an impressive talent roster than included the Spinners, a reformed group of Moonglows featuring the young Marvin Gaye, bluesman Eddie Burns and Johnny Bristol, who would later play an integral role in Walker's artistic development (for both better and worse).

Walker's three Harvey singles typified his already fully matured blasting approach. "Twist Lackawanna," his debut, was a relentless dance instrumental, while its flip, "Willie's Blues," had the dubious distinction of being the only Harvey-era track that didn't turn up later on a Motown LP. Its follow-up was the atmospheric "Cleo's Mood," which strutted to hitdom when reissued by Soul in 1966.

"Willie Woods was writin' that tune one night," says Walker. "We was at a club, and we was playin' it. This was before we was famous. And we was fiddlin' around with it, and he looked at me, and he said 'What about this tune?'"

"I said, 'Boy, that's a bad tune!' And this chick walked across, and I said, 'Mmhmm! Ol' Cleo's back!' Just like that, I don't know if the girl was named Cleo, but we always called her Cleo."

The final issue on Harvey paired "Good Rockin'," which sounded a lot like Jimmy Forrest's seminal "Night Train" with the boiler pushed to full throttle, backed with the similarly searing "Brainwasher (Part 2)" (part one had graced the flip of "Cleo's Mood"). But Fuqua's promising Tri-Phi empire had fallen on hard times.

"The record company kinda broke up then. They couldn't really hang onto it, 'cause they didn't have enough money to handle it," says the saxist. "We cut a few other tunes, but then they merged with Motown. And I walked over to Motown and talked with Mr. Gordy.

"He said, 'Well, you wanna cut records, huh?'

"I said, 'Yeah, I wanna blow a little bit!'

"So he signed me up, and the first thing I did was 'Monkey Jump.'"

"Monkey Jump," released in August 1964, perpetuated Walker's string of driving instrumentals, and its flip, "Satan's Blues," showcased Woods' fluid lead guitar in addition to Walker on a downtempo 12-bar item.

But it was Walker's rough-hewn debut as a vocalist that put him on the national map, in a rare instance of a dance step existing prior to the song that immortalized it.

"I was watchin' 'em when they came out with this new dance. They was doin' the Karate too, but this dance kinda got to me. They was goin' across the floor like they was shootin'. So I called couple of 'em, I said, 'What are you doin' now? What kind of junk is this?'

"The girl looked at me and said, 'Man, that's the Shotgun!'

"I said, 'The Shotgun?!?'

"They said, 'You better write a tune to that! That's what's happenin'!'"

"So I said okay, and went on and wrote the thing, 'Shotgun.' I called Mr. Gordy up – at that point you could call him and talk to him – so I called him up, and he said, 'Yeah, what's happenin'?'

"I said, 'Well, I've got a tune called "Shotgun"!'

"And he fell out and went to laughin' and said, 'Come on in and record it.' And we went on in and did it, and it come to be a great tune."

"Shotgun" immediately blasted its way to the top of the R&B charts and made #4 pop in February 1965, earning the saxist a live appearance on a Dean Jones-hosted segment of the NBC-TV program Hullabaloo and kicking off a slew of similar dance floor favorites from Walker ("Shotgun's" flip, "Hot Cha," was a charming rhumba-influenced number), beginning with "Do The Boomerang" (#10 R&B) and the double-sided hit "Shake And Fingerpop"/ "Cleo's Back," which both made it to #7 R&B. The latter was obviously a very similar sequel to "Cleo's Mood," with crisp guitar from Woods more to the fore. A reissue of "Cleo's Mood" climbed to #14 R&B in its own right.

The modern hitmaking machine was running at peak production capacity. "It was rough! They had quite a few people there that was strong," says Walker. "It was a big thing, man, when you walked into Motown then, at that time. Oh, man, it was just like heaven! You walk in there, everybody was makin' hits."

"So, you know, you had to go in the studio and go to work. You didn't go there and sit down. You didn't have people goin' there sayin', 'Oh, I'm a big star,' you know, and have a chip on their shoulder. Because when they walked in the door, somebody was kickin' a record. They was kickin' you in the hips! And when that guy would open the studio doors, you'd go in there and go to work. Nobody would have to tell you to go to work. You'd just go in there and go to work."

Most of Walker's releases to this point had nominally been produced by engineer Lawrence Horn and bossman Berry Gordy himself, but perennial Motown hitmakers Brian and Eddie Holland and Lamont Dozier took an interest in the hornman in early 1966, writing and producing Walker's next major smash, "(I'm A) Road Runner," which rose to the #4 R&B slot in May of that year. Compared to his previous output, this was a highly produced effort, with plenty of unusual chord changes and heavy band augmentation.

"I always run in and out of the studio, so Brian Holland and Dozier, they was kinda the ones that wrote the tune, they called me when I was comin' in. He says, 'Hey man, where's your horn?'

"I said, 'Well, I left it in the car, I left it at home, I think.'

"He said, 'From now on, when you come to the studio, always bring your horn!'

"I said, 'Alright, sir,'

"And then he told me, 'Look, I got a tune for you.'

"I said, 'What's the name of it?'

"He said, 'The same thing you're doing. "Road Runner".'

"So I said, 'The next time I come in, I'll record it.' So we went on a road trip, and when we came back in, I came in the door runnin' again. And he said, 'You ready?'

"I said, 'Yeah I'm ready,' and we went right in the studio and cut it."

Walker plundered the Motown vaults for his next pair of hits, "How Sweet It Is" and "Money (That's What I Want)," which had helped to launch Gordy's empire when it was first cut by Barrett Strong for Tamla in 1960. "How Sweet It Is," a major hit for Marvin Gaye only a year-and-a-half earlier, actually bettered Gaye's original on the soul charts by one position (Walker's cover made it to #3).

Both hits benefitted from a supercharged party atmosphere that sounded as if the sides had been cut at a live concert, but that wasn't quite the case. "It was kinda live. When I did it, they was there," says the saxist. "They was cuttin' it, and I said 'Cut it to my arrangements.' And we was doin' it to my arrangements, and everybody said, 'This is a party! This ain't no cuttin' no record,' so they went to doin' it like a party. And it turned out to be a big smash. Sometimes you luck up on those things. They just don't come all the time."

The B-side of "How Sweet It Is," "Nothing But Soul," was an upbeat instrumental that experimented with overdubbing Walker's throbbing solos atop one another and never found its way onto an album.

Walker's first three LPs, released in rapid succession during 1965-66, coupled the expected hits with B-sides and a few otherwise unavailable items. *Shotgun's* obscurities included such romping instrumentals as "Tune Up," "Tally Ho" and "Ain't It The Truth," which opened with some dubbed-on studio repartee and a taste of the blues before getting down to funky business.

Road Runner was full of goodies: "Ame Cherie (Soul Darling)" sported a kicking soul groove and knockout high-register blowing, and "Anyway You Wanta" and "Baby You Know You Ain't Right" were in much the same mode. There was also an updated cover of bluesman Freddy King's "San-Ho-Zay" and another pseudo-live instrumental, "Last Call," that boasted a relentless drive that recalled the work of '50s sax great Rusty Bryant.

But the album's standout cut was the jazzy "Mutiny," containing some of the most compellingly muscular blowing Walker ever committed to tape. The All Stars were augmented on "Mutiny" with a special guest on bass supplying extra inspiration: James Jamerson from Motown's house band, the Funk Brothers.

"We was doin' the tune, and the Motown band came in. That's how it was, and Jamerson picked it up and started playing the bass to it. Lawrence Horn said, 'Why don't y'all cut it like that?' We was doin' it a different way, and he said, 'Why don't you cut it the way he's startin' the tune? That sounds good!' I said, 'Well, don't make me no difference. Cut it!'

"We didn't rehearse it or nothin', Jamerson just fell in and went to playin' it, and looked like everybody fell in their place, and we just cut the tune on down."

Soul Session, which was issued between *Shotgun* and *Road Runner*, was all-instrumental and utterly red-hot, apparently comprised of sides from Walker's association with Harvey Fugua a few years earlier such as "Eight Hour Drag," "Decidedly," "Mark Anthony (Speaks)," "Shake Everything," "Hewbie Steps Out," "Everybody Get Together" and "Three Four Three". There was also an inexplicable reading of the hoary standard "Moonlight In Vermont" and the snappy "Us," which owed a great deal to Phil Upchurch's "You Can't Sit Down". Overall, the set shows what a tight little unit the All Stars were, Thomas's fatback organ pushing hard against Woods's effective rhythm guitar lines and the solid backbeat of drummer Graves.

Walker's first two hits of 1967 were both pulled from earlier albums. "Pucker Up Buttercup," an absolutely savage dance raver, managed a #11 R&B showing , while "Shoot Your Shot," from the saxman's debut LP, was an obvious knockoff of "Shotgun" but still made it to #33 on the R&B charts. Walker's biggest smash that year found him once again plundering the Jobete catalog, reviving the Supremes' million seller of two-and-a-half years before, "Come See About Me," to the #8 R&B mark. 1967 also brought Walker's first legitimate live album, which didn't contain any unfamiliar titles.

The saxist apparently got lost in Motown's incredible success during 1968, or perhaps his unadulterated bluesy brand of Detroit soul didn't jibe with the increasingly slick sounds the label was concentrating on. Whatever the reason, Walker's only hit that year was the aptly titled "Hip City," one of those funky travelogues that James Brown was so fond of, with an exceptionally memorable sax hook. Much like his previous hit "Money" in its fake live setting and two-sided format, part two of "Hip City" jumped to #7 R&B.

Just before Christmas, Soul issued another rocker, the delectable "Home Cookin'," which only managed a #19 R&B showing but inspired another exceptional album by the same name. The set's highlights included the torrid "The Things I'd Do For You" and "Baby Ain't You Shame," the playful novelty "Sweet Daddy Deacon," and a welcome revival of Buster Brown's "Fannie Mae," Walker's makeover as a vocalist was now so complete that there was only one instrumental on the entire collection, the inspiring "Sweet Soul".

But most important to Walker's immediate fortunes was the second track on side one, which apparently wasn't considered anything too marketable at the time of "Home Cookin'"'s issue in January of '69. "What Does It Take (To Win Your Love)" placed Walker in the unfamiliar role of balladeer.

"Johnny Bristol was tryin' to get me to do the tune, and I turned it down," says Walker. "I said, 'Oh, man, I don't want to cut that tune.' So he said, 'okay,' He didn't say nothin'. So I didn't cut the tune.

"And it was a year later, I came back in at the time we was cuttin' "Hip City". So I came in the door, and he was standin' up there lookin' at me just as funny, silly, you know. I said 'what's happenin', Brits?'

"He said, 'Nothin' to it. What's goin' on?'

"I said, 'Oh, everythin's mellow. What're you doin' here?'

"He said, 'I'm waitin' on you to cut this tune!'

"I said, 'What tune?'

"He said, '"What Does It Take (To Win Your Love)". If you turn me down, I'll be here next year!'

"I said, 'Come on, man,' So we went on in and cut that tune. And that was a big one. I said, 'I'm glad I cut it.' I didn't think I could do it. I really didn't. But he pushed it on me, so I did it."

Berry Gordy belatedly recognized the song's potential and pressed it as a 45 in April of '69, and the slickly produced soul ballad, which represented the first time Walker was backed by violins, became the saxist's second and final #1 R&B smash, equalling "Shotgun"'s pop success by achieving the #4 slot.

But as undeniably brilliant as "What Does It Take" was, it meant the end of the All Stars as a cozily self-contained recording unit. Under Bristol's savvy production wing, Walker increasingly became one more Motown cog, subject to whatever advanced production techniques were deemed necessary, and with a few notable exceptions, the sax-man's subsequent output suffered in comparison to what had come before.

The sudden success of "What Does It Take" apparently took everyone by such surprise that the Harvey-era "Brainwasher (Part 1)" was exhumed from the vaults to serve as a B-side. The hornman's next Soul LP, *Gotta Hold On To This Feeling*, sported the same sort of hastily assembled feel as well, and shortly after it was issued in November of '69, the title was switched to *What Does It Take To Win Your Love*, complete with psychedelic artwork, to commemorate the song's continued success. Six other selections were retreads from past albums, and covers of Creedence Clearwater Revival's "Proud Mary" and the Guess Who's "These Eyes" didn't distinguish themselves aesthetically either (although the latter was a mammoth soul hit, reaching #3 R&B).

The set's remaining three tracks were attractive compromises between Walker's patented earthy approach and the string-sweetened Motown sound of 1969, especially "I've Got To Find A Way To Win Maria Back," where Walker's mournful vocal effort and blistering sax breaks combined with a sympathetic if massive arrangement to create a truly moving performance. "Gotta Hold On To This Feeling" another huge R&B seller at #2 and "Clinging To The Thought That She's Coming Back" were almost as good, certainly the pinnacle of the softer, more refined Junior. Walker was coping admirably with the increased emphasis on his vocal ability.

The saxman tallied his last Top 10 soul hit for close to two years in July 1970 with "Do You See My Love (For You Growing)," penned by Bristol and his one-time duet partner, Jackie Beavers. Another slice of admirable if unspectacular assembly-line soul, it hit #3 R&B. But the album that it lead off, *A Gasssss*, presaged the beginning of the end quality-wise, with uninspired covers of unsuitable rock ditties like Blood, Sweat and Tears' "And When I Die," Neil Diamond's "Holly Holy" (which didn't exactly inspire Walker's fans either; its #33 R&B showing was his weakest in four years), and the Beatles' "Hey Jude," where Walker's signature squeals on the introduction sounded hopelessly out of place. Even the home-grown material was less than first-rate, with only "Carry Your Own Load" and a pair of instrumentals, "Groove And Move" and "At A Saturday Matinee," rising above the mediocrity level.

Another live set was also released in 1970, and it steadfastly proved that Walker still possessed his familiar gutsy growl when all the syrup was stripped away. Besides the anticipated hits that constituted the bulk of the package, Walker served up impressive vocal renditions of the Temptations' "(I Know) I'm Losing You" and Chris Kenner's "Something You Got," supported by his eminently tight (and still uncredited) little crew of All Stars.

Jazz Crusaders reedman Wilton Felder penned "Way Back Home," and the song's lighter-than-air quality totally undermined Walker's chitlin' circuit raunch on both the vocal version and its instrumental flip, while "Take Me Girl, I'm Ready" found Walker's fragile vocal effort overwhelmed by an unwieldy vocal choir. But both 1971 singles sold fairly well to the faithful, though hardly on a par with Walker's glory years.

Bristol fed Walker an unpalatable diet of unwisely chosen covers and undistinguished originals for his 1971 *Rainbow Funk* LP, which came with a trendy gatefold cover and truly bizarre artwork that couldn't quite mask the overall insipidness of its contents. There were horrific remakes of the Beatles' "Something" (Walker's valiant attempt to croon this one is downright painful), Joe Cocker's "Feeling Alright" and the Temptations' "Psychedelic Shack," and the few originals weren't much better. Only a revival of the Bristol/Fuqua oldie "These Things Will Keep Me Loving You" approached listenability.

Perhaps sensing a subtle shift in the saxman's demographics, Bristol emphasized Walker's instrumental talents on his next collection, *Moody Jr.*, and the strategy paid off in the short run when "Walk In The Night" scored as Walker's final Top 10 R&B hit. But too much of the overproduced LP sounded like aimless, glossy background fodder, including the hit – the very antithesis of Walker's once vital, engrossing sound.

It took an infusion of eager new blood at the production helm to resurrect Walker's recording fortunes, and while it didn't do nearly as well as it should have on the sales front, 1973's *Peace and Understanding Is Hard To Find* boasted some of the best Walker cuts in years. There were no less than five producers listed, including most importantly, Walker himself.

"I Ain't Goin' Nowhere," the two-part "Gimme That Beat" and the title tune all virtually glowed with the resonant energy that had been systematically drained from Walker's most recent efforts. Even longtime All Star organist Victor Thomas was credited as co-writer on two cooking cuts, "Soul Clappin'" and "Country Boy," and Johnny Nash's "I Can See Clearly Now" proved a worthy vehicle for Walker's tenor (even if Carole King's "It's Too Late" didn't). Unfortunately, Walker had all but worn out his welcome with the record-buying public – for the first time since "Monkey Jump" back in 1964, two 45s from the fine LP didn't even crack the charts.

After a series of five singles over a span of 1974-77 resulted in one minor seller ("I'm So Glad" in '76) and three misses (including the endearingly titled "Dancin' Liked They Do On Soul Train" in 1974, which should have at least garnered a few spins from Don Cornelius), Walker finally jumped the Good Ship Motown, briefly landing with fellow Gordy exile Norman Whitfield's self-named label in 1979 for a very minor hit, "Wishing On A Star". But the sax great actually got far more promotional mileage out of his guest solo of Foreigner's rock smash, "Urgent," than for any of his own later work.

The trademark high-register squeal of Junior Walker's groundbreaking saxophone style will always be remembered by R&B enthusiasts, impressionable young saxophonists and high-steppers alike, and the earthy good-time vitality of his many classic Motown recordings will stand as his considerable legacy. And although his ebullient, good-natured personality doesn't quite allow for bragging, Walker seems engagingly aware of his exalted position in the history of soul.

"It's just like Satchmo," says Walker. "You hear Satchmo, and you know him. And you hear Junior Walker, and I guess you just know him."

"And that's good. I'm glad everybody knows me."

Sources:

Joel Whitburn's *Top R&B Singles 1942-1988*, published by Record Research, Inc. 1988

The Motown Story by Don Waller, published by Charles Scribner's Sons, 1985

Where Did Our Love Go by Nelson George, published by St. Martin's Press, 1985

16

They're For Real: Freddie Gorman and the Originals
by Steve Towne

Led by Freddie Gorman, The Originals were one of the many Motown acts who, despite some splendid records, never joined the front line of acts. Their story begins pre-Motown, and takes them through a number of label changes until they ended up on Gordy's Soul label in 1967. Their dancer "Suspicion" became the lead off track for the Debutante label second collection in 1998, and they finally got a retrospective album of their material released by Motown around the same time. This piece by Steve Towne first appeared in Goldmine *in September 1981.*

R&B has grown throughout the '70s, expanding into a sophisticated urban sound with many of its roots still intact, undoubtedly because many R&B veteran producers, arrangers, and performers got their starts singing doo-wop in our cities during the '50s and early '60s. Rather than being cast aside as "has beens" after a few years, rhythm and blues institutions like the Dells, Impressions, O' Jays, Temptations and Aretha Franklin can still be found in R&B charts today, still selling strong after 20 some-odd years in the business.

A particularly pretty pop ballad titled "Love Has Seen Us Through," was recently recorded by Freddie Gorman, who is an example of an R&B performer who has been at it since the '50s. Although Gorman is not as well known outside of Detroit as he should be, hopefully "Love Has Seen Us Through" and Gorman's own label, Rene, based in Los Angeles will provide a second start for this great R&B veteran.

Gorman started, as so many other young urban blacks did in the '50s, in a street corner group. In a recent interview, he remembers, "Yeah, we were just some guys who would get together and rehearse. We were all into a group thing bash in Detroit. We'd be out singing on the street corner until someone's mom came to look for them or the police ran us off. After that I got hooked up with a little high school group called the Quailtones. I had met James Marlin who was a singer from the East Side of Detroit where we were all from. James and I put the group together and James brought in his cousin Ted Scruggs, and I had known Sonny Sanders and I knew he could sing, so I brought in Sonny. Johnny Franklin was our bass singer. He had a tremendous bass voice like Melvin Franklin of the Temptations although they're not related. We'd rehearse everyday. I guess we were waiting for someone to look through the window and *discover* us."

Someone did look through that proverbial window, literally. Sax Kari a local record store owner and saxophone player looked out his record store window and discovered the Quailtones. After organizing a couple of original tunes and recording them, "Roxanna"/ "Tears of Love" by Sax Kari and the Quailtones was sold to Josie, a subsidiary of New York's Jubilee Records, and was released in the spring of 1955. Shortly thereafter, the record sank without a trace. Gorman says "Actually Sax should have been the producer and manager. I wrote 'Tears Of Love' with him and I wrote the B side 'Roxanna,' too but I didn't get any credit as a writer on either one of those. But whenever I see Sax again I'll ask him about that (laughs). We were all kids back then you know. We were into the Diablos and the Spaniels and all the groups out at that time. We liked them all. We sang on some of the same talent shows together with the Diablos, who were very big in Detroit before Motown."

Shortly after their record the Quailtones disbanded in traditional fashion. Freddie explains "We began in school. We all went to Cass High, but as we got older the guys were getting married and going out on their own and getting jobs. I think it just boiled down to out of the basic five guys, Sonny and I were the two that were serious, so we stayed with the business."

Being serious about the music business doesn't guarantee a living, so Freddie left school and went to work for the post office. "That's how I first met Berry Gordy," recalls Gorman. "I delivered mail to his mother's house." But the vocal group bug persisted. Explains Freddie, "I was in a group and we called ourselves the Fidelitones. That group was myself, Sonny Sanders, Brian Holland and a guy. I can't remember his name now but we called him Bosco. He sang bass. There was never a release on that group but I wrote two songs for us. We recorded them and I know we were really up about them. Berry recorded them but this was before he had formed Motown. Then Berry sold the masters to some major company and they were supposed to release the record but they never released it. They're in somebody's can right now. In fact, I'm trying to find out about them. They were done so well for the time."

At about this time, another streetcorner aggregation, the Voicemasters, was coming into contact with Berry Gordy through his sister Gwen and her label Anna. In fact, the very first record, Anna 101, was "Hope And Pray" by the Voicemasters. The group consisted of Ty Hunter, Lamont Dozier, David Ruffin, Walter Gaines and C.P. Spencer. Veterans all, Gaines and Spencer had joined the 5 Jets (Deluxe) during the late '50s and then when that broke up, that pair, plus long time friend Hank Dixon and two others, formed the 5 Stars. They had a record on George Goldner's Mark-X label around 1958.

In early 1958 another Detroit streetcorner group, the Romeos, whose members included Ty Hunter and Lamont Dozier, had a release on Atco. "Fine Fine Baby" went nowhere. Dozier and Hunter joined by Ruffin Gaines and Spencer went straight to Gwen Gordy and her label, Anna. Hank Dixon had been called by Uncle Sam, but the Voicemasters with their soon-to-be all-star lineup, had a local Detroit hit, the beautiful ballad, "Needed (For Lovers Only)". Throughout 1960 and 1961, the Voicemasters had releases on Anna as billed by their different lead singers, Hunter, Ruffin and Dozier. "Everything About You" by Ty Hunter and the Voicemasters even made the national R&B charts in the summer of 1960.

Meanwhile, Freddie Gorman was exercising his skills as a songwriter. Gorman remembers, "I was writing and working on my single thing as a single artist. I realised writing songs was a gift, so I got off into that. Eddie Holland had sung with me and Sonny Sanders in the Fidelitones and when Eddie met Berry Gordy, we went over to Motown. Eddie then went solo and Sonny joined the Satintones. I ran into Brian Holland working on a tune one day that Georgia Dobbins had suggested a title for. She came up with the title "Please Mr Postman," so with me working at the post office it was very easy for me to write the lyrics. I just used things that had happened to me carrying mail. Brian and I had started writing for the Marvelettes with "Please Mr Postman," and right after that Lamont Dozier joined us."

The songwriting team of Holland, Dozier and Gorman wrote some of Motown's first hits, including the Marvelettes' "Someday, Someway", "Strange I Know", "Forever", Mary Wells' "Old Love", and the Supremes' "I Want A Guy". Joined by Bob Bateman, a friend from the Satintones, they wrote "Playboy" and "Twistin' Postman". All these have that classic early Motown sound and gave Motown some of its first big hits.

By late '61 Gorman's solo career got off to a start with "The Day Will Come" on Motown's subsidiary label, Miracle. The songs has a nice melody and suggests what Brook Benton might have sounded like had he recorded for Motown. Gorman worked for Motown for two more years as a songwriter, but things got rougher as Motown got bigger. Freddie explains: "In the beginning, Motown was a really big family thing. Everyone worked together. But it changed when it got to be a big business. I was still working at the post office at the time and Brian, Lamont and myself had never had a contract or anything linking us together. It was more or less a handshake, that kind of thing. I would get off work and I would come down to Hitsville on the boulevard about 5 p.m. Brian and Lamont would be working all day, so when I would get there, they were ready to leave. So finally, Eddie Holland started writing with Brian and Lamont."

Goran left and started his solo career fresh with another company, Ed Wingate's Golden World / Ric Tic label. In 1965, Gorman's first record for Ric Tic, "In A Bad Way", was a local hit in Detroit. The follow-up, "Just Can't Get It Out Of My Mind", was not as successful but Gorman was still writing up a storm, this time for a white group, the Reflections.

Gorman says, "I wrote 'Just Like Romeo & Juliet' with Bob Hamilton. That did very well. I'd like to see that tune done again. Bob came up with the idea and my brother, Sonny Sanders, did the arrangement. Sonny came to Ric Tic from Motown too." Also at this time a lot of the Motown house band was at Ric Tic at night picking up some extra money, much to Berry Gordy's aggravation. "I didn't have anything to do with that," says Gorman. "At that time at Ric Tic we had a lot of big hits coming out and Motown had to notice us. We were on the other side of town cranking them out."

Sanders eventually left Detroit for Chicago and greener pastures with Carl Davis at Brunswick Records and later Chi-Sound Productions. Gordy eliminated his competition by buying Golden World/Ric Tic and Gorman went back into singing, this time successfully.

He remembers, "Lamont Dozier introduced me to the Voicemasters. That was Walter Gaines, Hank Dixon and C. P. Spencer at the time. We had all seen each other around for years, but never really knew each other. Lamont wanted to produce the group so he brought us back to Motown. There were no hard feelings about me having worked at Ric Tic, at least Berry never said anything. Lamont started by producing a song called "We Got A Way Out Love" but we never got to finish it the way Lamont wanted, with all the hassles he was having with Motown at that time. Our first release as the Originals was "Goodnight Irene", the old Leadbelly song that was produced by Clarence Paul, who also worked with Stevie Wonder. We had Joe Stubbs with us at that time." Stubbs, brother of Levi Stubbs of the Four Tops, was the soulful lead on one of the earliest Detroit soul hits, "You're So Fine", by the Falcons.

Gorman stated, "Joe was with us about eight months. He was there trying to do something with Motown and they suggested putting him with us. Ty Hunter was also with us when we first formed, but he had contractual obligations to Chess; they wouldn't let him go. So when Joe left there was the four of us."

"We've Got A Way Out Love" did get released in early 1969, but didn't make the charts. Its follow-up "Green Grow The Lilacs" didn't make the charts either, but "Green Grow The Lilacs" seems better organized than "We've Got A Way Out Love". Maybe, like Gorman says, they were kind of in a 5th Dimension bag, but it did probably deserve more attention than it got. Between "Goodnight Irene" and "Green Grow The Lilacs", the Originals managed to keep busy.

Recalls Gorman. "The Originals did a lot of background work behind Diana Ross and the Supremes, Jimmy Ruffin, just about everybody. We did 'What Becomes Of The Broken Hearted' for Jimmy as well as 'I've Passed This Way Before' and 'Gonna Give Her All The Love I Got', and we did 'For Once In My Life' with Stevie Wonder, Marvin Gaye's 'Chained' and David Ruffin's 'My Whole World Ended', to name a few. We even doubled as females [*laughs*]."

The Originals finally saw daylight with the smash hit "Baby I'm For Real". Gorman says, "'Baby I'm For Real' was written and produced by Marvin Gaye and his wife, Anna. Marvin had liked our sound for a long time and thought he could do something with us. The unique thing about 'Baby I'm For Real' was that all four of us took some parts of the lead. A lot of people told me they thought it was one person but I never understood how they heard it that way."

"Baby I'm For Real" was a beautifully loose-versed ballad that peaked at No 14 on *Billboard*'s pop charts. The Originals took to the road opening for headliner Bobby Taylor, formerly of Bobby Taylor & the Vancouvers.

"The Bells" did even better in the early part of 1970, reaching No 12 in the pop charts and was every bit as beautiful as its predecessor. Marvin Gaye came up with another beautiful melody and the group outdid itself vocally, combining tight harmonies with another shared lead and a spoken bridge. This time the Originals toured the country as headliners. Motown also released the group's second LP *Portrait of The Originals*, featuring "The Bells". Previously, the Originals had released the LP *Green Grow The Lilacs*, but with the success of "Baby I'm For Real" the title was changed (though the songs remained the same).

Throughout 1970, the Originals made the charts with two other releases. "We Can Make It Baby", released in the summer, was not as strong a song as the previous hits, although written by Marvin Gaye. It creates a tension that never seems to be resolved, although the group's trademark of switching lead singers during the verses is as great as ever.

The winter of 1970-'71 saw "God Bless Whoever Sent You" try to battle into the top 50. It deserved better. "God Bless Whoever Sent You" has a beautifully catchy hook that is complemented by a very happy lyric. You can almost see the smiles on the guys' faces. Throughout the early '70s the Originals' success declined. Motown put out two more albums and several singles, but none of them seemed to click with the public.

In 1972 C.P. Spencer left the group. Gorman takes up the story, "C.P stepped out to pursue a solo career. That's when we got Ty Hunter back. When Ty got out of his contract with Chess, the Originals were well on their way, with four singers, so Ty joined up with Glass House on Invictus. They had several hits, but by 1972 Glass House wasn't doin' that much. They about folded up so we got Ty back with us."

Even with Ty Hunter's return, the hits didn't come. In 1974 the group made the move to L.A. to be closer to the Motown company and its producers. The result was an album entitled *California Sunset*, an artistically satisfying compliment to the Originals' style, due particularly to the group's reassociation with Lamont Dozier, who produced the LP. Gorman remarks, "Lamont kind of got us back on our feet."

By late 1975 the Originals changed direction with the uptempo tune, "Everybody's Gotta Do Something", a stab at a social conscious theme about lack of work in the inner city. Picking up where the Temptations had left off with their series of similar tunes and themes, the Originals sound very competent at their new style, if not particularly distinctive.

Following this, the Originals turned to disco, with much improved results. Gorman comments, "The last album we had at Motown was *Down to Love Town*. We had a disco hit of that in the winter of 1976-77. It stayed at number one on the disco charts for six weeks and we're still together."

Indeed they are! After a short stint at Fantasy Records, which produced several disappointing singles and one album in the late '70s, the future is still uncertain. Gorman says, "C.P. Spencer came back about '77 or '78 and we're still very tight. I have a new record out, "Love Has Seen Us Through" on my own label, Rene. The distribution has been picked up by LAX in Los Angeles, so things are looking up, and Hamilton Bohannon has recently produced a new album for the Originals on Phase II. And guess what the tune is? None other than 'Please Mr. Postman'."

Overshadowing the new album by the Originals was the untimely death at age 40 of Ty Hunter on February 24th, 1981. It's always sad when a group with such a long and successful history loses a key member, but with the new album, the Originals plan to stay together. The album, *Yesterday and Today* is dedicated to Ty.

17
Stevie Wonder
by John Rockwell

Anyone who has ever spent time in the company of Stevie Wonder will testify to the man's tremendous personality and talent. When I was lucky enough to get the chance to run his British Fan Club upon the demise of The Tamla Motown Appreciation Society, I jumped at it. During Stevie's next few visits to these shores, including the Uptight *tour, I was able to spend as much time as I was able with him. We were of a very similar age, and were able to connect on more than just musical levels. Stevie was very well looked after by his travelling tutor Ted Hull, and his musical director Clarence Paul, both of who cared for him on a very personal level. Stevie loved getting to Britain, and loved playing club dates where he could feel the close attention of the audiences. Every single moment was fun for him, and consequently for those around him. Everyone was aware of his prodigious talents, but perhaps we were never aware of just how strong and independent a figure he would become in the story of Motown. This John Rockwell piece is from* The Rolling Stone Illustrated History Of Rock And Roll, *published in 1992 by Plexus. It serves as a succinct overview of Stevie's career and his strengths.*

In rough outline, Stevie Wonder's career goes like this: born Steveland Judkins (or Morris – his father's name was Judkins, but Wonder says that Morris was on the birth certificate) on May 13th, 1950, in Saginaw, Michigan, he was raised as Steveland Morris in Detroit. At the age of ten, he was introduced by Ronnie White of the Miracles to Berry Gordy's Hitsville, U.S.A.; his stage name changed to Little Stevie Wonder at about the same time Hitsville, U.S.A. became Motown.

Wonder had his first hit – it went to Number One – in "Fingertips – Pt. 2" in 1963. At that time his audience was consistently integrated; in 1964 the Rolling Stones were his opening act. His adolescence was spent turning out a steady succession of singles and albums, many of which did well on the pop as well as the rhythm & blues charts. But he didn't have another Number One single until "Superstition" in 1972, after the exposure gained from opening for the Stones during their American Tour that year. The albums *Music Of My Mind, Talking Book* (both 1972) and *Innerversions* (1973) were enormous successes, both critically and commercially, and sealed Wonder's status as the most influential and acclaimed black musician of the early Seventies. On August 6th, 1973, he was almost killed in an automobile accident while on tour in North Carolina. A log from a truck smashed through the front window of the car in which he was a passenger and struck him in the forehead. Already blind since infancy, he lost his sense of smell in the accident but apparently emerged otherwise unscathed. In 1974 he won five Grammy awards, then in 1975 five more, and that August was reported to have signed a seven-year, $13 million contact with Motown, at that point one of the most lucrative in the history of the record business. (It later turned out he didn't actually sign the document until April 1976.) His 1974 album, much of it written before his 1973 accident, was called *Fulfillingness' First Finale.*

Since two years passed before the release of *Songs in the Key of Life*, the 1974 album might have really looked like a finale. But actually *Songs* seems now to better fulfill that role. Its blend of hit singles and ballads echoed Wonder's pattern of the past and sustained his commercial dominance and artistic influence. But apart from a retrospective package in 1977, *Looking Back*, it would be more than three years until the next Stevie Wonder album, *Journey Through the Secret Life of Plants,* a mostly meandering two-disc soundtrack of mood music that failed to top the charts. After that came *Hotter Than July* (1980), the soundtrack for *The Woman in Red* (1984), *In Square Circle* (1985), *Characters* (1987) and the soundtrack for Spike Lee's *Jungle Fever* (1991), with the long-mooted *Conversation Piece* still in preparation as of spring 1992.

Even at the peak of his mass appeal, from 1972 to 1976, Wonder occasioned a certain puzzlement. He isn't consistent; he has a distressing predilection for cosmic meanderings and soupy sentimentality. But listening to his albums in sequence is an instructive experience; it indicates that Wonder is perhaps most comfortable as a live performer and that his gifts are more constrained by the confines of a studio than those of some artists. It also suggests that the supposedly sharp break in his career around 1971, when he reached legal maturity and renegotiated his Motown contract to obtain a far-reaching artistic freedom, needs to be partially reevaluated. Certainly the post-1971 Wonder records are more innovative than those that preceded them. But the same polarities in his art can be observed from the beginning.

Wonder's first singles appeared in the fall of 1962, but he didn't make an impact until the summer of 1963, with "Fingertips" and the *Little Stevie Wonder the 12 Year Old Genius* album that contained it. Both were distinguished by two things apart from Wonder's raw talent. First, "Fingertips" and the album were recorded live, which is hardly customary for new artists or hit singles; second, both caught Wonder right at the end of his prepubescence.

The first image of Little Stevie Wonder was of a loose-limbed, tambourine-shaking, harmonica-blowing natural child of music, and it was the image that has defined his large-scale concerts ever since. At Wonder's first major U.S. appearance after his accident, at Madison Square Garden in March 1974, it was the uptempo material that got the biggest cheers and the long, rhapsodic, building, repetitive improvisations that constituted the night's emotional high points. In particular, his concert version of "Living For The City," with the chorus repeated over and over in terraced levels of intensity, surpassed anything Wonder has ever done on record, and that's not to say he hasn't made wonderful records. Spike Lee's use of the 1973 studio version of that song in the crack-den scene of *Jungle Fever*, with the musical climax cut short to suit the film's needs, attained no such comparable impact – and was still far and away the most powerful moment of the soundtrack.

Recording careers are made in the studio, however, and Wonder's recorded product in his adolescence mostly derived from the Motown hit factory of the Sixties. The fact that his first big hit came when he was thirteen meant that Wonder couldn't count on a protracted boy-soprano career like that of Michael Jackson. Almost immediately his voice began to crack, and although his next few albums contain occasional soprano outtakes inserted incongruously into the rest, he was mostly a high baritone/low tenor from then on. His voice now is full of tenor lightness, but he lacks the range to exploit high notes or the desire to cultivate a Smokey Robinson falsetto.

The records of this period are highly variable, ranging from curious emulations of the then popular "surf sound" – he even appeared in two of that era's surf film epics. *Muscle Beach Party* and *Bikini Beach* – to an inevitable homage to Ray Charles and a Christmas album. The hit singles of his adolescence include punchy R&B ("Uptight (Everything's Alright)," "I Was Made To Love Her"), brassy pop ("For Once in My Life"), sentimental ballads ("My Cherie Amour"), even a Dylan tune ("Blowin' in the Wind"), long before Motown discovered social consciousness.

This is a far more varied output than that of most Motown artists during the Sixties, but Wonder was still deeply enmeshed in the Motown system: the company controlled his publishing, masterminded his arrangements and recording sessions, booked his tours, held his money in trust and doled out an allowance ($2.50 per week when he was thirteen). Many of the songs Stevie sang were composed by staff writers; those he wrote were generally co-credited to such Motown regulars as Sylvia Moy and Henry Cosby. Just who wrote what in this period remains a mystery. Moy and Cosby, for instance are credited on "Upright" along with "S. Judkins," yet Wonder himself once said this was the first song he ever wrote. What is clear is that Motown executives and producers had much to do with how the records actually sounded. "They would have the rhythm worked out," Wonder later recalled, "and I would just come to the session and play the piano."

That doesn't mean, however, that some of Wonder's later characteristics weren't already in evidence. There was the childlike ebullience of his fast tunes and the unabashed sentimentality of his slow numbers (no matter that at first he confined himself to the stock banalities of teen-drama love, only later to lap over into universal brotherhood). There was his omnivorous ability to devour diverse influences and put his own stylistic stamp on the results – from the basics of gospel, blues, rhythm & blues and soul to Dylan, the surf sound, jazz and adult white pop, and finally to rock, electronic music and African ethnicity.

Still by his late teens Wonder had reached a ceiling on what he could accomplish within the traditional Motown strictures. A live album released in early 1970 dramatizes that fact, with its turgid arrangements continually weighing down his inherent gifts. "All I'm trying to do is get myself together," he remarks in the introduction to one song. All I'm trying to do is do my own thing." *Signed Sealed and Delivered* from later in 1970 was the first album Wonder produced himself, and it amounted to a return to his old "Uptight" R&B roots. But the key shift came the next year, when he turned twenty-one and got control of his $1-million trust fund. His new, laboriously negotiated 120-page contract was a precedent-shattering event at Motown. The company would continue to distribute his records, but Wonder gained complete artistic freedom, control of his publishing and a far higher royalty rate. *Where I'm Coming From* (1971) only partially fulfilled the promise of this new freedom. But with *Music of My Mind* the next year, Stevie Wonder could be counted as a mature artist. The maturity expressed itself in several ways. The records weren't "concept albums," but they were conceived as entities, the songs flowing together organically. The lyrics now embraced social, political and mystical concerns, and even his stock love-and-sex themes were deepened to include domesticity and religiousness. Musically, Wonder, aided in the early seventies by producers Robert Margouleff and Malcolm Cecil, started to exploit the potential of the modern studio, particularly for overdubbing. He was now able to play most of the instruments, with only occasional guitar solos, horn, string or percussion supplementation and backup singing by others. Most crucially, both the shape and the color of his music had matured. Its shape, no longer bound to the rigid confines of the three-minute hit single, increasingly reflected the expansive spontaneity of his live performances. The music's color was defined above all through Wonder's fascination with synthesizers, the clavinet, electric pianos and organs and, more recently, samplers and MIDI-interfaced computer technology. They lent his work, particularly the uptempo material, a twangy insistence that was unmistakably personal without ever lapsing into silly technocratic display.

While Wonder has never seemed emptily virtuosic, in the Eighties he did lapse into a self-conscious perfectionism that limited his output. Although his big hits remained lively R&B material like "Higher Ground," Boogie On Reggae Woman" and "You Haven't Done Nothin'," his albums have contained a disproportionate amount of balladic ramblings, faceless soundtracks and banal ruminations. There was a solid level of craftsmanship, but Wonder perhaps inevitably failed to extend the extraordinary innovation that marked his work in the early and mid-Seventies. Some critics complain about his self-indulgence and bleary universal-love sentimentality, especially after the release of *Journey Through the Secret Life of Plants*. These are unquestionably parts of his maturity, but his early records prove they're nothing new. After the lively *Hotter Than July* in

1980, nothing he subsequently accomplished surpassed his soundtrack for *Jungle Fever* of 1991, knocked out with liberating speed in just a month. Yet that, in turn, paled before *Living for the City*, from 1974.

Despite some stagnation in the last decade, what is ultimately exciting about Wonder's music – and what still makes his potential for growth more promising than that of more settled artists – is his unpredictable openness to a new sounds and new styles. Not that he chases after every trend; his venture into rap in *Jungle Fever* came years after other non-rappers had taken that plunge. But his responses are fresh, and what he has already accomplished is enormous. One imagines he will keep plugging away, striking the chord of critical and popular success every few years and proceeding on his own way in between. Isolated from the "real" world by race, blindness and success even as he is linked to it by his own extraordinary acuteness, Wonder is probably too original for guaranteed, comfortable acceptance. Which, of course, constitutes his ultimate strength.

Stevie Wonder in Paris with the Motown Revue, being set up
by a mischievous photographer!

18
David Ruffin & Eddie Kendricks and The Temptations
by Spencer Leigh

The story of The Temptations is a long and sad one. With all but Otis Williams of the original five now deceased, it is difficult to view events without considerable heartache. Experienced writer and broadcaster Spencer Leigh met David Ruffin and Eddie Kendricks in 1991, at a time when they weren't with the group. This interview turned out to be Ruffin's last, as it was only a few days before his drug-related death.

The Temptations have always been one of my favourite Motown groups, and their records certainly haven't dated at all. The group has recorded in many different styles, but they are best-known for their sweet love ballads from the mid-Sixties and their psychedelic fund from the early Seventies.

The other Motown groups always had a leader. The Four Tops were Levi Stubbs plus backing vocalists; the Supremes centered around Diana Ross, and the Vandellas around Martha Reeves; and when you think of the Miracles, don't you think of Smokey Robinson first? The Temptations were different: each of them could have had a career in his own right, and part of their appeal was the way they swapped vocalists in the middle of a verse.

Individual Temptations tended not to stay for long: they all had the urge (the temptation, perhaps!) to pursue a solo career. David Ruffin and Eddie Kendricks, in particular, had solo hits, and they appeared as a duo with Hall and Oates at Live Aid. Together with another Temptation, Dennis Edwards, they created a stage show which paid tribute to the Motown group and also featured their individual successes.

In May 1991 this roadshow came to Southport, and an interview was arranged for me with David and Eddie at the hotel before the show. David suggested that the interview should take place in his room. I had to ring from the room next door, so that he could swiftly open the door and let me in. He seemed twitchy and uncomfortable, and had a similar ritual for when Eddie joined him. "This is a man playing at rock stars!", I thought. "There's no need for him to be this paranoid unless…."

Well, the 'unless' happened. Within a few days of returning to the States, David Ruffin died as a result of his drug habits. What follows may be the last interview he ever gave. It includes several references to the Lord – but what would the Good Lord have thought of cocaine?

Spencer Leigh: *David, the place you were born in has the marvellous name of Whyknot.*
David Ruffin ("DR"): Yeah, Whyknot, Mississippi, and Jimmy was born in Collinsville. It does exist, It's on the Mississippi/Alabama state line. Why is in Mississippi and Knot is in Alabama!
Were both you and your brother Jimmy singing from an early age?
DR: Yeah, we used to be the Ruffin Family – with my sister, my oldest brother Quincy, and my father – and we used to open shows for Mahalia Jackson, the Five Blind Boys, the Clara Ward Singers and Rosette Tharpe. If anyone has that album that we made as the Ruffin Brothers, there is a picture of me when I was six years old in Mobile, Alabama, on a show then. We were singing spirituals. Mahalia Jackson was a very, very dynamite lady and I learnt a lot from her.
How did you come to be in Detroit?

DR: I left home at 14 years old and went to Memphis. I was chauffeuring a limousine for a minister, and I put myself through school – Booker T. Washington High School in Memphis, Tennessee – and then I left Memphis and went to Little Rock, Arkansas, and the minister and I worked down there for a while. I came back to Memphis and joined the Dixie Nightingales, and I started travelling a lot with the spiritual groups. After that I worked with the Soul Stirrers, after Johnnie Taylor left, for a short time.

I stopped singing spiritual because the minister and I were not selling enough ads for our paper to afford to keep me out on the road, and he suggested that I could make some money and support myself better by singing blues songs. I was 15 at the time. I went to Hot Spring, Arkansas with Phineas Newborn Snr., who was a great jazz player, and I played at the Fifty Grand ballroom/casino. Then I went to Detroit, Michigan, where I met Berry Gordy. I had some solo records before I joined the Temptations. I joined them as a drummer, but I was looking forward to singing tenor. My man, Eddie Kendricks, over there, he was singing so good, and he taught me a lot.

Eddie, I think you were in the Primes first of all.

Eddie Kendricks ("EK"): Well, we were called the Cavaliers, actually, and in Cleveland we met Milton Jenkins, who changed our names to the Primes. We met this girl group whom we changed to the Primettes, and so we became a brother and sister group. They were Diana Ross, Mary Wilson, Florence Ballard and Barbara Martin. I had no idea that we would be big. We knew we had the talent, and I guess what happened was up to the Lord.

How did you come by the name of the Temptations?

EK: I have no idea how that happened. I'd like to know myself!

DR: Billie Jean Brown named the group. She was Berry Gordy's secretary at Motown Records.

EK: I do know that there was another group called the Temptations, and they had a record called "Barbara". I have no idea as to how we got the name.

One of the first Temptations' records which you sing on is "The Way You Do The Things You Do". Do you remember getting that song?

EK: We were at the Apollo, and Smokey and Bobby Rogers brought us the song. We thought it was a good song, and with our talent, our voices and things, we made it happen.

And you co-wrote "The Girl's Alright With Me".

EK: These things just happen. I saw a girl in a newspaper and I thought she was very pretty, and that gave me an idea. Everyday things make a song.

Why didn't Smokey Robinson keep "My Girl" for himself?

DR: I've known Smokey since I was 16, we all used to live together, Smokey knew my voice and he knew that everybody had a song to sing and I didn't have one, so he wanted to write one for me. "My Girl" came out, and then he had "My Baby" and "Since I Lost My Baby".

I love that bit in the middle where the Temptations are harmonising and you then come in with 'ooohs'. Was that spontaneous or had you worked it out?

DR: It was spontaneous. My mind was telling me to sing one thing but I couldn't think of the words and I just held the note. Later on, I said, "We'll have to go back", and they said, "No, we're going to keep that". Mistakes do pay off in this business sometimes.

And what about the dance routines?

EK: That was Paul Williams. Although we put in bits and pieces, he was the main man. It was hard work to get them right, but later on we could look at it as a nice picture and say "Yeah". We were not a stand-up group, although we could have stood and sung with anybody. We were a show group. I would like to think that we gave the people what they wanted.

Although "My Girl" was a No. 1 hit in America for you, over here it was a Top 10 hit for Otis Redding. What did you think of Otis's version?

DR: Oh, Otis was great, he was a pioneer. And he didn't only do "My Girl", he did "My

Baby" as well. He and I were very close. Otis was into horses, and so was I. We both had motorcycles.

What about "Get Ready"?

EK: I thought that we did a good job of performing Smokey's songs, for both Smokey Robinson and Motown. I think, to be honest, he thought we couldn't perform some of them as well as we could.

DR: Writers have an idea of how they would like it to be recorded. Eddie had a very good tune, "Way Back In The Hills Of West Virginia", that he had for me. He just thought that it would suit me better.

David, on "Ain't Too Proud To Beg", your voice was rougher than it had been previously. What had been said to you in the studio?

DR: I wasn't any rougher! I don't know what kind of voice I have, but if you write a song, you can tell me if you want it soft or hard or churchy, and I can do that. Basically, I suppose it is just the feeling I get for a song.

And you're really screaming at the end of "(I Know) I'm Losing You".

DR: A lot of those songs were recorded when we came off tours. We would come into town, go home and then go into the studios the next day, so you are trying to get the notes out, but I can be Ol' Rough Voice if I've been on a tour. On that record, Norman Whitfield was bringing something out of me. He was coaxing me to the point where I get angry.

EK: Sometimes the producer won't have it any other way. He knows what he wants and he wants to push you so that you sing like that. He doesn't want you singing like "My Girl" or "Since I Lost My Baby".

When I spoke to Jimmy, he said that he had recorded "Beauty Is Only Skin Deep" first but it wasn't released, and the song was passed over to you and the Temptations. Did you have any qualms about taking your brother's song?

DR: No, record companies play tricks with you. After I left the Temptations, I did a lot of demos for a lot of people. I did a lot for Stevie Wonder. I would be thinking that I was cutting the songs for an album and then later on, I would be travelling somewhere and I would hear his records. But I didn't mind. Sure, it hurts when those things happen, but I tried to keep going in the right direction. Sometimes I would be taking the low road, but it doesn't mean that the low road isn't taking you where you should be going. I don't have to get to the mountain top before anybody else. You see, I think God works in mysterious ways. If he gives you something, you have to use it to your full ability, but he also doesn't want you to misuse it.

You've both mentioned the Good Lord. Isn't it surprising that the Temptations never cut a gospel album?

DR: We did many gospel songs. "I know you want to leave me, But I refuse to let you go, If I have to beg, plead for your sympathy, I don't mind 'cause you mean that much to me." Take every 'baby' or 'girl' or 'love' away from our songs and you will have a spiritual song. "Get ready 'cause here I come", "The Lord's alright with me", "Loneliness made me realise, it's the Lord that I need". It's just that the message that the song has for marketing reasons has to be 'girl' or 'baby' or 'I love you'.

But the general public would never hear them that way.

EK: I agree because they were written in a special way, but every song is the truth, no matter how another person might hear it, and gospel is the only truth. We didn't sing songs about fiction.

The Beatles were very good for Motown in that they praised your records.

EK: I think we were very good for the Beatles too! These songs are good for the Rolling Stones and Rod Stewart today. They got a wider audience and a bigger push.

DR: When Rod Stewart first came to Detroit, I used to sing with him because I wasn't in the group at the time . He used to play there and come back, and he did better all the time. Our Jimmy's ex-wife, Shirley, used to cook dinner for Mick Jagger whenever he came to Detroit. In 1975, Mick Jagger was down in my basement when I was rehearsing "Walk Away From Love" and he asked me to sing "Ain't Too Proud To Beg" with my band. I told him to sing it himself 'cause I was too tired, and a few months later he got a platinum record with the song.

In the Sixties, you did a Ready, Steady, Go! *special in this country.*

DR: Yes, with Dusty Springfield. We came over about 15 days early to promote the Motown tour. I remember Paul Williams sitting in the Cumberland Hotel and making up the routine for the Supremes and "Stop! In The Name Of Love". He was trying it out with me and Melvin Franklin! We did the TV show and then they sent us back to the States. We should have been on the tour, but as I say, this business plays tricks on you. God works in mysterious ways, and I think he has taken care of us very well.

Why did you leave the Temptations?

DR: Because in every man's life, there comes a time when he has to step forth and deal with his own destiny. It was the will of God that I should step out and do the kind of things that Michael Jackson was doing later on. I was able to record by myself and produce and write, I could exercise all my talents. God said that anything that was trying to pull you down had to be beneath you. When you are lifted up, you are drawn unto him. I am very glad that I am lifted up and feel so close to him. Other than that, I would have perished by now.

When David left the group, the Temptations seems to change their sound.

EK: Well, we had lost one of the cogs on the wheel with David, but it was able to roll again once we found Dennis Edwards. We could have done the same sort of songs, but "Cloud Nine" was the producer's idea. He wanted to change everything and we had to go along with it. We were a love song group and there was an uproar about us singing those kind of songs. Eventually we went back to what we could do best. "Just My Imagination" was good for us, it was such a sweet song and we needed it, 'cause we were caught up in "Cloud Nine" and "Psychedelic Shack", which was my exit from the group. That was in '71, and here we are 20 years later, and the songs that we had all those years ago are the best songs.

After you left, you make disco records like "Keep On Truckin'".

EK: I do what the producers want. I'm a singer. When you have a contract, you have to go with what is wanted. It was successful for them and it was successful for me too.

David, you made an album with your brother, My Brother's Keeper. *Was that an enjoyable experience?*

DR: Very much so. That was dedicated to my mother and father. My mother died when I was 11 months old and there was only one picture taken of her, and I never saw it until I was 28 years old. Jimmy knew where it was, but I had never seen it before. I suggested to Jimmy that we do an album in their honour. We chose songs that we particularly liked. It is a spiritual album, with "Stand By Me" – message songs, anyway.

And now you're part of a revue doing Temptations' songs.

DR: We have a nine-piece band that is travelling with us. We have three background singers and we dance as well as ever. We all have our solo spots where we do our own songs. If I can get up there and I can make someone forget about his troubles, then that makes me feel great, that I have accomplished something. I am sure that we will all get together one time as the Temptations before it is all over and done with, one more time again. It will not be for making money, but just for singing and harmonising together.

David Ruffin and Eddie Kendricks, thank you very much.

DR: Thank you very much for giving us your time, and God bless.

What Motown Means To Me
Spencer Leigh's Top Ten Motown Tracks

1. "Money (That's What I Want)" – Barrett Strong (1959)
In 1959 this was a really obscure UK release and you'd be one of the in crowd if you even knew about it. The song was taken up by the British beat groups – notably the Stones and the Beatles – but Barrett Strong's original remains the best. Nowadays it is heard in one TV documentary after another and it has been featured, inevitably, in the Nick Leeson film, Rogue Trader. *Did Berry Gordy ever write truer words?*

2. "Please Mr Postman" – The Marvelettes (1961)
When I told my wife, I was compiling a Top 10 of Motown discs, she said, "You'll have to include 'Please Mr. Postman' as it's the story of your life." Millions of us wait for the postman and this song captures the tension of wondering what's in the mail. The scuttlebutt has it that the Marvelettes wrote it themselves but other writers got attached to the credits, which became common practice later on and alienated fine talents like Edwin Starr. Gladys Horton's lead vocal ("Delivah the lettah, The soonah the bettah") is terrific and she had the potential, if not the inclination, to be a solo star.

3. "Do You Love Me?" – The Contours (1962)
Go into a Merseyside pub and you may be cornered by Faron of Faron's Flamingos telling you that Brian Poole stole his hit record. Faron's Flamingos may have been the first UK act to cover a Motown song, but it is ridiculous for Faron to claim "Do You Love Me?" as his own and hold a vendetta against Brian Poole for 36 years.

4. "Fingertips (Parts 1 and 2)" – Little Stevie Wonder (1963)
Although this record was high on the US charts, British DJs would play it apologetically. David Jacobs and Sam Costa couldn't understand what it was all about, and it seemed to me like a curio from outer space, far, far stranger than "Purple People Eater". Now it just sounds amazing – a young boy revelling in his talent and the audience loving every moment. Note the spontaneity, the evidence being bassist Larry Moses shouting, "What key? What key?"

5. "Every Little Bit Hurts" – Brenda Holloway (1964)
I've known this soul ballad for some time but I'd ignored it until last year. Then Billy J. Kramer and the Dakotas topped a mammoth package in the US and the Dakotas' Eddie Mooney returned to the UK raving about one of the supporting artists, Brenda Holloway. I started playing "Every Little Bit Hurts" and realised that it was an absolute gem.

6. "Dancing in the Street" – Martha and the Vandellas (1964)
You could question the political motivation of this record – instead of rioting in the streets, everyone got to dance instead – but this is among the most infectious records ever made. Martha Reeves always sounded good but she never sounded better than this. First time out, the record only made No.28 on the UK charts and when I saw Martha with the Supremes, the Miracles and Stevie Wonder in April 1965, I doubt if there were 500 in the Liverpool Empire. The promoters had added Georgie Fame to the bill in the hope of selling more seats.

7. "My Girl" – The Temptations (1965)
To me, the song is always first and what separates good Motown records from great ones

are the songs themselves. Smokey Robinson's wrote okay up-tempo songs ("Mickey's Monkey") but stunning love ballads ("The Tracks Of My Tears", "You've Really Got A Hold On Me"). The imagery is simpler and less imaginative than "The Way You Do The Things You Do" but it is equally effective and the record is blessed with a Sam' Cooke-slanted vocal from David Ruffin. Surprisingly, the Tempts' version wasn't a UK hit at first but Otis Redding took the song into the charts.

8. "Reach Out I'll Be There" – The Four Tops (1966)
Levi Stubbs' stentorian tones meet the Motown Wall of Sound on this masterpiece, written and produced by Holland-Dozier-Holland. It sounds as though every decent musician in Detroit was in the studio but the flutes provide some subtlety. Perhaps it was simply friendship, but I wonder why Levi Stubbs never went solo – his occasional solo efforts (eg as the maneating houseplant in Little Shop Of Horrors*) didn't do him justice.*

9. "I Second That Emotion" – Smokey Robinson and the Miracles (1967)
I was sold on the title. Smokey didn't have to sing a note.

10. "Let's Get It On" – Marvin Gaye (1973)
Marvin Gaye's career is full of high moments (literally) and this, woolly hat notwithstanding, is the most carnal of all his Motown records. Sinuous, sensuous and sensitive, "Let's Get It On" is one of the few records to exploit the joys of sex. The lyrics aren't great ("If the spirit moves you, let me groove you"), but when you're as ecstatic as this, you're lost in emotion. Gaye repeated the process with "Sexual Healing" (1982), surely the best record by a Motown artist after leaving the label.

Lamont Dozier & Norman Whitfield
by Paul Zollo

The quality of the songwriting is usually agreed to have been the key factor in Motown's success, and this has been recognised on several occasions in the U.S. magazines Performing Songwriter *and* Song Talk. *Paul Zollo is one of the key writers for both publications and I have chosen two of his pieces to represent the best of Motown's composing teams. Lamont Dozier was, of course, part of the famous Holland/Dozier/Holland writing and production team, credited by many as being the single most important factor in "The Sound Of Motown". The Dozier piece comes from the Autumn 1988 issue of* Song Talk. *Norman Whitfield came to prominence shortly after the HDH golden era, but he was instrumental in steering the company towards a gutsier and harder approach more appropriate to the late sixties. The Whitfield piece comes from the Winter 1991 issue of* Song Talk.

19
Lamont Dozier: On Songwriting

Lamont Dozier is one-third of the legendary Holland-Dozier-Holland songwriting team, the most successful songwriting group, with the exception of the Beatles, in the history of popular music. Lamont is also the Chairman of the Board of Directors of the National Academy of Songwriters.

The Prominence of Melody

Melodies in songs are not as prominent as I'd like them to be. But I think melodies are more on a surge now than they used to be. We've run the gamut. It comes and goes in cycles. I think it's coming back.

The nature of people is to walk down the street and whistle a tune. So with that in mind, I think we're going to have melody. People will buy a good melody if it's there.

When writing, if I get a gut reaction from a melody, if it moves me, then I know it's good. I never pick a melody unless I've slept on it, so to speak. I may write a melody today and then I'll let it sit by itself for two or three days. I'll put it down, ignore it, come back to it, in two or three days, and if it still hits me, I know it's good. It's like hearing it for the first time.

If a melody comes back to me, if I start humming it, if it's made a mark on my unconscious in some way, then I'll know it's melodic and I'll continue.

A melody doesn't necessarily need a big range to be strong. You can take a minor melody that has no really significant highlights to it – it can be a down kind of melody – but if it has a haunting refrain that is so infectious that it stirs the spirit, that's what makes a great melody.

Listening to Standards

When I listen to some of the old tunes, by Richard Rodgers or Cole Porter or Irving Berlin, their melodies stand up today. You can pick them up anytime, if you're a music lover; those melodies have been around for years. There's a reason why. They carry a certain mystique about them and a feeling that grabs you right away.

I've always had this philosophy that if I don't like it, nobody's going to like it. If I sit down at the piano, and a melody hits me right off, if I can hum it, then I know I've got a good melody. "Stop In The Name Of Love" is a good example of a strong melody we wrote.

But the melody isn't the only important part of a song. There's a marriage between the melody and the music – the chords you use that the melody has to stand on – that must be strong. And you have to have the lyrics that work with that melody – there are those three elements, and if you have all three, you will have a song that can stand the test of time.

People still write great melodies but not as much. In these days of "Get the money and run-music" as I call it, we have a tendency to overlook some things. I think some writers might find a lush melody to be square. In this age of rap and disposable music, there's not a great emphasis on writing great melodies. But there are still serious writers who tend to take their craft seriously and put in the time to come up with a great melody.

The Demands of the Marketplace

The executives at the record companies want something that is gonna sell. And it's hard to stick to a craft if nobody wants it. So you find yourself between a rock and a hard place. You want to write good melodies, but you want to survive and you want people to hear the stuff. You wind up joining the bandwagon.

But for the few that have the heart to stick with their own personal convictions as far as melodies go, who stick to their guns as far as writing good songs regardless of who likes them, I think in the long-run, they're the ones who are going to contribute the most to keep the music flourishing.

People do have an inherent need to hear good melodies. They want to hear them. If they hear nothing else than what they hear, they get brainwashed into thinking that this is what is happening. They turn on the radio and they're led by what they hear.

The Predominance of Rhythm

Rhythm is very important as far as dance records go. America's in love with 4/4 time, especially when it comes to dance. When it comes to listening or ballads, it can be in 6/8 or any other type of beat – a mambo rhythm. I just cut a thing with a mambo feel that has a 4/4 type of undercurrent. Just to make it different.

A song doesn't have to have a backbeat to be a hit. A lot of ballads don't have a backbeat. You get the feel often of a backbeat without hearing a fat snare. If you have the guitar strum on 2 and 4, you get the same feel without the obvious backbeat. You get the feeling of the backbeat even without it. If you eliminate the backbeat, people will still feel it in 4/4 time.

When it comes to dance, throughout history, the 4/4 beat is easiest to follow. Rhythm always came first in the Motown songs. The rhythm carried the feeling of the song across. It's very important for the melody to sit on something rhythmically infectious that will carry the melody. If the melody doesn't have a good rhythm to sit on, it falls apart, and there's no continuity.

Making Song Demos

At Motown we would make finished records of the songs as our demos. Then we'd take our voices off and add the singer's voice. Nowadays you do have to make fully-produced demos. A lot of people, unfortunately, can't hear your goods unless they hear the whole ball of wax. The day of the piano-voice demo is just about gone. There's very few people around who can still do that, unfortunately.

Another reason is because of dance music. The public is so indoctrinated into listening to dance and rhythms, that you have to have the rhythm that you are trying to sell full-blast on your tape. There's no other way to describe it. You have to hear it.

Marketing Your Songs

Writers should put just as much time into marketing their songs as writing, if not more. You have to keep the deal you've made with yourself to get the song out. No stone should go unturned. Because you really don't know where your good fortune is going to come from. It really doesn't matter how big a company is or how small. If there's an avenue there, something could blossom. If a company can make enough noise locally you can get the attention of the majors.

You have to know everything you can about the workings of the business. You have do it all yourself. There's so much competition, so many people wanting to get into this business, that you have to make sure you are on top of your own affairs in your life. You can't leave it to anybody else.

You can go to song-pluggers and pay them and then you wait around for the phone to ring to see if they've got anything going. By that time you can go stark-raving mad. You can do the same thing they do yourself. You have to go to clubs and meet the powers that be yourself.

Staying Aware

You have to write from your heart, but at the same time you have to keep abreast of the trends. You have to do both. I always have, I think that every writer owes it to the public to at least know what it is they're responding to.

Every note has been played. Every backbeat has been beat, so to speak. You can only learn from your peers. You might come up with something different, but music is not something I invented. It was here long before any of us were here. So there's nothing wrong with listening to other work. Listen to the great writers of the past, present and future. If you're serious about having a career, you have to listen to everything, all types of music – from opera through country-western. There are so many facets of music. If you're serious about a career in music, you have to have the adaptability to adjust to whatever it is you're called on to write. You go into your library of knowledge and dig down deep inside of yourself to come up with the right thing.

I don't think about commercial concerns when I first come up with something. When I sit down at the piano, I try to come up with something that moves me. Writing is a very personal thing. Then you invite the other people in – the influences of the marketplace. You adjust it to make it something that can be commercial and potentially a big hit. But it all starts with the heart, with writing that moves you.

20

The Motown Memories of Norman Whitfield:
The Legendary Writer of "War", "I Heard It Through The Grapevine" and "Just My Imagination" Looks Back
by Paul Zollo

"Words and melodies are forever," said Norman Whitfield, a man whose own work bears out this truth. With his partner Barrett Strong, he has written many of the world's most lasting and soulful songs, classics such as "I Heard It Through The Grapevine," "Just My Imagination," "War," "Papa Was A Rolling Stone," "Smilin' Faces" and so many more.

More than anything, these masterpieces emerged from the fierce, fighting environment of Motown, where Whitfield & Strong had to compete against prolific geniuses such as Smokey Robinson and Holland-Dozier-Holland.

The first song that Strong and Whitfield wrote together was "I Heard It Through The Grapevine" which stands as the Motown single with the second longest run at Number One. It's one of the most recorded songs in the history of Jobete Music, having appeared in the Top 100 a total of five times. Artists who have recorded it include the Temptations, Ike and Tina Turner, Creedence Clearwater Revival, The Undisputed Truth, Gladys Knight and the Pips, Elton John, and many more.

In 1971, Strong and Whitfield parted ways. Strong moved to California to launch a solo career, and released two albums on Capitol. Whitfield kept working, writing and producing. He scored a hit in the late seventies with his title track for the movie *Car Wash* and its soundtrack, which he wrote and produced. He's the father of three sons, all of whom work in the music industry, and he presently lives in North Hollywood, California.

This interview was conducted in the Hollywood offices of *SongTalk*, where Norman came to talk, dressed as if ready for a basketball game. Three nights later he and Barrett Strong were reunited for the first time in about twenty years and finally received a little bit of the recognition they have long deserved, winning the Lifetime Achievement Award from the National Academy of Songwriters.

Norman Whitfield ("NW"): I was born and raised in Harlem, New York, I left there when I was fourteen years old. Came out to California with my family to attend my grandmother's funeral. And on the way back, my father's car broke down and we wound up in Detroit.

We stayed there for most of my early career. That was where the actual interest developed to become a songwriter or to have something to do with the business that would be lucrative enough [*laughs*] to keep me interested.

Paul Zollo ("PZ"): *Did you play any instruments as a kid?*

NW: Yeah. I played congas and bongos. Percussion, mostly. And I just did it at my own leisure time. It wasn't a serious effort. I was around sixteen or seventeen then.

PZ: *What kind of music were you listening to then?*

NW: Jazz. A lot of my friends played jazz, but they were on an absolute elite level. These people went on to become very big in the jazz industry. But they were just my friends and they would allow me to come by and listen. Cause I don't have any formal musical training. It was done basically by a *desire*…. and then I worked at it. I worked in a service station for quite a few years. [*Laughs*] And I'm a professional pool shooter. That's how I paid for my kids. [*Laughs*]

PZ: *When did you decide to make music your career?*

NW: When I saw Smokey Robinson driving in a Cadillac. To be absolutely point-blank. That's what inspired me. And I actually ran up to him one day. I scared him a little bit, I ran up behind him and asked him, after he was half-way frightened by then, "How do you get started?" And he gave me the most ridiculous answer I've ever heard in my entire life. He said "Make your own bed, brother, because you've got to sleep in it." [*Laughter*]

I later dethroned him dealing with the Temptations. [*Laughs*]

You know, the Motown experience was really quite an experience. There was an absolute philosophy of music over there.

This was the Berry Gordy period: The Hollands, Dozier, so on.

PZ: *Is this when you met Barrett Strong?*

NW: I knew him before I ever got in the business. Barrett is the guy who wrote and played "Money" a long time ago, and it was a Number One record. It was on a very small label called Anna Records. Berry Gordy produced and co-wrote the song.

I was like anybody else. I was very young and I had seen him perform. And we got to know each other, because I was hanging around Motown long before they let me participate, writing and producing. And we had some run-ins with some girls.... [*Laughs*]

PZ: *Did you and he begin collaborating on your own or did Berry Gordy team you up?*

NW: We kind of got together on our own. I was down in one of the Motown rehearsal rooms and ....he was much more familiar with the Motown thing than I was, to be honest with you, but what happened was that I had a hit record on Thelma Records called "I've Gotten Over You" and Berry Gordy sent his A&R director to find out who I was. The song got picked up by a larger label and Berry made me an offer. He said, "Look, man, why don't you come over here, we've got this big machine over here, you'll probably love it and it'll give you a chance to make a lot of money..."

Of course, I was only making fifteen dollars a week then when I went with Berry Gordy. And another fifteen dollars a week he'd pay me for any royalties. Which I didn't mind, because I knew in order to make money, you needed to be around a situation where there was some real money being made. And it was an opportunity. The absolute opportunity of a lifetime.

I was down in the rehearsal hall one day, as I was saying, and Barrett came in and we started talking. We talked about some old times...girls, you know...We were never really very fond of each other. There was a subtle rivalry there because of the ...girls. We liked similar girls. The only difference was that I had the girls and he was always trying to get them.

We sat down. I said, "Look. I've got quite a few hit records." I played him a few things, I said "If you are interested, I can at least guarantee you a hundred thousand dollars a year. To write together." He said, "Well.... yeah. Sounds pretty good." I said, "I can only guarantee you verbally, I can't put it on paper because it would have a lot to do with how much we would put into it." So it worked out pretty well. From that point on, we were writing.

PZ: *What was the first song that you wrote together?*

NW: "I Heard It Through The Grapevine". There's a tremendous story behind that song and nobody knows the story. Barrett doesn't even know the story.

PZ: *Can you share that story with us?*

NW: I wish I could. It's a story in itself because of the political obstacles and things that happened. And I personally wouldn't want to incriminate Berry Gordy. He's like a father to me. It would be something very special for you guys to have but I've got to be honest with you, there's a deal pending on it and I wouldn't want to dilute the value of it.

Other than the fact that it has been a song that, since day one, Barrett and myself, we've always had a very strong feeling for this song. And I guess it didn't transcend to other people till later on. Because the first version was done on Marvin Gaye, but it never got released. Then I did it on Gladys Knight and the Pips and it went to Number One. I had just come off their first hit record for Motown called "Everybody Needs Love" and it was a perfect chance for me to take a song that Barrett and I had felt *so strongly* about, and put it on an artist who just came off a hit record.

I personally went and looked up where the saying "Heard it through the grapevine" came from. It went all the way back to Confederate black soldiers. They had a grapevine in order to pass on their words and experiences to each other.

PZ: *You wrote the songs with Strong and produced them alone?*

NW: Yes. I shared in the writing but I always produced alone. Kind of like a solo. I'm such a loner when it comes to music. I think it would be a strain for somebody to produce with me because there are so many things that I envision. What my mind can conceive, I can achieve. I've lived by that code for a long time.

PZ: *Does that make it hard to write with someone else?*

NW: No, because I've come to a certain level of writing. I've mastered every style of writing there is.

PZ: *Where did you and Barrett write your songs?*

NW: At home, or in the office, or at his house. And Barrett is a very good piano player and a lot of time, from being a percussionist, I can figure the rhythm out, and he'd be struggling with a little piano lick and trying to keep the intensity up. When you go over it so many times, it gets hard, especially when you're writing uptempo songs.

When we first did a song called "Cloud Nine" on the Temptations, I started studying African rhythms on my own, and I wanted to know how to make a song have as much impact without using a regular 2/4 or 4/4 backbeat. And it turned out to be very successful. It went to Number Two or Three.

PZ: *So can you have a hit without a backbeat?*

NW: Yes. It has to do with the feeling. Of course, nowadays, the kids are pretty much dance-oriented and the records don't have as much substance. But it's something you have to learn to live with.

Melodies and good lyrics are forever. That's the philosophy we were raised on. Also that competition breeds champions. We had a *very* competitive atmosphere at Motown. *Very.* But in some cases it made people stronger. In my case it made me stronger. I went through a tremendous amount of adversity. I don't even want to *go into it! [Laughs]* I was really like the new kid on the block. Everybody else was pretty much established there. But I managed to hang in there and make my way. I was probably the fastest growing producer in the history of Motown. At least, that's what Berry Gordy told me. *[Laughs]*

I also worked in Quality Control. Because Berry discovered, when I first got there, that I have an absolutely perfect ear in terms of picking hits. So he gave me the job in Quality Control which would justify the fifteen dollars. *[Laughs]*

PZ: *Did you pick a lot of hits?*

NW: Oh, I picked many of them. All the way from "Where Did Our Love Go" to The Originals. I mean, a lot of hit records. But I enjoyed the work. It was an evaluating experience for me. In a small room with a desk and turntables. We'd have discs made from the tapes, have the disc sent upstairs, they'd pile up on the desk and I'd sit there and evaluate them.

I enjoyed it because I *felt* something. And when I felt something, I was always right. An alarm would go off inside me emotionally when I would hear something special.

PZ: *Would you do that with your own work as well?*

NW: Later on it came like that. Because I realized I had to be the recipient of the bad news, and the good news for Smokey Robinson when he sent up "My Girl". You know? It came up, I had to evaluate it, *[laughs]* I had to take it into Berry Gordy, I said "Berry Gordy, I do not have a record to submit at this time. This record is *absolutely a smash.*"

And then I was trying to regroup myself. But he came back with "It's Growing" for The Temptations *[laughs]* and I had to bow down once again and say, "I don't have anything inside of me, to make me say, "You know, Norman, you're really going to have to step into this." And eventually I changed the sound. And Smokey was doing records that I thought were not as *intense* or as lyrically strong, and I got a chance to beat him out. And then once I beat him out, nobody ever got a chance to have The Temptations again while I was there.

One record did. "All I Need," which was a record by Frank Wilson, Berry Gordy and a lot of people. That record beat out "I'm Losing You". He told me "I'm Losing You" was just an okay record, and I said, "'I'm Losing You' is a smash, and with all due respect, I'm not going to make any more records until you can show me that this record is not everything I think it is." *With all* due respect for Berry, because he is the head honcho. But I've always been very much outspoken. I'm a person of real conviction. When I make records I make records to please me and I cut what I feel inside as opposed to cutting trendy things that you hear on the radio. That's why I did *Car Wash* and why I worked with a group that I put together and groomed for about a year, Rose Royce. And they had about eleven hit records.

PZ: *Your songs all have a timeless quality to them; they sound as good today as ever. Can you explain how you can write a song that will last?*

NW: Yes. It has everything to do with the standard that was instilled by Berry Gordy. In other words, if you knew that you had to be six-foot in order to be a participant in the game, you wouldn't go in there at five-nine or five-eight. If it was a six-foot game, you would have to be six-foot or more.

In other words, there was no sense turning in things that were basically mediocre.

And the standard was so high, the competition put the edge on it, and would carry you over. And I enjoyed it. I enjoyed it. I actually found out that when the going got tough, the tough got going. And I wasn't like that in school. When I played basketball, I would react just the opposite. But with music, there was a certain tenaciousness inside of me and something that would always drive me to make something very special out of a common situation.

PZ: *Do you remember writing "Just My Imagination"?*

NW: Yeah. I wrote that in Barrett Strong's basement. We kind of felt that it was a step back, because we had just come off of "Can't Get Next To You". And we've always enjoyed driving the other groups crazy because we were the leaders. We would take the Temptations and make a left turn even with everyone saying, "Well, you know they're gonna turn right again," so we'd just go left. That's part of being a front-runner and being the best in the field. You are allowed to be innovative and do anything you want as long as you keep in mind the standard.

PZ: *Would you sometimes bring in a title or an idea you came up with on your own?*

NW: Well, it can work many ways because when you have a verbal pact, it doesn't matter who contributes the most. Because it can be the fact that somebody's in the room with you that can keep you in line in terms of your creativity. You might be trying to prove a point without saying it.

From a creative point, you know, I've mastered my mind. I think it's about nineteen years... I can absolutely envision a song before I cut it. I can hear the instruments. It doesn't happen as much now, basically, because I'm not under that kind of *intense* pressure. You know: *"The Temps gotta have it! Do Jimmy Ruffin, you gotta do Gladys Knight and the Pips..... Edwin Starr,"* all these people... I had fun doing Rare Earth, too. They were the first white group I ever did. They were very soulful. They had a lot of fire. Tremendous people chemistry. They respected me and I enjoyed what they did. "I'm Losing You" was another record I did on them. It was a big hit, Number Three in the country.

PZ: *Did you like doing "War" with Edwin Starr?*

NW: Yeah. I also had offered the song to the Rare Earth. You know, I did it on The Temptations first. It was a much different version. The college polls showed that this song was the most popular song around. And it wasn't in a single form. Then I cut a track that was strong enough to be a single, and I tried to give it to the Rare Earth. And they refused it. They said, "We want to play on our own records." And Edwin was walking down the hall and I said, "Edwin, I got a song for you." When we got ready to dub it in, I got a couple of classes of school kids to share the experience with him, of them coming to Motown. They were between nine and eleven. I did that from time to time, because I realise there was no vision there, because of the poverty.

PZ: *Did you like Springsteen's version of "War"?*

NW: Yeah. I was very thrilled when I heard it because I thought it was really quite a compliment to have it on his first live album. I was very excited and very grateful.

PZ: *Did you like the Rolling Stones' version of "Just My Imagination"?*

NW: [*laughs*] Well, it was different. And I can't say that I absolutely liked it. I can say that I accepted the fact that they did it because they were who they were. And it was such a beautiful song – it was very close to me and Barrett, you know – when I heard it, Mick Jagger had such a different rendition, it totally caught us by surprise. I think we held our heads down for a few girls. After a while you start accepting that somebody else has a different rendition of it. But it was anything but romantic. But it did pretty good in the dollars and cents category.

PZ: *Where did the groove for "Papa Was A Rolling Stone" come from?*

NW: First I'd better say this: The Temptations didn't do the first version of it. The Undisputed Truth did. And it did about three hundred thousand. And I thought there was more to the song. So I went and cut it a whole different way, because I wanted to stay away from the original version. And The Temptations were a *little reluctant* because they felt it was a used tune. Eventually we saw eye to eye and we worked on it *very* hard and got excellent results on it.

PZ: *Do you have a favorite song that you've written?*

NW: It's not "I Heard It Through The Grapevine". Because that one was written and produced with the same intensity as all the songs we did.

It's one of my favorites. The phenomenal success it has had is undeniable. I like a song very much like "Too Busy Thinking About My Baby" which Marvin Gaye did, it did a quiet two million.

One of my favorite songs that I've ever written is a song called "Ooh Boy" that I did on Rose Royce. It went to Number Three. I love "I'm Losing You". I thought the song had pie-in-the-face, so to speak. It said what it said and it said it so cleverly.

PZ: *Why did you and Barrett stop working together?*

NW: I could be gentle or I could be rough. I choose to be graceful. He had an attorney that felt like Barrett could be doing more and getting more money. Even though many times I offered to get him a producer's contract. Like I say, I don't produce with anybody... *He* had never shown any sign of being discontented in any way. He disappeared. I didn't know. I was still putting his name on records. Then I saw the announcement that he had gone to CBS and took on a writing, producing and singing career.

CBS called me and asked if I was interested in coming over. Meanwhile, I had turned in the new album on the Temptations, *Masterpiece*. I wrote every song on that. But I have a tremendous amount of respect for Barrett. He has good judgment and good tastebuds. I enjoyed working with him. We both made a lot of money and we made a lot of people happy. But the inevitable is that nothing lasts forever. But it didn't end on a sour note.

PZ: *One thing that is forever as you said, are great songs. How does it feel to have written standards?*

NW: I'm still experiencing the thrill of it. It's phenomenal and I thank God that whatever He gave me, that the songs have longevity. And the people are really the people that make the songs what they are. We as writers, we only do what we do, and then we have to give it to the public. They're the ones who determine it you're a genius or a failure. So it's an exhilarating feeling. I've had it for so long, but I don't take it for granted. I try to remember what it took to get it to that level.

Lyrics and melodies are forever, but music can change. It changes with the times. I'm always going to be a chancy person and a nonconformist. I conform only to my feelings.

Motown's Girls
by Kingsley Abbott

Alongside the development of Motown in the early sixties, there was the pure pop mainstream. After the wilderness years of the "Bobby" era circa '61/2, producers began to take notice of the success of girl groups that had begun in the fifties with The Chantels and The Bobbettes and had come to full fruition with The Shirelles and Phil Spector's groups. Here was a rich bandwagon to be jumped on, and any studio or producer worth his salt searched around for young girls with the right look. Voices were a bonus, as there were experienced session singers who could actually make the records if the front-line girls couldn't sing. Berry Gordy was quick to notice what was happening, and put great efforts into The Marvelettes, who delivered Motown's first national number one with "Please Mr. Postman". Their subsequent singles and albums stayed close to the pop mainstream formulas of dance songs and teen romance. Berry also developed other groups like Martha & The Vandellas and The Velvelettes; indeed, Martha's early albums often included copies of national girl group hits. However it was The Supremes who, after a very faltering start, proved to be Berry's masterstroke. Their career development mirrored Mr. Gordy's vision for the entire company. They became the spearhead for a concerted effort to broaden Motown's appeal to cover the entire mainstream of popular entertainment. As well as groups, Berry Gordy was also anxious to cover all the bases by having successful female soloists too. After some early sixties cul-de-sacs with artists like Mabel John and Linda Griner, Berry concentrated on nurturing Mary Wells, whose steady rise to stardom must have been very satisfying for the company. However her early departure from the fold left somewhat of a void, that was only ever partially filled by Kim Weston and Brenda Holloway until the eventual re-marketing of Diana Ross as a solo star.

The common factor between all the acts was the desire of the company to present its songs in glamorous TV friendly packaging. The acts were cosseted, chaperoned and groomed into the Motown mould. Those whose faces and temperaments fitted best usually went on to long term success, but, as we shall see, there were some who fell by the wayside...

21

The Silk and Soul of Mary Wells
by Steve Towne and Chris Beachley

The rare Oriole British issues remain highly desirable.

Mary Wells was one of the first artists whose career intimated that all was not sweetness and light at Motown's hit factory. After realising Mary's star potential Berry Gordy showcased her talents on a run of Smokey Robinson-produced singles including the beautiful "Two Lovers" and the breakthrough worldwide hit "My Guy". However, instead of company and artist building on this success together, the relationship between Mary and Motown rapidly deteriorated, with both parties ending up losers. This piece, from the little known US fanzine It Will Stand, *tells Mary's cautionary tale with full reference to her wonderful music. It was written before Mary's untimely death.*

In the early sixties, while Berry Gordy was trying to get the gears to mesh for Motown, the biggest consistent hit maker he had was Mary Wells. Between the Spring of '62 and the Spring of '64 the team of songwriter-producer "Smokey" Robinson and singer Mary Wells could hardly miss. Mary Wells' smooth and intimate style of singing set the pace for later soul singers like Diana Ross, Natalie Cole and Donna Summer.

Born in Detroit, Michigan on May 13, 1943, Mary grew up on Detroit's West side near Wayne College. Of her childhood, she says, "There were three of us, but my two older brothers got married early, so I was like an only child. But I grew up without a father, so we were poor. I wasn't the best dressed kid in school 'cause we never had too much money, but I never looked bad because I would always stay neat and clean. My mother had to do a lot of domestic work and I helped out when I became around twelve years old. I wanted to do something to help her because I had seen a lot of her youth fading away from not being able to enjoy life other than working day in and day out.

"I'd been singing in church since I was three or four years old, so when I went to North Western High School I sang in the choir, but most of my learning experiences were in church. Besides church, there were plenty of people I was listening to sing on the radio like Sam Cooke, Etta James, Jackie Wilson, Ruth Brown and people like that who were out then. Singing looked so glamorous and so great, it inspired me a lot."

During high school people began taking notice of Mary Wells' singing ability. Mary says, "A couple of The Temptations, Melvin and Richard Street, and I went to school together. Richard is one of the newest members now but he was one of the guys that was singing years ago with them, before they went over to Motown. (He later sang with the Monitors – V.I.P.) We were managed by this lady, Johnnie Mae Matthews and her firm. She was a singer who knew a lot about the record business, but I don't think financially she was capable of handling the whole situation."

"I eventually left because The Temptations were signed to her longer and she was more involved with them. Meanwhile I ran into Robert Bateman, one of the early songwriters for the Marvelettes (co-author of "Please Mr. Postman" and "Playboy") who worked at Motown. He took me over there and I met with Berry Gordy, so I got with Motown."

Mary Wells' first recording with Motown was "Bye Bye Baby"/ "Please Forgive Me". The A-side, "Bye Bye Baby", was written by seventeen year old Ms. Wells as a poem, but sung in an exciting up-tempo raw gospel style – the style that still lends itself to some nice dancing (Carolina's style!). It made it as high as No. 45 on *Billboard*'s Pop charts and No. 8 on *Billboard*'s R & B charts in the Winter of 1960-61. The B-side, "Please Forgive Me", was slower and not as pleasing a song.

By late Summer 1961 Mary was back on the charts with her second song, the frankly mediocre "I Don't Want To Take A Chance". Surprisingly this did even better, going to No. 33 Pop and No. 9 R & B on *Billboard*'s charts.

After "Strange Love"/"Come To Me" failed to excite the record buyer, there were the first of a string of hits for Ms. Wells produced by William "Smokey" Robinson, "The One Who Really Loves You". This was Motown's third top ten pop hit and it established Mary Wells as Motown's most consistent hit maker. Ms. Wells comments, "That was when 'Smokey' started writing songs for me. 'The One Who Really Loves You', 'You Beat Me To The Punch' and those tunes, he was going to release on himself but he said that he was having so much success with me, more so than with The Miracles at the time, that he continued to write for me."

And succeed he did, writing three top ten hits, "The One Who Really Loves You" in the Spring. "You Beat Me To The Punch" in late Summer and "Two Lovers" in the winter of 1962. These medium tempo tunes are a perfect example of Mary Wells and early Motown at their best. The cha cha type rhythms are carried along perfectly by her sexy – smooth vocals. She says, "What I was really doing was projecting a softness because that's the type of tunes they were if you're singing something hard, you're going to push harder, but if you're singing something soft with soul, you're going to sing it with feeling. It's the way the melody goes that makes you want to sing it softer. You listen to the words and melody and it comes out natural. You don't say I'm going to project like this or sing this part softer, or build it up here, you just feel it. That's what they call soul."

Success made Mary Wells one of the headliners of The Motown Review tours and presented new problems. She says, "Performing in church and peforming on stage, Rock & Roll, Rhythm & Blues, whatever, is much different. I had to learn how to really perform. Back then they didn't have any people at Motown that trained you. They got more sophisticated after I left. but they didn't have anyone when I was there, so you had to learn yourself, or get people yourself to teach you. In the early days it was just like a family, everybody participated. Diana Ross sang background on a number of my songs and I did some things with The Temptations. As a matter of fact, Berry signed The Temptations and at the time he wasn't particularly interested in them. I told him I thought they could be really great, so I took them on the road with me. They got such good publicity that I took the newspapers back to Berry to show him that the guys had a lot goin'. But the guys who sang most of my backgrounds were called The Love-Tones. ("For This I Thank You" – Gino Parks and Love-Tones). These were some guys who grew up and sang with my older brothers. They had a lot of jazz flavor in their voices and could sing great harmony. I started pushing for them to record, because you see people with talent and you figure they could do something themselves. They eventually went on the road with me to get people familiar with their voices, but the lead singer got stabbed to death and they kind of fell apart after that."

Released in the Spring of 1963, "Laughing Boy" was not quite as successful as its predecessor, making it only in the top twenty. The sound on "Laughing Boy" is very urban, a real city sound much like the guitar sound and rhythm of "I Need A Change" by The Miracles. Also in this mode is "Your Old Standby", which just made it into the Pop Top 40, but was every bit as good as "Laughing Boy". Flip over "Your Old Standby" and you'll find a beautifully sung "Smokey" Robinson composed ballad, "What Love Has Joined Together". This song is probably better known from The Temptations' stage shows of the mid-sixties.

"What's Easy For Two Is So Hard For One" from the Fall of 1963 sounds like it was written exclusively for Mary. From the opening, "Well, Well, Well, Well" to the chorus, "But Two Can Easily Do" this song has a smoothly irresistable feel. The original A-side, "You Lost The Sweetest Boy", was one of the few Holland, Dozier, Holland songs recorded by Mary Wells and was picked up by radio first, but "What's Easy For Two" was definitely the stronger side.

This brings us to the Spring of 1964 and her first No. 1 record, "My Guy". "I had really been able to establish myself as a name act with that one. Although, I've really found some enjoyment in every last one of my songs because it's like trying to decide which one of your children you love best. You love them all." (The *Mary Wells Greatest Hits* LP entered the charts two months after the "My Guy" 45 made it's mark. Then "My Guy" was put on the next two LP's. *My Guy* – Motown 617 and *Vintage Stock* – Motown 653… hence, "My Guy" was obviously someone's favorite! From the *Vintage Stock* LP you'll find that "Honey Boy", "Everybody Needs Love", and a superb version of "When I'm Gone" are excellent for some nice listening or dancing.)

After a Top 20 double-sided hit duet with Marvin Gaye, "Once Upon A Time"/ "What's The Matter With You Baby", Mary Wells left Motown. The most common explanation for her departure was a rumor of a large sum of money and a movie contract offer from 20th Century which Mary Wells flatly denies.

Mary explains, "I left Motown because I was having problems. I was told it was a family situation and that's the way I believed. I felt I had a lot of hit records at the time and I deserved more. I wasn't as business-inclined as I am now because I always did business from the heart. You don't tell people that it's a family business and you're family, and then you're left out. I was hurt, but I could have said later for that family thing, we'll write up a new contract, this is what I want and it would be strictly business."

WVON, Chicago's major R & B radio station played "He's The One I Love" from Mary's album *My Guy* throughout the Summer of 1964 and had a sizeable turntable hit with it. The *My Guy* LP, far from being one hit and eleven pieces of junk, is a fairly solid album. It contains the previously mentioned "He's The One I Love", the beautifully sung "Whisper You Love Me Boy" and "He Holds His Own", predecessors of the Supremes' flip sides and probably written for Mary, plus the nice & danceable "Does He Love Me". Side B is Motown's attempt to slip Mary Wells into an acceptable white night club sound by doing standards like "You Do Something To Me" and "I Only Have Eyes For You". This makes for some pretty dull listening – even sadder, this would happen again later.

Discographers show no releases for Motown #'s 1061 and 1065, but it is thought those numbers were held for "Guaranteed For A Lifetime" and "Whisper You Love Me Boy".

By the Fall of 1964 Mary Wells was back on the charts with her first single for 20th Century, the Robert Bateman produced "Ain't It The Truth" / "Stop Taking Me For Granted". "Ain't It The Truth" went Top 40 and was a nice medium-tempo record. "Stop Taking Me For Granted" is classic Mary Wells, beautifully sung with a very tasty arrangement and another nice dance tune.

In regards to 20th Century, Ms. Wells says, "20th Century didn't know how to promote black music. They weren't one on one with me as far as what to do with me. At Motown a lot of the artists could sit up and discuss different ideas. Berry Gordy is a smart man who is able to see talent and put a lot of people with talent and ideas together. I would discuss ideas with someone at Motown that maybe I wasn't able to do and it would get back to Berry Gordy and he might use it on Diana Ross or someone else. I couldn't do that with other companies, but I was young and didn't realise it at the time. Giving ideas to different record executives or producers outside of Motown was like talking to a brick wall. At Motown we didn't look at it like business."

After "Ain't It The Truth" peaked at No. 45, "Use Your Head" did even better making it in the Top 30 in January 1965 and denting the R & B charts for two weeks. In the follow up, "Never Never Leave Me", Mary's voice sits like a gem in the lush ballad arrangement. This one should have been big, but 20th Century seemed to be losing interest in her, with this and her last two releases doing worse (chartwise) than the one before. 20th Century, in a desperate attempt to get Mary back into the pop marketplace, followed with an LP of Mary singing pop arrangements of Beatle songs (*Mary Wells Sings Love Songs to the Beatles*) with predictably little success.

By early 1966 Mary's recording career was back in capable hands when she teamed up with Chicago producer/writers Carl Davis, Gerald Sims and Sonny Sanders after a move to Atco records. This brought about the sparkling and infectious smash hit, "Dear Lover". Both sides are great female soul with the driving flip, "Can't You See (You're Losing Me)" even getting some pop play. "Dear Lover" went to No. 6 on the R & B charts and became a mainstay on the Beach Music jukeboxes, but the follow up Atco records by her failed to click nationally even though "Such A Sweet Thing" and "Fancy Free"/ "Me & My Baby" might get dancers up on the floor. Her LP on Atco *Two Sides of Mary Wells* showed a weak production of Deon Jackson's classic "Love Makes The World Go Round", remakes of Wilson Pickett, Otis Redding, and Supremes tunes with the "other" side being remakes of old standards including, believe it or not, "Girl From Ipanema". Wasting her talent on junk like that and misguided projects like the Beatles LP is what slowed down Mary's career.

In 1968 Mary Wells switched companies again, this time going to Jubilee Records. She says, "I went with Jubilee because I wanted to start writing again and producing so I went in and started writing. They didn't have too many producers around then like they have now, that I thought were capable of producing me as an artist."

"The Doctor" is a laid back Southern soul sounding ballad with some standout guitar picking. It was written by Mary and her then husband Cecil Womack (Cecil had sung with brothers Bobby, Curtis and Harry as the Valentinos in the early sixties ("Looking For A Love" and "It's All Over Now" – SAR).

Although the promotion at Jubilee was done by Mary and her husband Cecil calling disc jockeys, "The Doctor" still made No. 22 on R & B charts and crossed over to Pop making it to No. 65. The follow-up records at Jubilee, "Never Give A Man The World" and "Dig The Way I Feel" showed up minimally on the R & B charts in late 1969. Mary stayed with Jubilee until 1975 when she switched to Warner Bros. Nothing for WB/ Reprise got any chart action and Mary Wells has been in semi-retirement for most of the seventies in order to raise a family. She has three children from her marriage to Cecil Womack.

Mary says, "My children think it's just great that I'm going back out and singing. They read in black history books about their mother being a famous singer and their friends' mothers know of me and they say why don't you start back up singing. That kind of made me feel guilty. Recently, I recorded four sides and I've been talking to different record companies and performing concerts and at night clubs. There seems to be a lot of interest in the records but we haven't decided on which record company we would be going with. But there should be a record coming out in a couple of months. The records are sort of like some of the older things I did, sort of with feeling. The instrumentation is up-to-date. I think a lot of music today doesn't have what it used to have, that innocent, natural feeling of the artist being into the music. We used to communicate more with the people because we were the people. Some singers today have had it pretty easy. I've always worked hard to make a better living so I could see my family smile. I think that's why God gave me a lot of success. My mother always told me to think about others and now that I have children I think about them too. I don't like to see my family do without, so that's what keeps me going."

22

The Marvelettes: Holding On
by David Cole

Even Berry Gordy was not averse to bandwagon jumping.

The Marvelettes came to Motown as fresh, naïve girls, at a time when Berry Gordy was still very aware of the need for a young company to cover all the market bases. They became his "girl group", and rode the early sixties wave created by The Shirelles and others. As their career progressed, they grew from cutesy teenage girlie popsters into a sophisticated soul group, but ultimately faded from view as company attention was switched to The Supremes. This piece comes from David Cole and his superb soul magazine In The Basement, *(Subscription details from Astrascope, 193 Queens Park Road, Brighton, BN2 2ZA) which is well worth seeking out.*

The Supremes may be better known to pop-pickers, so may Martha Reeves & the Vandellas, but the group to have Motown's first Number One on the *Billboard* Hot 100 was the Marvelettes. (N.B. Even the Miracles' "Shop Around" from nine months earlier only made the #2 slot.) What's more, it sat at the very top of the R&B chart for no less than seven weeks. The song was "Please Mr. Postman", a seemingly five-person writing collaboration including major input from original group member, Georgia Dobbins.

The five girls who were to form the first Marvelettes' line-up were got together by Gladys Horton and, in addition to Georgia Dobbins, fresh out of school, were three classmates from the high school at Inkster, a suburb some 35 miles from Detroit – Katherine Anderson, Juanita Cowart and Georgeanna Tillman. Because Gladys had no real confidence in their singing abilities, they called themselves the Casinyets, a contraction of "can't sing yet", but she did have enough faith to put them in a school-sponsored talent contest, singing a number written by Georgia, "Come To Me". Although they only came fourth, that was sufficient to award them the prize of an audition at Motown.

For their audition, they sang popular numbers from the Shirelles, Chantels and Bobettes, but listeners Robert Bateman and Brian Holland asked to hear original material. As a result they went away determined to keep up the momentum by returning post-haste with a new song. Georgia Dobbins decided to call up a friend, William Garrett, whom she knew to be a prolific songwriter and, going through his portfolio, she lighted on "Please Mr. Postman". When Garrett sang it to her, it turned out to be a blues – not exactly what she wanted. In return for a writing credit, she took the title away from Garrett and went home to write a new number using that and its theme. Sadly, Georgia was not to share in the group's success however. Her mother was not well and in need of constant care and she decided she should quit the group. As a result, it was Gladys Horton who took the lead vocal and Wanda Young – about to leave Inkster High for nursing school – that took over as Georgia's replacement when they returned to face Bateman and Holland a month later.

The guys liked the song and, in "cleaning it up", also took songwriting credit, alongside Originals' group member Freddie Gorman. They took the girls straight into the studio to record it but Berry Gordy did not like the name "Casinyets". After several attempts at alternatives, it was he who decanted on Marvelettes. For the flip, Holland and Bateman chose a song they had written with James Young Jr., "So Long Baby", and for this, lead vocals were taken by Wanda Young.

The follow-up was to retain the "Postman" theme but "Twistin' Postman" failed to emulate the success of the debut hit, only spending six weeks on the R&B chart and stalling at #13. Top Ten success soon returned with "Playboy" (which informed sources advise was written by Gladys Horton and not the team of Dobbins-Holland-Bateman-Stevenson, as credited by Motown) and its successors, "Beechwood 4-5789", its flip, "Someday, Someway" and a third single, "Strange I Know". Around this time, Juanita Cowart left the group for reasons undocumented, and the girls decided to continue without a replacement, although at-the-time Supreme, Florence Ballard, sometimes augmented the line-up, as she did on occasion when another group member was absent for sickness or any other reason.

After the success of the Berry Gordy-penned "My Daddy Knows Best", culled as a single in July 1963 from *The Marvelous Marvelettes* album, Smokey Robinson expressed a wish to work with the group. Already hot, not just with his own Miracles' group but with a string of hits for Mary Wells, Robinson's first writing expressly for the girls was "As Long As I Know He's Mine", issued in the middle of October 1963. At the same time as cutting that single, the girls had been in the studios with Holland-Dozier-Holland. Together, they came up with a song and production that owed more to Phil Spector than Motown. "Too Hurt To Cry, Too Much In Love To Say Goodbye" was so unlike anything Motown had ever done and way removed from the Marvelettes, so it was issued as by the Darnells. Despite double-tracking Gladys Horton's vocals, the "mystery" Darnells were recognised by fans as the Marvelettes. Motown got letters and the marketing of another girl group called the Darnells was dropped. The sad thing is that the Darnells' number, issued just two weeks after "As Long As I Know He's Mine", proved an unjustified flop.

The ties between the Marvelettes and the Miracles were cemented when Wanda Young married Miracle, Bobby Rogers. Whether or not this was why Smokey Robinson decided that his compositions for the girls were more suited to the voice of Wanda than Gladys will never be certain but it was Wanda that fronted "You're My Remedy". Nevertheless Gladys was back on lead for the Holland-Whitfield song "Too Many Fish In The Sea", a number chosen by the girls in preference to "Where Did Our Love Go" which they had also been offered but decided was too plain.

A further reduction took place early in 1965 when Georgeanna Tillman left to marry Billy Gordon of the Contours. (She sadly died of lupus in 1980.) Again the girls chose not to look for a replacement but to continue as a trio. Wanda was now very much lead singer and the hits become more consistent: "I'll Keep Holding On" and "Danger Heartbreak Dead Ahead", both penned by Mickey Stevenson and Ivy Jo Hunter plus, on "Danger...", Clarence Paul, and a trio from Smokey: "Don't Mess With Bill", "You're The One" and "The Hunter Gets Captured By The Game". That last number, which climbed right to #2 on the r&b chart and has now been recorded by numerous artists, nearly got shelved. Motown's "powers that be" thought it a little "too jazzy," certainly for the Marvelettes. Smokey disagreed and fought hard for its release. (Whilst he may have been vindicated, a remake of the Ruby & the Romantics' Van McCoy-penned hit from three years earlier, "When You're Young And In Love", was chosen as the follow-up.)

Though the hits continued – notably "My Baby Must Be A Magician", for which Temptation Melvin Franklin was brought in for a deep-voiced introduction – Gladys Horton's domestic life was causing problems and she decided to quit. (Her husband had been a trumpeter with the Joe Tex band and resented her success. She saw leaving the group as a way of maintaining the marriage but it was not to be and she ended up having to raise her three sons, one handicapped, as a single mother.) Her replacement Ann Bogan, stayed with the group from late 1968 through 1969 before moving on to become a member of Love, Peace & Happiness as part of the New Birth "conglomeration". Katherine decided to call it a day at that point but Wanda still wanted to be a singer. Smokey Robinson worked on Wanda's [first] solo project but Motown decided to release the resultant LP as "The Return of The Marvelettes", the sleeve featuring three women on horseback with only Wanda's face out of shadow. Doubtless this misjudged sop to Wanda's talents left her rather disillusioned and she decided to pursue no further recording at that time.

By the mid-1980's, with children grown up, Gladys Horton was anxious to re-form the group and approached Katherine and Wanda with this in mind. Katherine was heavily involved in community work and not anxious to return to performing and Wanda had become somewhat reclusive and not keen on the idea of having to leave her native Detroit. Undaunted, Gladys found Echo Johnson and Jean McClain and it was that line-up who signed with Ian Levine's Motorcity label at the outset of his 1989 Motown "reunion" project. (Levine also managed to persuade Wanda out of retirement sufficiently to include her in the group for recording purposes.) However, after the girls' first Motorcity single, "Holding On With Both Hands", Echo Johnson and Jean McCluin were replaced by Jackie and Regina Hollemon.

The Motorcity idea may have gone sour but, to this day, Gladys is undaunted and still sees a future for the Marvelettes, still performs and is writing a book entitled "Letter From The Postman". Katherine too, whilst not yet lured back into performing, often gives live radio interviews on the history of the group, including a recent appearance on Jamaican radio, whilst on the island attending a golf tournament hosted by Johnny Bristol.

Last year, the Marvelettes received a Pioneer Award from the Rhythm & Blues Foundation and Frances Bough, the President of the SMV [Supremes, Marvelettes, Vandellas] fan club – enthusiastically supported by the club's Larry Cotton – is currently campaigning frantically to have the group inducted to The Rock & Roll Hall of Fame. This is not just a worthy campaign but an essential one which should be supported. There are strong indications of ultimate success – though not this year – but testimonials and letters of advocacy are required by the nominating committee. The President of The Rock & Roll Hall Of Fame is Seymour Stein, who is also President of Elektra Entertainment Group. His address is 75 Rockerfeller Plaza, New York, NY 10019, so you know where to write!

David Cole would like to acknowledge Larry Cotton for inspiring this feature and checking the facts, also Fred Bronson, whose liner notes to the Marvelettes' double-cd Deliver-The Singles 1961-1971 *(Motown 37463-6259-2) were invaluable.*

In The Basement magazine editor's David Cole's
Sixties Motown Top Twenty

DC's criteria... Only one song per act – Must have been released on 45 – Must have been issued prior to 31/12/69

"Oh Little Boy (What Did You Do To Me)" – Mary Wells	Motown 1056
"Baby I'm For Real" – The Originals	Soul 35066
"Love Me All The Way" – Kim Weston	Tamla 54076
"If Your Mother Only Knew" – The Miracles	Tamla 54069
"Together Till The End of Time" – Brenda Holloway	Tamla 54125
"My Smile is Just A Frown (Turned Upside Down)" – Carolyn Crawford	
	Motown 1064
"The Touch of Time" – Barbara McNair	Motown 1087
"Never Say No To Your Baby" – Hit Pack	Soul 35010
"As Long As There is L-O-V-E, Love" – Jimmy Ruffin	Soul 35016
"I Wouldn't Change The Man He Is" – Blinky	Motown 1134
"Does Your Mama Know About Me" – Bobby Taylor and the Vancouvers	
	Gordy 7Q69
"I Want To Go Back There Again" – Chris Clark	VIP 25041
"Envious" – Linda Grainer	Motown 1037
"I Got A Feeling" – Barbara Randolph	Soul 35038
"Locking Up My Heart" – The Marvelettes	Tamla 54077
"If Cleopatra Took A Chance" – Eddie Holland	Motown 1030
"Greetings (This is Uncle Sam)" – The Monitors	VIP 25032
"You Love Is Wonderful" – Hattie Littles	Gordy 7007
"Since I Lost My Baby" – The Temptations	Gordy 7043
"My Baby Loves Me" – Martha and the Vandellas	Gordy 7048

23

Brenda Holloway On The Rebound
by David Cole

When Mary Wells left Motown, it was thought for awhile that Brenda Holloway was going to be the star to replace her. However, certain things militated against this, with her being based in Los Angeles foremost. She was not at the hub of the organisation at the right time, and whilst she recorded some great soulful sounds in LA, often with Frank Wilson, she never hit the outright commerciality to break her as a big star on a national or international basis. It is also interesting to remember that, by the time she started with Motown in 1964, she was already an experienced session singer with her sister Patrice around the Californian independent labels. Her motivation to be sucked into the Detroit-based machine may well have been less than others. This article is also from In The Basement.*

Brenda Holloway was born on 21 June 1946 in Atascadero, a small town on the southern edge of the Santa Lucia mountain range, roughly mid-way between the Californian cities of San Francisco and Los Angeles. One of three children, her younger sister is singer/songwriter, Patrice Holloway. Raised by their mother, the family unit moved to the Watts district of Los Angeles when she was two years old and there Brenda began to utilise her obvious musical talents. Encouraged by her mother and influenced by her Spanish grandfather, she took violin and cello lessons, becoming proficient in both instruments and sparking off an ambition to become a concert violinist. At the same time, her vocalising was also getting her noticed, thanks to a lady who lived across the street and who urged her to sing in the local church. Through this, she met the man who would later become Motown's West Coast representative, Hal Davis, who, together with partner, Marc Gordon – who would later marry 5th Dimension's Florence LaRue – was an aspiring record producer. (He had also cut records of his own, including "Read The Book of Love" released on Del-Fi in 1960.)

As a result, Brenda began singing backgrounds for Hal and Marc's productions and, aged fifteen, she cut her own first solo single, the Jesse James composed "Hey Fool", flipped by "Echo", a song penned by Brenda, sister Patrice and one Ken Harris. Leased to the Hollywood-based Donna label, it was issued early in 1962. Two further singles on Donna appeared that same year, "Game of Love" and "I'll Give My Life". Donna also released a single in 1962 by the Wattesians – "I'll Find Myself A Guy" – a group comprising Brenda, plus other session singers at the time.

A year later, duetting with Hal Davis, Brenda Holloway recorded "It's You" for another local label, Minasa, issued as Hal & Brenda and which was also released on Snap with the same (6714) catalogue number. This was rapidly followed by another duet, "I Get A Feeling" for In-Sound, where the place of Hal Davis was taken by Gloria Jones, and the names on the label became "Bonnie & Clyde". The In-Sound label was distributed by the larger Era records, who quickly reissued the single under their own imprint, in turn renaming Bonnie & Clyde as the Soul Mates and flipping the disc to make "I Want A Boyfriend (Girlfriend)" the A-Side. Additionally, Brenda featured as part of another duet, this time with Jess Harris for the Brevit label and a coupling of the Frank Robinson-penned "Gonna Make You Mine" with Brenda and Patrice's "I Never Knew You Looked So Good Until I Quit You". Both sides were produced by Hal David.

Ask Brenda to name her idols of all time and top of the list will be Mary Wells, alongside the influences of jazz stylists, Morgana King and Sarah Vaughan. She would sing along to all Mary's hits and dream of being a Motown star. Learning of a dee-jay convention taking place in Los Angeles early 1964 and encouraged by Hal Davis, she saw her main chance to fulfil that dream. Wearing an outfit dedicated to be both figure-hugging and ooze stardom, she gatecrashed the event and, with the inevitable playing of a Mary Wells' record, Brenda got her chance to sing along and duly impressed her main-aim convention attendee, Berry Gordy Jr. By the end of the day and having secured her mother's approval, she had her Motown recording contract.

From the start, it would be clear Brenda Holloway would not be a conventional Motown artist. As the first signee to be based on the West Coast, she was not immediately steeped in the indoctrination of the "Motown makeover" department. Her mother had taught her the arts of choosing the right clothes, grooming and deportment (although she has subsequently confessed she still had a lot to learn at the time, particularly about stage presence). Additionally, her initial recordings were cut in Los Angeles, with Hal Davis and Marc Gordon still at the production helm. Thus, the first item offered up to Gordy was far removed from the expected pop/soul/dance sounds of Detroit's Motown studios, being a sophisticated, intense beat-ballad penned by Ed Cobb, "Every Little Bit Hurts", with Brenda's vocals showing a maturity way beyond her seventeen years, doubtless due to what Brenda has described as "something of a sad childhood." Gordy hesitated at putting out a ballad on a debut artist but, for once, he allowed himself to be overruled and the judgement of others proved to be correct. The song took off immediately, hitting #13 on the *Billboard* pop charts – the magazine published no R&B listings at the time – and peaking at #3 on the *Cashbox* r&b chart. Additionally, the success led Era to dig out "I Ain't Gonna Take You Back", which they issued as by Brenda Holloway & the Carrolls on their Catch subsidiary.

Further West Coast recordings followed; an album on the strength of the hit and an even more intense second single, again from the pen of Ed Cobb, "I'll Always Love You". (Instructions that promotion should be concentrated principally on the latest Supremes' effort, resulted in it being less commercially successful than it deserved.) Furthermore, Brenda got the chance to step into the shoes of her idol. Mary Wells had left Motown and her intended follow up to "My Guy", "When I'm Gone", had been canned. Smokey Robinson's song was deemed too good to be thrown away and the powers-that-be decided it would be right for Brenda. So, in January 1965, she made her first trip to Motown's Detroit Studies for the recording. A practical joke, intended by Berry Gordy to be a "welcome" for Brenda into the Motown family, involved her being buried in the snow but the joke backfired, Brenda was not amused and thenceforth was perceived as being somewhat aloof. (From Brenda's point of view, her immaculate grooming was being sacrificed by a childish jape.)

If that was a personal low-spot, the same year also saw a high-spot. At the instigation of her friend, Jackie DeShannon she became the only female vocalist to accompany the Beatles on their tour of North America, appearing to acclaim in New York (Shea Stadium), Toronto, Atlanta, Houston, Chicago, Minneapolis, Portland, San Diego, Los Angeles (Hollywood Bowl) and San Francisco. This led to her being in demand for numerous television and nightclub appearances and, later, being the ideal artist to record a promotional single, encouraging children not to neglect their studies, "Play It Cool (Stay In School)". Nevertheless, Brenda began to have the feeling she was not being afforded much more than cursory attention by Motown. While others had regular producers in the studios, Brenda found herself working with Smokey Robinson, Berry Gordy, Hal Davis, Marc Gordon, Frank Wilson, Mickey Stevenson and Hank Cosby, to name but a few, all in the space of a year. Many of her songs were left to gather dust and one in particular, Smokey Robinson's "Till Johnny Comes", a favourite of Brenda's, was pulled at the last minute after having been given a catalogue number and release date. Three months later, a rip-roaring "Just Look What You've Been Done", penned by Frank Wilson and R. Dean Taylor and produced by Wilson, took Brenda to #21 R&B and #69 Pop but she remained disillusioned.

Her stage act was getting very sexy. "My skin couldn't breathe unless it was exposed," she was on record as saying. "My costumes were made for sex appeal. I was influenced by Tina Turner." Smokey Robinson reportedly told her to tone her act down and Berry Gordy, in collaboration with Frank Wilson, did the same for a song she and sister Patrice had written, "You've Made Me So Very Happy". Written as a rock number with Tina Turner in mind, whilst it could be said to have been sanitised by the Gordy/Wilson input, it is hard to imagine it would have been more successful for Brenda [#40 r&b, #39 pop] had it been given a "Tina treatment". That said, two years later its rock undercurrents were seized on by Blood, Sweat and Tears, as David Clayton-Thomas' blue-eyed soul vocals took the song to #2 pop and #46 r&b and a Grammy nomination for the song-writing team.

"Just Look What You've Done" and "You've Made Me So Very Happy" were the only two singles issued on Brenda in 1967, despite their chart successes. The 1964 album, *Every Little Bit Hurts*, had been her only LP release. Further albums, *Hurtin' And Cryin'*, mooted for November 1965 issue and *Brenda Holloway* – possibly a "live" set – sched-uled for a year later, were shelved. Songs promised to her would be snapped-up by the likes of Gladys Knight; there was an on-going personality clash with Diana Ross and the decline in health of her friend, Tammi Terrell, affected her deeply. "I will always love Motown and you," a well-balanced, lengthy letter of protest about her situation within the Company, which she had written to Berry Gordy shortly after the release of "You've Made Me So Very Happy", went unheeded and in the latter part of 1968, in the middle of a Smokey Robinson-fronted Detroit recording session, her patience snapped. She returned to the West Coast to sit out her contract, leaving more than fifty documented recordings to gather dust in Motown's vaults. (One such, "Reconsider", a.k.a. "Think it Over (Before You Break My Heart)" – a driving pounder on the lines of Ashford & Simpson's "Starting The Hurt All Over Again" – leaked out in the U.K. and has subse-quently become such a popular tune that Brenda has to include it in her act for British audiences.)

Smokey Robinson attempted to get Brenda back but seemingly, Berry Gordy saw nothing wrong with his treatment of Brenda and ignored her departure. However, when contract renewal time came up in 1969, he tried to get her to re-sign but she refused. As a result, Motown's publicity machine suggested Brenda had quit the secular world to devote her time to the church but this, at that time, was more of a prophetic statement than the actual truth.

(By way of an aside, in the summer of 1968, a single appeared on the Liberty label by one Brendetta Davis, entitled "I Can't Make it Without Him". Co-penned and produced by Barry White, this heavily-orchestrated beat-ballad is fronted by a lady with appar-ently very similar vocal inflections to Brenda Holloway and many sources have been convinced it is the lady herself. However, the flip, a version of "Until You Were Gone", sounds far less like her. Brenda has recently confirmed she and Brendetta Davis are definitely not one and the same, although admitted that another song from around the same time, "Under Construction", sitting in the Bronco/Mustang labels' vaults, is indeed her recording)

In 1969, Brenda Holloway became the first ex-Motowner to take court action against the Company over alleged mis-appropriation of funds, in particular charging underpay-ment of royalties. The courts found in her favour. The same year, she married preacher Alfred Davis and began the dedication to the church which Gordy's press statements had ironically "prophesied". However, her secular recording activities were not put on ice until after sessions in 1972 with Eddie and Brian Holland's Music Merchant label, which she bowed in with the first catalogue number (1001) although in actuality, not the label's earliest release. The single boasted an A-side not too far removed from a typical UK entry to the Eurovision Song Contest, "Let Love Grow", with a much better "Some Quiet Place (To Rest My Mind)" on the flip. Although she cut further sides for the Hollands, they were not released, probably because internal and external pressures were causing a conflict between her increasingly religious background and the secular recording work, resulting in her getting the reputation of "being difficult". Ultimately, the church won and Brenda settled down – perhaps somewhat resignedly – to the life of a preacher's wife and, in time, raising their four daughters, Beoir, Unita, Christy and Dontese. (She is now a grandmother five times over.)

1980 saw a return on wax by way of the album, *Brand New*, recorded for the gospel-orientated Birthright label, based in Pasadena, California. Described by Brenda as [being] "Thrown together" and "the worst mistake in my career" – something that would doubtless be hotly-disputed by her many fans – the album was partly arranged and produced by Gil Askey, who had done his own fair share of work at Motown. Musical support featured, among others, Keni Burke and Greg Poree, while vocal support included contributions from sister, Patrice, and former Smokey Robinson backing singer Ivory Hudson. Alongside the directly religious songs, the album includes versions of "You'll Never Walk Alone" and, at Brenda's insistence, "You Make Me Feel Brand New", slightly revised to fit the requisite religious message.

Eventually freed of an unhappy eighteen year-long marriage, Brenda began to blossom again. She emerged from self-imposed retirement at the end of the eighties and became an early signing to Ian Levine's s UK-based Nightmare/Motorcity labels, as part of his (ex-) Motown reunion project. Her outings included "On The Rebound", a duet with Jimmy Ruffin, a critically-acclaimed "Give Me A Little Inspiration" and a re-vamp of "You've Made Me So Very Happy", which was reworked to imply the "You" in question is Jesus Christ. Unlike some other signings, Brenda has nothing but good words for Levine and his project and perhaps it provided the impetus needed to set the set the lady back on the road of regular performing. As a result, Brenda has been doing numerous radio interviews and personal appearances to get her name back into the spotlight, and has been touring the USA with the likes of Brenton Wood and Al Wilson – her act usually includes a tribute to Mary Wells – and also with the Ronnie Milsap Review. In addition, she made highly-acclaimed UK visits in 1997 and 1998 alongside Kim Weston.

As well as recording with the Ronnie Milsap Review, she has been back in the studio for her own sessions with Billy Preston producing. Unfortunately, these have been curtailed by Preston's imprisonment on drug charges but, hopefully, they can be picked up on elsewhere. The name of Brenda Holloway has been absent from record labels' new product for far too long.

24

The Velvelettes: Motown's Earthy Soulful Girl Group Sound
by Steve Towne and Max Oates

The Velvelettes are another Motown girl group that, despite having put out some of the label's best remembered songs, never got their due credit. Possibly through personnel changes and the lack of a distinctly recognisable lead voice, The Velvelettes somehow missed the boat. They were allowed several great singles, but never rated an album issue in the sixties. This has been partially rectified by an excellent retrospective album from Motown in the late nineties which gives the group some late but deserved public recognition from the company. This article was first published in Goldmine *in September 1986.*

In 1964, Motown president Berry Gordy had one of those typical promotions that record companies in those days often tried out on the public. He staged a "Battle of the Stars" between two of his then lesser-known groups – the Velvelettes and the Supremes – at the old Graystone Ballroom in Detroit. The winner would be determined by audience response. The winner? Well, it wasn't the Supremes.

Cal Gill, who was the Velvelettes' superb forceful lead, explained to Maury Ewalt of the *Detroit Free Press* why her group won: "We had a more earthy soulful sound that appealed to the Detroit audience." The irony is that the Supremes would go on to become one of the biggest acts of the '60s while the Velvelettes are recalled today as an obscure Motown act best known for three classic recordings, "Needle In A Haystack" (1964), "He Was Really Saying Something" (1964), and "These Things Will Keep Me Loving You" (1968).

The roots of the Velvelettes began in Flint, Mich., in the late '50s when cousins Bertha and Norma Barbee formed a singing group called the Barbees. Bertha Barbee McNeal recalls:

"Norma and I are first cousins. Our dads are brothers. We have an uncle named Simon Barbee, who would sing at different places in Flint – teas, churches etc. When Norma and I were teenagers, probably I was about 15 and Norma was much younger, maybe 13, he wanted some background singers to travel with him around Flint and sing. So Norma and I and another cousin named Joyce would sing background harmony with our uncle around Flint. We did this for about two or three years. After a while, we became known in Flint. We even got to a point where we were giving our own shows."

Norma Barbee Fairhurst picks up the story:

"We recorded a song at this time, it must have been around 1957, by the name of "Que Pasa?" Mickey Stevenson wrote that song. He was producer at that time. We recorded the song in Bill Lamb's basement." Bertha said, "He was a very famous disc jockey in Detroit. He was so kind. It was a very small type of place but it was very exciting".

The record, "Que Pasa?" backed with "The Wind" by the Barbees, appeared on the Stepp label briefly and sank into obscurity, just as hundreds of thousands of small productions before and since. "The Wind" is not the same song as recorded by the Diablos.

The Barbees began to fade as the girls continued their education. Bertha recalls:

"I left Flint, Mich., and transferred to Western Michigan State University, so at this time the Barbees sort of petered out. One evening I was sitting at the piano in the Student Center and I was playing some of our old Barbee songs. Mildred Gill and about four or five other gals were around the piano sort of liking the songs, and somebody said, Hey, why don't we start a group."

Mildred Gill Arbor picks up the story:

"To start with, we did a little sock hop on the campus. We got together with a bunch of AKA (Alpha Kappa Alpha) members, about 12 of us, and it was like a little choir. But that was just for fun. Later I told Bertha my sister sings and there's another little girl that's a friend of my sister's and she sings too. I said that we had sung at church and what have you. Then Bertha tells me she's got a cousin who sings, so she calls her cousin Norma and one day we all get together and rehearsed for a little party here at Western. We sang in the Student Center. There were five of us to start with and we sang in five-part harmony and it was really something."

Mildred's sister Caldin recalls:

"There were the five of us, myself, Caldin (or Carol) Gill, Bertha Barbee, Mildred Gill, Norma Barbee, and Betty Kelly, who later joined Martha and the Vandellas. First we needed a name. We felt confident that we had a smooth harmony blend so we thought of the description velvet. And then we just extended it to Velvelettes."

Not really looking for a record label, they nonetheless wound up on one of the hottest – Motown. Bertha remembers:

"Berry Gordy's nephew, Bob Bullock, went to Western and heard us singing at one of the functions. Alpha fraternity had a talent show and we won first prize and Bob Bullock heard us and encouraged us to go down to Motown. Only he called Motown ahead and cleared the way."

Another twist of fate helped. "They had turned us down," says Caldin. "The audition was on a Saturday and this gal who was a receptionist said, 'I'm sorry, but we don't have auditions on Saturdays and you girls can't go in.' We pleaded, we came all the way from Kalamazoo and she acted like she never heard of Kalamazoo. She said, 'Kalama-whoo?' So we turned around, we had tears in our eyes, this is the truth, and we were about ready to go out the door. Just then the recording studio door opens and just like out of the heavens, out walks Mickey Stevenson. He remembers Norma and myself and says, "Hi, Norma, Bertha, what are you doing here?""

The Velvelettes' first record was on a small Motown subsidiary, I.P.G. Records, in 1963. "There He Goes" backed with "That's The Reason Why" made little noise either locally or nationally, but Bertha has fond memories:

"I will always remember my cousin Norma coming over to the house when we were in the Barbees and saying, 'Bertha, I've just written a song.' She didn't call it "There He Goes" but she sung the melody and she had all the words, so she really should have gotten credit. It really wasn't a job to us, it was big fun and they knew it. They took advantage of us, the writers and producers."

Norma continues: "They never really talked to us about that. They just took it. We just thought it was supposed to be done that way. We went into the studio with a whole bunch of songs we had created that were taken away from us."

Caldin picks up the thought:

"But they were slick; we were used at that time. The writers were young, ambitious people, so if they saw an opportunity, they would capitalize on it."

Though "There He Goes" never really took off, the Velvelettes kept busy. Caldin remembers:

"We had done some recording for Motown, but they didn't want to interfere too much and didn't want to pressure us, mainly because I was still in high school. We did background on Stevie Wonder's 'Fingertips.' Stevie was very supportive. They paid us $15 for an hours work. We were so impressed by this little boy. When we would go to Motown, he'd just be sitting out front playing his harmonica. He was 13 or maybe even younger than that, and we were just in the studio one day and they needed somebody to do background, so we did it."

In 1964 the Velvelettes lost Betty Kelly. Caldin recalls:

"Betty Kelly had a chance to join Martha and the Vandellas. I never will forget, she called me on the phone. We had done some recording at Motown, and she called me and said that she had an opportunity to sing with the Vandellas because one of the members was going to leave and she had the same physical appearance and wore the same size clothes. So I just encouraged her to go ahead, to go for it, because it was the opportunity of a lifetime for her." (Kelly stayed with the Vandellas until 1967, when she left to pursue a solo career.)

Also in 1964 the Velvelettes came out with their second release, "Needle In A Haystack," on Motown's newly formed V.I.P. label. The girls were down to Cal Gill, Bertha Barbee, and Norma Barbee, because Mildred Barbee was expecting a child and couldn't attend the session. "Haystack" became their biggest hit, reaching No. 45 on Billboard's Pop Hot 100 chart in late 1964.

Bertha remembers:

"That took lots of practice. We must have heard that song a million times."

Norma recalls:

"We helped with the background, but Norman Whitfield wrote "Needle In A Haystack". It wasn't as rhythm 'n' bluesy as I think that I personally wanted to sing. But probably luckily so, because that really had a cross-over audience. Both white and black liked it."

About "Needle In A Haystack," Bertha remembers:

"I thought we did about 17 takes on 'Needles.' Mildred thought it was about 13. I know it was in the teens. We found out how much it was costing us against our royalties, about $4,000 dollars per dub that we did. It was a very large sum of money, and it was put on our account as a debt. Once we realized that, you should have seen how quickly we learned our tunes. *(laughs)*.

"Needle in A Haystack" has a knocked out slap-dance rhythm similar to the Supremes of late 1954, but in defense of the sound, it is sung with much more of an R&B sound than the Supremes. Caldin recalls:

"I remember Berry Gordy making a statement at that time, up in the room where they did the playback. He said, "The Motown sound is bottom. You know, we have to feel the music in our feet, when we're dancin'."" He wouldn't hesitate to let a writer know that that's what our sound was. And then the musicians. One of the baddest bass players at that time was James Jamerson. Earl Van Dyke was the famous keyboard player and Paul Riser was the trombonist. And Benny Bongo, he was on a lot of Marvin Gaye tunes. A lot of the artists had spiritual backgrounds. A lot of them started in the churches."

Mildred adds:

"I think that great sound came from the structure of the building. It was a big mansion-like house of West Grand Boulevard. The basement was where the recording studio was set up. Norman Whitfield and all the writers at Motown were assigned a room and he would be in there creating. He'd play these simple melodies and we would pick up on the right away. Once he would establish a story, then he would give us a sheet of paper with the lyrics on it. Sometimes, however, those lyrics were not complete, so we had to fill in. So we did have significant input to the songs we recorded. Then we would all work together on the backgrounds. We would put our ideas together. I really believe that's why Motown was impressed with us. We were full of talent. We were going to college, were writing, and we all played piano."

With the success of "Needle" the Velvelettes hit the road. Mildred remembers:

"We went out and promoted 'Needle In A Haystack.' I believe the promotion period was about six months, but between the promotion, we were back in the studio recording new songs."

Caldin adds:

"Going on the road brought our attention to Maxine Powell. She was a charm teacher at Motown. She along with Motown choreographer "Cholly" Atkins was the reason artists got special attention on the road. Maxine Powell taught us how to come up on stage, present ourselves, and depart in a very lady-like fashion. She told us this profession is 'one third glamour and two thirds work'."

Bertha remembers Ms. Powell:

"She was our chaperone. Motown made sure all the girl groups had a chaperone on the road. She would wake us up in the morning, put on our makeup, do our nails, get our clothes pressed, take us out to eat – she did literally everything. It was kinda' nice."

Caldin remembers:

"Diana Ross's mother was our chaperone on the Dick Clark tour. She also was a wonderful lady and did a great job." (Motown experts may recall this was the tour in which the Supremes started out at the bottom with the Velvelettes and before it was over were on the top of the bill with the No. 1 record in the country, "Where Did Our Love Go?")

Sometimes the road can take its toll, but in the case of the Velvelettes, the road became an education, Bertha says:

"We went on the Dick Clark tour and that was a very big experience. And then we went to the Apollo Theater in New York and Flip Wilson emceed the show. And this was before he had ever been heard of on T.V. We really didn't know the significance of the Apollo Theater at the time, until we got there. It was quite a thrill."

Motown has been compared many times to a tight-knit family. This feeling was extended to the Velvelettes. Bertha says:

"Berry Gordy would call meetings of all the artists and would instil that this was a family. He would make you feel very non-competitive with the other groups."

Mildred says:

"We used to go down to St Antoine and Farnsworth and Marvin Gaye would be down there and I had two small children and we would be rehearsing and doing choreography and he would be busy changing my daughter's diapers and feeding them milk. I had no babysitter, so I would have to take my kids to the studio with me."

Adds Norma:

"Marvin was very supportive. He'd just motivate us. He and his wife lived upstairs in the building with Berry Gordy's father and mother and we went up there to visit a few times and Marvin was always a very nice, charming gentleman."

The Velvelettes next record and probably their best was "He Was Really Sayin' Something". The group at this time consisted of the Gill sisters and the Barbee cousins. The tune entered the *Billboard* Hot 100 chart on Jan. 30, 1965, and died at No. 64. The record was a stronger soul hit because it lasted two months and went as high as 21 on *Billboard*'s soul chart. The record cooked. From the opening piano and bari sax to the do-wah-dah-wah-dah's, this is one of Motown's toughest dance tracks. Simple and direct.

Bertha recalls:

"'He Was Really Sayin Something,' I love it. I think the beat was more R&B, it was more funky. You could really dance off it. It told a story and it was fun to sing."

"Norman Whitfield," says Mildred, "the writer of the tune, his basic foundation of the tune was so simple, that some of your more complicated writers like Holland, Dozier, Holland would make fun of his tunes. But he wouldn't let that frustrate him. The first time he played, 'Really Sayin' Something' I asked him what was the theme of the song and he said, 'Well you know, you were walking down the street and this guy starts following you and he starts rappin' to you, and you really like what he's sayin'. So he was kinda really sayin' something, you know.' And I said, 'wow, I love it.'"

By 1965 Caldin was the only original Velvelette left. "I was the last one to get married," she recalls. "I was the youngest. Late in our career I had to get two other girls because we had another request to go on a Dick Clark tour. Motown would not let Dick Clark know that the Velvelettes had split up. So the Velvelettes kept going and made more records, but basically we did a lot of road shows. One of the new girls was Sandra

Tilley, who was from Cleveland, Ohio. Basically she was a dedicated Motown fan. She was dating Duke Fakir of the Four Tops, and he told her there was an opening in the Velvelettes. Sandra came up to Detroit and auditioned. She was a very good singer."

Sandra appeared with Cal and another new member, Annette McMillan on the group's next release, "Lonely Lonely Girl Am I" backed with "I'm The Exception To The Rule". Neither side is particularly memorable so it is not surprising that neither charted when released in May 1965. Two more sides by the Gill-Tilley-McMillan Velvelettes were released in late 1965, "Since You've Been Loving Me" backed with "A Bird In The Hand Is Worth Two In The Bush". But Motown was saddling the group with smooth Supremes sound-alikes; it was obvious that the Velvelettes deserved punchier material.

In 1966, the trio got a moderate hit on Motown's Soul label with "These Things Will Keep Me Loving You," which charted for three weeks on *Billboard*'s soul survey in October. The recording dated back to when the Gill sisters and the Barbee cousins were the Velvelettes, but Motown added Sandra Tilley's and Annette McMillan's vocals to the mix. The song, basically produced and written by Harvey Fuqua and Johnny Bristol, was another Supremes style of song that wasn't compatible to the distinctive strengths of the Velvelettes.

Caldin Gill kept the Velvelettes going for three more years, despite the fact that the group had no more recordings out to keep their name in the picture. In 1969 Cal got married to Richard Street, who was a long time Motown artist, having sung with a Temptation predecessor group, the Distants, and having sung with the Monitors. Later he would join the Temptations. He put pressure on Cal to disband the group, saying that "there can only be one star in this household and that is me." The Velvelettes thus passed into history, but they left a bold mark on the story of Motown and '60s soul music.

Unlike other singers who often find themselves short on skills once their singing careers are over, the Velvelettes always took their educations seriously. Today Mildred Gill Arbor is a registered nurse working in the operating room of McLaren Hospital and resides in Flint, Mich. Bertha Barbee McNeal is a junior high school teacher in Kalamazoo instructing music to seventh and eight graders. Norma Barbee Fairhurst is currently employed by television station WGRT, of Flint, in the accounting department. Caldin Gill Street currently is employed by the Upjohn Company of Kalamazoo, working in Employee Development. Betty Kelly works for a bank on the West Coast. Annette McMillian lives in Detroit. Sandra Tilley after leaving the Velvelettes sang in Martha Reeves and the Vandellas. In 1982 she died of a brain aneurism in a Las Vegas club.

In early 1984, the Gill sisters and the Barbee cousins reunited to form a new Velvelettes, and in November of that year they returned to Detroit's famed Fox Theater on the Motown Motortown revival show. The shared the bill with Martha Reeves, Junior Walker, Eddie Kendricks, Kim Weston, and Mary Wells and reportedly it was some show. The group today makes occasional weekend appearances in the Detroit area and Canada.

25

Martha Reeves: An Interview
by Bill Randle

When Martha's fascinating autobiography Dancing In The Street *was published (sadly to date in the US only), I was delighted to find myself pictured behind her in a shot taken at a* Ready Steady Go! *rehearsal. It brought back a wealth of memories of a woman who represents the early spirit of Motown to me. Martha had all the determination, single mindedness and talent that imbued the company and brought it the success it deserved. At the same time, she was always delightful to fans and she, Betty Kelly and Ros Ashford were tremendous fun to be around.*

This 1991 radio interview was conducted by Bill Randle, and gives an excellent overview of Martha's views on early Motown, her visits to Britain and her career as a whole.

Bill Randle: With me today is … the beautiful Martha Reeves.
Martha Reeves: Hi Bill.
Bill: It is really nice to see you back in England again, and the tour is going very well…
Martha: It is always a pleasure to come here; it is like coming home.
Bill: Did you ever expect these Motown records to last as long as they have?
Martha: No. I'm really overwhelmed with our careers, when we started out we didn't know what our music would do. We'd just sing because we loved doing it; and to actually perform and have people sing along with us, young people that weren't even born when we recorded the songs, they join in and have such a good time. Our music is truly fun-making, and fun to do.
Bill: It's certainly timeless … When you were with Motown in those early days, did you ever expect the company to become the major force that they did in the music business?
Martha: When I heard Smokey Robinson And The Miracles and The Marvelettes, I wanted to be a part of Motown. I was working at a nightclub, I was Martha LaVelle, and I was doing 'Happy Hour' at The Twenty Grand. William Stevenson came in, and said 'You've got something. Take my card and come to Motown records'. Well I showed up the next day at nine o'clock, when all the secretaries showed up. Unfortunately there was no A & R secretary. Just fourteen guys: Smokey Robinson, Stevie Wonder, Holland, Dozier, Holland. A lot of guys that were actually just writing songs, and not really keeping records. I was asked what I was doing there by William Stevenson. I said I came for the audition. He said, 'You were meant to take my card and call to make an appointment'. He said, 'I'll tell you what, answer the phone, I'll be right back'. So no-one ever knew that I was a singer in the beginning, because I started answering the phone. And I'd say, 'Yes A & R department, William Stevenson's office'. And they'd say, 'Who are you?' Because it was new to them that the A & R department had a secretary. And I was able to meet a lot of musicians, like James Jamerson, Benny Benjamin, Earl Van Dyke, Jo Hunter, to name a few. And I think that's why we got some of the best tracks from Motown because I got those guys their cheques.
Bill: The material you got from Holland, Dozier, Holland was absolutely superb and the run of hits, once they started with 'Come And Get These Memories', never seemed to stop, for almost ten years …
Martha: …Holland, Dozier, Holland were all singers. Eddie Holland had 'Jamie' out, which went to number one. Brian Holland had a record out, but it wasn't a seller at all

and Lamont Dozier had a record out, 'What Goes up Must Come Down'. And they decided that they didn't want to be artists, cause it was kinda hard work, and they were shy guys. They were all good looking too. They make you real nervous, and I'd always ask them to leave the studio, and not to look at me so hard while I'm trying to sing. Our first ballad 'Love (Makes Me Do Foolish Things)' was one where I actually asked them to *leave* the studio. Leave the picture window, and let me sing.

Bill: You were also used exclusively by Marvin Gaye as backing vocalist, and helped launch his career.

Martha: Well, that's about being at the right place at the right time. The Andantes, Jackie, Louvain and Marlene, were the regular back-up singers. One of my jobs was to call up people for sessions. I remember calling up Marvin Gaye a lot for drumming sessions. At first I didn't know he was a singer. He was specially attractive; but he hid his beauty, with a hat over his eyes, a pipe in his mouth and some dark glasses. He was real quiet. But I knew he was an excellent drummer. So when Benny Benjamin, the regular drummer, wasn't available I'd call Marvin Gaye. And Mickey, my boss William Stevenson said one time, 'Martha, I'm gonna have a session tonight, call The Andantes'. Well you didn't go back to Mickey and say, 'I can't find The Andantes'. They were in Chicago recording for the CHESS label, and I knew that Rosalyn, Annette and I had been with The Del-phis and recorded 'Won't You Let Me Know' with J. J. Barnes, and our answer to him 'I'll Let You Know'; it didn't really sell, just local in Detroit and Chicago. I called Annette, at the hospital where she still works. And I called Rosalyn, from Michigan Bell where she is now a computer specialist, and asked them if they would come on down and give me a hand, singing back-up. When I told them it was gonna be just five dollars for their work, they were happy because any money to add to your regular nine to five salary worked. Before Motown I was working at the cleaners, hoping we could get a break, and singing in the nightclubs at the weekends. We recorded 'Stubborn Kind of Fellow', 'Hitch Hike', 'Pride And Joy' and a whole Marvin Gaye album. We are featured on the back of his *Stubborn Kind of Fellow* album. You'll notice my voice kinda sticks out. I love Marvin so, I sung my best for him. I had it reputed on one of the albums that I was trying to steal his glory; but nobody could steal Marvin Gaye's glory. I think it was just something to make the reader take note. But I love Marvin so much, although I was never a personal friend of his. I always admired him from afar, and he knew he had a friend in me. I didn't think we were ever compensated monetary for singing behind him. We just did it because we loved him so ...

We loved one another, and when the company grew the family sort of spread out. We looked after each other in the first days. I've been asked time and time again if we were ever jealous of maybe The Supremes, The Marvelettes or other acts that excelled over us; but I feel we've got a good place in the business. I feel that we've had a very good share of fans, record sales and Hit Records ... We cheered each other on, and I'm still in awe of the talents of Stevie Wonder, Diana Ross, Mary Wilson, The Four Tops, Temptations; to name just a few.

Bill: I remember speaking to Esther Gordy a couple of years ago, and she said when Berry (Gordy) heard 'Come And Get These Memories', he said 'That's the Motown Sound ...

Martha: Ooh – that's sweet, I didn't know that.

Bill: He said 'That's the sound I've been looking for ...'

Martha: I think it shows off our good harmonies, that Rosalyn, Annette and I had over the years. And I knew that instantly. We didn't go to school together. We're not the same age. We didn't live in the same neighbourhood. I didn't know them. They were the Del-phis, and they had a girl leave, and I replaced her, and I wasn't lead singer. So when I got with them, and we had instant harmony, I knew we had something, so when I called them to Motown, I just knew that Motown would love us...

When I first heard 'Dancing In The Street' it was a Marvin Gaye rendition, he wrote it along with Ivy Hunter and, William Stevenson. When I heard Marvin's version it was in a male key ... I thought it was a good song but not my key. So they said 'O.K. Martha, give it your treatment', and I came up with the melody. I didn't like the song at first, to be honest; but when I put myself into it and made it my own, it became like the *anthem*, and everybody when they hear it gets up and dances. I love the excitement, and the magic of it still works today.

Bill: It came out at a very important time in the States with the racial problems that were happening over there at the time ....

Martha: I had been in Rio De Janeiro, and danced in the street. I'd been to New Orleans, Louisiana, and I'd danced in the street. But after riots it was just awful in America. We were involved in Detroit; left Detroit, went to New Jersey and the riots broke out in New Jersey. We left New Jersey and went to South Carolina... We were mistaken on The Motown Revue for Martin Luther King's movement ... A lot of times we'd pull up places and be met with double barrelled shotgun. 'Get back on that bus!'... They didn't understand that we were there to bring music, so we'd be chased around and shot at.

Everything! When the riots broke out we didn't know what to do ... We felt helpless. We got on the radio, with James Brown, in New Jersey and made announcements to people to go home, and take care of their families. To stop shooting, stop looting the stores. And protect themselves, 'cause it's not a time to steal, shoot and kill one another. 'Dancing In The Street' came out just after that, and it helped people just to calm down...

Bill: Things were happening so fast it must have been difficult to keep up with the changes ...

Martha: Well it was difficult; but we were right in the middle of it ... And because of our music being The Sound of Young America, and being filled with just love ... Nothing to incite riots, nothing to make you feel bad about another person. We identified with a lot of women who had had little disappointments. Like 'In My Lonely Room' helped me a lot. 'Come And Get These Memories' helped a lot of girls in school. I got lots of letters saying, 'Yes, I sent my boyfriend his teddy bear back and I sent him a copy of your record.' It was a young time for me, and a lot of young ladies helped solve some of their heart problems with our music. Then to have wonderful things like 'Ready For Love' and 'Bless You'... You know what makes me feel so good? To hear Dusty Springfield and Tina Turner doing 'A Love Like Yours (Don't Come Knocking Everyday)', 'cause that was special. Brian Holland was singing in the back of The Vandellas, and it just has a wonderful feeling ...

Bill: Motown's move to Los Angeles seemed to leave a lot of people in the lurch in Detroit ... I think you were one of the ones that decided to stay in Detroit ...

Martha: You know – I called Motown, after a few months with no response. I asked to speak to Berry (Gordy), because we'd been very close in the first days, and as the company grew we didn't talk as often as I would have liked... I asked to speak to him, and one of the receptionists finally said 'Don't you know the company has moved to Los Angeles?'. I wasn't aware of it ... I was very disappointed. I had a son, my son is now twenty-one years old so I can kinda mark the time by his age. There I was waiting for another hit record... but missing my communication with Berry Gordy. I had to go on to another label, and I went to MCA. MCA was located in Los Angeles, so I made the move as well. I was out there for twelve years of my son's young life. Thank God, my parents, Ruby and Elijah, took care of my son; but it was a big disappointment to me that Motown moved. But I knew why. The company had grown so large, it was too big for Detroit. They couldn't really service all of us, 'cause we'd all grown to such proportions and Berry had to be the wise man, that he was, and single out maybe his best advantage, which was Diana Ross, and she has certainly proved herself as an artist. Unfortunately we lost Florence Ballard, and Mary Wilson is still standing her own: she's still strong ....

But we had to grow up. Hurry up and grow up, and go on to bigger and better things. I think my MCA album, with Richard Perry, will always be one of my favourites. My first solo effort, 'Wild Night', is now on *Thelma And Louise*, after all those years, it is now a hit. And the music just keeps on going on. It keeps me alive …

Bill: The music you made is absolutely wonderful …

Martha: You know I'm fortunate. My father played the guitar and sang. My mum idolised Billie Holiday. She used to wear camellias in her hair, 'cause she loved Billie Holiday so. She used to sing her songs, and I guess I am the epitome of her dreams … so she encouraged me as a child. She always told me 'Never sing a song unless you mean it from your heart'. And I know I've got some emotions in some of my songs …. I've always wanted to be a jazz singer. In fact Martha LaVelle, who I was before Motown …, wanted to be a jazz singer. But Motown had another rhythm and blues thing going, so I adapted to it, and was very good at it … But my whole desire in my heart is to be as moving and soul-stirring as Billie Holiday, Dinah Washington, Ella Fitzgerald, Sarah Vaughan, Carmen McRae…

Bill: Who were your favourites at Motown?

Martha: Everyone was my favourite. It was like a family truly. The competition came maybe in the '70s, when everybody kinda had to go on their own, and hold their own. If a Motown act was on the show they usually took it over. I've seen The Temptations compete with The Vibrations, The Okays, The Flamingos, to name just a few. I've seen The Supremes compete with The Crystals, The Ronettes, The Shirelles. Whenever a Motown act was on, I loved them all… The Marvelettes, I must say, were the most helpful in our career. You can't find a heart bigger than Gladys Horton.

Bill: Gladys is currently working on a book; tell me about your book.

Martha: Well Bill, I've been writing my book since 1962, and I'm a good secretary. I've kept good notes. There are still a lot of revelations. For instance in 1991, Rosalyn, Annette and myself, all settled our law suits with Motown. It wasn't that they didn't want to pay us; but we had to go through procedures like anyone in business … so in the future I'll be receiving royalties. Well before that settlement I had my mind all confused because we had done good work and I thought we should be compensated. A lot of artists are walking around today saying because of their negotiations, and not knowing show business they didn't get a fair shake. Well you have to spend time. It's protocol … It's a little hardship; but the minute Berry Gordy heard about my law suit – it was six years after I had applied for my royalties, his people who guard his personal life wouldn't let him know I was actually asking – he said, 'Martha, what's happening?'. I said, 'I'd like to have some accounting, 'cause I have grandchildren now'.

I've a two-year-old grandchild, named Lala, Lauren Ashley, and I have a little grandson named Eric Jnr., that, my son has blessed me with. 'And I want to secure their futures.' I figured this is an investment as well. It's pleasure; but it's business too … I have grown up, thank God for that, I'll always be child-minded; but I've grown up. And I had to go through the channels it takes to get to your business. I feel better now, so I can write my book with peace of mind, knowing I'm no longer on the dark side, where I'm going to do something and not get compensated. I feel good about Berry Gordy, 'cause we've sat now for two or three meetings. Hours upon hours reminiscing about the good times. He's writing a book too. A lot of the things about our careers he had forgotten because … look at all the artists he's made. Look at all the millionaires he's made. So I had to get some time for myself. I pushed and shoved past all the secretaries, and the people who stop you from seeing him. Berry's our own, he made us … And after speaking to him, he's still an alright guy. I didn't know we'd be famous. I didn't. I was never the prettiest in my class. I was never the brightest. I might have been the best singer. I might have remembered the poems in English better than anyone else. But I didn't think that I would ever excel. I was captain of the cheering team, a little bit rowdy. I was in all of the clubs at school … I was in the special chorus. I sang the 'Hallelujah' at my graduation, but I never thought I had star quality. I never thought I would be famous. Then all of a sudden I look around and I'm famous. I'm on television. I'm in London. I'm on the BBC. I'm on *Ready, Steady, Go*. And I go 'WOW'. I meet the Beatles. I meet the Rolling Stones. We go on tour with Georgie Fame I meet the beautiful Dusty Springfield, and she brings us to England, and introduces us to Vicki Wickham, who was one of the producers of British T.V… It happened so fast, and I didn't realise what was happening to us. But look how long it has lasted. We've been touring the U.K. since 1964, and I look forward to it every year. It's work of course; but it's like a holiday, and I can look forward to it. If I do right all year, the reward is being able to come to England, and see a lot of my lovely friends and see this wonderful country. Can I take the liberty of saying it's like a second home?

Bill: I'm sure it must be after all, these years, you probably know it as well as we do…

Martha: I've seen some changes here, some wonderful changes here … I feel a real closeness to a lot of our friends here.

26
Kim Weston – A Thrill A Moment
by David Cole

Motown was very keen, even desperate, to find a Mary Wells clone in 1964, and Kim Weston was one singer who got the makeover treatment. She stayed with the company for around four years, during which time she cut some fabulous tracks including her best known duet with Marvin Gaye "It Takes Two". She was pushed out on the gig circuit, including tours to Britain, but with no major record sales resulting. Another singer who recorded mainly in Los Angeles, she apparently was somewhat disdainful of the up-tempo pop tunes from H-D-H and Smokey that were pushed her way, and wanted to work within the soul ballad market.

Of all the female solo artistes to pass through the Motown books, Kim Weston arguably possessed the finest voice in terms of depth, resonance and quality. The torchy, jazz-inflected vocals were often not most suited to the material she was given at the label but she always gave of her best, even if the chart rewards were few.

"Kim" Weston was born Agatha Natalie Weston in the Paradise Valley area of Detroit, on December 20, 1939. As a teenager, despite playing piano and directing the church choir, her main ambition was to be a professional swimmer and, ironically, it was her swimming coach who directed her into singing, suggesting this would improve her breath control. Thus, graduating from high school aged 17, she joined gospel group, the Wright Specials, coached by the Rev. James Cleveland, and immediately gained professional experience performing alongside the likes of the Caravans, Staple Singers and Mighty Clouds of Joy. It was also as a member of the Wright Specials that she made her first foray into the Motown studios, where the group cut two singles issued on the company's Divinity subsidiary in 1962 and 1963: "That's What He Is To Me" c/w "Pilgrim of Sorrow" and "Ninety-Nine And A Half Won't Do" c/w "I Won't Go Back'.

Kim's vocal abilities were singled out by one Johnny Thornton, who was looking for a singer to demo some songs he aimed to present to Motown via his cousins, Eddie and Brian Holland. The Hollands hated the songs but loved the singer and successfully recommended to Berry Gordy that she be signed-up. She was immediately – late 1962 – sent out on the road with the Motown Revue, reportedly being unnerved by the screams of audience response to the stage antics of fellow performers, the Contours. The tour completed, she took the first trip into the Studios to cut the original version of "It Should Have Been Me" (featuring an over-loud Diane Ross among the back-up vocals). The song, written by Norman Whitfield and William "Mickey" Stevenson and produced by Whitfield, flopped but southern-based dee-jays started to play the flip, "Love Me All The Way", a strong torchy ballad penned by Stevenson and Barney Ales and produced by Stevenson. The result was a #24 *Billboard* R&B hit.

The follow-up, "Just Loving You", failed due to poor promotion – at the time all the company's efforts when it come to female soloists were behind Mary Wells – but when Wells began moves to leave the label in mid-1964, hot on the success of the Smokey Robinson-penned, "My Guy", the field was open for a successor. Brenda Holloway would be given Robinson's "When I'm Gone". Originally intended as Wells' "My Guy" follow-up, and Kim Weston was rushed into the studios to record another Robinson song, "Looking For The Right Guy". The lilting, pop-style, number would have been ideal for

Wells but it was a little too lightweight for Kim to get her teeth into and perhaps too similar and too soon for it to be picked-up by radio stations as the "My Guy" follow-up. So Kim went back to Mickey Stevenson songs and production work, kicking-off by turning down "Dancing In The Street" in favour of a deep ballad, "A Little More Love".

With Wells gone from the company, Motown had to find a new duettist for their top male vocalist Marvin Gaye. The first choice was Oma Heard, a slight Mary Wells sound-alike whose "Lifetime Man" had just been released as a single on the VIP label. Four songs were cut but set aside, not to see the light of day until 1990, instead, the company decided to try a Weston/Gaye pairing, scoring immediately with "What Good Am I Without You". Nevertheless, more solo recordings would follow before the big return with Gaye, "It Takes Two", released in December 1966 and lifted from the *Take Two* album, just about the only Marvin Gaye recording not yet reissued in cd format for some unapparent reason. (An earlier set, *Side By Side* was shelved completely.)

"A Thrill A Moment", on which Kim had songwriting input, is a classy beat ballad which she has described as a personal favourite. It heralded her transfer from the Tamla to Gordy label, where she was to score in September 1965 with "Take Me in Your Arms (Rock Me A Little While)", going #4 *Billboard* r&b and coming from the hot songwriting pens of Holland-Dozier-Holland. Even so, this was not the kind of material she liked to record. "I loved the ballads – that is all I wanted to sing," she is on record as saying and, indeed, between the hit and its successful but similar follow-up, "Helpless", she enjoyed a supper-club tour of Las Vegas, Reno and Lake Tahoe as support for Billy Eckstine.

An album, *Take Me In Your Arms*, was scheduled but not issued. By this time, Kim Weston and Mickey Stevenson were husband-and-wife and Stevenson was having "troubles" with Motown, where he had risen to a position as Director of A&R. Those "troubles" were due to a reported million-dollar offer from MGM. Conscious of the career rise nurtured by Motown, Stevenson, who had been a staunch Motown loyalist advised Berry Gordy of the offer, asking for the opportunity to stay with the label on the condition he be allowed to get stock in the company. Gordy refused and Stevenson consequently left, taking Kim with him and, shortly after, songwriter/producer/arranger, Clarence Paul.

Kim's first outing for MGM, "I Got What You Need", was sheer mock-Motown but with her first album came an ambition fulfilled – ten standards and show songs allowing full rein to her jazz style, backed by a band comprising musicians from Count Basie's orchestra, with whom she had recently performed at New York's "Riverboat" venue. The album, cited by Kim as her "best ever recording", was a personal triumph but by no means a commercial success. So her singles stayed in a more R&B vein, including the northern favourite, "You're Just The Kind of Guy", actually the flip to "Nobody".

By this time, Kim was diversifying into theatre work, both acting and producing, so it was logical that her second MGM album, *This Is America*, would be a concept set, linking the many facets of American life at the time. *Billboard* writer Nat Hentoff wrote in the liner notes: "To achieve this quality of dramatic truth ... requires a woman who has explored her own sense of self... I hope everybody in America hears this album ... [It] ought to be given to the young because it is living history, firmly based on a continually hard-won heritage while looking ahead to further frontiers of freedom which have to be conquered..." Pretentious? Possibly; and the album was a little over-the-top but it gave the world "Lift Ev'ry Voice And Sing", with words written by poet, James Weldon Johnson and set to music by J. Rosamond Johnson. The song rapidly became adopted as "The Black National Anthem" and Kim's reprise of the number at the 1972 "Wattstax" concert is a highlight of the companion film issued a year later.

Kim has stated that, at the time she initially recorded "Lift Ev'ry Voice And Sing", she had become disillusioned with the general behaviour of black people, particularly its youth. She felt that black communities had begun to move away from being caring units and, naturally, she gravitated towards the community work being set up by the Rev. Jesse Jackson's "Operation Breadbasket". (Jackson's pressure on black disc-jockeys to keep playing the "anthem", resulted in it being reissued on the Pride label in 1970, where it become a #50 R&B hit.)

In the meantime, Kim had left MGM in favour of Johnny Nash's Banyan Tree label and a Weston/Nash duet album, on which their voices melted together in more satisfying style than her duets with Marvin Gaye, due possibly to the freer reign given to Mickey Stevenson's production work. A solo single coupling the theme from the film *Changes* with a fine version of Joni Mitchell's "Both Sides Now", was also issued.

She moved on again later that same year (1969), when Stevenson formed his own People label, cutting Kim on single with a version of the Marvelettes' hit "Danger Heartbreak Dead Ahead", at the suggestion of Clarence Paul. As with the MGM period, the album took a far more jazz/standard road, with songs such as "Windmills Of Your Mind", "Eleanor Rigby" and "Sound of Silence".

Promised their own Mikim label by Stax boss, Al Bell, in 1971, the Stevensons joined the (by then) Gulf & Western subsidiary. Two singles were issued on Mikim, as the lady's vocals took a more earthy turn, allowing the true gospel influences to come through, perhaps for the first time. An album, not including either of the singles but with eleven stunners including a deep working of "When Something Is Wrong With My Baby", a torchy "Buy Myself A Man" and a dual-paced gospelly "The Choice Is Up To You", was issued on Volt and, in 1974, a further single appeared on Enterprise. (*Memo to Stax/Ace: there are at least four tracks from this period of Kim's career not yet available on CD.*)

By this time, Kim's priorities had shifted from being a performing artiste "out-front" to dee-jaying on radio in her home city of Detroit and to working for the under-privileged community in that city. Immersed in fund-raisers and her community work, she recorded a 1975 tribute to the city, "Detroit That's My Home Town", released on her own Rahkim label, and, in 1976, founded the Festivals of the Performing Arts, a summer programme for the city's youth.

An "impossible to find" album recorded in 1976 with a group known as the Hastings Street Jazz Experience, recreating Detroit jazz sounds from the 1930s and 1940s, was the lady's lost studio work for just over a decade until in 1987, she agreed to be Ian Levine's first ex-Motowner on his Nightmare label, bringing along the Velvelettes, Mary Wells, Mary Wilson and Brenda Holloway in her wake and leading to the inspiration for rebuilding a new Motown under the guise of Motorcity records. Kim's vocals were as strong as ever but, for the most part, the material did not do the voice justice. Only "My Heart's Not Made Of Stone" and "Just One Man For Me", which Ian Levine composed with Sylvia Moy, having been inspired by Odyssey's "Native New Yorker", really reached the standards Kim deserved and re-makes of "Helpless" and "It Should Have Been Me" were probably not too much of a joy to record, although she has said, as tactfully as possible, "... I could deal with it, it wasn't too tasteless."

(A 1989 tour of Britain by Motorcity artists reportedly found Kim exercising her community skills by playing the "mother hen", soothing nerves and ensuring no egos got out of hand to the detriment of fellow performers!)

By 1992, the Motorcity bubble had burst and Kim has returned to doing good works. Recent rumours have suggested she has not been in the best of health, but the latest information suggests she has happily now recovered. Vocally, Kim has always offered "a thrill a moment" and it would be good to think that she is fit and well and that another trip into the studios may not be far off.

27
Cindy Birdsong remembers...
by Kingsley Abbott

As an original member of Patti La Belle and The Bluebells, Cindy Birdsong was an experienced performer when she joined The Supremes as the replacement for Florence Ballard. I met her first when she was a Bluebell, and we corresponded on a reasonably regular basis until she became a busy Supreme. She was always a warm and approachable lady, as were all The Bluebells, and it was a pleasure for me to renew our acquaintance especially for this book. She chatted easily and happily about those early days:

"Early on with The Bluebells, they were pioneering times when we were all struggling to make a name for ourselves. We were very young, and just of out doing sock hops. We started to get a bit of a name, but even then The Bluebells never really moved out of the chitlin circuit in the U.S. We only ever travelled to Jamaica and to you in England.

"Over in England, you had your music more compartmentalised than we did here in The States. Here we linked all music together more than you did, so when we came over we met people who really dug what we were doing. I remember that we played some small, really small clubs in basements where the atmosphere was great and really intimate. *[Ed.: Indeed, I believe I recall seeing them in clubs like The Flamingo and The Scene in London where they would put on an incredible show.]* We met lots of people, like you I guess, and we had Reg and his band backing us up all the time. *[Ed. Elton John and Bluesology who were very often the back up band for visiting U.S. R&B/Soul acts.]* We were very happy visiting England. The Bluebells were like sisters. We were very close and supportive of each other – really a close relationship. We always gave 100 percent in our shows. We once played a show to an audience of one in Asbury Park, New Jersey. There had been a mix up with the publicity by the organisers. They said we would get paid if we did the show, so we did it. And do you know, we really enjoyed that show a lot, and so did the one guy!! Another time we did the first of two shows in a small club in New York without the band. They were late getting there for some reason, so we did the whole show accapella. That was good too!

"I got real busy when I became a Supreme. We were often still on the road but it was a very different experience as we had all the back-up people. There was already a whole structure behind us, which we needed as we were playing places like Vegas. As well as knowing people, we didn't have any of the language problems that we did elsewhere. All the menus, instructions and conversations were in English, which made it much better for us. As with The Bluebells, we always gave 100 percent in our act, and I also found that I had a good relationship with Mary and Diana as well.

"The night that I particularly remember was when we played your Talk Of The Town. So many people came especially to see us. Bill Crosby, Michael Caine, Paul McCartney and Vanessa Redgrave and the whole of the Redgrave family came. Also Sharon Tate came with Roman Polanski. I think that they had just got married that very day.

"Another thing I remember about when I was with Mary and Diana was when we were on Dick Clark's radio show in New York City. We weren't all on together but he had us on the show on subsequent weeks I believe. He asked us all the same questions, and one of these was about our favourite Supreme song to sing. Well, quite independently we all gave the same answer! It was 'I Hear A Symphony', which was a great love song. I loved doing it even though I hadn't recorded it. It was one from Flo's time. My favourite songs from The Bluebells days were 'Down The Aisle' and 'One Phone Call'. I also liked doing the standards like 'Danny Boy' and 'You'll Never Walk Alone'.

"I'm still in touch with Mary Wilson on a reasonably regular basis, and with Diana but not so often. However just this year I met up with The Bluebells again when we were inducted into The R&B Hall of Fame in February. I had not seen Sarah and Nona for maybe 30 years, and we all sung together again. We did 'You'll Never Walk Alone' and it was wonderful.

"Thank you for letting me look back like this. Looking back is good. I have no regrets at all. I'd never want to take away from those great times. It was a high time in my life. I'm in the ministry now, and I've had other even higher times since then!"

28
Florence Ballard: Come & Get These Memories

Of all the ex-Motowners Flo "Blondie" Ballard was one of the ones who arguably got the rawest deal. As the original organiser and driving force behind The Supremes (then The Primettes), she was gradually relegated into a backseat position as Berry Gordy became more and more infatuated, musically and personally, with Diana Ross. Flo eventually got a settlement from the company, but hardly one that was generous in the circumstances. By 1975 news broke that she was living on welfare and the worst instincts of the gutter press sprung into action in the US. Partly to counter the various mis-representations, Flo granted a US television interview, and the following comprises the most germane extracts from it. Some of the questions can be seen as somewhat leading. The interview was conducted less than a year before Flo's untimely death at a time when she was prone to heavy mood swings, so total accuracy in her answers should not be necessarily expected. This was originally published in "Come And Get These Memories", one of the many interesting booklets produced by Mike Critchley for his Motown and Motorcity Fan Club.

As the interview started, in the background played "Put on A Happy Face", a Supremes recording by Diana, Mary & Flo.

Interviewer: Florence Ballard, what is your reaction when you hear music like that...?
Florence Ballard: ... Well listening to the records that were recorded with Mary and Diana – I love listening to the records; but it took me a long time to *want* to listen to them.
Int: You went a long time, and wouldn't listen to them?
Flo: ... I had mental anguish, and a whole bunch of other mental problems.
Int: Just too bitter, wasn't it?
Flo: It was bitterness. – And just hearing the records. – I guess inside I wanted to still be there, and I couldn't. And it seemed to just... tear me up inside.
Int: ...You left The Supremes in what? – 1967?
Flo: Yes.
Int: After how many years with The Supremes?
Flo: As a group, we were together from the age of fifteen, up until 1967.
Int: O.K., that's been eight years, and a story appeared lately that you're now separated from your husband. You have three children, and you're on 'Aid to Dependant Child' and your plight has received Nationwide attention... I'd like to go back to the early days. ...The other two girls were Mary Wilson and Diana Ross.
Flo: Yes.
Int: You came together as children, didn't you? How did that happen?
Flo: Ummm... Well...There was a man by the name of Milton Jenkins. He looked interested in my voice. He was managing a group called The Primes, which consisted of Eddie Kendricks and Paul Williams, who are The Temptations.... I used to stand in and sing along. I was asked by Paul and Eddie, did I know any other girls who sang...I said "Sure". I knew Mary, 'cause Mary and I went to Elementary School together; and Diana lived in The Brewster Projects, not far from me. So I contacted them, and that's how we started.
Int: It must have been just a dream when you learned that you were going to become recording stars. Even in those days Florence, there were stories... that The Supremes

were making millions of dollars... You never ever saw the millions of dollars, did you?

Flo: No, I didn't... We received an allowance, $225 dollars a week. The other monies was supposedly put into savings accounts, stocks, bonds, or whatever.

Int: When you say supposedly... What do you mean by that?

Flo: Well the monies that we made on engagements, we never saw this money. It was sent back to Detroit... To Motown.... And that was the last I heard of it.

Int: Didn't you have an attorney in those days? Did you sign a contract? Did you have legal advice? With all the people that were around you, wasn't there one person that said "Florence, this is what you should do"... Was there nobody like that?

Flo: No, there wasn't.

Int: Tell me, where was all your trust and faith? Was every ounce of your trust in Berry Gordy?

Flo: Yes, I trusted Berry Gordy. I was sure that he would take care of the money... and I believed that the savings accounts, and the stocks, and the bonds were there.

Int: Have you any idea how much money The Supremes made in those years? You had eight gold records in two years... and $5,000 dollars a night was not an uncommon fee for you.... Have you any idea how much money you made?

Flo: No, because I didn't receive any royalty statements. And I never saw any of the contracts that we had for different clubs.

Int: You signed a contract, didn't you?

Flo: Just the recording contract; but there were other contracts that negotiated us to perform in night clubs.

Int: In other words, you didn't get a ton of money, and then squander it?

Flo: No.

Int: What do you think of Berry Gordy today?

Flo: I dislike him... because I trusted him so much. ... And I also had a lot of respect for him at that time... And after all this happened, I found that I'd put my trust and faith in his man, and the money wasn't there...

Int: Tell me, what was it like when you were travelling around with The Supremes? ... A Superstardom is a very difficult thing to come by; but you achieved that status. How did it feel?

Flo: It was beautiful.... The travelling, going to the The Far East, Tokyo, Puerto Rico, London,... Places like that. ... Meeting different types of people.... It was just beautiful.

Int: Travelling in a limousine all the time, luxury automobiles, fur coats.

Flo: Well not all the time, we did have a lot of bus rides also.

Int: That was beautiful, right?

Flo: Oh yeah.

Int: When could you see that it was all going to end, at least for you?

Flo: Well, ... It was mentioned to me... that if Diana wanted to be a single artist, that I wouldn't stand in her way.... That's exactly what I said.... I did not say that I would leave the group. And after that it just kept going on and on... "Florence, you're a millionaire, and you're just twenty four years old, you can retire anytime you want"... So I got the feeling that I wasn't wanted or needed....

Int: But you're the one that came up with the name "The Supremes."

Flo: Yes.

Int: You brought the group together. You invented the name.

Flo: Yes.

Int: Then you were told "Florence, the group doesn't sound right, and you promised us that you wouldn't stand in anyone's way"... So you're telling me that you felt you weren't wanted any more... When did that happen?

Flo: It was the end of '65 or '66.

Int: So how many really great years of supposedly making lots of money?

Flo: Well I think… Well as far as making money, you mean… Ummm, since "Where Did Our Love Go", 'cause that's what started it all…

Int: That's three or four years when you were really on top?

Flo: Yeah.

Int: And you believed you had a million dollars… And you felt you weren't wanted, so you agreed to leave?

Flo: Right… I was told to leave.

Int:… Florence there have been reports over the years when you were on top, that there were frictions involving yourself and Mary and Diana Ross… You wanna talk about that.

Flo:… Well, I can only explain that like this… We did grow up together. And as far as I'm concerned, when you're around your family, your brothers and your sisters. There bound to be some kind of friction, and that's all it was… Like two sisters having just a little disagreement.

Int: In other words you spent so much time together… you travelled together, you lived together.

Flo: Yes.

Int: So there was no more than the normal amount of friction?

Flo: Yeah… That's all it was.

Int: Tell me about today… You talk with Diana or Mary, or even Cindy Birdsong? Are you in contact with them.

Flo: I've received postcards from Mary Wilson… And she would stop by and say hi if she's in Detroit.

Int: And what have you been doing since you left the group eight years ago?

Flo: Well, I have three children, and I've been trying to do my best seeing that they're alright… And I've suffered, like I said before, a lot of mental angish… I've been to doctors, and I've spent my life trying to come out of this nightmare… It seemed to me like I was dreaming…

Int: You just couldn't believe that you were up so high, and then down so low.

Flo: Right!

Int: I'm sure it must have been a terrible ordeal.

Flo: Then I kept saying to myself… Well at least couldn't I have just kept my home, if nothing else… For my children's sake… Couldn't it at least have been paid for… It goes over and over in my mind.

Int: What you're saying Florence, is that you went through a period when you didn't want to help yourself. It's a self-pity sort of thing that all of us have experienced…

Flo: Sure, I went through lots of different kinds of anxieties…

Int: What about today? What are you going to do with the rest of your life?

Flo: Well, this year I'm feeling a little better. I'm gonna do something. I haven't made a definite decision… as of yet. But I do intend to work, and do the best I can for my children.

Int: You have a great voice, and a great sense of showmanship. And Florence, you're only thirty one. Why waste that? Why don't you share that with the people.

Flo: I think that eventually I will.

Int: Since your story got out to the nation, haven't there been some people that have called the house and said "I remember you, Florence. I'll give you a chance."…

Flo: Oh yes, I got a call from New York… Well it's not definite. Not yet. But when I get this cast and everything off my leg, I'll be calling New York.

Int: A lot of our viewers might think, why don't you just go to New York and start singing… What would all be involved in putting together … 'The Florence Ballard Show'…?

Flo: Well first of all, I'd have to have my voice conditioned again… A little training, and then there's the music. You've got to get the feeling again, which probably wouldn't be so hard. The voice and the music. You have to have music written out for a whole big show... You can't just jump up and say "I'm gonna sing". You can't do it like that, it takes a lot of work.

Int: Do you really want to do it?

Flo: Yes.

Int: You know something, you're a lot more at ease, right this minute than you were when we started the interview.

Flo: Really... Well I often think, what would I do the first time I went on stage. I know I'd be so nervous; but then I say, once you are out there and you're facing the crowd: it's easier.... The feeling kinda goes away.

Int: ...Doesn't the applause really get you going?

Flo: Yes it does... When you know that the people are with you. It kind of relaxes you.

Int: Do you want to do it alone, or do you want another group?

Flo: I'd like to try it alone... Just to see what sort of projection I can feel comfortable with.

Int: What about the lawsuit you've got going with Motown?

Flo: At this moment, I'm not at liberty to discuss that.

Int: Tell me about your kids.

Flo: Oh they're beautiful... But then I think all children are. They can do the bop, and I can't.

The baby is two years old, and the twins... they'll be seven this year. They like to sing and dance a lot... I guess I was like that too as a child...

Within a year of this interview, Florence died at Mound Carmel Mercy Hospital in Detroit, from a heart attack brought on by coronary thrombosis. The solo album that Flo recorded with ABC has still not seen release.

29

The Girls, Part Two
by Gerri Hirshey

A rare French EP with a great cover.

The Supremes were one of the greatest Motown success stories, although their break-through was a long time coming initially. After a period of time being known at the company as the "no-hit Supremes", 1964 saw them teamed with Holland, Dozier and Holland at a time when that team were at their hottest. The hits flowed easily, and represented Motown's most commercial tilt at the white mass market. Immediately the company sought to capitalise on their appeal, and widen it by pushing the group towards thematic albums and show tunes. It was one of the furthest points away from the company's roots, but at the same time was closest to Berry Gordy's dream. This piece is formed from extracts from the chapter "The Girls, Part 2" from Gerri Hirshey's 1984 book Nowhere To Run. *Gerri's "fly on the wall" approach reveals something of the girls behind the Supremes.*

Whilst still in high school, Diana Ross worked as a busgirl at Hudson's department store. It covered a full square block on Woodward Avenue, with four restaurants and fifteen selling floors. On the street level, a brass-buttoned doorman opened limousine doors for the wives of auto barons from Grosse Pointe and Bloomfield Hills. To get to her post, Diana walked along plush-carpeted aisles, down wood-panelled halls. She remembers pulling her coat over the dowdy uniform that, despite the starch, hung on her bony frame like a sack. On her breaks she studied the manikins, and between her job and school she taught herself to sew.

"I'd see all these beautiful things and come home and make them," she says. "There's a picture somewhere of the Supremes' first look-alike outfits. I sewed them myself. They were black and gold, and we had a string of gold fake pearls from the dime store."

In the beginning Diana, Mary, and Florence shopped for fabric and patterns for all the local talent shows and those first days at Motown.

"You remember those balloon dresses? The skirt looked like a balloon? We made some of those in a very bright floundered print. And we had these bright orange shoes with big flowers stuck on the front of them."

Long before the Supremes had a distinct sound, Diana had them working hard on a look. "Personal style," she explains, "is a real important expression of self."

For the Supremes, and for the record company they came to represent, style would all but supplant soul. By the late sixties Berry Gordy's stylistic aspirations would set the Supremes in New York's Copacabana, sporting cutesy straw boaters and rattling nary an ice cube with perky renditions of "The Boy from Ipanema" and "Put on a Happy Face." By then style was the province of the Artists Development Department. But long before the ministrations of wardrobe mistresses, makeup artists, and hairstylists, the teenage Diana worked out an exhausting regimen on her own.

"I didn't feel I was college material," she says. "I didn't know what I wanted to do in school, couldn't select a career or anything. Really, all I wanted to do was sing and wear pretty clothes."

She credits her success in achieving that goal in large part to her mother, Ernestine Ross, who always understood. "She believed in me more than anyone, until I met Berry Gordy. If I said I wanted to do something – be a singer, a model, a fashion designer – she said, 'Go for it. Go ahead.'

"I was doing everything then. I'd go to school in the morning, then come home and work at Hudson's in the evening, so I'd have to change into my uniform. And I went to modelling school on the weekends. And then I was studying cosmetology to do hair, which was time-consuming. You know, you used heat on black hair then."

Her grandfather, who lived with them, clucked at the passing parade of garment bags, fashion magazines, sewing notions, and hair potions. "Daughter," he would say, "where *are* you going?"

Her parents asked the same question when a tall, handsome young man named Paul Williams came calling to ask if their daughter could be in a sister group that would per- form with his group, the Primes (later to become the Temptations). Shortly after, the Supremes began their career as the Primettes .

"We were singing all the time anyway," Diana says. "Not exactly on street corners. But out of doors. Everybody had their little record players outside on long cords. Nobody had air conditioners in those days, especially in the projects, and everybody would sit outside all the time. The first batch was Betty [Travis], Mary [Wilson], Florence [Ballard], and myself. Betty left to go steady. Then we got Barbara [Martin], and she got married. At one point Florence's mother took her out of the group because she wasn't doing well in school. We were in high school then. We were just *courting* Motown, you know. Making pests of ourselves. Mary and I started doing duets. We picked songs and did harmony but we needed our old girl friend. The two of us begged and persuaded Florence's mother to let her come back to the group. We promised we would help her with her schoolwork."

It was no secret that Florence Ballard had the most distinctive voice, a clear, high tenor that soared above Mary Wilson's alto and was far more sensual than Diana's ade- noidal keening.

"Some of the first stuff we tried was the Drifters' 'There Goes My Baby,'" Diana says. "And one Ray Charles song. 'Night Time Is the Right Time.' Oh, I had a very high voice, and very nasal. I was listening to 'You Can't Hurry Love' the other night...

"*Yew can't hurry luvvvv, naw, yew jushavtowait ...*" Pinching her nose with her fingers, she imitates herself and giggles.

"Since I had such a high sound, we'd always pick the singers to imitate, like Frankie Lymon."

The Primettes started getting a little work. They sang backup on some Eddie Floyd sessions, and at record hops they appeared with the Primes. Sometimes they found themselves on the same bill with that raucous gospel shouter Wilson Pickett, who was then fronting the Falcons. It was only through the intercession of Diana's former neighbour Smokey Robinson that they got an audition at Motown. It would be a fair trade-off since Smokey and his Miracles quickly appropriated the Primettes' accompanist, guitar player Marv Tarplin. Whenever possible, the girls dogged the Motown offices. Gordy steadfastly refused to record them until they were through with high school, tossing them only handclapping session chores at $2.50 a shot.

Their first record, "I Want a Guy," flopped in 1961; "Let Me Go the Right Way" reached only number ninety. It wasn't until Gordy teamed the Supremes with the writing/production team of Holland-Dozier-Holland that they hit the formula that would net eleven number one singles.

"It was funny," Diana remembers. "Mrs. Edwards had to practically twist Dick Clark's arm to get him to take us on his tour, Dick Clark's Cavalcade of Stars. Gene Pitney was starring, people like that. We were the 'and others.' I guess that was 1964. We started out opening the show 'cause no one knew us. But 'Where Did Our Love Go?' broke while we were out there, and by the time we got back we were closing the show."

By the end of that tour Clark was glad to renegotiate the Supremes' contract. "Where Did Our Love Go?" was followed by four successive number one hits: "Baby Love," "Come See About Me," "Stop in the Name of Love," and "Back in My Arms Again." As the Beatles continued to crash the American charts, the Supremes box-stepped into the British Hit Parade; by 1966 they had five number one hits there. Gordy saw a world market opening up. And as his product became less black and more processed, there were enticing new possibilities at home as well.

With the Supremes especially, the Motown sound made a sharp right turn, heading, with good speed, to the lucrative circuit of white supper clubs and Vegas casinos. Besides the straight, four-beats-to-a-measure rhythm of their own hits, the Supremes followed Gordy's directives on how to court the mink and monogram crowd with a repertoire of standards." While chaperones and beauticians fussed with gowns, wigs, and mink eyelashes, Gordy turned to a canny showbiz vet named Maurice King to work out the act itself.

King is an energetic retirement-age gentleman, still Pops to those he has taught. He says he couldn't leave Detroit and his ailing mother when Motown moved West, and since that time he has been special consultant to Gladys Knight and the Pips.

At the time King was also musical director of the Fox Theater (from 1951 to 1958). The audiences there were packed with teenagers like Eddie Floyd, Diana Ross, Wilson Pickett, and the future Temptations. King's move to Motown, however, came through a connection at the Flame.

"Berry's sisters Gwen and Anna owned the concession there. You know, it was an enterprising family. I saw them nightly, and Berry quite often. He heard I had a private studio. He had some cute teenage singers. But he was smart enough to know he needed *acts*."

King's studio wasn't unlike the studios of the gospel quartet coaches who rented out front parlours in Harlem.

"You'd secure a place in homes that had pianos and things. They'd rent you their front suite. At first this is the way the Temptations, Mary Wells, and the Supremes all rehearsed. The Temptations were scheduled at ten in the morning, and the Supremes would be scheduled at noon. And they'd meet going in and out. One day Berry came to me and said, 'Why are you rehearsin' your brains out in somebody's front hall? Why don't you just come on into the company and teach them all?'"

And Motown's fabled Artists Development Department was founded.

"That included a vocal coach, the choreographer Cholly Atkins, and me. I was executive musical director. I had a great assistant named Johnny Allen, and there were a couple of piano accompanists. There was a lady in charge of the girls' wardrobe, makeup and so on, a Mrs. Paul. Harvey Fuqua was director of the whole department. Now say a group had a smash record. Well, they'd have to do a performance. They got to do twelve songs. So while the producers may have taught them the hit record, I have to get them prepared to do the eleven others. We used to say that I was responsible for the in-person how-they-sounded stuff and Cholly Atkins was responsible for how they looked."

Atkins gave the Supremes their sideways head-over-the-shoulder stance, the stylised hand gestures. Maurice King would work up the order of the songs, the pacing of a show, even the between-song patter delivered breathlessly by the doe-eyed Miss Ross. Berry Gordy took a personal, almost obsessive interest in the nightclub productions and would not permit the slightest change without his approval. When the Supremes secured that prized first gig at the Copa in New York, King took them out to four or five other club engagements beforehand.

"By the time the Supremes got to the Copa it was no guesswork, sweetie," King says. "It was all cut-and-dried. Now in the Copa the age-group is maybe twenty to sixty. So they do their records but a lot of show tunes, too. And some real Las Vegas things. And I'd give them a little transition."

"Well, now that you've heard some of our very favourite songs – and we sure hope you enjoyed them – we just wonder if maybe you've heard this one....

"Ooooohwooowooooo."

"They'd fly into the introduction of 'Baby Love' like that, and I want to tell you the audience *screamed*. Because they were hungry and waiting for it. We knew just how long to make them wait." King chuckles. "It's all in the timing, honey."

If an act didn't talk those little transitions well, Maurice King would rewrite them so they could sing them. Gordy would watch rehearsals and shows, and he could be extremely rough if an act wasn't polished to his satisfaction.

"There's one little thing Berry Gordy used to say to a lot of the acts," King says. "And I thought that it was maybe a little cruel at the time. But it was true. He'd say, 'If you can't talk to the people out there, you're gonna have to sing and dance like *hell* to fill up the space.'"

This was particularly painful for some kids from the projects, facing a tuxed white cafe crowd. They could sing beautifully, but theirs was not the type of English spoken at bridge clubs. Gladys Knight was a good talker, Mr. King recalls. So was Martha Reeves since Martha was never afraid. Diana Ross was very good. She could deliver her lines without stumbling even if Gordy had rewritten them five minutes before curtain. As a vocal coach King never suspected she'd be the one to make it on sheer, raw talent. But Diana Ross always had that theatrical presence. It won her an Oscar nomination for her portrayal of Billie Holiday in *Lady Sings the Blues*.

"The lady works," King says. "The lady has always worked very, very hard."

I'm gonna make you love me, as the song says. After all these years, Diana Ross is the first to tell you that she still has to work, even sweat, to win the applause.

✳ ✳ ✳ ✳ ✳

When Diana and I spoke in 1982, Florence Ballard, the "quiet Supreme," had been dead for six years. Florence liked to say that despite all her years singing with the Supremes, she had never revealed her true voice. She said she started singing at her father's knee. He played guitar, and he played deep blues.

"I'd sing with him," she said. "You know, the public hasn't really heard me."

During the peak years she rarely spoke up in group interviews. In the studio Lamont Dozier, who supervised backup vocals for the Supremes, moved the mike farther away from Florence's arresting tenor lest it out-muscle and outsoul Diana's lead.

"Flo had the pipes," one ex-Motown staffer told me. "But Diana had the poise."

Once she had left the Supremes in 1967, Florence Ballard tried it as a solo, briefly, on ABC Records, with no success. Out of place again, the voice wandered forlornly through soppy show tunes or ill-crafted pop vehicles.

In the interviews she gave at intervals after leaving the group until her death in 1976, the voice was, in hindsight, impossibly blue. At first the quotes were stiffened with anger and wounded pride; progressively the words grew weaker, and the circumstances more ominous.

Eighteen months after she had left the Supremes, *Ebony* magazine visited Miss Ballard in her home on Buena Vista Avenue in Detroit, just across the street from Diana Ross and a few houses away from Mary Wilson. As she answered the reporter's questions, she rolled up the ranch mink sleeves of her at-home gown in order to heat up bottles for her infant twin girls.

"I've told people over and over again," she said, "that we didn't have any 'fight.' We had arguments and things just like sisters have because we grew up just like sisters and we were together all those years. Now as far as the so-called 'jealousy' is concerned, Mary Wilson and I always knew that Diana had the most commercial type voice, so she took most of the leads. We knew that all along ... so I just wish people wouldn't read more into my leaving than is actually there. All I have to say is that I wish the group all the success in the world. They're doing their thing, and Flo Ballard is going to do hers."

She added that her husband. Thomas Chapman, Berry Gordy's former chauffeur, had great plans for her. The same Mr. Chapman would appear in later newspaper interviews as a vigilant duenna, stopping his wife's more pithy responses with warnings like "Mr. Gordy wouldn't like that." Chapman was undaunted by the fact that Flo's first ABC releases, "It Doesn't Matter How I Say It" and "Love Ain't Love," were flops. He told interviewers of the deals he had arranged and the important people he knew.

"I believe I can make it," Flo insisted. "I wonder if people know how many flops the Supremes had before we made it big?"

On certain subjects, *Ebony* reported, Miss Ballard "maintained secrecy." There are no details of the "illnesses" that caused her to miss shows, no comments on the serious truancies that did her in. After failing to make a date at the Hollywood Bowl and a high-stakes run at the Flamingo Hotel in Las Vegas, Florence was asked to leave by Berry Gordy and was replaced by Cindy Birdsong, who had been singing with Patti LaBelle and the Bluebells.

In place of juicy revelations, *Ebony* was obliged to flesh out the report with a description of Flo's home. The house was large, with a Wedgwood blue interior and a "feel" of Oriental splendour. The drapes were velvet; the upholstery was deeply sculpted; the crystal chandeliers were tinted. A "unique" table hung suspended from the ceiling by a chain. All in all, fewer more intimate details were learned except for this: "Her husband is the only person known to have any influence on Flo now. He is completely in charge, except Flo has told him flatly that she'll have nothing to do with trading in their 1968 Eldorado for a 1969 Cadillac limousine."

Chapman had put in heavy mileage from the front seat of Berry Gordy's limousine; for years Florence had ridden in back. Now she was uneasy with the whole idea.

"Suppose I wanted to drive downtown and buy something," she said. "I'd look stupid sitting up there driving a big limousine. '

Shortly after, in 1970, *The Michigan Chronicle* found Mrs. Chapman counting out change to buy a head of cabbage and a box of cornmeal mix. At twenty-seven, she was broke, had lost her home, pawned her jewelry. The quiet Supreme complained to the press about mysterious harassing phone calls and threats of "public humiliation."

"Someone was always talking about exposing me," she said, "which is funny now that I think of it. I didn't even have a reputation."

She said that it was often pointed out to her, in heated corporate moments, that after all, she had never finished school eleventh grade. She would not say directly who her tormentors were, but she did not accuse her old girl friends.

"I was in such a bad state for a while, almost to the point of being bedridden," she explained. "For a year I didn't set foot out of the house. I guess I can't really accuse my close acquaintances of being fair-weather friends because I just withdrew into a shell."

In 1971 she emerged to file a lawsuit against Motown for $8.7 million, charging conspiracy in ousting her from the Supremes and failure to report the group's earnings accurately. The suit was dismissed in court as groundless.

Over the next few years she was mugged, robbed and separated from her husband. By January 1975, to support her three daughters, she was forced to appeal to the Aid to Dependent Families with Children program, a form of welfare. She told a reporter that she was looking for work, perhaps as a receptionist. "It's something around people," she explained.

She was alone, on February 21, 1976, when she called her mother at 3:00 A.M. to ask her to keep the children awhile longer. She complained of shortness of breath. At thirty-two she weighed 198 pounds and was reportedly on medication for high blood pressure.

Some hours later Thomas Chapman called Florence's youngest sister, Linda, to tell her that he had found Florence lying on the floor. She was conscious but had difficulty speaking. She could not move her legs.

Dr. Werner Spitz, medical examiner, later reported that she had been admitted to Mount Carmel Mercy Hospital complaining of a numbness in the extremities. He stated that the patient had ingested an unknown amount of pills and had consumed alcohol. She died at 10:05 A.M. of cardiac arrest. And for the first time in nearly a decade, hysteria marked the public appearance of Florence Ballard.

Weeping fans tore at the flowers and wreaths. One terrified funeral home attendant grabbed the base of a stripped floral arrangement and brandished it as a spear to fend off the crowd. The organ played the Supremes' "farewell" song, "Someday We'll Be Together." The Four Tops and Marv Johnson were pallbearers. The eulogy, in the New Bethel Baptist Church, was delivered by Aretha Franklin's father, the Reverend C. L. Franklin. Berry Gordy did not attend. There was tension in the church as Diana Ross was escorted from her limousine by a cordon of bodyguards. She was photographed holding one of Florence's daughters.

"I love you, Blondie" was the message on the satin banner of the flowers that Diana had ordered.

✳ ✳ ✳ ✳ ✳ ✳

The third Supreme, Mary Wilson, lives in Los Angeles now. She has another set of good, good girlfriends. Some are from the business; some, not.

"And this," she says, "is where the ladies lunch."

On this warm, unusually clear afternoon Mary has driven us to a small Japanese restaurant, a quiet place that shares a parking lot with some gas pumps. She and her friends find it very relaxed. They settle into the soothing half dark, knowing just what they want. They take a moment to admire the beauty and precision of the Japanese still life on their stoneware plates, then tear into them with good cheer. They drink sweet plum wine and pale green tea. Mary says they sit here for hours, dishing and scolding, boosting and bitching.

"Two plum wines, please."

"Will there be more to your group?"

"Just a duet today," Mary tells the waitress, musing aloud as the wine arrives.

Girl groups were surely a phenomenon in the sixties, a fad if you will. But if you think about it, it doesn't take a record company or some Svengali producer to make one. "Just a few good, good friends sitting around," Mary says. "Everybody has her voice. After a while you fall into parts naturally. And when the harmony's right, girl talk's a real pretty song."

Formal performance music doesn't fill her days the way it once did. As an alto she was best suited to group work. She's done some solo work, mainly in Europe, but just now she's on a sabbatical from supper clubs and TV shows. But she says she does not go long without checking in with that familiar circle of voices.

"The girls. I could not live without them," she says. "You know, you love men in those wild up-and-down ways. But the girls will get you through it *all* every day, if you know what I mean. They are always right *there*."

She raises her glass.

"To the girls?"

"To the girls."

Mary still misses her girl friend Florence. But so much happened to stomp on the spirit of the buoyant, soulful schoolgirl she came up with, it's almost as if *that* Florence had died before her body did. There have been so many rumours about how and why she died. Mary says that no one has gotten it quite right yet. Someone has to. But for now ...

"It's always a very touchy thing for me to talk about. I feel sad because there's so much about Flo – so much talent the girl had – that will never be known. She was a *great* singer. But no one will ever really know that. That Broadway play *Dreamgirls* was dead on, you know. Florence sings – sang – just like that."

"Well, it just tore me up," Mary says. "The guy next to me kept giving me hankies. I just fell like I was transported back to 1965, and my heart just went back there, and the tears were coming out. I couldn't stop them. I mean, I had makeup on, I was trying to be cool, to be Mary, the Supreme, and I just boohooed my way through it and made a mess of myself."

Unlike Diana, who took offence without having seen the show, Mary says she was curious and ultimately pleased. "I'm sitting there, just thinking it's going to be a play based on our experience, but not on *us*," she says. "Well, it *was* us. It hit me like a bolt. I was sitting with all these people, and everybody was watching my life."

"That show was much more about Motown than the Supremes," Mary Wilson says. "It was a marvellous idea they had at Motown. Reminds me of the Hollywood days when they took over a star and completely groomed them."

It was a disappointment but no surprise to Mary that friendships had to suffer.

"In the beginning, I'd go to fight for Diane in a minute. And she'd go to fight for me. We were inseparable, like sisters. And Flo, the same. I mean, *we* could get angry at each other, but nobody else could. By the time the name changed [to Diana Ross' and the Supremes] it had already gotten out of our hands. It was already Motown. It was all business, period. And you know, Motown was growing, growing so very fast. It happens in a lot of situations where you have a small business and then it becomes a big business. A lot of things are taken out of your control."

She found it a bit degrading to be a millionaire in her early twenties and unable to withdraw bank funds to buy herself a car without the written permission of Berry Gordy. In 1977 Mary sued her former employers, contending they had taken financial advantage of her being a minor and charging that those underage agreements still allowed Gordy to authorise withdrawals from her own savings. Special permission had to be sought for large purchases such as real estate or cars. In addition, she charged that funds were withheld over long periods while she received only $200 to $300 per week. As part of her legal struggle, Mary Wilson came away with 50 percent of the rights to usage and interest in the group's name. The whole business was messy and painful, but she says she came through with her sense of humour intact.

"Florence found it all very difficult," she says. "And surely most of the other acts did, too. We could not really grasp how we could be so important. Then, all of a sudden, we become nothing, and the company itself is the star. This really hurt a lot of people. But it was only natural. I'm sure it happens in every big corporation that started as a family-type hole in the wall."

Money and fame weren't the issues to high school girls in the beginning. Motown was the club everyone wanted to join.

"It was just cool, you know?" Mary says. "And if you are sixteen, cool is the meaning of life itself."

After school she and Diana and Florence took turns at the mirror, practising long, even strokes of eyeliner, blotting the kinds of lipstick that came in flavours, the air heady with the scents of cologne and scorched hair. Diana wielded a rattail comb like a field marshal's baton; she always had the inside track on the latest 'do and considered it her business to work out the battle dress when another girl group picked a clean three-part-harmony fight at a neighbourhood rec centre.

"Fondas think they're so tough. Hah!"

Florence was head cheerleader. She sat there in her clingy Orlon sweater, conjuring pep. "They can't outdo us. You just see who they clap for the loudest tonight. You just see."

"Awriiiight!"

"But first, girl, fix that hem."

The girls were at a similar powwow at Mary's apartment when they first heard themselves on the radio.

"All of a sudden, we were screaming," Mary says, " 'Mom, Mom, come here, listen to *this*! This is us!'"

The noise travelled fast around the Brewster projects. Diana, Mary, and Flo had made the club, had earned the right to sport its colours. The new, redesigned Motown label was midnight blue with a map of the Motor City super-imposed.

"We became heroes of the project overnight. You were hearing, 'Hey, Mary lives there.' You walk by, and they yell, 'Hey, Mary, right on! Hey, Diane, hey, Flo.' I think it was the best experience I ever had in my life. It was probably more exciting than our first million seller."

That first gold single, "Where Did Our Love Go?", convinced them that they were really going to make it. And at Motown, Mary said, it made them *the girls*. Other groups, like the Marvelettes and the Vandellas, were girls, of course, but already distinctions were being made as it became clear the Supremes best fitted Berry Gordy's optimum requirements for Top Ten crossover success. "We weren't as – well, masculine is the wrong word. Maybe tough. The Vandellas were a bit more soulful than us, let's put it that way. More R&B than us; they'd move more, with different kinds of gyrations."

Hip sliding was not in the Supremes' repertoire of stage moves. In fact, they hardly moved at all, except for the celebrated hand gestures taught them by Cholly Atkins. Done in perfect, elbow-length-white-glove synchrony, those moves are a bit harder than they looked.

After laying aside a chopstick, Mary demonstrates the famous traffic cop gesture that signalled the chorus of "Stop in the Name of Love." Berry Gordy and Temptations Paul Williams and Melvin Franklin helped them invent it on the spot. The hit was so new that there was no choreography when a sudden live TV show in England came up. All six repaired to a cramped TV studio men's room to work it out.

"STOP! Oh, no, not like that. Bring the arm up close to the body; try not to bend your elbow way out. That's it, palm out. Not in front of your face, girl. They always have to be able to see your face."

A startled waitress observes my lesson discreetly, then wonders if more plum wine wouldn't be nice.

"Cholly gave the Temptations all those great acrobatic steps. But since we were girls, we were restricted, so we worked on the hand motions."

Even offstage the girls were shown new, more proper forms of body language by an etiquette instructor named Mrs. Johnson. (Ed. Possibly meaning Miss Maxine Powell)

"She'd teach us how to get in and out of a car correctly. You know, you're supposed to put your leg in and scoot your behind in, never bend over, never have your rear showing. But every time we'd get out of her class and she'd go out and get into her car we'd die laughing. Because she did just the opposite of what she taught us."

Fittings for gowns and wigs were a part of the regimen. Songs were not presented to them until all three parts had been tailored to their voices.

"The guy who handled lead vocals was Eddie Holland. He had a way with lyrics and melody that was compatible with the Supremes' sound, and the Four Tops'. Why, I don't know. It's just like going to a tailor. Somebody just happens to fit your things perfectly. It was Eddie on lead vocals and melodies. Brian Holland took care of the tracks and overall composition. Lamont Dozier also did tracks and melodies and handled backgrounds. It worked for the Vandellas and for the Tempts. Most of the success is due to their giving us the right material, knowing what each lead singer could do and pushing them. Eddie pushed Levi [Stubbs of the Four Tops] and Diane an awful lot because both of them were very stubborn. And Eddie was the kind of guy who said, 'Hey, man, this is the way *I* want you to sing it.' The artist had to sing it his way, and thank God, we did."

They obeyed their producer, Mary says, because they flat-out adored Berry Gordy.

"We stuck to him so close, all three of us, that if he stopped in his tracks, we'd all pile up behind him. The guy happens to really know what he's doing. People would die to be around him. All the artists would like to be his favourite. And once he started referring to the Supremes as *the* girls, once it was clear where we stood in his eyes, most of the other girls really didn't like us. I mean, Flo and I could hang out together with the other girls and be comfortable. But it was very difficult for the other girl groups to like Diane."

In terms of glamour Ross was clearly the front-runner with her manikin's figure and devotion to style. But vocally the others had sized her up and found her lacking. To build her leads, she was coached individually, often by Berry Gordy himself. Sometimes she would be given tapes of other Motown artists, Like Brenda Holloway, to study. Mary points out that even on the Supremes' last single together, if you listen closely, you can hear Motown staffer Johnny Bristol leading Diana through the vocal on "Someday We'll Be Together," cueing her with phrases like "you tell 'em" and "sing it *pretty*."

Before the name change, before Flo's departure and all those blue times, the Supremes had a lot of fun on the road. They were still star-struck enough to feel faint when their road manager arranged for them to meet Sam Cooke one night while he was playing the Flame in Detroit. During one long tour, desperate for just an afternoon's freedom, they persuaded Diana's mother, then their chaperone, to let Jackie Wilson "babysit" while she went to lunch.

"Oh, sure, I'll watch them little girls like a hawk," he told her.

"Jackie Wilson and the Dells," Mary says. "Some baby-sitters, huh? We all behaved, of course, but it was a pretty funny concept. On those big tours you couldn't fool around. You'd only have time between shows. When those movies were playing. So maybe you could squeeze in lunch or go to someone's dressing room and play cards. You couldn't be hanging around the guys, though that's what we really wanted to do."

For America's sweethearts it was a PG-rated existence.

"We really became what Berry had imagined." Mary says. "And the message to all those guys was loud and clear. You can look, but don't even think about touching. We were off limits to fans and to other performers."

Rolling a transparent coral fish egg around with a chopstick, Mary giggles. "I should tell you what really happened when the Supremes met the Beatles."

The Supremes were in New York to do the *Ed Sullivan Show*. In town to do their historic Shea Stadium concerts, the Beatles had turned a few blocks near she Warwick Hotel into a riot zone. In the midst of all the volcanic hype, management for both groups thought it would be nice if these seven Top Ten heavyweights got together.

"Of course, the Beatles couldn't get out of their hotel," Mary recalls. "So in between one of the rehearsals for the *Sullivan Show*, we went for a limousine to go over there."

Inside the car the Supremes primped a bit for their presentation.

"Oh, we had our little outfits, you know. I had on my chinchilla, Diane had on her mink, and Florence had her fox and our little gloves. *Ooooweee*, my dear, we were just *so* chic."

They had to struggle to maintain their smiles when the door opened to the Beatles' suite.

"There's all these guys laying around; they looked like slobs. Maybe they were totally out of their heads, I don't know. Just sitting in their jeans, looking raunchy. They took one look at *us*, and they freaked."

The visit lasted only minutes. John Lennon retreated to a corner, wall-eyed with terror.

"He said maybe three words. Paul talked to us for a few minutes. We were whispering to our people, 'Get us out of here,' and they were saying to their people, 'Get them out of here.' Eventually, about five minutes later, we left."

She didn't think much about it until she ran into George Harrison about ten years ago. Yes, he said, the Beatles were mighty freaked. He laughed and explained.

"When you girls came up, we thought the Supremes were gonna be three hip black girls. And you girls come up there in your little fur coats and all prissy and everything. We were *so* paranoid."

It's getting late, and behind the counter the sushi chef is hanging up his array of scabbards. In between the talk and the choreography lessons, a sizeable pyramid of tuna and yellowtail has gone untouched. We decide to have it packed up and head out, blinking, into the bright afternoon.

Mary can't find her car keys, digging through a welter of notebooks, mascara, cleaners' tickets, and the like. We are doing a Lucy-and-Ethel with the carton of fish and her purse contents when she leans against the car and laughs.

"You know something? For years, I didn't have to carry around so much as a Kleenex. Or a key or even a purse. There was always someone there, trailing after me. It's pretty funny when you think about it. I am always pulling these little scenes, losing keys and whatnot. After all that's gone down, I guess it's not a terrible side effect, huh? That I can't get used to carrying my little freight?"

In the spring of 1983 the Supremes – Diana Ross, Mary Wilson, and Cindy Birdsong – were reunited, briefly, for the finale of the two-hour TV special celebrating Motown's twenty-fifth anniversary. Those present at the taping saw Diana Ross shove her old friend Mary Wilson and knock the mike out of her hand. Smokey Robinson was dispatched from the wings to airbrush the awkward moment with his considerable charm. When the show was aired, it drew an audience rating double that of any show in the time slot; the dickey moment had been neatly spliced out of the tape. Speaking to *People* magazine shortly after, Mary Wilson politely characterised Diana's behaviour as not "a personal thing."

Mary went on to a summer of small revival shows with a reconstituted set of Supremes. Diana Ross held a free concert in Central Park that cost the city of New York $650,000 in damages and police overtime. More than a quarter of a million people stood in the downpour of a predicted rainstorm, yet before she cancelled the show until the next night, Diana was moved to ask them, "Do you love me?"

The show went on the following night, and afterward roving youths, working in packs, robbed and beat the exiting crowd and passers-by in streets surrounding the park. In the wake of the civic uproar in her adopted home, Diana flew to LA to appear on the *Tonight Show*. She showed Johnny footage of how she calmed the crowd; no mention was made of what one radio station was calling "the night New York got mugged."

The majority of the perpetrators were identified as unemployed minority youths – kids who could not have gone unnoticed in previous park concerts by Elton John and Simon and Garfunkel. No one could blame Diana Ross for their crimes, but when Anaid, her production company, and Paramount, which co-produced and televised the concert, announced there were no profits, the press was less than sympathetic. Despite having sold world film and video rights to the event, the concert backers claimed to have lost money; the city of New York would not get its promised 7.5 percent of the profits, nor would the children of New York get the playground Diana had pledged to build in Central Park. *People* magazine ran a full-page photo of New York's Mayor Koch holding out his empty palm. Days later, Diana and "Hizzoner" kissed and made up at a news conference when she presented a check for $250,000 "out of my own pocket" for a playground to be named in her honour.

"Yes, you put pressure on me," she told the press. But she insisted that she had intended to ante up regardless. Building the playground, she explained, was always very real in her mind. Like so many other wonderful things in her life, it had started as a dream.

PART 3

A selection of British issues circa '64/5. All well played, but still in good condition.

30
Motown: Produced by Berry Gordy, Jr.
by Nick Brown

Part 1: The Early Years

The history of Berry Gordy's myriad record labels is long and complicated. When we look at the history of British releases, it becomes a little less daunting. However, in the interests of gaining a fuller insight of the whole Motown story, we have turned to a multi-sectioned tour-de-force article that originally appeared in Record Collector *magazine over several issues in 1994/5. Nick Brown's research and presentation was meticulous, and it is befitting of the articles' worth that they can now be brought together in one place. Nick has been a keen Northern Soul collector since becoming involved in the scene in the Seventies. He now DJs regularly around London, enjoys a regular slot at Stoke-on-Trent, and has written for fanzines such as* Shades Of Soul *as well as* Record Collector. *His work is representative of the high regard for, and knowledge of, Motown that is shown in Britain.*

Motown Records, and its stable of spin-off labels, remains one of the most unlikely success stories in the history of popular music. There were thousands of American indie labels in the '50s and '60s, most of which collapsed after their initial batch of singles didn't sell or were catapulted into disaster when they couldn't keep pace with the demand for their first hit.

But Motown didn't go down that way. Instead Berry Gordy's small company grew into the most profitable black-owned corporation in America. It launched the careers of dozens of stars, from Smokey Robinson and Diana Ross to Stevie Wonder and Michael Jackson. Its hit-factory production-line marketing strategy sometimes offended diehard R&B fans by tailoring its output to the white pop audience. But no-one could argue with its success...

Soul purists sometimes dismiss Motown out of hand. The thirst for the obscure which characterises so much of the Northern Soul collecting scene sits uncomfortably with the familiar image of the multi-national Motown business empire, formed by a boss whose artistic skills and management technique left a bad taste in many fans' mouths.

Yet at the same time, Motown surely ranks among the most beloved of labels among fans, not only for its great recordings, but also because it represents one of the routes alone which all soul collectors, including the most diehard lover of obscurities, took their first faltering steps. It's even been claimed that without Motown there would never have been such a thing as Northern Soul. Perhaps that's an overstatement, but there's no doubt that the company's influence on collectors has been enormous.

No Motown collection made up solely of British releases can be considered complete; in fact, only a fraction of the company's U.S. output up to the end of 1966 (the era covered by this series) was issued in Britain. As a result, hardcore Motown collectors have tended to concentrate on the U.S. catalogue instead of (or as well as) the British one, augmenting them with the occasional foreign rarity never issued in either territory.

Meanwhile there's been a groundswell of interest in Motown from Northern Soul fans in recent years. They've come to appreciate that many of the U.S.-only releases from

Motown's first few years are not simply a difficult challenge for the collector, but are also excellent records in their own right. The pillaging of the early U.S. Motown catalogue by Northern Soul specialists has seen prices for many of these items rocket in the past five year or so, while the more traditional British Motown collectors who are perfectly *au fait* with talk of TMGs, HLUs, Orioles and Stateside red-and-whites, have scratched their heads in puzzlement when they've been faced with names like Rayber, Melody, Tri Phi, Linda Griner and the Satintones.

The aim of this series is to guide the collector through this maze by describing the story of Motown's launch and growth and pointing out the many collector's gems which are there for the taking. Motown is an enormous subject, and its beginnings are still sketchy enough to have crammed many reference books with vagueness and inaccuracies. These articles will give collectors a clearer picture of one of the greatest record companies in the history of popular music.

Motown was built on the efforts of two people, Berry Gordy and Raynoma Liles (later Berry's second wife). Berry was an ex-boxer from a black middle-class entrepreneurial background who wanted to work in the entertainment business. His first move was to set up a Jazz record shop, the 3d Jazz Mart. But despite financial support from his family, it failed, partly because he misjudged his market – a lesson he never forgot in later years. After a brief stint at Ford he returned to the music business in 1957, writing songs with his sister Gwen and her boyfriend Billy Davis (alias Tyran Carlo).

Berry managed to hawk one of their songs, "Reet Petite", to Nat Tarnopol, an associate of Jackie Wilson's manager. Wilson recorded the song with enormous success and so Berry, Green and Billy were invited to write more material for him, including "That's Why (I Love You So)", "I'll Be Satisfied", "To Be Loved" and "We Have Love". The trio's writing royalties were depressingly small and slow in coming, however, and Berry began to toy with the idea of forming his own independent label, realising that control was the key to financial success. Before long he was looking for artists, musicians and writers with whom he could build a roster of talent.

If Berry's contribution to the partnership was his business instinct then Raynoma Liles supplied the musical expertise which put the finishing touches to the Motown sound. Born Raynoma Mayberry in 1937, she was given piano lessons at the age of six, and grew up experimenting with her own compositions and arrangements, while absorbing a whole range of musical influences from jazz and classical to the mainstream pop of Mario Lanza. By the time she graduated she could boast a tremendous knowledge of musical theory and an instinctive knack for arranging.

When her 1955 marriage to Charles Liles collapsed, she looked once again to music for an escape route. With her sister Alice she formed a duo called Alice and Ray. In early 1958, they won a talent contest at the Twenty Grand (an important Detroit nightclub): one of their prizes was an audition with Berry, who was sufficiently impressed to include them on his list of potential vocal groups, alongside the Five Stars, the Satintones and the Miracles.

Those three outfits occupied much of Gordy's time in the late '50s. He produced "Oh Shucks" a single by the Five Stars for the small Detroit label, Mark X. Their next effort, "Magic", was the first recording made by Berry and Raynoma as partners, but it was never issued except as a bootleg in 1991. Almost certainly Gordy's Five Stars were the same group who released "Blabber Mouth" / "Baby Baby" on End 1028 in July 1958 as End and Mark X were both owned by George Goldner and Berry had a deal to release Miracles material through End at the same time; but apart from this they do not seem to have recorded anything else.

The individual members of the Five Stars (Billy Davis, Crathman (CP) Spencer, Henry Dixon and Walter Gaines) stayed with Berry, however, resurfacing in later

Motown groups or working as backroom boys for the label. Sonny Sanders and Robert Bateman of the Satintones also ended up in the backroom, having cut their teeth on the group's early singles, where they backed up the tenor of James Ellis or the soulful gruffness of Vernon Williams.

The most important of Gordy's initial clutch of groups though, was the Miracles. William 'Smokey' Robinson formed his first group, the Five Chimes, at Detroit's Northern High School, as a means of meeting girls. After numerous personnel changes, the group settled down to a line-up of Smokey, Warren 'Pete' Moore, Ronnie White, Bobby Rogers, and Emerson 'Sonny' Rogers and changed their name to the Matadors to sound tougher…

Berry's first signing became the most successful of Motown's initial crop of artists, thanks to the special relationship which grew up between the gifted Robinson and his mentor. Berry coached Smokey in songwriting and production techniques, sharpening his songs and ironing out the contradictions and inconsistencies which resulted from Smokey's "if it rhymes, write it" approach. Gradually, Smokey was able to turn his original ideas into saleable ideas, producing million-sellers which ultimately led to the "America's greatest living poet" accolades (mistaken as they might have been) sent his way by rock musicians like Bob Dylan.

While Berry Gordy worked one-on-one with Smokey, Raynoma Liles' job was to coach the groups in matters of harmony, arrangement and musical theory, as well as writing out songs and lead sheets (the definitive copy of a song in sheet music form, used for copyright registration and by session musicians). Meanwhile, she formed her own group, the Cute Teens (Alice and Ray plus Marlene Nero and an old girlfriend of Berry's called Mamie), who recorded "From This Day Forward" for Aladdin. This was just one of the licensing deals which maintained a steady flow of cash for Gordy's enterprises in the days before Motown was set up.

Meanwhile, brothers Brian and Eddie Holland had joined the circle of artists congregating around Berry. Eddie functioned as both songwriter and singer, using his uncanny vocal similarity to Jackie Wilson to perform demos of the Gordy/Davis/Gordy songs written specially for the "Reet Petite" hitmaker. In April 1958, Eddie released his own songs, "You" and "Little Miss Ruby", both Berry Gordy productions, as a single on Mercury. Around the same time, another Berry Gordy production, "Shock", appeared on the small Detroit independent Kudo, credited to Brian Holland – though it's actually thought to feature Eddie's vocal

Gerry also produced Marv Johnson's 1958 debut single, "Once Upon A Time", again for Kudo, and three other records for the label. He also undertook numerous writing assignments for United Artists and Coral, and produced the first record published by Jobete Music, Herman Griffin's "I Need You" on HOB. That label was owned by Detroit entrepreneur Mike Hanks (later a fierce rival of Berry's), who was connected with the House Of Beauty – or HOB – where Raynoma had her hair done.

Jobete was the first Motown publishing company, named after JOy, BErry and TErry, the three children from Berry's first marriage. A range of companies followed, including Stein and Van Stoch, a name Berry hoped would sound like a Jewish, Tin Pan Alley company with loads of pedigree. While Berry wrote, produced and struck deals with established labels, his groups practised day and night, perfecting their acts. But these were unstable times for the fledgling company, which survived hand-to-mouth, with frequent moves from one set of borrowed premises to another. When Berry's sister Louyce got fed up with them using her house for their all-day and all-night rehearsals, they moved to 5139 St. Antoine, where Gwen Gordy and Billy Davis were operating the Anna label. After a few months they moved again, this time to Raynoma's house at 2040 Blaine Street, where the Motown story moved into a new gear.

Each of Berry Gordy's short-lived deals with established labels took a lot of effort to clinch and yielded small returns. Berry, Raynoma, the Miracles and the rest were still freelance performers, songwriters and producers. Forming a fully independent label was still beyond their financial reach, so as a half-way house Raynoma suggested establishing a "music company". Their customers would be singers who needed songs or songwriters who needed singers. Their service would be turning whatever the customer delivered into a finished demo, which the customer could hawk to record labels. The first advertisements on local radio drew an immediate response and soon Rayber was born.

The Rayber (from RAYnoma and BERry) music service turned out to be a rich source of talented performers and songwriters, many of whom remained at Motown when it began operating as a fully-fledged record label. They included Mary Wells and Mickey Stevenson, who came with his own group, the Mello-Dees (Stevenson, Joe Myles, Carl Jones and Stan Braceley). Initially, they backed Herman Griffin (another Rayberite), but when Stevenson quit singing to concentrate on producing, they changed their name to the Love Tones and became the in-house male backing group, sometimes credited (as on records by Mary Wells and Gino Parks), but more often not. Over the next few years, they provided almost all the label's male backing vocals.

Louvain Demps, who formed the in-house female backing group, the Andantes, was the very first Rayber customer, while Wade Jones and the late Eugene Remus both arrived via Rayber, recorded a solitary single under the Gordy's auspices, and then vanished. Mabel John (sister of '50s R&B star Little Willie John) also took this route to Motown, having heard about the service from Berry's mother who worked at the same insurance office as her.

Income from the service ($100 per song, payable in instalments) provided the first regular music business salaries, small though they were, for any of Berry's employees. Meanwhile, new customers kept arriving, needing songs, or vocal groups and musicians to provide backings on their demos. All this activity whipped up the atmosphere until Raynoma's house was a pit of frenzied, non-stop, day-and-night creativity!

Rayber's demos were recorded on a three-track basement studio lent by Detroit DJ Bristoe Bryant, while the core group for backing vocals (usually Robert Bateman, Brian Holland, Sonny Sanders and Raynoma) became known as the Rayber Voices. The looseness of their line-up is a testament to the spirit of energetic creative collaboration: within the first few years of Motown's formation, virtually every vocalist who passed through the company's doors performed as a Rayber Voice. Income from the company facilitated a move from Raynoma's house to new premises, set aside specifically for musical activity. At 1719 Gladstone (the first address to appear on a Tamla record label), Brian Holland and Robert Bateman constructed a demo studio in the back bedroom, and the creative flow continued unabated. Working for Rayber was excellent experience for the artists, and it helped Berry to strike his major label licensing deals.

By autumn 1958, Rayber was flourishing. After more cash disputes with Nat Tarnopol, Berry was finally convinced that he was in a position to set up an independent label. In her autobiography, Raynoma recalls encouraging him, as does Smokey in his. Berry took some persuading, but the reward was enticing – financial and creative control. The Motown story was about to begin in earnest.

The $800 loan is one of the more famous incidents in Motown's history, but the bare statement, "Berry borrowed $800 from his family to start a record label", hardly tells the full story. $800 was Raynoma and Berry's precise estimate of the recording, pressing and promotional costs of one planned release, namely Marv Johnson's "Come To Me". The money was borrowed from the Ber-Berry Co-Op, the Gordy family savings fund (named after parents Bertha and Berry Snr.) into which family members contributed $10 per week. The $800 loan was a gamble, because if the record flopped, there would not be enough money for a second. The extent of the gamble is highlighted even more sharply by the fact that Berry and Ray turned down an offer from Detroit night club owner

George Kelly of a $10,000 investment (not loan!) in exchange for half-ownership of the new label, because sharing ownership would have defeated the object of striking out on their own.

"Come To Me" and its B-side, "Whisper", were recorded in a single day at United Sound, Detroit's best-equipped recording studio, with a session musician line-up which reads like a who's who of the Motown sound: Thomas Beans Bowles (baritone sax and flute), Joe Messina (guitar), Benny Benjamin (drums), Marv Johnson (piano and vocals) and the great James Jamerson on bass. Backing vocals were added by the Rayber Voices, alias Robert Bateman, Brian Holland and Raynoma (who also played tambourine). Berry negotiated with United Artists for national distribution and managed to secure an undreamed-of $3,000 advance for the master, plus the rights to local distribution on his own label. It was the green light for the birth of their own label, which they christened Tamla; their dream of total control, from conception to distribution, had been realised.

Tamla records was inaugurated legally in January 1959, alongside the Jobete publishing company, and was named as a partnership in both Raynoma's name and Berry's (though shortly afterwards, Berry convinced Ray to change the papers from both their names to just his, as a formality, "for tax purposes"). Local distribution was done from the back of Berry's car, and everybody lent a hand.

Berry and Smokey nearly crashed on the icy January roads when they were travelling to pick up the first Tamla singles from the pressing plant in Owosso, Michigan, 50 miles from Detroit. Meanwhile, the United Artists copies of "Come To Me" were selling well, and the first quarterly royalty payment from UA was more than ten times the original advance. Ensuing royalty cheques were even larger. The gamble had paid off, and now Tamla could operate with increasing independence. Berry still relied on major labels to some extent – not as an outlet for talent, but more as a rich source of income. Of the nine records released locally on Tamla and sister label Motown, five were given national release through established majors in 1959, and two more in 1960, after which all Motown records were released solely on Gordy-owned labels. Meanwhile, the success of "Come To Me" (which reached No. 6 on the *Billboard* R&B chart) persuaded UA to offer Marv Johnson a full contract (which lasted until 1965) for records that would still be produced by Berry Gordy, but would be issued nationally by UA and not Tamla. Berry capitalised on UA's approval of the Marv Johnson 45 by leasing the second Tamla release, Eddie Holland's "Merry-Go-Round", to them as well, and for a year Eddie was signed by UA on the same terms as Marv Johnson.

All this success produced healthy profits for Berry, offsetting the disappointment of his second label, Rayber whose first release (by Wade Jones) flopped so resoundingly that no other record appeared under that logo. The income paid for a move to 2648 West Grand Boulevard in the mid-to-late summer of 1959.

The new house was in a business district, which meant that they could now operate legally and openly for the first time. It had a kitchen which could be used as a control room, a garage which would make a great recording studio, a living room and dining room which could be set aside for accounts and sales departments – and best of all, a toilet which produced a fantastic echo effect. It only required some redecorating, which was duly carried out by Raynoma, the Miracles and the Satintones – typical of the family spirit which ran through everything at Motown in the early years.

The house was christened with a ludicrously optimistic name for a company with just a single hit to its credit, but the name stuck, came true and became a legend. It was called "Hitsville USA".

Part 2: Anna, Tri-Phi, Harvey and Check-Mate

In any number of reference books, you'll find lists of the record labels owned and run by Berry Gordy. Tamla and Motown are familiar to almost everyone, while soul specialists will instantly recognise labels like Gordy, Soul and VIP.

There is another batch of American soul labels, however, which were linked to the Motown empire but were never officially part of it. The most important of those was undoubtedly Anna, the home of early singles by artists like Barrett Strong and Joe Tex.

One important misconception must be cleared up from the start. Berry did not own Anna records: in fact, he never had a real say in the running of the label. It was his sister, Gwen and her boyfriend, Billy Davis, who owned and ran it, and the two companies were quite separate entities until Anna folded in early 1961 and Berry bought up many of the staff and artists' contracts for Tamla. Netherthenless, the companies were in close contact and its rich reservoir of talent marks Anna out for a crucial role in Motown's history.

Billy Davis was a vital figure in the early Motown story, as it was through him that Berry gained many of his contacts in New York and, especially, Chicago. Born and raised in Detroit, Davis was the manager of the Four Tops (yes, the same group!) in 1956, when he secured a recording deal for the group with Chess. In exchange, Chess acquired the rights to two of his songs, "See Saw" and "A Kiss From Your Lips", which became R&B hits for the Moonglows and the Flamingos respectively.

For the next few years Davis divided his activities between Chicago and Detroit, setting up the Anna label with Gwen Gordy in 1958 in Detroit, and collaborating with her and Berry on songs for Jackie Wilson who was signed to the Chicago-based Brunswick label.

At various times, Anna's records were distributed by Chess (in Chicago), Gone and End (both in New York), and Berry Gordy seems to have used Anna's connections to secure the release of the Miracles' singles on End and Chess, and the Ron and Bill single (Smokey Robinson and fellow Miracle Ronnie White in an intentional – and actually very good – Everly Brothers pastiche) on Chess's Argo subsidiary. When Anna finally collapsed in 1961, Gwen and Billy split up, and Chess gave Billy the job of opening and operating a Chess subsidiary in Detroit, called Check-Mate. When this entirely non-Motown label folded in 1963, Davis' links with Motown ensured that it proved an invaluable source of artists for Berry's future operations.

Most Anna recordings were of the style known to collectors as "transition", a mixture of doo-wop and early soul, where you can hear the '50s vocal group stumbling into the future. The Voice Masters' singles on Anna epitomised this "transition", but not everything on the label fitted into that category. Some, like the Hill Sisters' "Hit And Run Away Love" were flat, '50s-rooted pop slowies, while others, like David Ruffin's shouter "One of These Days" and Lamont Anthony's "Benny The Skinny Man" (originally released as "Popeye The Sailor Man" but withdrawn for copyright reasons) were good early soul dancers, which now attract attention from Northern Soul collectors.

Only three of the Anna singles – numbers 1111, 1115 and 1116, to be precise – were actually Motown recordings produced by Berry Gordy and his team. Another, the Hill Sisters' side mentioned above, was co-written by Berry but not produced by him. That means that the single usually recognised as being the second U.K. Motown release, Paul Gayten's "The Hunch", is not actually a Motown record at all – British collectors take note!

Anna introduced the world to two figures who were to loom large in the Motown story. Lamont Dozier, later part of the Holland/Dozier/Holland team, recorded for Anna under the name of Lamont Anthony, while Johnny Bristol, an important producer at Motown in the '60s, performed in the duo Johnny and Jackey with Jackey Beavers, who himself became a Northern Soul hero for his performances and production work on a range of Detroit labels in the 1960s.

When Anna ceased operations, some of the label's artists – like Ruben Fort, Lamont Anthony and David Ruffin – followed Billy Davis to Check-Mate, where they joined a roster which included several other future Motown acts. Notable among them were the Del-Phis, who recorded two sides for the label with Gloria Williams on lead, before Martha Reeves joined the group, eventually, of course they became the Vandellas.

Ty Hunter and the Voicemasters (Walter Gaines, C.P. Spencer, Ty Hunter, Lamont Dozier and David Ruffin) also made the move from Anna to Check-Mate. Hunter and Lament Dozier had both begun their singing careers with the Romeos on Detroit label Fox and then Atco in 1957 and Hunter later joined Crathman Spencer (ex-Five Stars) in Freddie Gorman's group, the Originals – themselves very successful on Motown's Soul subsidiary.

Check-Mate releases by all these artists are subject to increasing attention from Motown collectors and rare soul fans alike, and prices seem set to show a steady growth over the coming years. The label never really took off, however, and Chess abandoned the project after little more than a year, at which point Davis moved to Chicago to become a full-time Chess employee.

With Anna out of action, and Billy Davis involved with Check-Mate, co-owner Gwen Gordy decided to set up another label, Tri Phi, with her new boyfriend, Harvey Fuqua. Harvey had been at Chess with the final line-up of his famous doo-wop group, the Moonglows, who split up in 1960. Leonard Chess arranged for Harvey to meet Gwen, reckoning that her business connections would make her an ideal business partner for Fuqua, who was now at a loose end.

Johnny and Jackey followed Owen to the new label and its subsidiary, Harvey, while Gordy and Fuqua also made several new signings, included Junior Walker and the All-Stars (Walker on sax, Vic Thomas on organ, James Graves on drums and Willie Woods on guitar), Shorty Long and the Spinners.

The Spinners (Henry Fambrough, Robert 'Bobby' Smith, Billy Henderson, Pervis Jackson and George W. Dixon, who was replaced in 1962 by Edgar 'Chico' Edwards) were already a polished night-club act by the time they joined the label, and they released the only Tri Phi record to have any significant chart success: "That's What Little Girls Are Made For", which reached No. 19 on the *Cashbox* R&B chart in July 1961. That was also the only Harvey/Tri Phi record released in the U.K., and British collectors need to be reminded that this is no more a Motown recording than Paul Gayten's "The Hunch"!

The group moved to Motown in 1963, after Berry saw them perform comic impersonations of all the top Motown acts, one after another, during a show at the Twenty Grand. Their arrival at Motown coincided with – and probably inspired – the hiring of choreographer Cholly Atkins, who began polishing up the stage routines for which Motown acts were to become famous. At the same time, Gordy inaugurated the Artists Development Department, via which Motown acts (particularly the female ones) were instructed in poise, etiquette and elegant manners.

Back to Tri-Phi, however: despite the appearance of further pop records by artists like the Davenport Sisters, there is plenty to interest the early soul fan in the label's roster. For example, the Challengers III featured Ann Bogan, Harvey Fuqua's some-time duet partner, who went on to replace Gladys Horton as the lead singer of the Marvelettes in 1968. Harvey's own Tri-Phi release, "Any Way You Wanta", was bootlegged on the Pittsburgh soul scene in the early '70s, and it was subsequently such a big success on the early '90s "all-nighter" scene in Britain that those vintage bootlegs enjoyed another lease of life. The counterfeits are quite obviously modern pressings with a fine groove and a bulbous rim. Original Tri-Phi 45s have a broad, flat run-in.

Tri-Phi and Harvey were doomed to a short life because of the problems that Gwen

Gordy and Harvey Fuqua faced in getting distributors to pay their bills on time, so they could pay the pressing plants. By mid-1963, both labels had gone bankrupt. The co-founders, by this time a married couple as well as business partners, duly moved to Berry Gordy's Motown stable, taking with them artists contracts and recording masters which paid handsome dividends in the years to come.

Part 3: Tamla
(Additional information by Martin Koppel)

Almost every British collector is familiar with the name of Motown's Tamla Records subsidiary – if only because so many U.K. releases from Berry Gordy's Detroit soul stable were issued here on Tamla Motown. In the States, meanwhile, Tamla was a distinct label in its own right, the home of some of the best-selling artists of the '60s and '70s.

Tamla's name, which was adapted from Debbie Reynolds' film and chart hit "Tammy", demonstrated from the start that Berry Gordy had crossover pop success in mind. But the label's early U.S. releases were hardly likely to dent the national pop charts.

In fact, they were strictly local releases, some of which were licensed to major labels for national distribution. The others like the Satintones' debut 45, Chico Leverett's solo effort and the instrumental by the Swinging Tigers (Beans Bowles, Motown's number one sax man until Mike Terry's arrival in 1961 plus a band of Motown session musicians) are particularly rare as they weren't leased for national consumption. The Downbeats' high quality dancer, "Your Baby's Back", was at least reissued in 1962, but copies of the first run in 1959 are so rare that it's been omitted from many past discographies.

Another problem for the new Tamla collector is the apparent haphazardness of the labels numbering system. It jumps from a three-figure system to a four-figure one, then to a totally unrelated five-figure one which looks as if it is in mid-series (collectors often ask what happened to the releases between 54001 and 54024) and then offers multiple releases on the same number.

These discrepancies were caused by administrative errors, which were cleared up when Billie Jean Brown (later the first head of Quality Control) was hired to assist Berry Gordy's co-founder, Raynoma Liles, and reorganised the tape library in 1960. But the jumps in the numbering system aren't so easy to explain.

The first two Tamla singles were numbered 101 and 102, which makes perfect sense. But the third, by Nick & the Jaguars, bore the number 5501. This seems to be part of a different numbering system entirely, which links Gordy's publishing company Jobete's releases on different labels. Motown researcher Ron Murphy has discovered a Jobete-published record by the Biscaynes on the previously unknown label, Ridge, with the number 6601, which suggests that there may have been a short-lived numbering system which went 1101, 2201, 3301 etc. during 1959. Bryan Brent's Gordy-produced "Vacation Time" was issued on Penny 2201 around this time which lends weight to the theory.

After these three singles the main Tamla numbering sequence began – with the number 54024. The "missing numbers" from 54001 onwards aren't Gordy productions which were leased out to other labels, as some people have supposed, as the numbers don't seem to tally up. Then there's the suggestion that the first number in Tamla's five-figure catalogue series 54024 was a sentimental reminder of the first hit song written by Berry, Jackie Wilson's 'Reet Petite" which was released on Brunswick 55024.

In recent years, however, evidence has surfaced that 55024 wasn't actually the starting point of the Tamla numbering sequence after all. Barrett Strong's "Let's Rock", bearing the catalogue numbers Tamla MT 54021/54022, was first mentioned in the "Hitsville

USA" box set booklet by Janie Bradford, a Motown staff writer who was involved in the making of Strong's classic hit single "Money". Gradually it emerged that a couple of collectors did in fact own copies of this previously unknown release.

Aural evidence suggested that besides Barrett Strong, the record also featured the voice of Raynoma Liles. Dave Marsh's book *The New Book of Rock Lists* says outright that the entire story is a fake; but collectors who own copies of the "Barrett Strong" single think otherwise. To add to the confusion there's also a Miracles bootleg 45 with the number 54022 "Embraceable You"/ "After All".

Once they'd established a numbering system that made some kind of sense Tamla were free to look for hit singles. At first, these had to come "second-hand," via licensing deals with other companies. But that all changed when Gordy began recording at Hitsville, his all-purpose office and studio.

Barrett Strong's "Money (That's What I Want)" was written about a week after the move to Hitsville, during a jam session that involved Motown staff writer Janie Bradford, Berry, Raynoma, Robert Bateman, Sonny Sanders, Brian and Eddie Holland and Strong, who was simply visiting for the afternoon. As soon as he'd sniffed the possibility of a hit song, Gordy ran an unbroken three-day recording session which ran through scores of aborted attempts at "Money" before they hit the manic take he was looking for.

As usual, Tamla released the record in Detroit, while another label – this time Gwen Gordy's Anna, which held Strong's contract – got national distribution. The single sold slowly on Tamla but became a huge hit when the Anna release appeared some five months later, reaching No. 8 on the *Cashbox* R&B chart. Income from the sales of "Money" probably aided the setting-up of Tamla's new sister label, Motown (named after Detroit's nickname of "Motortown", established experimentally in September 1959, and operative by Spring 1960); and for Tamla itself, it marked a definite turning point.

For the first time, Berry was able to give his next release on the label (some seven months later) a national release on Tamla, without relying on any major label for coast-to-coast distribution. The record in question, Tamla 54028, was the first of a number of complicated releases which epitomise Motown's early days, when innovation and experimentation produced a fresh new product but also provoked indecision over different versions of potential hit songs. The Miracles' "The Feeling Is So Fine" was initially coupled with "You Can Depend On Me", but was withdrawn in a matter of weeks or even days. "Feeling" was replaced with "Way Over There" and the B-side title was shortened to "Depend On Me". "Way Over There" (running time 2:40 master no. H55501) was then removed in favour of a different, tidier take of the song with added strings (running time 2:48 master no. H55501 T-3) and backed with the same version of "Depend On Me". And to make life even more complicated, all these releases shared the same catalogue number Tamla 54028!

Three months after the final version reached the shops, the Miracles' next release went through a similar process – albeit with sensational results. "Shop Around" was originally pressed with the master number 45-H55518 A-2 in the run-out groove, as a relaxed, uptempo dance record. About a week later, Berry hit upon an idea for an entirely new treatment of the song. He woke up the Miracles with 3am telephone calls telling them to get to the studio and booked musicians for an immediate session. The Miracles grudgingly turned up, re-recorded the song and produced one of the all-time Motown classics.

The improved vocal performance wasn't the only difference between the two versions. Berry produced the track with a heavy, chopping backbeat – a decisive move towards the stomping, on-the-fours upbeat which became a trademark of the Motown sound. "Shop Around" was Motown's biggest hit to date, a million-seller which fulfilled Berry's dream of crossover success by reaching No. 2 on the pop charts.

From that point on, most Miracles U.S. 45s were also released in the U.K., either on single or LP, but a few slipped through the net. For example "Mighty Good Lovin'" was a good uptempo dancer in the "Shop Around" mould which surprisingly didn't make the R&B charts. It's not only a desirable rarity today, but a track with the potential to make an impact on the Northern Soul scene.

Tamla's next big success came with the Marvelettes. The group (Gladys Horton, Wanda Young, Katherine Anderson and Georgeanna Dobbins) were brought to Motown by Robert Bateman after they'd won a talent contest at their high school in Inkster, Michigan, where the prize was a Motown audition. After changing their name from the Marvels and losing Georgeanna who left to look after her mother, they recorded "Please Mr Postman", a song written by an Inkster friend, William Garrett, as a blues song and remodelled by Georgeanna. The record was a huge hit, which gave Motown its long-awaited first pop No. 1, and enjoyed a five-week residency at the top of the *Cashbox* R&B chart.

Astonishingly, Berry Gordy did little to capitalise on the girls' success. The superb "I Want A Guy" was hidden away as the B-side of the derivative cash-in "Twistin' Postman", which deservedly only made No. 34 in the Top 40. "Playboy" and "Beechwood 4-5789" did rather better, but after that the Marvelettes didn't reach the *Billboard* Top 40 again until December 1964, with "Too Many Fish In The Sea". Maybe the Marvelettes were overshadowed by Berry Gordy's growing determination to secure a hit with the Supremes (who at the time were having disastrous flops), but whatever the reason, the Marvelettes don't seem to have enjoyed their stay at Motown. They had to fight for attention from the in-house writers and producers, while they watched the label's other girl groups being feted and courted. Insult was added to injury when Berry threw in the group's name as a stake in a gambling match – and lost it. In some ways, the Marvelettes' treatment exposed the first cracks in the Motown family spirit. But their more positive legacy was a series of excellent singles which are now surprisingly hard to find.

The problems which bedevilled the Marvelettes didn't hinder the progress of Marvin Gaye, who is often claimed (somewhat unfairly) to have had his path at Motown smoothed by being married to Anna Gordy, another of Berry Gordy's sisters. Gaye was one of the artists who came to Motown via Harvey/Tri Phi, but he actually arrived before the mass exodus when those labels collapsed. A native of Washington DC, he wanted to emulate his heroes Dean Martin and Perry Como. After singing in various DC groups, including the Marquees who recorded for Okeh, he met Harvey Fuqua in 1958 and became lead tenor in his group the Moonglows. When they split in 1960, Harvey and Marvin went to Detroit where Harvey set up Tri Phi records with Gwen Gordy. Marvin did some session drumming for the label and recorded some vocal performances which were never released, before wangling his way into Motown as a session drummer.

His dream of becoming the black Perry Como fitted in surprisingly well with his new boss and Marvin was soon allowed to make an LP of supper-club standards, *The Soulful Moods Of Marvin Gaye*, which bombed. The promo-only 45 which accompanied this album featuring "Witchcraft" and "Masquerade (Is Over)" was actually Marvin's first single – crediting him as Marvin Gay. His first commercial 45 "Let Your Conscience Be Your Guide" was in a similar vein, albeit with an impressive Jackie Wilson-style dancer on the flip, and the formula was maintained for "Sandman" and "Soldier's Plea".

In the midst of the highly competitive Motown set-up, Marvin was alarmed to see that his records weren't selling, while R&B artists like the Miracles and the Marvelettes were topping the charts. He was essentially forced to contemplate a change of style and his first attempt as a R&B singer, "Stubborn Kind Of Fellow" (which featured the Vandellas on backing vocals) was a resounding smash. So was "Pride & Joy", which Marvin dedicated to Anna Gordy and which charted in June 1963, the month the couple were married. All his subsequent 45s sold well despite his initial discomfort with the R&B style.

Eleven-year-old Steveland Morris, alias Steven Judkins but better known as (Little)

Stevie Wonder was introduced to Motown in 1962. The connection was Ronnie White of the Miracles, whose brother Gerald was a friend of Stevie's. He auditioned spectacularly by playing every instrument in the studio, and was signed immediately to Tamla, but Gordy and his staff didn't know exactly what to do with him at first. Apart from the fluke success of "Fingertips", a live jam session which became a No. 1 Pop and R&B single, the hits were slow to come, and Stevie didn't score another major hit until "Uptight (Everything's Alright)" in 1965.

Most of his flops from the intervening period were issued on British 45s or LPs, but those that didn't include the club favourite "La La La La La", and the attractive, mid-tempo "Pretty Little Angel", which was cancelled and replaced with "Kiss Me Baby". Some demo copies of that first pressing do exist, but they'll prove tough to track down.

The Supremes had a similarly agonising gestation period, when they cut two records for Tamla before being shifted to Motown. The first, "I Want A Guy", is not up to the standard of the Marvelettes' version, but that doesn't mean it's not good! It is, however, very rare, and its status as the "first Supremes record" makes it highly collectable. "Buttered Popcorn", with its eyebrow-raising lyrics, is a treat for Florence Ballard fans, as it was the only Supremes record on which she sang lead. It proved that her voice was by far the best of the three.

Kim Weston's stay at Tamla resulted in the first Tamla Motown 45 to feature A- and B-sides from different U.S. records, namely TMG 511, "I'm Still Loving You"/"Just Loving You". Another excellent mid-tempo dancer of hers, "Feel Alright Tonight", didn't make it to Britain at all, and is set to receive close attention from Northern Soul collectors.

L.A. singer Brenda Holloway, a veteran of seven record labels by the age of 17, met Berry at a disc jockeys' conference in 1964. She went on to record three non-U.K. tracks at Tamla: a strong ballad ("Sad Song") and a decent pair of mid-tempo dancers on Tamla 54121. Most interesting to collectors, however, is the Tamla special pressing which features her giving a "school is cool" public service announcement to the youth of Detroit. This promo-only disc is exceptionally rare, and all the more desirable for its first-class "Golden Age of Motown" production, stomping upbeat and all.

Mable John was one of the first artists to join Motown – and also one of the first to leave it in protest, around 1962, when she discovered that her R&B style didn't fit in with Berry's increasingly pop tendencies. All her earthy, tough-voiced R&B recordings were somewhat under-promoted, and none of them made it as far as a British single.

Herman Griffin's marriage to Mary Wells was one of the first of many romantic unions which cemented the family atmosphere at Motown. Others included Smokey Robinson and Claudette Rogers, Bobby Rogers (Miracles) and Wanda Young (Marvelettes), Billy Gordon (Contours) and Georgeanna Dobbins (Marvelettes, Johnny Bristol and Iris Gordy, Marvin Gaye and Anna Gordy, and Mickey Stevenson and Kim Weston.

Though Griffin was one of the first Motowners, he didn't last long, possibly because, like Mable John, his poor-selling R&B singles didn't match the emerging company image. The same may be true of R&B artists "Singing" Sammy Ward, Gino Parks and Little Otis. Nothing by any of these artists made the *Cashbox* R&B Top 100, not even the bought-in Chicago recording, "I Out-Duked The Dukes" – Little Otis' answer record to the million-selling "Duke of Earl". Sammy Ward's R&B movers and Gino Parks' frantic shaker "Fire" are now in-demand items among fans of early soul music. Of these, perhaps the one to watch most closely is Ward's "Don't Take it Away", which with its kicking rhythm and cool jerking keyboard sound is ripe for serious Northern Soul interest.

Parks left Motown with producer Eddie Singleton around 1965, recording a Northern Soul in-demander, "Nerves of Steel", for the Capitol subsidiary Crazy Horse and some unreleased material on his next label, Shrine. Ward, meanwhile, left Motown for the Detroit independent Groove City and released one of the true Northern Soul classics,

"Sister Lee", under the name of Sam Ward.

The disappearance of these artists from the Motown catalogue was a sign of the company shedding its R&B skin and preparing for a new generation of pop-orientated soul acts, to build on the success and experience of the early years. The records by Mickey Woods, Mickey McCullers and Saundra Mallett marked the beginnings of this second generation. Woods' second Tamla single, "Cupid", was an excellent mid-tempo soul effort, featuring one of the finest string arrangements on any Motown record.

Mickey McCullers' "Same Old Story" is the sort of haunting, atmospheric, mid-tempo record which is crying out for wider Northern Soul exposure. It sold badly on first release, and even when it was reissued on VIP two years later, the company still had no luck selling it. Saundra Mallett's sole Tamla single, on which she was backed by the Vandellas, is very rare indeed. Its release was poorly promoted, partly because the singer was too young to go on the road, and only a handful of copies have survived. Saundra Mallett later became Saundra Edwards and teamed up with the Downbeats to become the Elgins, who recorded for Motown's VIP subsidiary. The flip of her Tamla 45, "It's Gonna Be Hard Times" was reissued on their *Darling Baby* LP (UK number TML 11081) in 1968.

The Saundra Mallett single appeared in July 1962, by which time Tamla was set firmly on its hitmaking path. Marvin Gaye's "Stubborn Kind of Fellow" was issued the same month, followed soon by acknowledged classics like the Miracles' "You've Really Got a Hold On Me" and "Mickey's Monkey".

Looking through the Tamla discography to the end of 1966, what's remarkable is the consistency of the names behind the hits: only Brenda Holloway and then the Isley Brothers were added to the Tamla roster between the summer of 1963 and December 1966. The ratio of hits to flops during that time speaks volumes for Berry Gordy's quality control.

Part 4: The Motown Label
(Additional information from Martin Koppel)

Alongside Tamla, Motown was the flagship of Berry Gordy's Detroit soul empire. During the '60s, it amassed a remarkable collection of worldwide hits by artists like the Supremes, the Four Tops and Mary Wells. But like Tamla, Motown's early years were a time of obscure local pressings, withdrawn 45s and chart flops.

The Motown label began life in September 1959 with the only Miracles record ever to appear under this logo: a pair of primitive test pressings of "Bad Girl"/ "I Love You Baby", given the catalogue numbers Motown G1/G2 and TLX 2207. "Bad Girl" was actually leased by Berry Gordy for national consumption on Chess, so these demos were intended either as demos for Chess to hear, or more likely as prototype copies for a simultaneous local Motown release, following the pattern of early Tamla issues. There's no evidence to suggest that "Bad Girl" was ever given a full issue on Motown.

In the event, no record on the Motown label was ever leased out to another larger company for national airing. Early Motown numbers are therefore as hard to obtain as early Tamla 7"s, but there is no national alternative for the collector to fall back on. Exactly how rare they are is clear from the Satintones' output. Not one of their records appeared on the *Cashbox* R&B Top 100, but they all featured first-rate vocal group performances and most have some potential for Northern Soul exposure, where they remain little-known. Their first two Motown singles, "My Beloved" and "A Love That Can Never Be", were each released with and without dubbed-on strings, with the latter (Motown 1006) being complicated further by the fact that the original A-side "Tomorrow And Always" – an answer to the Shirelles' "Will You Still Love Me Tomorrow" – had to be withdrawn for copyright reasons and replaced with "Angel".

All the Satintones' 45s were good, mid-tempo soul performances – particularly "A Love That Can Never Be" with its tuxedo-sharp vocal interplay, and the excellent stepper "I Know How It Feels", with its sparkling echo and moody feel – so it's a shame that their projected LP, *The Satintones Sing*, never saw the light of day. The group dissolved around 1962 and vocalist Robert Bateman concentrated on producing, teaming up with Brian Holland to form "Brianbert", Motown's first important production team, which became "Sonbrianbert" (or "Sonbrybert") when the pair were joined by Bateman's fellow Satintone, Sonny Sanders.

The second commercial release on Motown was Eugene Remus' highly rare single, "You Never Miss A Good Thing", issued in a variety of forms. He seems to have simply come to Motown via its Rayber music service, cut the record and disappeared again. Next came Richard "Popcorn" Wylie, songwriter and session pianist at Motown from pre-Hitsville days, who issued the uptempo "Shimmy Gully" and, later, a decent instrumental version of Barrett Strong's hit "Money". Though more successful than Eugene Remus, he scored no hits, and in mid-1962 he moved to Epic, eventually carving out a career writing and producing Northern Soul classics for what seems like half the soul acts in Detroit.

Debbie Dean, Motown's first white female signing, cut a few reasonable sellers (including an answer to the Miracles' "Shop Around"), as did Henry Lumpkin, whose gravelly angst-packed voice graced a couple of worthwhile dancers, including "Don't Leave Me". But Motown's attempts at gospel (the Golden Harmoneers), high-quality blues (Amos Milburn) and Christmas novelties (the Twistin' Kings – Beans Bowles and his session musicians again!) all failed to make an impact.

It was left to Eddie Holland and Mary Wells to provide the chart action (and much-needed revenue, for the label). Astonishingly, apart from Mary Wells' seven chart entries, Eddie Holland's "Jamie" was the only Motown record to hit the *Billboard* Top 40 until the Supremes broke through with "When The Lovelight Starts Shining Through His Eyes" four years after the label was launched. It seems fair to say that Mary Wells kept the label afloat, which emphasises the impact of her acrimonious departure.

Her first 45, "Bye Bye Baby", was her own composition, which she had wanted the Rayber Music Company to turn into a demo for her or else sell to Jackie Wilson. Suitably impressed, Berry signed her and put the record out himself. It reached No. 17 on the R&B charts during a stay of 21 weeks, preparing the way for her next effort, "I Don't Want To Take A Chance", which peaked at No. 33. After a slight blip with the follow-up (only five weeks on the R&B charts), all her records became big sellers, with the No. 1 hit "My Guy" marking the beginning of Motown's Golden Age – and the end of her stay at Motown. After demanding a new contract on the grounds that her existing agreement was signed when she was a minor, Wells's last two proposed singles were shelved (or possibly never even recorded), prompting her to join 20th Century Fox and later Atco, where her career tailed off.

Until the Supremes became chart regulars, Eddie Holland was regarded as the label's biggest hope. His first hit, "Jamie", exists in two versions, though the only difference appears to be the running time printed on the label. U.K. releases for Eddie's follow-ups were somewhat erratic – though odd A-sides did find their way onto compilation EPs and the like – which leaves collectors no option but to track down his U.S. issues. Probably the most significant of these is "On The Outside Looking In", a monster-hit on the Northern Soul scene thanks to its blasting brass, handclap beat and girly backing from the Andantes. "Just A Few More Days" and "If Cleopatra Took A Chance" have also been in strong demand from Northern Soul collectors for many years, with the latter sporting a delightful aura of unrequited love – "If queens can fall in love, then why can't you?", Eddie asks his heart throb – set against the sort of Egyptian-sounding music which accompanies dancing girls and banquet scenes in Hollywood "Cleopatra" films. Eddie Holland's output is a good starting point for any U.S. Motown collection, as all his records repay the effort needed to track them down.

Equally under-represented in terms of U.K. output is the highly talented Carolyn Crawford, whose fine "When Someone's Good To You" only hints at the quality of much of her other material. Carolyn went to the label in 1963 at the age of 14, after winning that year's annual Motown talent contest. The much-loved "My Smile Is Just A Frown" found a place on the reissue album, *Motown Memories*, though its U.S.-only flip, "I'll Come Running", is definitely worth a listen. Easily her best record, though, was "Devil In His Heart", which sadly missed out on a British single, but at least made it onto the rare "Hitsville U.S.A." EP. Its B-side, "Forget About Me", is one of the biggest Motown rediscoveries of recent years. It's a restless, intense piece of mid-tempo soul, with a pounding tom-tom beat and the world-weary lyrics: "I loved you but it wasn't smart to tell you/You made a big issue out of everything I said." Demand is high for this dancefloor gem, and its price is rising.

Linda Griner's "Goodbye Cruel Love" is possibly the rarest Motown single to have been issued commercially, and easily the rarest sought-after by collectors today. Linda joined the Motown stable at the age of 16, after becoming friendly with Berry. Written and produced by Smokey Robinson, "Goodbye Cruel Love" suffers from a few too-obvious rhymes, but these are more than compensated for by its sparkling rhythm production. On its release, it suffered from poor promotion, with demo copies misprinting the title as "Goodbye Cruel World", thus losing the wit of Smokey's favourite songwriting trick of punning on a well-known phrase.

Its poor sales have provoked debate as to whether demos or stock copies are rarer (they are probably equally scarce) while its Canadian release on Tamla is now super-rare. After recording only one single for Motown, Linda changed her name to Lyn Roman for a sizeable hit with "Stop, I Don't Need No Sympathy" on Brunswick, before recording for Dot, Epie, Ichiban and other labels.

The Supremes had a touch more success at Motown than Linda, though interestingly enough, their first Motown single is by far the rarest record on the label, and is many times scarcer than "Goodbye Cruel Love"! "I Want A Guy" was originally scheduled for release as Motown 1008, but was transferred to Tamla at the last minute, with the Contours' debut single becoming its replacement. The few Motown copies of "I Want A Guy" which escaped can be counted on about half the fingers of one hand. With two flops on Tamla, the Supremes returned to Motown, where Berry devoted his best efforts to securing a hit with them.

In fact, their fortunes crystallise much of what happened at Motown as a whole: why it succeeded and why it ultimately went rotten. At first the group members were all equal, taking turns at singing lead and occupying the centre spot in publicity photos, but Berry recognised that Diana (no longer Diane) had the greatest star potential (despite having the weakest voice, as the shared lead on "Breathtaking Guy" clearly shows), plus the best stage image and, most important of all, the greatest desire to be a crossover pop star, whatever it took.

Berry and Smokey split production duties on their first attempts at recording the group, but it was only after the girls were given to Holland-Dozier-Holland that they scored a hit – in the shape of "Lovelight" – after which everything they did was a phenomenal success, apart from "Run, Run, Run". A relative disappointment, that single reached only No 22 on the *Cashbox* R&B chart, and is more sought-after for its flipside, "I'm Giving You Your Freedom", a promising dancer which never reached the U.K.

Then, "Where Did Our Love Go" started an astonishing run of five consecutive pop No. 1s, setting the Supremes on course towards becoming the third biggest-selling act of the '60s in the U.S., topped only by Elvis and the Beatles. Berry's concentration on the Supremes paid dividends in terms of sales, but was a major cause of splits within, and defections from, his company. Other Motown artists found their careers pushed aside or put on hold as Berry ploughed more and more effort into the group, who'd embarrassingly failed to score a hit for so long they'd earned the nickname of "The No-Hit Supremes", making the favouritism even more pronounced.

Tensions within the group also grew, as Mary and Flo effectively became back-up singers for Ross. To minimise competition with Diana's vocal, Flo was sometimes required to stand nearly 20 feet away from the microphone during recording sessions.

Soon, the Supremes gained the reputation of being prepared to record anything which might net them enormous sales. The Copacabana performances and show tunes LPs make most soul fans recoil in horror, and help to explain the suspicion about Motown in soul circles. "Baby Love" was a record so trite and twee that Brian Holland confessed he could hardly bring himself to write it, while Mary recalled shedding many tears at the thought of the lightweight rubbish they were expected to record. The situation worsened when Berry and Diana became personally entwined, and by July 1967, matters had gotten so bad that Flo and Mary apparently heard about the name change to "Diana Ross & the Supremes" through the grapevine.

In that same month, Flo was kicked out of the group, though the official line was that she left because of ill health (she had started drinking heavily in 1966). The first Mary knew of this was when Cindy Birdsong arrived to audition for the vacant place. Flo's solo career failed and the girl who had formed the biggest-selling girl group of all time slid into homelessness and welfare dependency, dying in abject poverty in 1976.

The story of the Supremes is a perfect example of how what Smokey Robinson called the "chaotic fun, chaotic love and chaotic togetherness" of the early days had gone sour by the late '60s. By then, Motown was a place full of backstabbing, ambition, discontent and poor industrial relations, as the many defections, feuds and disputes about royalties and restrictive contracts testify. It is this image of Motown as a kind of faceless corporate body which had its employees at the bottom of its list of priorities which has put so many soul fans off the label.

Indeed, some individuals go so far as to claim that Motown – and the Supremes, in particular – betrayed Soul music in some way. However, its important to say that the Supremes pop records were also instrumental in bringing soul music to the attention of millions, and their early recordings, at least still reveal a group which was in good harmony, both personal and vocal.

The Four Tops were an altogether happier group, boasting the same line-up – Levi Stubbs, Renaldo Obie Benson, Duke Fakir and Lawrence Payton – as when they formed as the Four Aims in 1954. At Motown, their faultless vocals combined with the production skills of Holland-Dozier-Holland at their creative peak to produce some of the most outstanding records the company ever put out.

Originally signed by Berry in 1963 to the Workshop Jazz label, they recorded an unreleased (until 1999) LP of jazz and easy listening. before they were assigned to the H-D-H team at Motown, where their first record, "What Goes Up" – an over-the-top, almost tongue-in-cheek blues slowie – sold poorly. In fact, it was over a year before another Four Tops record appeared, after the band had been fetched from the audience at a Temptations show at the Twenty Grand to record "Baby I Need Your Loving" in the early hours of the night.

This single was followed up by two further mid-tempo epics, of which one, "Ask The Lonely", was one of the most-played Motown tracks in Northern Soul clubs. In fact, its club success prompted a revival of interest in the Four Tops, as Northern Soul collectors realised the exceptional quality of some of their records, which they'd previously ignored in favour of rarer material.

To round up this instalment, it's worth mentioning a few other tracks on Motown which U.K.-only collectors might otherwise miss. Tammi Terrell's "Hold Me Oh My Darling" is an attractive mid-to-uptempo production; the Morrocco Muzik Makers' "Back To School Again"/ "Pig Knuckles" couples a pair of gritty R&B instrumentals; and Connie Van Dyke's "It Hurt Me Too" is a heartfelt soul version of the flip of Marvin Gaye's "Stubborn Kind of Fellow", recorded by one of Motown's white signings (no relation to Earl Van Dyke!).

Finally, a warning: the Easy Listening croonings of Tony Martin, Bobby Breen, Sammy Turner and Billy Eckstine are of little value to soul fans, except as evidence of Berry's continuing ambitions to reach the pop market. However, some do feature fine arrangements or productions, which will no doubt be of interest to Motown specialists. Try Bobby Breen's "Here Comes That Heartache" – an excellent production by New York recruit Eddie Singleton.

Part 5: Miracle and Mel-o-dy
Miracle

It might have been the income from the Miracles' huge hit, "Shop Around", which helped Berry Gordy realise that it was possible to launch a third label, alongside Motown and Tamla. Whatever the reason, January 1961 duly saw the first single on the new Miracle label.

Miracle is fascinating for early Motown collectors. It showed that the Motown sound was beginning to gel, much to the delight of later Soul fans, while the label also saw the recording debut of a number of important Motown artists, including Jimmy Ruffin, the Valadiers and the Temptations. Not only that: the extraordinary rarity of most of its output stems from the fact that none of the dozen records released on the label appeared on any national chart, pop or R&B.

Jimmy Ruffin's vinyl debut, a pacy dancer with a snappy brass riff, has been a sizeable Northern Soul club favourite for some years now and is very difficult to find. Little Iva, meanwhile, who had the second release on Miracle, was Gordy's original Motown partner, Raynoma Liles, the band were Motown session musicians and the "Continental Strut" was just that – an R&B instrumental, and a very good one too. The other side, "When I Needed You", was a touching doo-wop ballad written by Raynoma for Berry after the miscarriage of their first child in 1958.

Gino Parks' version of Ron & Bill's "Don't Say Bye Bye" is even rarer. In fact, it's never been seen (even by Parks himself), and the same goes for Andre Williams' "Rosa Lee", so it's likely that neither single was ever issued.

The Temptations' first two attempts, on Miracle 5 and 12, were attractive, if a little hard-edged, uptempo dancers of the sort. Copies are not too difficult to find (in rare Motown terms, at least) but demand from collectors is high.

Motown was often criticised in the '60s for ignoring social issues and concentrating only on hitting the pop charts, but the Valadiers' "Greetings, This Is Uncle Sam" (later resurrected by the Monitors) was an ironic comment on the Army draft letter, an all too real shadow over the lives of many of Motown's young customers. The Valadiers' flipside, "Take A Chance", was a fairly high quality doo-wop effort which commands high prices on the American market.

One of the real gems on the label came next. The Equadors' "Someone To Call My Own" is little known outside specialist Motown circles, but the value of this first-class mid-tempo dancer from a very good soul group is sure to rise. The label's next three releases were all white doo-wop efforts and highlighted again Berry's desire to cross over to the pop charts. Both sides of the Freddie Gorman record on Miracle 11, however, were a return to whole-hearted dance-soul. The fine mid tempo "The Day Will Come" (also cut by Mary Wells for her *Two Lovers* LP) was backed by the uptempo "Just For You", a coupling which is in strong demand.

The Miracle label wound up after just eleven months (though singles were reportedly still being pressed in 1963) – partly, it seems, to make way for the Gordy label, whose first release appeared some five months later and who took on board a number of Miracle acts. Most of its meagre output is still a long way from realising its full potential on the collectors' market.

Mel-o-dy

Motown's other small label of the early '60s was Mel-o-dy. The first five releases were good but little-known soul-dance records, and all of them are rare – one or two extremely so. The Creations' "This is Our Night" is a case in point: a solid mid-tempo soul sound by a group whose identity has long since been forgotten.

Lamont Dozier's final attempt as a Motown performer was something of a milestone, as it was also the first Holland-Dozier-Holland collaboration, with Eddie Holland replacing Freddie Gorman in the Holland-Dozier-Holland writing/production team after Freddie's move to Ed Wingate's rival Ric Tic studios. "Dearest One" was not only important in historical terms, but also an excellent record into the bargain. Surprisingly, the record remains little known outside serious Motown circles.

The Vells record is rather more familiar, perhaps because the group were later renamed the Vandellas, having changed their name from the Del-Phis because they were still under contract by that name to the Check-Mate label. Their thumping dancer, "You'll Never Cherish A Love So True", was the first record to feature Martha Reeves as a member of the group, though Gloria Williams remained the lead vocalist. When it flopped, Gloria quit the music business, leaving behind Martha, Rosalind Ashford and Annette Sterling.

The single happened because Martha had landed a job as secretary and receptionist to Mickey Stevenson (physically getting inside Hitsville was the key for unsigned hopefuls!) and was biding her time waiting for the chance to record, while singing back-up with the Del-Phis on a number of other labels. When Mary Wells failed to turn up for a session, Martha was allowed to round up the Del-Phis as a replacement. Exactly the same happened again for the group's appearance as the Beljeans on Gordy 7009 (though only Rosalind and Annette sang on this one). Only after that were they allowed to record in their own right, as Martha & the Vandellas.

Other budding Motown superstars resorted to pseudonyms. The mysterious Pirates who issued Mel-o-dy 105 were actually the Temptations, cutting a good, uptempo dancer. The label's big rarity, however, is the Charters' "Trouble Lover" on Mel-o-dy 104. Practically nothing is known about them, and the only surviving copy of their reputedly excellent soul dancer was unearthed only in the 1980s, making it one of the truly heavyweight rarities and a jewel in the crown of any Motown collection.

From Mel-o-dy 106 onwards, the label took a sharp change of direction, being devoted exclusively to white folk or country music, none of which is of interest to soul fans. Ironically, these records proved far less popular with the white pop market than the soul releases on Berry Gordy's other labels.

If Motown collectors are aware of the Workshop Jazz subsidiary at all, it's probably only for the fact that it almost released the first Four Tops LP, *Breaking Through*, in 1964. In fact, Workshop Jazz also issued seven singles in 1962 and 1963.

The label seems to have been set up as a means of attracting top jazz musicians to

Motown, so that they would then be available to Gordy as sessionmen. Few of the Workshop Jazz releases sold at all well, but prices for the singles are still relatively low, as they're only of interest to jazz specialists and Motown completists, and don't have any real relevance to Motown's history as a soul empire.

Part 6: Gordy, V.I.P and Soul

Although it seems to be comparatively rare today, accusations of bribery – or 'payola' – were rife in 1950s and '60s America, and proved to be a constant source of concern for DJs and schedulers. Radio stations became extremely wary of over-exposing any one label, however good its music. To counteract this, labels developed off-shoots: Atlantic had Atco, Cotillion plus several others; Chess had Checker, Cadet and Argo; VeeJay had Tollie; and Mercury had Blue Rock.

As head of a growing soul empire, Berry Gordy had little choice but to employ the same business tactics, establishing three Motown subsidiaries, Gordy, V.I.P. and Soul, between 1962 and 1964. None ever looked in danger of overshadowing its parent company, either commercially or musically, but all produced some classic recordings among which are several of the most collectable soul singles from the '60s.

Although he was as keen as his rivals to flood the airwaves with product, Berry clearly had an ulterior motive when he set up Gordy. In late 1962, he got word that his ex-wife, Thelma Coleman, was planning to set up a record label in Detroit, possibly using the "Gordy" name. To sabotage her efforts, he immediately filed an application for his own Gordy offshoot, forcing Coleman to choose a new name for her company, Thelma.

The two companies had much in common: both issued their first record in March 1962, both enjoyed commercial success and both are popular with collectors today, with Thelma being the most collectable Detroit label after Motown and its subsidiaries. But there's another interesting coincidence, too: the first release from both labels was, in a manner of speaking, a Temptations record.

Now regarded as one of the true soul greats, the Temptations had their roots in a late '50s vocal quartet, the Cavaliers, who were formed in Birmingham, Alabama around the nucleus of Eddie Kendricks and Paul Williams. After Willie Waller quit the group, they renamed themselves the Primes, before shedding Kell Osbourne and moving to Detroit, where they became the 'brother' outfit to the Primettes – later the Supremes – and met the Distants, featuring Otis Williams, Eldridge 'Al' Bryant, Melvin Franklin, Richard Street and James Crawford.

Bryant, Williams and Franklin teamed up with the two Primes to form the Elgins (not the mid-60s V.I.P. group), who Berry found and signed in 1960, changing their name to the Temptations. Street and Crawford continued with the Distants, recruiting replacements and releasing an impossibly rare record on Thelma, the beautiful mid-tempo "Answer Me", which was given a more widespread release on New York's Harmon label. When this record went nowhere, Street joined Motown's Quality Control department, before fronting the Monitors and eventually replacing Paul Williams in the Temptations. The young Norman Whitfield, who had written and produced "Answer Me", came along too, and became a Motown producer, working on hits by the Temptations and the Velvelettes, among others.

Meanwhile, the Temptations proper had been shifted from the defunct Miracle label to the new Gordy imprint, which issued their "Dream Come True" debut as its first release in March 1962. The response from the public was lukewarm and, in fact, none of their first four singles for the label was able to break into the R&B charts. Among them was Smokey's first production with the group, "I Want A Love I Can See", a Northern Soul rediscovery which marks the debut of Eldridge Bryant's replacement, David Ruffin.

All of these tracks made it onto the Tempts' first U.K. LP, but none appeared as a single, except "I Want A Love I Can See", which became a U.K. B-side nearly five years later. After they finally hit with Smokey's "The Way You Do The Things You Do", all their U.S. 45s were given a U.K. release, except their label-credited back-up to Liz Lands' "Midnight Johnny" and a number of uncredited stand-ins for the Love Tones. Puzzlingly, a fine mid-tempo version of the Eddie Holland side, "I Couldn't Cry If I Wanted To", was also denied a British release.

The other ex-Miracle label group, the Valadiers, recorded only two non-hits on the Gordy label, before slipping from the Midtown catalogue. "I Found A Girl" is well known to U.K. collectors, thanks to its release on Oriole, but "Because I Love Her" remains virtually unknown – amazing, considering its exceptional quality. Where "Found" hurriedly jerks along, "Because" flows smoothly, with a group vocal rivalling any other contemporary Motown act for soulfulness. Pounding kettle drums and Raymona's Ondioline – a primitive synthesiser which appeared on most early Motown recordings – lend the record a dynamic and exotic feel, making it a perfect candidate for future Northern Soul attention.

After leaving Motown, the group (Stuart Avig, Jerry Light, Art Glasser and Marty Coleman) combined with the Sunliners from Detroit's famed Golden World label to form the Latin Counts, while in 1964 Avig also recorded a solo Northern Soul winner, "Angelina"/"King For A Day", on Ed Wingate's tiny J&W label, under the pseudonym "Stewart Ames".

The Contours – Billy Gordon, Joe Billingslea, Billy Hoggs, Hubert Johnson, Sylvester Potts and, at various times, Dennis Edwards and Joe Stubbs – complete a trio of male vocal groups transferred to Gordy from other labels, having started out with two incredibly rare records on Motown, "Whole Lotta Woman" and "The Stretch". Loud and raucous, they were signed as a novelty act on the recommendation of Jackie Wilson, Hubert's cousin.

Despite their gimmicky aspect, their Gordy 45s all earned a U.K. release in some form, apart from "You Get Ugly" and "Pa I Need A Car", a fine example of Berry's desire to identify his sales market and target it ruthlessly – in this case, late-teen males. The same approach can be seen on records like the Supremes' "She's Seventeen" (aimed at 16-year-old girls) and the Twisting Kings' "Xmas Twist", which is the sort of thing you see middle-aged diplomats dancing to in archive footage. Berry's more blatant targeting rarely seems to have worked, but in general his marketing was spot on, and very thoroughly followed through.

It has been estimated that nearly 10,000 tracks were recorded at Motown between 1964 and 1966 alone, of which only a few hundred were issued. Some of the unissued records have been unearthed over the years, and the stunning quality of some, like Marvin Originals' "Suspicion", and the Temptations' "Forever In My Heart", hints at the wealth of musical treasures which may remain in Motown's vaults.

Records were not only voted on at regular Monday morning meetings, but played to the local teenagers who gathered every day after school on the Hitsville front lawn. Several children made it inside the building to become regular – if unofficial – quality control advisors, being paid in sweets and soft drinks. One or two even did an occasional backing session, while Martha Reeves managed to get a job there as a secretary.

Early sessions for her Del-Phis mainly involved stand-in work for the Andantes, backing artists like Hattie Littles, LaBrenda Ben and Marvin Gaye, who later returned the favour by playing piano on "Dancing In The Street". After standing in for Mary Wells once again, on "I'll Have To Let Him Go", the group was allowed to release the recording under their own name of the Vandellas, taken from Van Dyke Street – where Martha's mother lived – and Della Reese, an idol of Martha's. The record teamed them with Holland-Dozier-Holland for a Northern Soul classic which marked the beginning of the "Golden-Age" Motown sound. After that, all U.S. releases credited to the Vandellas became U.K. 45s, a distinction unmatched by any other big-selling Motown act.

Kim Weston's phenomenal 45, "Helpless", has always enjoyed cult status on the Northern Soul scene, but non-U.K. dance sounds – like "A Thrill A Moment" (which sounds years ahead of its time), "I'll Never See My Love Again" and Tamla's "Feel Alright Tonight" – confirm her as a firm dancefloor favourite.

On his return from United Artists, where his career had tailed off after 1963, Marv Johnston cut two poor sellers, "Why Do You Want To Let Me Go" and "I Miss You Baby (How I Miss You)". As with Weston's "A Thrill A Moment", neither reached *Cashbox*'s R&B Top 100, and only the most alert collectors tend to notice that the famous name disguises quite a rarity. Both sides of Johnson's release on Gordy 7051 are in fact belting "Golden Age" dancers, though neither gained a British release at the time.

Harder to spot are the Marvelettes, who appear on Gordy disguised as the Darnells, in an attempt to recreate the Spector sound, complete with castanets and mile-wide echo. The track was included on the U.K. LP, *R&B Chartmakers Vol. III*, while its flip, a semi-instrumental featuring Lamont Dozier, Eddie Hendricks, Brian Holland and some of the Marvelettes, was recycled from the B-side of the H-D-H/Four Tops/ Andantes record on Motown 1054. Similarly disguised is Robert L. Gordy, Berry's brother, who recorded a 45 for Carlton in Motown's earliest days, as well as a couple of singles on Anna, a single for Tamla and the Gordy novelty disc, "Hold On Pearl", under the alias of Bob Kayli. His Tamla 45 is a weak novelty answer to Jimmy Dean's hit, "Big Bad John", but its uptempo flip is welcome in many early soul collections. Discouraged by poor sales, Robert followed an administrative career at Motown. He took over responsibility for Jobete publishing in 1965 after the death of his sister Loucye, who had been given the job when Raynoma left in 1963 to set up a Jobete office in New York.

The Stylers record, a surf car/death/novelty disc (!) would be pretty unwelcome at most Northern Soul allnighters, but is hard for Motown completists to track down, and does at least have an acceptable white doo-wop flip. Little is known about Tommy Good except that he was a talented white vocalist. Lee & the Leopards were signed from Fortune Records, Detroit's biggest and most important R&B independent, in the late '50s and early '60s, but their move to Motown gained them little in terms of commercial success.

Hattie Littles is another great favourite of Motown specialists. A tough-voiced blues vocalist from the deep South, she seems to have recorded endless Motown sessions, with virtually nothing appearing commercially. At least a dozen unreleased acetates have been found to date, several of which are well worth a listen. Hattie worked at Motown for some years, doing a lot of work with Marvin Gaye as the opening act on his tours, but she had little joy in commercial terms, perhaps because her records were too bluesy and not pop enough. Nonetheless, all her singles made an impact on the Northern Soul scene similar to that made by Liz Lands' "Midnight Johnny".

This record crossed over from "Motown collectable" status to "Northern Soul giant" at the end of the eighties. Lands was a singer of Spanish or Latin descent, with a bit of Red Indian blood thrown in for good measure, and had a very wide vocal range. Originally signed to Motown's Divinity label, she was involved in Civil Rights work with Martin Luther King and issued a single mourning President Kennedy's assassination ("May What He Loved For Live"), an event which hit everyone at Motown hard. These records do not threaten to follow in the footsteps of the uncharacteristically worldly "Midnight Johnny", which provides an essential introduction to the kind of early Motown "rediscoveries" which made their mark on the Northern Soul scene.

V.I.P.

The V.I.P. label was set up at the beginning of 1964 and seems to have been intended as an outlet for Motown's many white acts. Certainly, Joanne & the Triangles (sugary teen pop), the Hornets ("Kiss" echoes the Beatles' "I Want To Hold Your Hand"), Ray Oddis (self-explanatory novelty) and Danny Day have little place in a soul collection, though other white acts such as the Headliners ("You're Bad News"), the Dalton Boys ("I've Been Cheated"), the six-year-old Little Lisa ("Hang On Bill"), Rick, Robin & Him ("'Cause You Know Me") and staff writer R. Dean Taylor have contributed in-demand Northern Soul sounds.

The Lewis Sisters made two records which were later picked up by British clubs, as well as singing back-ups for Chris Clark, V.I.P.'s best and most successful white act. They also wrote under their married names of (Kay) Miller – Little Lisa's mum – and (Helen) Masters, as well as appearing in the film *Lady Sings The Blues*.

Among this array of white acts were several formidable black artists, including the Vows, whose "Tell Me" has become one of the biggest allnighter sounds, and features a lead vocal by Morris "Too Darn Soulful" Chestnut, a long-established favourite for his solo recordings. And the A-side, "Buttered Popcorn", was actually by legendary Detroit soul artist/producer, Richard "Popcorn" Wylie.

Oma Heard recorded an LP of duets with Marvin Gaye after Mary Wells's departure left him without a female singing partner. The album remained unissued (though tracks from it are included on the Marvin Gaye box set), and Oma was eventually fired, apparently for being overweight. Afterwards, she became a top L.A session singer, recording as Oma Heard, Oma Page and Oma Drake. Her delicious, husky-voiced V.I.P. floater, "Mr. Lonely Heart", has considerable potential for club exposure.

George Kerr's group, the Serenaders, were one of Raymona's discoveries during her stay (or perhaps exile) in New York, and featured lead vocals from Timothy Wilson, a long-time favourite of soul fans for his solo recordings on Veep, Blue Rock and Buddah. The astonishingly good "If Your Heart Says Yes" whisks along like a roman candle, spiralling through several key changes and exploding with ringing xylophones and sprays of harmony.

The label's big gun for collectors, however, is the only credited release by the Andantes – Louvain Demps, Jackie Hicks, Marlene Barrow and, periodically, soul favourite Pat Lewis. "Like A Nightmare" is virtually the Vandellas' "Heatwave" with different words, and given that song's success, it's a shame the Andantes weren't given the chance to cross over from backing group to soul stars. On reflection, it may have been the similarity of styles which made Motown change its mind about releasing it. Motown legend has it that the withdrawn copies are now propping up a skyscraper in downtown Detroit!

The Monitors featured ex-Distant Richard Street, together with Sandra Fagin, John 'Maurice' Fagin and Warren Harris. Although their revival of the Valadiers' "Greetings" scraped into the Top 100 for one week, all their other efforts flopped, though their non-U.K. tracks like "Since I Lost You Girl" and "Don't Put Off Until Tomorrow" shouldn't be overlooked.

Perhaps V.I.P.'s most successful act were the Velvelettes, who were discovered at a fraternity dance a year after their formation at Western Michigan University. The group were put together by Rob Bullock, a nephew of Berry and a fellow student of the two group's members, Mildred Gill and Bertha Barbee (the line-up was completed by Carolyn 'Cal' Gill, Norma Barbee and Betty Kelly). Bullock took them to Detroit to audition, but despite failing, Mickey Stevenson was sufficiently impressed to produce a single, which was issued by the Detroit IPG label (Independent Producers Group). This rare 45 features a delicate mid-tempo lament for a lost boyfriend, backed with a sassy dancer along the lines of the Marvelettes' "Too Strong To Be Strung Along" which benefits from harmonica contribution from Little Stevie Wonder.

The Velvelettes sang some backing vocals for Motown, and after Mildred Gill and Betty Kelly left the group (Betty joined the Vandellas in 1963), they cut "Needle In A

Haystack" and "He Was Really Sayin' Somethin'".

With Sandra Tilley and Annette MacMillan drafted in as replacements, the group was assigned to Norman Whitfield, who produced the Northern Soul classic "Lonely Lonely Girl Am I", which reached No. 34 on the R&B chart during a two-week stay. A post-poned follow-up, "A Bird In The Hand (Is Worth Two In The Bush)", emerged, while "These Things Will Keep Me Loving You" (a 1964 Bertha, Norma and Cal recording with vocals by Sandra and Annette dubbed on) was also cancelled and rescheduled for the Soul label. Sadly, the girls failed to match the success of other Motown girl groups, and when their contract expired they simply left – leaving behind them some of the most respected soul offerings of their kind.

Soul

While V.I.P. was a label full of contradictions, providing an outlet for both determinedly lightweight pop and full-bodied soul recordings, the Soul label enjoyed a consistent cat-alogue of resolutely R&B-orientated dance sounds. When Tri-Phi folded, Soul inherited acts like Junior Walker, the Merced Blue Notes and Shorty Long, who issued a highly-recommended non-UK dancer in the shape of "It's A Crying Shame", as well as his two all-time classics, "Devil With The Blue Dress" and "Function at the Junction". Long was also MC for the Motortown Revue, and was in close contact with keyboardist and band-leader Earl Van Dyke – who in turn was responsible for instrumental club classics like "Soul Stomp" and "Six By Six".

Soul also scheduled one-off 45s from Californian instrumental combo, the Merced Blue Notes, the Hit Pack (an obscure white group), the Freeman Brothers, and Frances Nero, the winner of 1964's annual Motown talent contest (previous winners were LaBrenda Ben in 1962 and Carolyn Crawford a year later), who beat Northern Soul favourite Ronnie McNeir into second place. The award brought Nero a Motown contract, and her "Keep on Lovin' Me", has long been a dancefloor great. The New York-based black group, the Freeman Brothers, whose Soul 45, "My Baby", is a recent arrival on the club scene, also recorded for Mala and Sprout and can boast one of the rarest-ever deep soul 45s (especially in demand in Japan), "You Got Me On A String" (International Allied).

Another Soul signing, Frank Wilson, was responsible for what is without a doubt one of the great collectables in any field: "Do I Love You", only two or three copies of which are thought to survive. As one of Motown's crowning glories and a celebrated rarity, "Do I Love You" provides a very fitting conclusion to this survey of the label's early years. Of course, the "Golden Age" could not last forever and by 1967, many of those responsible for Motown's initial success were no longer around to share its fruits or contribute to its further success.

Barrett Strong had left for Veejay; Beans Bowles and Janie Bradford had followed suit following bitter arguments with Berry Gordy; and Kim Weston and Brenda Holloway departed when their careers were put on hold to make way for the Supremes, with Weston taking with her both her husband Mickey Stevenson (a past Motown stalwart) and Carolyn Crawford (a hope for its future).

The New York Jobete office, which Raynoma had set up after her separation from Berry, failed, apparently because of lack of support from Detroit HQ. In a desperate attempt to improve the label's cashflow, Raynoma had copies of Mary Wells' "My Guy" repressed and, as a result, she was forced out of the company on the bewildering charge of bootlegging Motown product. She took with her Eddie Singleton, Gino Parks and Frances Nero, setting up Shrine Records in Washington D.C., where the spectre of Berry still seemed to pursue them.

The artists who fell away quickly had their places filled – by accountants, who increasingly called the tune, even in creative matters. Those who remained found themselves caught up in vicious personal squabbles, with toe-treading competition replacing the friendly rivalry which had spurred them on in the early years. In place of incentives – $1,000 for a No. 1, plus the automatic right to produce the next record by the artist you scored the hit with – came a scramble not so much to get ahead but to prevent yourself from being trampled underfoot by rivals. The production-line approach, which led Berry to adopt ideas like a Quality Control department, had gone overboard, and artists felt undervalued and isolated from their boss, who spent much time in L.A., looking into the film industry. Worse still, the artists felt distanced from each other, particularly after the company moved from Hitsville to the faceless, ten-storey Donovan Building in March 1968.

But the biggest blow was the loss of Holland-Dozier-Holland, who staged a go-slow in 1966 when they realised that their stream of Top 40 hits was unlikely to be rewarded with a profit-sharing deal. After two years of law-suits, they set up their own label, Invictus.

Before the glitter of the "Golden Age" faded, Motown assured itself a place in history, and touched the lives of millions of music lovers. It would take many thousands of words to tell the label's story in full, and a lifetime to collect every record it ever issued – but wouldn't now be a good time to start?

Nick Brown's Motown Top Ten

1. "Baby, I Need Your Lovin'" – Four Tops
Hard to choose a single winner and "Ask the Lonely" comes pretty close, but I think this is Motown's most perfectly accomplished record. Grace, style, and poise come together in a moment of infinite yearning. I like to throw this in when Dj-ing; nobody ever expects it and the reaction is always ecstatic. Pure perfection.

2. "I'll Keep On Holding On" – Marvelettes
This is another one that drives dancers absolutely mental, whether they're hardcore Northern Soulies or casual students who've never heard it before. One of the best records ever made full stop.

3. "Forget About Me" – Carolyn Crawford
Smashing tune, great production, inch-perfect arrangement and those devastating lyrics.

4. "Goodbye Cruel Love" – Linda Griner
An automatic choice, I suppose, for a Northern Soulie. I remember the moment I first heard this, at an allnighter in Chesterfeld in about 1988 and just panicking to find out what it was.

5. "Lonely Lover" – Marvin Gaye
One of the big bunch of unissued titles that turned up in the early eighties which revived my interest in Motown after considering it a bit passe when I first found Northern Soul. Now it's thankfully on a box set, but how this never came out originally, I cannot imagine. Absolutely faultless.

6. "If Your Heart Says Yes" – Serenaders
One of the earlier sounding Motown pieces that's become popular with Northern Soul collectors over the last ten years or so, and one of the best, too. This one's day will come.

7. "My World Is Empty Without You" – Supremes
Never thought I'd be putting a Supremes record in my top ten, but it's the backing track on this one that sets it apart. Absolutely no prisoners whatsoever.

8. "Lonely, Lonely Girl Am I" – Velvelettes
Golden age Motown par excellence and one of the most exciting records you could ever dance to. Turn the volume dial to 11, roll back the carpet and annihilate your shoe leather.

9. "A Love That Can Never Be" – Satintones
An elegant splendour of heartbreak and harmonies on this polished jewel of a record that never puts a foot wrong. Equally loved by early soul fans and doo-woppers. Extremely rare, but well worth the hunt.

10. "If Your Mother Only Knew" – Miracles
I'm a real sucker for that early '60s Motown sound with the tip-toe beat and doo-wop transition feel. Lovely strings on this one, and a fabulous bubbling rhythm that will put a smile all over your face.

Coda: "Do I Love You" – The 10,000 Dollar Question!
by Nick Brown

Written by Motown songwriter Frank Wilson in 1965, "Do I Love You (Indeed I Do)" was originally conceived for Marvin Gaye, but when the singer grew lukewarm about the project, Wilson was persuaded to have a go at recording it himself. After a handful of test pressings were made (Soul 35019), Frank asked Berry not to release it, as he felt he was essentially a producer rather than a singer, and was reluctant to get drawn into a role in which he wasn't comfortable.

In the mid-70s a copy of the disc, with Berry's hand-written comments on the label, fell into the hands of Motown historian, Tom DePierro, who stumbled across it while trawling through the Motown vaults to research a series of archive albums. He sold it to fellow Californian Simon Soussan, a Los Angeles resident who'd grown interested in Northern Soul while living in Leeds in the '60s. Acetates were sent to DJs at the legendary Wigan Casino allnighter in 1975, crediting the track to Eddie Foster (whose huge dancefloor hit, "I Never Knew", featured a similar wait-for-the-beat intro and string arrangement). Top DJ Soul Sam played the disc, but covered it up again – this time crediting it to Otis Clark. It was an instant success, but despite efforts to keep its identity secret, bootlegs appeared under the guise of Eddie Foster.

Together with a belated British Tamla Motown release (November 1979), this fake satiated demand for the track. Meanwhile, Soussan sold the only known original copy to Les McCutcheon (a former Northern Soul dealer who was by then a successful London music publisher and creator of the funk band, Shakatak), for the disclosed sum of £400, the highest price ever paid for a Northern Soul 45 at the time. Fuelled by rumours that multiple copies of "Do I Love You" were turning up, the single then passed to Nottingham collector Jonathan Woodcliffe for the lower sum of £250. In 1981, Woodcliffe's allegiance had shifted towards jazz funk and he exchanged the disc for £300-worth of 12"s with rare soul afficionado Kev Roberts, a renowned Northern Soul DJ from the Casino days.

"I came close to offloading the piece several times, due to rumours that X had found a load or Y was getting 100 copies", recalls Kev. "But I weathered the storm of controversy, and slowly its mystique and demand grew. In 1993, Tim Brown, then the U.K's most prominent collector, approached me, and I eventually sold this ultimate Northern Soul rarity for £3,300."

After DiPierro's immortal find, Ron Murphy, a Detroit native and Motown historian, unearthed a second copy which was sold to Tim Brown's partner at Goldmine/Anglo American, Martin Koppel, as part of a larger collection. *[Ed: The record has subsequently changed hands for even higher sums, begging questions of sanity amid certain collectors.]*

This kind of rarity places "Do I Love You" among other celebrated world collectables like the Five Sharps' "Stormy Weather"- and rightly so, as it is a truly superb recording capturing Motown's "Golden Age" at its very best. What's more, it also epitomises the Northern Soul scene, capturing the sheer joy of the atmosphere at an allnighter.

31
Hitsville Highpoints: 10 Favourite '60s Singles
by Timothy White

Timothy White is Editor of Billboard, *and a respected writer in many fields. His acclaimed books include:* The Nearest Faraway Place: Brian Wilson, The Beach Boys and The Southern California Experience.

"Please Mr Postman" – The Marvelettes	Tamla, 1961
"Actions Speak Louder Than Words" – Mabel John	Tamla, 196
"Beechwood 4-5789" – The Marvellettes	Tamla, 1962
"Stubborn Kind of Fellow" – Marvin Gaye	Tamla, 1962
"You Beat Me To The Punch" – Mary Wells	Motown, 1962
"Where Did Our Love Go" – The Supremes	Motown, 1964
"Going To A Go-Go" – The Miracles	Tamla, 1965
"Bernadette" – Four Tops	Motown, 1967
"I Was Made To Love Her" – Stevie Wonder	Tamla, 1967
"Ain't Nothing Like The Real Thing" – Marvin Gaye and Tammi Terrell	
	Tamla, 1968

32
Northern Soul and Motown
by Dave Rimmer

The fact that there can be a Motown reader book published in the new Millennium is to some extent due to the music's continued popularity on the Northern Soul scene. This music scene, now so well known to American soul artists, has kept '60s and '70s Soul music alive and is more popular than ever as a record collecting area. Whilst Motown's original popularity in the early '60s was without doubt rooted in London and the Home Counties, its long life and status now lies elsewhere. To support the scene there are many specialist magazines, and Dave Rimmer's Soulful Kinda Music *is one of these. Dave's article originally appeared in 1990, and has now been updated and re-written especially for this book.*

The "Northern Soul scene" as we know it, was born in the mid-Sixties in clubs all over the country which specialised in playing the latest UK release of Soul records. Amongst the Stax and Atlantic there were also a lot of records played on the Tamla Motown label.

The Twisted Wheel in Manchester is often quoted as *the* club where the Northern scene was born. This isn't strictly correct, it happened to be the Twisted Wheel that journalist Dave Godin was visiting when he coined the term "Northern Soul". There were of course other clubs around at the same time playing the same type of soul records, but when the Wheel was closed down at the beginning of the Seventies, the all night scene moved to the Golden Torch Ballroom, in Hanley, Stoke on Trent.

By this time the people who made up the scene had all had a thorough grounding in 1960s Tamla Motown. Let's face it, nobody became a Northern Soul fan straight away, we all started by buying the more easily available releases on Tamla Motown, Stax, Atlantic, Beacon, Action, and Soul City. It's only as your involvement in the scene increases that the emphasis switches to imports. That's what slowly started to happen at The Torch; as more and more rare and obscure records were sought out, the emphasis switched to imports rather than UK releases.

Eventually the emphasis of the whole scene changed to more obscure labels, but Motown was not ignored. Right through the seventies, Motown supplied the scene with reissues that were accepted straight away by the dancers (or was it the other way round, that the scene prompted the release of the records?). I'm talking about records like "Tell Me It's Just A Rumour" by the Isley Brothers, "There's A Ghost In My House" by R Dean Taylor, "The Zoo" by The Commodores, and "The Night" by Frankie Valli on the Motown subsidiary label Mowest. You can't ignore the fact that Motown also re-issued a considerable number of Ric-Tic tracks in the UK as well. They were all enormous hits at Wigan Casino, the main focus of the scene in the Seventies. In fact Wigan Casino used to hold regular allnighters on a Friday night when only Motown would be played, showing the influence the label had in those days.

It wasn't just confined to singles either. Tamla Motown recognised the love that the Northern Soul scene had for Motown's music when they released three albums that were aimed specifically at the Northern Soul Market. All three albums *Motown Memories: 16 Non Stop Tamla Hits* (STML 11200) *The San Remo Strings Swing* (STML 11216) and *Ric-Tic Relics* (STML11232) were compilations from the golden age. You could also perhaps include *The Best of The Fantastic Four* and *Soul Master* by Edwin Starr in that as well, although both got American releases.

The world's rarest Soul single is also a Motown release, or not as the case may be. Reputedly recorded as a demo version, "Do I Love You (Indeed I Do)" by Frank Wilson was actually pressed up on the Soul label and given a catalogue number, but then, for some reason, all the copies were destroyed – with the exception of perhaps three copies. One of which recently sold for in excess of £10,000. UK Tamla Motown released the single in the late seventies, and even copies of this are still so in demand that they regularly sell at £20, and it's even been bootlegged twice!

It wasn't just the Motown artists that exerted an influence on the music though. The musicians played just as important a part. Not just at Motown either, people like Mike Terry, and Richard "Popcorn" Wylie both worked at Motown at some stage during the sixties, but are probably better known for their work on other Detroit labels, either as songwriters, or arrangers, or producers. They were there during the formation of that Motown sound though. The "Funk" Brothers, the studio band led by Earl Van Dyke, featuring the bass playing of James Jamerson and the drumming of Benny Benjamin, were the heart and soul of Motown, and played on virtually every hit record to come out of Hitsville. Even they moonlighted though. A lot of the Ric-Tic releases sound very much like Motown records, mostly because it was the same backing band. Jackie Wilson had a hit with a Motown sound alike "Your Love Keeps Lifting Me (Higher And Higher)". We now know why it was such a good Motown sound-alike – it was the Motown house band backing him.

It has to be said though that as Motown lost their way in the seventies, very few seventies releases were played on the northern soul scene. The sixties were the business as far as dance music went though, and anyone who grew up in that period cannot deny the influence Motown had on their whole life.

It was generally assumed that as the eighties approached Motown had given up all its gems, and then the first of the unreleased tapes appeared. I have no real idea of their origin, or how all the original Motown acetates ended up in this country, but what a shot in the arm for the Northern Soul scene these turned out to be. It showed that there were still things waiting to be discovered, and to a certain degree that situation has continued right up to today with the two CDs that were released on the Debutante label *This is Northern Soul* Vols 1 & 2 in 1998, and were composed of several well established released tracks with about fifty per cent being previously unreleased recordings. It's also true to say that as the tempo and flavour of the Northern Soul scene has evolved, other Motown releases that wouldn't have been played years ago have become accepted and gone onto to become dancefloor favourites. Two that spring to mind from the last couple of years are "You Ain't Saying Nothing New" by Virgil Henry on Tamla, and "I Wonder Why (Nobody Loves Me)" by Billy Eckstine on Motown.

Motown's own reissue campaign has also produced some gems such as "Your Business My Pleasure" by the Miracles on the box set.

So here we are with Motown having celebrated their fortieth birthday and "new" records are still becoming huge records on the Northern Soul scene. I won't go as far as saying that without Motown there wouldn't be a Northern Soul scene, but without that Motown influence which existed right from the scene's beginning and has continued to today, I think the scene would be a much poorer place.

33
10 Motown Tracks
by Sharon Davis

Sharon Davis began as a Motown fan in the sixties, and went on to write Motown: The History (Guinness, 1988) – an extraordinary tour de force in anyone's eyes. She has also written books on Marvin Gaye, and most recently, Diana Ross.

In no particular order:
"I'll Always Love You" – Brenda Holloway
"Just Loving You" – Kim Weston
"Where Would I Be Without You" – Barbara McNair
"Let There Be Love" – Caston and Majors
"Back To Nowhere" – Valerie Simpson
"If You Should Walk Away" – Chris Clark
"'Cause We've Ended As Lovers" – Syreeta
"Try Love" – Gloria Jones
"Why Am I Loving You" – Debbie Dean
"Do You Know Where You're Going To?" – Thelma Houston

"Kingsley,
As requested and I've just realised they're all female vocalists! These were off the top of my head – Lord knows what would happen if I dug further for titles." S.D.

34

The Northern Soul of Berry Gordy
by Tim Brown

Continuing and underlining the importance of the Northern Soul scene to Motown, we are including this piece from Tim Brown which originally ran as a tailpiece in Record Collector *to the series of historical overviews by Nick Brown (no relation) in May 1995. Tim Brown is heavily involved in the record business, running Anglo-American (Nanholme Mill, Shawwood Road, Todmorden, Lancs. OL14 6DA) whose Goldmine label continually issues great collections of rare soul to an ever-eager public. He has added an additional section to the original piece especially for this book.*

It's easy for the casual observer to think that Northern Soul *is* the Motown sound; and to a certain extent, that's true. Motown's golden era of the mid-60s had a vast influence on soul, and black music in general, in a way that no other organisation, not even Stax/Atlantic, could match. A myriad of artists, producers, songwriters and labels raced to emulate Berry Gordy's success – and most failed, many abysmally so.

By the late '60s Motown had moved on creatively to a funkier sound epitomised by the Temptations "Psychedelic Shack" – much to the disapproval of mods and club-goers in the North of England, who yearned for the earlier, 'classic' sound. When they delved a little deeper, these enterprising DJs and collectors found they were already sitting on a treasure trove of obscure soul goodies, some on Motown-related labels, but the vast majority consisting of failed competition to Gordy's empire, recorded not only across the length and breadth of the U.S., but here as well.

The Northern Soul sound, then, can more accurately be identified as the sound of the Motown copyists. To a trained ear, only a small percentage of these 'would-be-Motowns' managed to capture Gordy's magic accurately, so many Northern Soul discs sound quite different from their sources of inspiration like "I Can't Help Myself" or "Uptight". The situation is further complicated by the fact that the Northern sound has shifted in several different directions over the years. In a successful attempt to prolong the dancefloor life of a scene reliant on undiscovered '60s obscurities, DJs have embraced other soul styles. There has been a downturn in tempo and a move towards the early, New York-influenced soul sound of 1961-64.

Despite all these subtleties and nuances, however, the classic Motown "on-the-fours" rhythm remains the archetypal Northern sound. What follows is an attempt to view the Motown archive in the context of the greatest underground club scene of them all.

Motown first hit these shores at the start of the '60s on the U.K. labels London-American, Fontana and Oriole. By the time Gordy's output was licensed to EMI's Stateside label in '63/'64, the Motown sound was not only carving its own identity but also starting to make a musical impact. But though the Detroit sound may have been rated by those "in the know" like the Beatles and Dusty Springfield, few Motown records charted in Britain – with the odd exceptions, like the Supremes and the Four Tops. Marvin Gaye, the Temptations and the Miracles, for instance, were conspicuously absent from our Top 20 until the late '60s.

Away from the pop charts, the mods fell in love with Motown – with the possible exception of the Supremes, who were deemed too commercial. By 1965, Gordy had his own U.K. label, Tamla Motown, the club scene played virtually all its danceable releases, and youngsters rapidly became familiar with names such as Kim Weston, Earl Van Dyke and

Brenda Holloway as well as the more famous artists. The mod phenomenon was London-based, with outlets in clubs like the Flamingo and the Scene. By 1967, the Hitsville sound was changing to keep up with the times, and the capital's nightspots shifted with it – or moved away from soul altogether, in favour of the burgeoning psychedelic scene.

In the North and Midlands, however, the love affair with the songs of Holland/Dozier/Holland ran deeper, fuelled by a growing realisation that a wealth of non-hit uptempo soul singles could keep the halcyon days of the mid-60s alive for the forseeable future. At first, the non-hit sides from Motown's U.K. output garnered attention, like the Velvelettes' "Needle In A Haystack" and Earl Van Dyke's "All For You" (ironically enough, a supreme rarity on its original U.S. label, Soul.) Soon, it became apparent that there was a rich seam of material on American labels waiting to be redis-covered, not least on Motown and its associates. During 1968 and '69, records like the Contours' "Just A Little Misunderstanding" and Marvin Gaye's "One More Heartache" were joined by import-only monsters such as "Heaven Must Have Sent You" by the Elgins (V.I.P.) or "Six By Six" by Earl Van Dyke (Soul).

This was the era of Manchester's Twisted Wheel club and the Mojo in Sheffield. Gradually, these sounds filtered through to the mainstream discotheques, and into the twitching ears of record companies and radio stations. This was the foundation for a curi-ous revival for Tamla Motown in Britain – which probably left the Detroit office totally bemused. All of a sudden, records like "This Old Heart Of Mine" and "Get Ready" were in the Top 20, years after their original release. Britain enjoyed a fully-fledged love affair with a sound that its American originators had largely discarded, inadvertently paving the way for ersatz-Motown hits for the likes of the Foundations and Johnny Johnson & the Bandwagon. Even as late as 1976, the U.K. charts were wallowing in records made in the style of the mid-60s, like Billy Ocean's "Love Really Hurts Without You".

By 1970, Tamla Motown was issuing more old material than contemporary record-ings. Sometimes, the label even put their eggs in two baskets, underpinning a new release with a 'Northern' B-side – the Spinners' "It's A Shame" came with "Sweet Thing", for example. Meanwhile, *Blues And Soul* journalist Dave Godin coined the phrase 'Northern Soul' to describe this whole throwback phenomenon, and the search was on for ever faster and rarer soul discs to satisfy the mushrooming crowds at all-night events (chris-tened 'allnighters'). Lesser U.S.-only hits from the Motown stable were snapped up, played to death and then tossed aside (together with those on acquired Detroit labels like Ric Tic and Golden World), at clubs like the Torch in Stoke, and the Highland Room at the Blackpool Mecca. Interest turned to other U.S. labels like OKeh and Mirwood, and Motown-related titles became less and less frequent visitors to the turntables.

The exception was its V.I.P. subsidiary which came under the spotlight: Debbie Dean's "Why Am I Loving You", the Dalton Boys' "I've Been Cheated", Rick Robin & Him's "'Cause You Know Me" and the Spinners' superb "She's Gonna Love Me At Sundown". Motown even re-released the Elgins' "Heaven Must Have Sent You" (V.I.P.) in the States after its success in Britain – talk about the tail wagging the dog! Occasionally, other releases like Frances Nero's "Keep On Loving Me" (Soul) or Eddie Holland's "Candy To Me" (Motown) would get a spin, but in 1973, there was one Motown title which took the scene by storm. The super-catchy "There's A Ghost In My House" by R. Dean Taylor, one of the many white artists on V.I.P., was actually much scarcer on its original label than many soul fans realise. Indeed many DJs at the time lifted the track off a Music For Pleasure budget compilation!

1973 also witnessed the birth of the Wigan Casino allnighter, the most famous of all Northern Soul venues – they even pulled R. Dean Taylor out of retirement for a live appearance. Motown's British outlet was still on the case, and "Ghost" raced to No. 3 in May 1974, backed with Taylor's other in-demander, the rattling "Let's Go Somewhere". The Northern scene's popularity reached its heyday in the mid-to-late '70s, with clubs stretched across England from Manchester to London, Torquay to Cleethorpes, and

Blackpool to Bristol. Allnighters were sweaty, 100mph affairs, fuelled by adrenalin and less natural stimulants, and there were a few unfamiliar Motown sides which could satisfy the demand for such upbeat dancers. There were exceptions, like the Originals' "Goodnight Irene" (Soul), or Edwin Starr's "Time" (Gordy), or even new discoveries: Tommy Good's "Baby I Miss You" (Gordy) and the Andantes' mega-rarity, "Like A Nightmare" (V.I.P.). But the mother of all Northern soul rarities was around the corner and at first, no-one realised it was a Motown disc.

By 1981, the Wigan Casino had passed away after lengthy death throes, and the Northern Soul scene had lost much of its status. The scene lurched on in the wilderness for a couple of years, and the '60s Motown archive was left behind in favour of '70s and '80s 'modern' rarities. It was the emergence of the 100 Club allnighters in London and Stafford's Top Of The World which gave the scene a fresh impetus, expanding upon the music's '60s roots. For the first time in years, a younger, enthusiastic generation joined the ranks of older collectors who were realising that Northern Soul was here to stay.

The music, too, broadened out, to encompass beat ballads, Latinesque Drifters-type productions, early '70s soul/funk sides labelled 'crossover', as well as a plethora of forgotten B-sides. Prices soared and no labels were riper for the picking than Tamla, Gordy and the rest of the Motown empire – for the first time, Miracle, Tri-Phi and Melody came into the picture. Throughout Northern Soul's '70s heyday, pre-1964 Motown was a definite 'no-no', but although the label itself was often quite derivative in those early days, this prejudice has now dissolved among Northern Soul collectors.

The stand-out dancefloor winners of recent years have been Linda Griner's "Good-by Cruel Love" (Motown), Eddie Holland's raucous "I'm On The Outside Looking In" (Motown) and Liz Lands' "Midnight Johnny" (Gordy; an even better unissued version of this track exists, by the way!). From the 1961/'62 period, DJs have embraced Jimmy Ruffin's debut, "Don't Feel Sorry For Me" (Miracle), Freddie Gorman's "Just For You" (Miracle) and Lamont Dozier's "Dearest One" (Melody). And special mention should be made of the novelty appeal of Harvey's "(Dance) Any Way You Wanta" on Tri-Phi.

As a revival, Barbara McNair's "You're Gonna Love My Baby" (Motown) has been far more popular than before; likewise, all three Carolyn Crawford's Motown 45s, and Kim Weston's Helpless" and "Take Me In Your Arms" (Gordy), have been overtaken in demand by "I'm Still Loving You" (Tamla) and "A Thrill A Moment" (Gordy). Fresh mileage has even been made from the earlier recordings of such major groups as the Miracles ("If Your Mother Only Knew" on Tamla) and the Temptations ("I Want A Love I Can See" on Gordy). It's a strange feature of the Northern scene that 25 years ago, these kind of recordings were considered too dated to be danceable.

In addition, there has been a wealth of unissued material brought to light, almost always from unauthorised sources – and there have been two particularly large finds over the years. Until recently, Motown itself paid scant attention to what was lurking in its vaults, other than material by its superstars. One notable exception was the exhuming of an unissued 1966 Contours cut, "Baby (Hit And Run)", some eight years later – arguably Motown's finest '60s find to date. Marvin Gaye has also attracted special attention since his death, with the excellent "Sweet Thing" and "Lonely World Without Your Love". Conversely, Motown ruined the reissue of the superb "Lonely Lover" by adding an '80s bassline. Less official are the copies in circulation of Chris Clark's cancelled V.I.P. version of "Do I Love You", the Originals' "Baby Have Mercy On Me" (Alias "Suspicion"), and the superlative Brenda Holloway side, "Reconsider".

So there we have it, Motown is as popular as ever. The changes of taste for Motown rarities over the years is a perfect musical barometer of this unique culture. As for the future, the best hope lies in the vast amount of unissued material lying dormant in Motown's vaults. Let's hope that Motown themselves care enough about their most loyal fans and make this lost music widely available at last.

35
The UK Concerts
by Jim Stewart

*A U.S. Revue programme that included great photos
of many of the rarer Motown acts.*

*In the early Sixties, British concerts by Motown artists were initially few and far
between. Until Motown singles began to make the charts with sufficient regularity, such
shows were often poorly attended, with just the knowledgeable few showing up. It is well
documented just how grateful Berry Gordy and his artists were for the early attention
that they got here in the UK, especially at a time when travelling around was not as
quick and easy as it is today. I got to as many of the shows as I could, given the incon-
venient demands of school and A-levels, and so I was delighted when Jim Stewart told
me of his sixties travels which took in many more shows than I ever managed. In this
specially written piece, he relives those exciting days, and gives an insight into some of
the early tours when success had to be worked extremely hard for. Nowadays Jim runs
a busy mail order record business from 37 Main Road, Hextable, Swanley, Kent BR8
7RA (01 322 613883) www.soulsearchingplus.co.uk – anyone enthused to seek out rare
Motown or other soul issue CDs would be advised to get in touch.*

Living in London during the Sixties, it was not difficult to see pop music live as the
local cinemas in the Granada and Astoria groups were always chosen by the promoters
of the package tours. These normally lasted three weeks, including six or seven dates in
the London area and consisted of a couple of American artists, supported by a number
of UK chart acts.

The first of the artists from the Motown group to tour was Marv Johnson. This was before most people were aware of the potential of the music coming from Detroit. Mary Wells and Kim Weston were the first acts to be promoted as Motown singers, however, and the contrast could not have been greater. Mary arrived with a blaze of publicity. "My Guy" was Motown's first UK top ten single, and she was "chosen" by the Beatles to support them on their tour in early 1964. Kim was added to the bill on Gerry and the Pacemakers tour to test the water, and she was almost unknown – even to the other members of the tour. Prior to the first show, the compere Bryan Burdon asked Kim how she would like to be introduced, she replied "Kim Weston from Tamla Motown". But when the introduction was made the audience was asked to give a warm welcome to "*Miss Pamela Motown*"; this she overcame to become one of the tour's successes.

It was not until the autumn of that year that I was fortunate to see my first performances by Motown artists. Martha and the Vandellas and The Supremes both made brief visits to appear on *Ready Steady Go!* and included one-off club dates in Soho; both in very small venues with tiny stages, packed to over capacity; it was just about possible to see their heads, but the atmosphere was electric. They were preaching to the already converted.

It was a different story for the first appearance by The Miracles – the Royal Albert Hall was the venue, on a Friday night early in December. The concert was being staged as one of a series of *Teen Beat* shows for broadcast by the BBC. Each of the acts did two slots consisting of about 12 minutes in the first half and a second slot in the second half which was filmed for inclusion in the TV broadcast the following week on BBC2. Brenda Lee was the headline act who did her full tour act in the recorded session only. The main attraction for most of the audience were The Yardbirds, who were at their peak chart-wise, together with Nashville Teens, but for me (having purchased the tickets to see Brenda Lee) it was the opportunity to see a full Motown stage routine. The previous shows had been so crowded it had only been possible to see the head and shoulders, and the artists did not have room to display the perfection of their dance routines. This was to be the only performance in the UK by Claudette Robinson as a Miracle, as she decided to quit the stage shows before the revue toured a few months later. All of the early hits, "Shop Around", "You've Really Got A Hold On Me", "Mickey's Monkey" and "That's What Love Is Made Of" (the new single) were included, and the movements and dance routines were unlike any previous acts I had seen – a taster for what 1965 was to bring.

The spring of 1965 was a milestone in the UK history of Motown. The label had been issued by EMI on Stateside for the previous couple of years, but now was the time to have their own identity. Merging the names of two American labels the name Tamla Motown was created. To coincide with this the first European tour by a Motown Revue was set and a Granada TV special with the artists from the tour, plus Dusty Springfield and The Temptations. Dusty acted as host to the television show (since issued on video as *Ready Steady Motown*), introducing and chatting to the artists, singing hits by others and dueting with Martha Reeves. It was a great production, received well by the press and should have given the tour the maximum publicity possible. I attended the opening night of the tour at Finsbury Park Astoria in March: both shows were sold out well in advance, as had the following night at Hammersmith. The atmosphere inside the theatre for the opening night was electric: everyone knew they were in for something special. I was in the front stalls and they were full of names from the music scene. Dusty was further along my row and Jonathan King was just behind.

Earl Van Dyke opened both halves with sets that included "All For You" and "Too Many Fish In The Sea"; these set the mood for the evening. Clarence Paul then introduced Martha And The Vandellas and the place erupted to the sound of "Heatwave". It was dance hits all the way, "Quicksand", "Wild One", together with a different routine for each song; the new single "Nowhere To Run" was explosive and closing with "Dancing In The Street", it was a perfect set. The first half was closed by Georgie Fame, who played a set of Flamingo favourites, and although the tempo of the show had dropped it was still held up by the expectation of the second half. After another brief set by Earl Van Dyke it was time for "Little" Stevie Wonder. His composure and confidence on stage belied his age and blindness as he danced around, always knowing exactly where to return to the microphone, with "Kiss Me Baby", "Hey Harmonica Man", "Workout Stevie Workout", "I Call It Pretty Music". The enthusiasm and musicianship built up to the final number "Fingertips", the excitement returned by the audience was equal to the Apollo recording. Unbelievable. A change to the running order printed in the programme followed; whoever provided the information must have assumed that chart hits dictated who would close, and was unaware that if the Miracles were on the bill they would always have that honour.

Already Motown's most successful act, with three US number one's, The Supremes needed very little introduction. Diana Ross, Mary Wilson and Florence Ballard were the perfect girl group. Stage routines that displayed rare precision, this was the first chance to see the now legendary introduction with the raised arm to "Stop! In The Name Of Love" – it brought the house down. "Baby Love", "Where Did Our Love Go", "Come See About Me" all delivered with such style and closing with a track from the *We Remember Sam Cooke* LP – "Shake". London had never seen a show like this before and it wasn't over!!! The Supremes left the stage and The Miracles replaced them, maintaining the standard with an act packed with American hits, "I Like It Like That", "Come On Do The Jerk", that invitation being delivered as if Smokey was enjoying himself as much as we were. Then came the only time during the evening that the tempo was allowed to drop, almost every song performed had been aimed at the dance-floor. This time, the heart was the target for the new single, "Ooh Baby Baby". You could have heard a pin drop as Smokey pleaded for another chance. The final number was exactly what we had hoped for: "Mickey's Monkey", with Smokey and Bobby Rogers working out frantically, and then joined by all of the other artists for a real Motown Revue finale. A night never to be forgotten.

Motown had started the British section of the tour on a high with the TV show and the London dates, but they were disillusioned by the time it closed, due to poor attendances outside of the capital. Martha And The Vandellas returned in March the following year for a tour, which confirmed their popularity, but it was the visit in September 1966 that was to change the London concert scene forever.

Brian Epstein had always stated that one of his ambitions was to see a theatre in London that could be compared to New York's Apollo in Harlem, where pop music, of any gender, would be at home. A place where music could be enjoyed seven nights a week in the centre of town. After long negotiations he bought The Saville Theatre in Shaftesbury Avenue and his dream became a reality. He had been in America during the summer of '66 and had seen an act that he knew was perfect to open it for him. They had an album due for release containing a title track that would finally establish Motown once and for all. The group were The Four Tops.

Once again the theatre was packed to capacity, for the first of the legendary "Sunday Night At The Saville" concerts, and when Tony Hall came on at the start of the show he said that the first house had been unlike any that London had previously seen...and he was right!!! Cliff Bennett And The Rebel Rousers opened with a tight R&B set that was perfect for the occasion, and fully appreciated by this audience.

From the opening bars of "Its The Same Old Song" everyone automatically rose to dance, clap and sing along to one great Four Tops song after another. The dance routine was as much a memorable part of their act as "The Temptation Walk" or "Shadows Steppin'". "Ask The Lonely" and "Baby I Need Your Loving" were next with a request to join in the singing. This was a Sunday night in church and Motown was the religion. The show contained all of the hits "Helpless", "I Can't Help Myself", "Something About You", every single included, plus the best of the album tracks. Then the moment everyone had been waiting for: "Reach Out I'll Be There", their first number one and the reaction was such that you could see Levi was completely overwhelmed by the evening. He said the group would stay as long as we wanted and went well beyond the time allocated for the show, promising to return as soon as possible. This was confirmed by Tony Hall, who also announced that Sunday concerts would become a regular feature at the theatre.

The promises were kept by both the Four Tops and Brian Epstein, with the group returning for a nation-wide tour in January 1967, and just a few weeks after the first "Sunday At The Saville" they started on a weekly basis attracting many great names for one-off shows over the next couple of years.

Package tours were a great opportunity to see between six and as many as ten acts in one show, but many acts had more to offer than the fifteen to twenty minute slots allowed, and the music scene was now moving in so many new and exciting directions that getting the balance right for a successful tour was becoming increasingly difficult. The Saville concerts changed that with the normal evening consisting of only two acts performing for between 45 and 75 minutes each. As more and more artists proved they had the ability to do so, the need to have such a large number on a package tour was obviously felt unnecessary as well as uneconomic. These shows gave many of the great names from both pop and soul music the chance to show their capabilities and were even more important to the emerging rock scene.

The Royal Albert Hall was the London venue for The Four Tops tour, supported by Madeline Bell and The Merseys, and although it was extremely difficult to achieve perfect sound due to the size of the venue, it did not matter as the singing by the audience virtually drowned the sound system. Once again it was a night to remember, repeated nightly throughout the tour with every show sold out and any doubts about Motown's appeal were gone.

Over the next few months Motown artists continued to visit for TV spots and the Saville had now replaced the small clubs as the venue to showcase their acts. Artists including Edwin Starr, now having signed to Motown following the belated chart success of his Ric-Tic recordings (they were always discotheque classics), was already building a relationship with fans that is just as strong today. Bobby Taylor And The Vancouver's and Chris Clark both used these shows to prove that great records and chart success still did not always go together. Chris also showed that a beautiful blonde could still deliver a very soulful sound. Jimmy Ruffin also appeared there starting a love affair with this country that lasts to this day.

Stevie Wonder was the next major act to tour, not at theatres but at Mecca Ballrooms, including Streatham Locarno. Thursday night was becoming soul night at Streatham, with Rufus Thomas, Edwin Starr, Ike And Tina Turner, amongst others appearing there, but the booking of Stevie took everyone by surprise. He was promoting "I'm Wondering" and had had a number of chart hits including "Uptight" and "I Was Made To Love Her" since his last tour with the revue. This was a young man, still only 17 years of age, making his brand of 'pretty music' and getting the crowds to dance. Once again the act relied on the singles, all delivered with style and perfection. He just could not fail and was proving he now had the stature to head his own nation-wide tour in the near future.

Then came a double header to remember. Having seen the Stax-Volt touring earlier in the year there was no way I was going to miss their second visit, this time with Sam And Dave headlining supported by Arthur Conley and Percy Sledge making his first appearance. But this coincided with Jr. Walker And The All Stars' only concert at the Saville.

Fortunately the tube connection between the two venues meant it was possible to see

Sam And Dave at Hammersmith Odeon at 5.30pm, and with the sound of Percy's "It Tears Me Up" still going around my head, make it to Shaftesbury Avenue in time for Jr Walker's 8.30 show. Jr. was everything you could have hoped for, once again playing a greatest hits sets of vocals such as "Road Runner", "How Sweet It Is", and "Shake And Fingerpop", plus instrumental gem "Cleo's Mood". One of the highlights was his forthcoming single "Come See About Me" – a heavy treatment of a Motown classic that he could now claim to be his own.

A couple of weeks after that weekend should have been one of the shows to die for. Once again The Saville had booked two major American acts to give their first UK performances on the same bill. Joe Tex was due to appear with Gladys Knight & The Pips, and bookings were so heavy for this that for the first time I had been unable to get good seats for the second show. Imagine the disappointment when at about 11.45am that Sunday morning Radio One announced that Joe Tex had pulled out as he had been given a slot on Ed Sullivan that same evening. This was the second time in a year that I had tickets to see him and he had cancelled. The theatre quickly arranged for Georgie Fame to take his place, and although I still felt cheated it was forgotten as soon as Gladys walked on the stage. Although she had only been with Motown a short while, with just one album and a couple of singles, Gladys had been performing and recording for years. In addition to the new hits "Take Me In your Arms", "Everybody Needs Love", the early songs, including "Giving Up", were equally well received but the biggest hit of the night was "I Heard It Through The Grapevine". How it was never a hit over here for her still amazes me. Throughout the performance The Pips kept up a faultless display of dancing. As we left the theatre the missing Joe Tex was completely forgotten, but not forgiven, until I saw him give one of the best shows ever in 1970.

January 1968 brought another change of direction for Motown in London, The Supremes having now become Diana Ross and the Supremes. Florence Ballard had been replaced by Cindy Birdsong, and they were about to start the first of three Motown residences at "The Talk Of The Town". I saw the show mid-way through the second week and the media could not shower enough praise on them for bridging the gap between pop and cabaret. You could not help but be impressed by their performance. It was so polished, perfect for this type of venue. The dance routines were brilliant, mixing comedy with the slick movements, but there were also two aspects that would change their concerts in the future. Over the previous five years they had amassed so many hits, that 'the medleys' were introduced to allow the inclusion of as many songs as possible, albeit in very small pieces, allowing more time to be devoted to show tunes and standards. This was the way Motown was going with the *Rodgers And Hart* and *Mellow Mood* albums, but you could only admire and enjoy the show, as they proved they were possibly the world's number one act. The success of that season, was rewarded not only with the release of a *Live At London's Talk Of The Town* LP and the appearances by The Temptations and Stevie Wonder at the same venue, but the invitation for Diana and the Supremes to appear in the Royal Variety Show later that year. When November came and they arrived to appear on the show the press still loved them. When the girls were rehearsing they had shown that they were unhappy about appearing with the Black And White Minstrels: the year had seen great racial tension in America and although the label were not outspoken on these matters, equally, they did not want to upset their friends at home.

I don't know if it had been planned prior to the visit or decided at the venue, but the highlight of their performance was to be "Somewhere" from *West Side Story*. Halfway through the song, Diana made a plea for harmony and racial equality throughout the world. How it was received within the theatre I don't know as I have never seen the performance, but the next day the tabloid press turned on the group for insulting the Royal Family, and using the most important event in UK entertainment for political gain and comparing it to the "black power salutes" at the Olympics earlier that year. There were even calls for their performance, or that song to be edited from the television broadcast and for the group to be banned from the Palladium.

The reason I never saw the televised show is that I had front row seats for the girls' return visit to the theatre on the following Sunday when it was being shown. The support acts that evening included The Fantastics, who I immediately recognised as a group I had seen on a number of occasions over the previous couple of years appearing as The Fabulous Impressions / Temptations / Drifters etc., doing a pretty similar act on each occasion, just increasing the number of songs made by the people they were supposed to be. This had obviously done them no harm as they now had their own name and had used those performances to polish up a fine act.

Diana and the Supremes were given a great reception from the off. Since I had seen them at the start of the year, their *Love Child* album had been issued and given another direction to the music, but everyone in the celebrity packed audience must have been waiting to see if they would dare the repeat the performance of "Somewhere". They did. As Diana completed the plea for peace, you could sense something happening within the theatre, and as one we stood and gave them a standing ovation, mid-way through the act, a very unusual event in those days. Any doubts they had about upsetting people were completely dispelled. The show tunes were still there and one memory that sticks with me that that evening is of the girls singing "Big Spender" with Cindy standing directly in front me, flicking a feather boa at me and inviting me to spend a little time with her: all I had left in my pocket was the return train ticket; I had done all of my big spending getting the front seats.

Stevie Wonder returned the following year, this time supported by The Foundations and The Flirtations, who I had also seen as The Fabulous Chiffons/Shirelles/Marvelettes, giving excellent performances that built up to the appearance of Stevie. He was maturing with each visit and for this one he had his biggest UK hit to date "For Once In My Life" this had given him an even wider audience. It was during this tour that "My Cherie Amour" started to emerge as the more popular side of the current single "I Don't Know Why" and, once it was officially flipped, it became one of his biggest hits. I saw the show from the front row at Croydon's Fairfield Hall and I was struck by his tremendous stage presence and the confident way he moved around the stage freely, often coming to the very edge without once checking where he was. Jr. Walker, Edwin Starr and Marv Johnson all visited the UK that same year, but mortgage payments meant something had to give, so I missed their shows.

The Temptations' long awaited UK debut finally took place at London's Talk Of The Town in January 1970. If The Supremes had opened the door to this venue then The Temptations blew it off – this must have been the first time funk had been played here. Dennis Edwards was lead on most of the singles now and he and the rest of the group gave us a night to remember, with all the hits included, plus selections from *Mellow Mood*. But the highlight for me was "Runaway Child Running Wild" which took the dance routines to a different level, with spotlights scanning the room like searchlights and the Tempts on the edge of the raised dancefloor looking for the runaway. Paul Williams was on stage that night, but he missed a number of the performances and the *Top Of The Pops* show with "flu".

Once again the season was a great success and Motown issued a "Live" album to celebrate it. They also did the same following Stevie Wonder's visit there later the same year, but I did not go to that show.

The Four Tops returned in the early summer for a tour, this time with Faith Brown, plus Johnny Johnson And The Bandwagon. They were still giving 100 percent and selling out every show. "MacArthur Park" was now a major number in their act, together with the "shake hands and love thy neighbour" theme. This was now becoming an integral part of most soul acts: as the '70s progressed, some artists used this as the finale stretching a great five minute number to fifteen or twenty minutes of tedium. Fortunately the Tops did not fall into this category.

The spring of 1971 was the next tour I saw. It was Stevie Wonder, and although this was now an annual event you always got something completely new. This tour was no exception: with Martha Reeves And The Vandellas supporting him it really was a case of the old and new sounds of Detroit. Martha was continuing in the original groove concentrating on singles, still generating as much excitement as on the early visits. For this tour she did not have a single ready, so Motown went back a couple of years and picked a very under-rated flip, edited out the spoken section in the middle, and "Forget Me Not" became her second biggest UK hit, and still remains a favourite to this day. Stevie, however, was experimenting with synthesisers, and introduced us to the Moog, singing and blowing into a length of tubing attached to his microphone that gave his voice a totally different sound. This was to be the route to independence and "Music Of My Mind". The black suit was missing for this trip, replaced by casual gear. It was clear he was making his own decisions.

The Four Tops and Martha Reeves were both back in 1972, touring together and getting rave reviews, but the next show I saw was the first tour by The Supremes, following Diana's solo career. Jean Terrell had replaced her and the hits were still coming, the tour sold out, and there were now two extremely successful acts instead of one. The early hits were condensed into medleys and "Up The Ladder" and "Stoned Love" (especially the long spoken introduction) were highlights.

Gladys Knight And The Pips were the final tour I saw during this period. Gladys sang a mix of Vee-Jay, Motown and the new album *Imagination*. This was a truly outstanding performance, and the group were at their peak. "Help Me Make It Through The Night" was the highlight for most of the audience, but for me it was the "offer, threat or promise" behind "If I Were Your Woman" – without doubt one of the best deliveries I have ever seen.

The number of shows I attended in that period was reduced due to a number of reasons: alternative demands on the finances; the reduction in the number of tours going to the old cinema circuits; preferring to do one large venue per town and the increasing difficulty in getting front seats for those I wanted to attend. I had been spoilt in the early days, especially by the Revue tour and The Saville concerts,… but weren't we all in one way or another…?

36

Ball of Confusion: The Second Golden Era of Motown
by Peter Doggett

This book is unashamedly rooted in Motown's golden era of the early- to mid-Sixties. I was always aware that this was limiting to a degree, and that some balance was desirable. Being of a slightly later generation than myself, Peter Doggett came upon Motown at the end of the sixties and only learnt of earlier goodies subsequently. His appreciation of his own golden era helps to remind us of a time when other soul labels had emerged to provide another vast expansion with the arrival of the Seventies. Peter was well known as the editor of Record Collector *for some 18 years, during which time he built it up to the esteemed position it holds today. Having recently stepped down from that post to take a freelance breather, Peter's fine writing and reviewing is sure to mean that he is as busy as he ever was.*

It was double English after lunch, and that Monday afternoon I was supposed to be with Wilfred Owen, for a "Strange Meeting" in the trenches of the First World War. But another battle hymn was pulsing through my brain. The poignant symbolism of Owen's poetry couldn't compete with the epigrams of Edwin Starr: "WAR! What's it good for? Absolutely NOTHING!". Good God y'all.

I wasn't the only distracted boy in that classroom. A geological cross-section of the 13-year-old mind in November 1970 would have revealed layers of sex and football, as hormones dashed directionless across the cortex, colliding in incoherent fantasies of sporting heroism and mysteriously vague orgies.

And then there was music. A transmitter tuned to our inner ears would have picked up traces of Led Zeppelin, Deep Purple, Emerson Lake & Palmer, Black Sabbath and the distant echo of the Beatles. But none of that was for me. I was different (obviously). An adolescent snob, I was already six years past my Infant school flirtation with Merseybeat, and convinced that "pop" was only meant for the lower orders (i.e. all my classmates). Me, I preferred classical, although I never listened to it.

So Edwin Starr has a lot to answer for. As the subtle rhetoric of his chorus lumbered across my mind, I began to think that maybe this pop music might have more to it than I'd ever imagined. It could match Wilfred Owen for political relevance, *and* it had a beat. It also sent an eerie shiver to the pit of my stomach, equalled only by my furtive flicking through my father's collection of *Amateur Photographer.*

Within a week, I'd exhumed an ancient valve radio from the loft, found fabulous 247 on the dial, and tuned into another dimension. Within two, I'd "borrowed" a copy of *Record Mirror* from the dentist's waiting-room, and discovered charts of the best-selling records across Britain and America.

There was Edwin Starr, sure enough, and his intellectually inspiring "War". In small print at the end of the line, it said "(Tamla Motown)". I checked the rest of the Top 50, and discovered the same mysterious annotation alongside several other titles – the Temptations with "Ball Of Confusion", Smokey Robinson & the Miracles' "Tears Of A Clown", the Four Tops' "Still Water", the Jackson 5's "I'll Be There". They had something else in common, these "Tamla Motowns" – I loved them all.

By accident, I'd stumbled upon the Second Golden Age of Motown – though I'd never heard about the First Golden Age. Nor could I fathom why the compilers of the American

Top 100 were so lazy that they listed some records as "Tamla" and some as "Motown". All that mattered was that whenever the magic words appeared at the end of a review in the *NME*, I was in for another pre-sexual shiver.

Adolescent pocket money in 1970 barely stretched to a music paper a week, never mind a single, and certainly not the enticing *Motown Chartbusters* albums that I tracked down in W.H. Smith's – prompting distant folk-memories of "My Guy" and "Baby Love" from my premature baptism in Berry Gordy's font. In my delicious innocence, I knew nothing and cared less about Gordy, Barrett Strong, Holland/Dozier/Holland and the other luminaries who built the Motown empire. That knowledge came later, ironically coinciding with the headlong decline in Motown's output that followed the Corporation's hitch-hike from Detroit to Los Angeles. In 1970 and 1971, Motown didn't need its history: its contemporary output was so strong that it made the past irrelevant.

The evidence? You can pick almost any black-labelled Tamla Motown 45 of the era, and be seduced not by a sound – the homogeneous production ethic of the mid-60s had long gone – but by quality control that had lost none of its stringent attention to detail. If the early years of Motown, from "Money" to "Reach Out, I'll Be There", created an identity that stretched around the globe, then the watchword of 1970 was diversity. From symphonic soul to proto-funk, Motown was covering all the bases, aided by the sharpest hooklines this side of an Invictus compilation.

Consider the talent at their disposal. Even without Diana Ross, the Supremes were the equal of their name. "Stoned Love" was ushered in with a whisper, and then whipped onto the dancefloor with a groove that extracted the essence of Stevie Wonder's "Uptight'. And Miss Ross? That November 1970 chart held the emotional bubble-bath of "Ain't No Mountain High Enough", revealing depths of passion that she'd carefully disguised in previous years. The following summer, "I'm Still Waiting" gave Motown their last UK No. 1 for seven years. Better still, those hits were separated by "Remember Me", another roller-coaster of doomed romance. "*Remember me as a good thing*", Ross cried out, as if she knew that her decade ahead would be filled with showbiz, not soul.

Other Motown veterans were enjoying momentary flurries of excellence – the Four Tops returning from the MOR of "It's All In The Game" with the atmospheric and haunting "Still Water", Martha Reeves & the Vandellas offering a surprisingly upbeat slant on the Vietnam War with "Forget Me Not", the Motown Spinners banished thoughts of bearded Liverpool folkies with "It's A Shame".

But the undoubted kings of the old brigade were the Temptations. David Ruffin was already gone by 1970, his solo career trickling into nonentity, though Eddie Kendricks' plaintive falsetto was an instant tie to the era of "The Way You Do The Things You Do". But even when Kendricks embarked on his own solo path in 1971, the faces mattered less than the masterplan of writer/producer Norman Whitfield. In 1969, he'd employed the Temps as his vehicle for exploring the limits of psychedelic soul. That uneasy hybrid climaxed in autumn 1970 with "Ball Of Confusion", a thrilling blend of political protest, blues motifs and funk sensibility which beat Sly Stone at his own game.

Just to prove that Whitfield respected Motown tradition, the group followed through with Kendricks' swansong, and perhaps the greatest soft-soul record ever to come out of Detroit – "Just My Imagination". Even while the company collapsed around him, Whitfield kept pushing the Temptations into new territory – the soul symphony of "Take A Look Around", and finally the epic landscape of "Papa Was A Rolling Stone", a blaxploitation masterpiece waiting for a movie. Whitfield revived another Motown tradition in the early '70s, sharing his songs around a stable of acts and inviting them to compete for the hit. It was a rare flop in Britain, but the Undisputed Truth's definitive reading of "Smiling Faces Sometimes" justified that approach – besides anticipating the soul paranoia of the O'Jays' "Back Stabbers" a full year later.

Maybe it was tough for anyone over the age of consent to admit that they'd fallen for a bunch of adolescent soul brothers from Gary, Indiana, fronted by a squeaking 12-year-old. But Paul Gambaccini in *Rolling Stone* called "I Want You Back" the greatest record of all time, and it wasn't even their best single. Their albums were patchy, in keeping with Motown's exploitative past, but even the tamest of their early 45s ("Maybe Tomorrow", say) was a gem. It helped that Michael Jackson was the most spontaneous, least studied soul singer in America – until his voice broke, his balls presumably dropped, and he began to understand what he was singing about. Fortunately that was after "I'll Be There" (pre-teen ballad ecstasy) and the remarkable "Mama's Pearl", which contains the most orgasmic moment in Motown history (as young Michael screams *got what you need, let's fall in love*" out of one of the final choruses).

Back in November 1970, the chart was about to bid farewell to Smokey Robinson & the Miracles' "Tears Of A Clown", which would have been the finest single of the year if it hadn't been recorded in 1967. Motown followed it with another superb reissue, "(Come Round Here) I'm The One You Need", though these niceties were lost on 13-year-olds who couldn't remember 1967. But when the company relented and issued some contemporary Miracles product, there was no obvious dip in quality. "I Don't Blame You At All" is almost forgotten today, but its tricksy melody, tension-filled arrangement and heart-piercing lead vocal stacks it up alongside Smokey's finest.

As befits the man whom Bob Dylan once called "America's finest living poet" (turns out he meant Arthur Rimbaud, who was neither American nor living), Smokey eased effortlessly from the Miracles into an ill-appreciated solo career. Records like "Just My Soul Responding", "Sweet Harmony", "Virgin Man" and "Vitamin X" were all ignored in Britain, but their excellence almost persuaded the lucky few that Motown had survived the turbulent early '70s intact.

That proved to be an illusion, as fleeting as this second wave of classic 45s. Even at 14, I could tell that late 1971 Motown wasn't a patch on its year-old predecessor. Whichever way you stacked the jukebox, 1970 won out. "Superstar" wasn't "Ball Of Confusion"; "Floy Joy" wasn't "Stoned Love"; "Surrender" certainly wasn't "Ain't No Mountain High Enough".

Industry politics hadn't registered, so I didn't know that Berry Gordy had asset-stripped Motown's Detroit home and shifted the contents to Hollywood. Nor did I realise that the company's heart had slipped off the lorry in mid-journey, or that vital cogs in Motown's engine (the Four Tops, Martha Reeves, Gladys Knight, the Spinners) were restlessly searching for another home. Ironically, the ignorance of Top 40 teenhood also ensured that I missed the two most positive entries on Motown's 1971 balance sheet. That was the year in which Stevie Wonder and Marvin Gaye declared effective independence from Berry Gordy's empire, gambling their individual futures on the conviction that their artistic intelligence weighed more than Gordy's faith in the bottom-line.

If British radio had been the battleground, then both stars would have lost first time out. Radio 1 effectively boycotted Marvin Gaye singles like "What's Going On", "Save The Children" and "Inner City Blues", and likewise overlooked Stevie Wonder's "Never Dreamed You'd Leave In Summer" and "Superwoman". Only in retrospect did Britain realise that in 1971, Marvin Gaye released *What's Going On,* a contender for the best soul LP of all time; while it took 1973's *Talking Book* to focus belated attention on Wonder's first two self-produced albums, *Where I'm Coming From* and *Music In My Mind.*

All those records still carried the Tamla Motown logo, persuading the faithful that maybe Gordy's label had retained its magic after the relocation. But their success, artistic and (in the States) commercial, proved the opposite: that inventive and challenging music could be made despite Gordy's vision. By the mid-70s, only Gaye, Wonder and that eternal maverick, Smokey Robinson, were still making Motown records worthy of the name; and all three men were beyond Berry Gordy's control. The irresistible magic of Motown was finally gone. But for one last fabulous fling in 1970/'71, Gordy's label had indeed proved itself to be the Sound of Young America.

37

Back Tracking Motown In The New Century
by Kingsley Abbott

Motown's recorded legacy is an extremely rich one. The well known hit tracks have been endlessly and unimaginatively re-packaged over the years, and the corporate machines that now own the back catalogue have generally shown very little interest until recently in any process of re-discovery or archaeology. That is not to say that there have not been interesting reissues over the last ten to fifteen years, but what there has been has been largely unheralded and lacking in continuity.

During the original vinyl era, Motown were never renowned for their albums. Everything appeared to be subservient to the single issues, reasonable in the first half of the sixties, as that was without doubt where the market was driven. Albums then appeared to be hastily slung together affairs, with the requisite two or three singles, their B-sides and a handful of fillers. The cover artwork did not appear to have had the designers burning the midnight oil either! Gradually however, as time rolled on, there were glimmers of interest in creating some interesting collections that would include some previously unissued material. A handful of decent retrospective collections were issued that showed the tip of the unreleased iceberg.

The advent of CDs, which for some companies gave the perfect format for re-marketing rare tracks, was largely ignored by the owners of the Motown vaults. Corporate lack of interest and vision was obviously to blame. Rather than put time and effort into maximising material for the new format, the easy options of re-packaging were taken. Some attempts were made in the early eighties with the advent of the Compact Command Performances series of re-packed hits of individual artists, but these were shoddily presented with only track lists to be found inside. The first cheaper Spectrum issues in the mid-eighties continued the same sparse theme with only the barest of notes, and somewhat strangely chosen and ordered contents. All the main artists were covered including, for the first time in the UK, a collection from The Detroit Spinners (550 408-2) that managed to miss off "Truly Yours" and "I'll Always Love You" despite covering 1961 to 1970. The Diana Ross and The Supremes two disc 25th Anniversary set (Tamla Motown ZD72512(2)) in 1986 managed a decent booklet and some genuinely rare tracks, and the Mary Wells splendid double set from 1993 (Motown Master Series 37463-6253-2) included eleven previously unreleased tracks from all stages of her Motown career. These hopeful signs were not to continue in any organised way, as releases other than standard hit packages since then have been erratic and variable. The cheap Spectrum series has continued with the re-release of the original Motown Chartbusters series of album collection, and has gone on to an ever-changing selection of presentation ideas from the Early Classics original dozen main artists issues of the mid-nineties to the more recent series of the lesser known acts. The sub-titles on these keep altering, as do the rarity of the tracks presented. For instance The Contours *Essential Collection* (544 259-2), splendid as it is, contained no unissued material from the extensive list that exists, whilst The Marvelettes equivalent (554 8592) contained six very tasty new tracks with classic Motown sounds. However the outside packaging made no mention of these goodies, and the short notes only mentioned it obliquely. Surely such releases ought to be trumpeted from the rooftops!

Slightly brighter were the two *This Is Northern Soul* volumes that emerged on the Debutante label in 1997/8 (530 818-2 and 530 814-2). Both had a good selection of twenty-four rare, unissued and collectable tracks, mouth-watering to any fan, but were so very poorly presented inside that they looked like bootlegs. Imagine how wonderful these could have been if Ace or Westside had been given the chance to issue them. On the subject of bootlegs, there have of course been some Motown ones of 'European' origin. A series of "Rare Tracks from Detroit" have shown little obvious theme other than rarity of value, whilst issues of Velvelettes, Elgins and Monitors material amongst others have been around. As is usually the case, they are very poorly presented and vastly overpriced. Perhaps the best recent disc was one that appeared quietly, actually on the Motown label, in 1998. Billed as *The Ultimate Rarities Collection 1: Motown Sings Motown Treasures* (530 960-2), the twenty-one tracks were well known songs sung by other acts from the roster. Included were some lovely performances, often very different to the well-known versions. There were rare acts as well as the stars, and the disc was beautifully presented in a foldout card sleeve with excellent notes and a total design concept to the whole package. At the time of writing there is no sign of a volume two.

The summer of 2000 has seen much more UK re-issue activity than of late, with the *Big Hits & Hard To Find Classics* three volumes re-emerging cheaply, and the first UK issue for the newer *Lost And Found* series. This series initially covers rarities from The Miracles, The Four Tops, Marvin Gaye and the Temptations, and the issues highlight the fact that they are the first issues of material from the vaults. However, at the same time, other back catalogue issues and rare collections are hitting the shops, and are showing a lack of planning and care, which can only be laid at the door of corporate management.

The end of 2000 has seen news of a series of new two-on-one album reissues from Motown's early big names, but there are some odd couplings, some missing albums, sparse packaging and a lack of new notes that could so easily have been rectified. Whilst it is lovely to catch up on rarities however they reach the market, how much more worthwhile it would all be if there was some, or any, continuity of releases, prices, labels, sleeve notes and presentation. Then someone might take the trouble to advertise the issues properly and get some decent sales. The 40th Anniversary got a pretty big campaign behind it, but all that was on offer was corporate re-packaging of the same old stuff, rather than taking the obvious opportunity to hitch some rare releases on as well. Such is the corporate mind: they neither know nor care. The legacy is great. It deserves better.

Kingsley Abbott's Top Ten

As I collected other writers' ten choices for this book, I happily thought that I would add mine in at the end. Having reached the moment, I now realise the difficulty of the choice that I was setting people. How do you set about choosing just ten from all the amazingly good music that appeared on Motown labels over the years? It is probably inevitable that worthy records will be missed. In the end, I decided to go for the ones that really grabbed me from the first listen, and that have stayed with me. Even then, I'm missing wonderful songs like "Reach Out" that I played maybe twenty times in a row when I brought it home. A brief reflection shows me that my choices often verge towards the rawer, rougher edges of early Motown. I am sometimes ill at ease with the perfect production, preferring the joys of slight imperfections. This would be why two of my all time favourite pop/soul singles elsewhere are "Candy" by The Astors and "Johnny My Boy" by The Ad-libs, and another love being Steely Dan's "My Old School". But back to Motown...

1. "Leaving Here" – Eddie Holland
It must be one of Motown's longest intros, and it is what grabbed me from the first second. Raw passion from everyone concerned. Please, someone explain to me why it was never a huge hit. I found it on my first Motown album A Collection Of 16 Original Big Hits – Vol 2 *on the Tamla label.*

2. "I'll Always Love You" – The Detroit Spinners.
In some people's eyes this will be rated as a regular run-of-the-mill song and production. For me it was a song that struck home, with a great melody on the verse and chorus. I love it!

3. "Dancing In The Street" – Martha and The Vandellas.
The anthem as far as I am concerned, with Martha giving such a powerful lead. Probably one of the best all round song/performance/production records ever, it just had to be in my ten. "Nowhere To Run' almost made it too.

4. "Ask The Lonely" – The Four Tops
Early Tops before they got launched on their incredible hit run. This was representative of the great harmonising that kept those four men together for so long. This comes from the era that also produced "Baby I Need Your Loving" and "Without the One You Love", both of which would probably make my twenty.

5. "It's The Same Old Song" – The Four Tops.
Accepting that it is a total rip off from their "I Can't Help Myself', this makes it because it was always better to dance to. The sort of record that someone like me (not a dancer, not now, not ever...) can let go with and make a total prat of themselves. There should be records that do this!

6. "As Long As I Know He's Mine" – The Marvelettes
Another great intro, and another from my Vol. 2 of Hits. *The Marvelettes made some great records for Motown, but got forgotten along the way. This crosses over well to the mainstream girl group sound, and is cute, cute, cute all the way.*

7. "Do As I Do" – Kim Weston
Originally released in the U.K. as a bonus 45 in a boxed set of singles, this is now avail-

able on a budget CD of the best of her work. A very sludgy production fails to obscure a great song and vocal. This one just edges out "Helpless" for me.

8. "The Way You Do The Things You Do" – The Temptations & The Underdogs.
OK, so I'm cheating, but it's my book. I had to have the song for all the obvious reasons, having loved The Temps cool version for years. I was surprised to hear The Underdogs version on a recently released compilation of rarities, as it is as different as chalk and cheese. The white four-piece band almost turns it into "Land Of 1000 Dances". I suspect that purists will hate me for including it, but I love the attacking contrast.

9. "Ooh Baby Baby" – The Miracles
Pure magic from one of the best voices and songwriters Motown ever had. Total toe-curling time. When Smokey's falsetto soars on this, it is like no other.

10. "How Sweet It Is (To Be Loved By You) – Jr. Walker & The All Stars
Motown's wonderful wild card helped remind the world that they could get down and dirty when they chose to. "Shotgun" or "Road Runner" could also be included, but I've chosen this one to illustrate the power of the Motown songwriting that allows good songs to be hits in very different versions.

Final Thoughts

This book was always conceived to deal with what we called "The Golden Era". The simplest way to define this has been to simply take the sixties as the time, but this has been exceeded in one or two instances. It does of course mean that certain Motown acts and key records simply don't get a look in. Whilst this may be a shame to some, it comes about through having to have a cut-off point somewhere. If we had tried to cover the whole story, it would have got cluttered and I would not have enjoyed the work on the book nearly so much. I remain unashamedly a fan of early and classic Motown, and I usually date my lessening of interest from when I saw "The Corporation" appearing in various places. It spoke volumes to me. However I am not so blinkered to claim that Motown never made any decent records after the sixties. The Jackson 5, The Commodores, Rick James and many others appeared after my focus period and made some great records, but for me at least they never had the edge or unique sounds that I link specifically with the sixties. Some have said that Motown became just another soul label; a follower rather than a leader, and I do have some sympathy with this view. However, others will point to records, concerts, events and continued experimentation that contradict it. Ultimately it is for each individual to decide.

The recorded legacy is an extremely rich one. There have been glimmers of hope with the appearance in the U.S. of compilations of The Velvelettes and The Originals and other retrospective sets. We should all hope, and lobby for, more of such issues. From my point of view, I would love to see a boxed set, or series of CDs, dealing specifically with the early days of Motown before the "golden" years. In the meantime, I hope that several things in this book will send you searching for some old sounds to play again, or to seek out some new purchases to enjoy the fabulous sounds that were Motown.

There is more than a tinge of sadness that so many of the giants of Motown are no longer with us, and that a number of them are very unwell. Despite all the reported problems that people had with the company along the way, the story of the growth of such a great organisation remains essentially one of talent, inspiration, co-operation and very hard work by so many people. Motown influences spread far and wide, both musically and in a much wider social and economic context. Such a growth is unlikely to ever be repeated on such a scale. Let us all celebrate the time that it did. It's a grand story.

Kingsley Abbott

APPENDICES

Appendix 1: UK discography

A selection of recent CD re-issues that allow collection of rarer tracks.

BRITISH SINGLES

7 INCH SINGLES

LONDON-AMERICAN

HLT 8856	Marv Johnson	Come To Me Whisper	5.1959
HLM 8998	Paul Gayten	The Hunch Hot Cross Buns	11.1959
HLT 9013	Marv Johnson	You Got What It Takes Don't Leave Me	12.1959
HLU 9088	Barrett Strong	Money (That's What I Want) Oh I Apologise	3.1960
HLT 9109	Marv Johnson	I Love The Way You Love Let Me Love You	4.1960
HLT 9165	Marv Johnson	All The Love I've Got Ain't Gonna Be That Way	7.1960
HLT 9187	Marv Johnson	You've Got To Move Two Mountains I Need You	9.1960
HLT 9265	Marv Johnson	Happy Days Baby Baby	1.1961
HLU 9276	The Miracles	Shop Around Who's Loving You	2.1961
HLT 9311	Marv Johnson	Merry-Go-Round Tell Me That You Love Me	3.1961
HLU 9366	The Miracles	Ain't It Baby The Only One I Love	6.1961

FONTANA

H 355	The Marvelettes	Please Mr. Postman So Long Baby	11.1961
H 384	The Miracles	What's So Good About Goodbye I've Been Good To You	2.1962
H 387	The Marvelettes	Twistin' Postman I Want A Guy	3.1962
H 387	Eddie Holland	Jamie Take A Chance On Me	3.1962

ORIOLE (Prefix: CBA)

1762	Mary Wells	You Beat Me To The Punch Old Love (Let's Try It Again)	9.1962
1763	The Contours	Do You Love Me? Move Mr. Man	9.1962
1764	The Marvelettes	Beechwood 4-5789 Someday, Some Way	9.196
1775	Mike & the Modifiers	I Found Myself A Brand New Baby It's Too Bad	10.1962
1795	The Miracles	You've Really Got A Hold On Me Happy Landing	1.1963
1796	Mary Wells	Two Lovers Operator	1.1963
1799	The Contours	Shake Sherry You Better Get In Line	2.1963
1803	Marvin Gaye	Stubborn Kind of Fellow It Hurt Me Too	2.1963
1808	Eddie Holland	If It's Love (It's Alright) It's Not Too Late	3.1963
1809	The Valadiers	I Found A Girl You'll Be Sorry Someday	3.1963
1814	Martha and the Vandellas	I'll Have To Let Him Go My Baby Won't Come Back	3.1963
1817	The Marvelettes	Locking Up My Heart Forever	4.1963
1819	Martha and The Vandellas	Come And Get These Memories Jealous Lover	4.1963
1829	Mary Wells	Laughing Boy Two Wrongs Don't Make A Right	5.1963
1831	The Contours	Don't Let Her Be Your Baby It Must Be Love	5.1963
1846	Marvin Gaye	Pride And Joy One Of These Days	7.1963
1847	Mary Wells	Your Old Standby What Love Has Joined Together	7.1963
1853	Little Stevie Wonder	Fingertips (Part 2) Fingertips (Part 1)	8.1963
1863	The Miracles	Mickey's Monkey Whatever Makes You Happy	9.1963

STATESIDE (Prefix: SS)

228	Martha and The Vandellas	Heatwave	10.1963
		A Love Like Yours (Don't Come Knocking Every Day)	
238	Little Stevie Wonder	Workout, Stevie Workout	11.1963
		Monkey Talk	
242	Mary Wells	You Lost The Sweetest Boy	11.1963
		What's Easy For Two (Is So Hard For One)	
243	Marvin Gaye	Can I Get A Witness	11.1963
		I'm Crazy 'Bout My Baby	
250	Martha and The Vandellas	Quicksand	1.1964
		Darling I Hum Our Song	
251	The Marvelettes	As Long As I Know He's Mine	1.1964
		Little Girl Blue	
257	The Supremes	When The Lovelight Starts Shining Thru His Eyes	1.1964
		Standing At The Crossroads Of Love	
263	The Miracles	I Gotta Dance To Stop From Crying	2.1964
		Such Is Love, Such Is Life	
272	Martha & The Vandellas	Live Wire	3.1964
		Old Love (Let's Try it Again)	
273	The Marvelettes	He's A Good Guy, Yes He Is	3.1964
		Goddess Of Love	
278	The Temptations	The Way You Do The Things You Do	4.1964
		Just Let Me Know	
282	The Miracles	(You Can't Let The Boy Overpower) The Man In You	4.1964
		Heartbreak Road	
284	Marvin Gaye	You're A Wonderful One	4.1964
		When I'm Alone I Cry	
285	Little Stevie Wonder	Castles in The Sand	4.1964
		Thank You (For Loving Me All The Way)	
288	Mary Wells	My Guy	5.1964
		Oh Little Boy (What Did You Do To Me?)	
299	The Contours	Can You Do It?	5.1964
		I'll Stand By You	
305	Martha & The Vandellas	In My Lonely Room	6.1964
		A Tear For The Girl	
307	Brenda Holloway	Every Little Bit Hurts	6.1964
		Land Of A Thousand Boys	
316	Mary Wells & Marvin Gaye	Once Upon A Time	7.1964
		What's The Matter With You Baby?	
319	The Temptations	I'll Be In Trouble	7.1964
		The Girl's Alright With Me	
323	Stevie Wonder	Hey Harmonica Man	8.1964
		This Little Girl	
324	The Miracles	I Like It Like That	8.1964
		You're So Fine And Sweet	
326	Marvin Gaye	Try It Baby	8.1964
		If My Heart Could Sing	
327	The Supremes	Where Did Our Love Go?	8.1964
		He Means The World To Me	
334	The Marvelettes	You're My Remedy	9.1964
		A Little Bit Of Sympathy, A Little Bit Of Love	
336	Four Tops	Baby, I Need Your Loving	9.1964
		Call On Me	
345	Martha & The Vandellas	Dancing in The Street	10.1964
		There He Is (At My Door)	
348	The Temptations	(Girl) Why You Wanna Make Me Blue?	10.1964
		Baby, Baby I Need You	
350	The Supremes	Baby Love	10.1964
		Ask Any Girl	
353	The Miracles	That's What Love Is Made Of	11.1964
		Would I Love You	

357	Earl Van Dyke & The Soul Brothers	Soul Stomp	11.1964
		Hot 'n' Tot	
359	Kim Weston	A Little More Love	11.1964
		Go Ahead And Laugh	
360	Marvin Gaye	How Sweet It Is (To Be Loved Loved By You)	11.1964
		Forever	
361	The Velvelettes	Needle In A Haystack	11.1964
		Should I Tell Them?	
363	Marvin Gaye & Kim Weston	What Good Am I Without You?	12.1964
		I Want You 'Round	
369	The Marvelettes	Too Many Fish In The Sea	1.1965
		A Need For Love	
371	The Four Tops	Without The One You Love (Life's Not Worthwhile)	1.1965
		Love Has Gone	
376	The Supremes	Come See About Me	1.1965
		Always In My Heart	
377	The Miracles	Come On Do The Jerk	1.1965
		Baby Don't You Go	
378	The Temptations	My Girl	1.1965
		Talkin' 'Bout Nobody But My Baby	
381	The Contours	Can You Jerk Like Me?	1.1965
		That Day When She Needed Me	
383	Martha & The Vandellas	Wild One	1.1965
		Dancing Slow	
384	Carolyn Crawford	When Someone's Good To You	2.1965
		My Heart	
387	The Velvelettes	He Was Really Sayin' Somethin'	2.1965
		Throw A Farewell Kiss	
394	Tony Martin	Talking To Your Picture	3.1965
		Our Rhapsody	

TAMLA MOTOWN (Prefix: TMG)

501	The Supremes	Stop! In The Name Of Love	3.1965
		I'm In Love Again	
502	Martha & The Vandellas	Nowhere To Run	3.1965
		Motoring	
503	The Miracles	Ooo Baby Baby	3.1965
		All That's Good	
504	The Temptations	It's Growing	3.1965
		What Love Has Joined Together	
505	Stevie Wonder	Kiss Me Baby	3.1965
		Tears In Vain	
506	Earl Van Dyke & The Soul Brothers	All For You	3.1965
		Too Many Fish In The Sea	
507	Four Tops	Ask The Lonely	3.1965
		Where Did You Go?	
508	Brenda Holloway	When I'm Gone	4.1965
		I've Been Good To You	
509	Jr Walker & The All Stars	Shotgun	4.1965
		Hot Cha	
510	Marvin Gaye	I'll Be Doggone	4.1965
		You've Been A Long Time Coming	
511	Kim Weston	I'm Still Loving You	4.1965
		Just Loving You	
512	Shorty Long	Out To Get You	4.1965
		It's A Crying Shame	
513	The Hit Pack	Never Say No To Your Baby	5.1965
		Let's Dance	
514	The Detroit Spinners	Sweet Thing	5.1965
		How Can I?	
515	Four Tops	I Can't Help Myself	5.1965
		Sad Souvenirs	
516	The Supremes	Back in My Arms Again	5.1965
		Whisper You Love Me Boy	
517	Choker Campbell & His Band	Mickey's Monkey	6.1965
		Pride And Joy	

No.	Artist	Titles	Date
518	The Marvelettes	I'll Keep Holding On / No Time For Tears	6.1965
519	Brenda Holloway	Operator / I'll Be Available	6.1965
520	Jr Walker & The All Stars	Do The Boomerang / Tune Up	7.1965
521	The Velvelettes	Lonely, Lonely Girl Am I / I'm The Exception To The Rule	7.1965
522	The Miracles	The Tracks of My Tears / Fork In The Road	7.1965
523	The Detroit Spinners	I'll Always Love You / Tomorrow May Never Come	7.1965
524	Marvin Gaye	Pretty Little Baby / Now That You've Won Me	8.1965
525	Marv Johnson	Why Do You Want To Let Me Go? / I'm Not A Plaything	8.1965
526	The Temptations	Since I Lost My Baby / You've Got To Earn It	8.1965
527	The Supremes	Nothing But Heartaches / He Holds His Own	8.1965
528	Four Tops	It's The Same Old Song / Your Love Is Amazing	8.1965
529	Jr Walker & The All Stars	Shake And Fingerpop / Cleo's Back	9.1965
530	Martha & The Vandellas	You've Been In Love Too Long / Love (Makes Me Do Foolish Things)	9.1965
531	The Contours	First I Look At The Purse / Searching For A Girl	9.1965
532	Stevie Wonder	High Heel Sneakers / Music Talk	9.1965
533	Billy Eckstine	Had You Been Around / Down To Earth	10.1965
534	Dorsey Burnette	Jimmy Brown / Everybody's Angel	10.1965
535	The Marvelettes	Danger Heartbreak Dead Ahead / Your Cheating Ways	10.1965
536	The Lewis Sisters	You Need Me / Moonlight On The Beach	10.1965
537	Tony Martin	The Bigger Your Heart Is / The Two Of Us	10.1965
538	Kim Weston	Take Me In Your Arms (Rock Me A Little While) / Don't Compare Me With Her	10.1965
539	Marvin Gaye	Ain't That Peculiar / She's Got To Be Real	11.1965
540	The Miracles	My Girl Has Gone / Since You Won My Heart	11.1965
541	The Temptations	My Baby / Don't Look Back	11.1965
542	Four Tops	Something About You / Darling I Hum Our Song	11.1965
543	The Supremes	I Hear A Symphony / Who Could Ever Doubt My Love	11.1965
544	Barbara McNair	You're Gonna Love My Baby / The Touch Of Time	1.1966
545	Stevie Wonder	Uptight (Everything's Alright) / Purple Raindrops	1.1966
546	The Marvelettes	Don't Mess With Bill / Anything You Wanna Do	1.1966
547	The Miracles	Going To A Go-Go / Choosey Beggar	2.1966
548	The Supremes	My World Is Empty Without You / Everything Is Good About You	2.1966
549	Martha & The Vandellas	My Baby Loves Me / Never Leave Your Baby's Side	2.1966
550	Jr Walker & The All Stars	Cleo's Mood / Baby, You Know You Ain't Right	2.1966
551	The Elgins	Put Yourself In My Place / Darling Baby	2.1966
502	Marvin Gaye	One More Heartache / When I Had Your Love	3.1966
553	Four Tops	Shake Me, Wake Me (When It's Over) / Just As Long As You Need Me	3.1966
554	Kim Weston	Helpless / A Love Like Yours (Don't Come Knockin' Every Day)	3.1966
555	The Isley Brothers	This Old Heart of Mine (Is Weak For Me) / There's No Love Left	3.1966
556	Brenda Holloway	Together 'Till The End of Time / Sad Song	3.1966
557	The Temptations	Get Ready / Fading Away	4.1966
558	Stevie Wonder	Nothing's Too Good For My Baby / With A Child's Heart	4.1966
559	Jr Walker & The All Stars	Road Runner / Shoot Your Shot	5.1966
560	The Supremes	Love Is Like An Itching In My Heart / He's All I Got	5.1966
561	Tammi Terrell	Come On And See Me / Baby, Don'tcha Worry	5.1966
562	The Marvelettes	You're The One / Paper Boy	5.1966
563	Marvin Gaye	Take This Heart Of Mine / Need Your Lovin' (Want You Back)	6.1966
564	The Contours	Determination / Just A Little Misunderstanding	6.1966
565	The Temptations	Ain't To Proud To Beg / You'll Lose A Precious Love	6.1966
566	The Isley Brothers	Take Some Time Out For Love / Who Could Ever Doubt My Love?	6.1966
567	Martha & The Vandellas	What Am I Going To Do Without Your Love / Go Ahead And Laugh	6.1966
568	Four Tops	Loving You Is Sweeter Than Ever / I Like Everything About You	7.1966
569	The Miracles	Whole Lotta Shakin' In My Heart (Since I Met You Girl) / Oh Be My Love	7.1966
570	Stevie Wonder	Blowin' In The Wind / Ain't That Asking For Trouble	8.1966
571	Jr Walker & The All Stars	How Sweet It Is (To Be Loved By You) / Nothing But Soul	8.1966
572	The Isley Brothers	I Guess I'll Always Love You / I Hear A Symphony	8.1966
573	Shorty Long	Function At The Junction / Call On Me	8.1966
574	Marvin Gaye	Little Darling (I Need You) / Hey Diddle Diddle	9.1966
575	The Supremes	You Can't Hurry Love / Put Yourself In My Place	9.1966
576	Gladys Knight & The Pips	Just Walk In My Shoes / Stepping Closer To Your Heart	9.1966
577	Jimmy Ruffin	What Becomes Of The Brokenhearted / Baby I've Got It	9.1966
578	The Temptations	Beauty Is Only Skin Deep / You're Not An Ordinary Girl	9.1966
579	Four Tops	Reach Out, I'll Be There / Until You Love Someone	10.1966
580	The Velvelettes	These Things Will Keep Me Loving You / Since You've Been Loving Me	10.1966

581	Brenda Holloway	Hurt A Little Everyday	11.1966
		Where Were You?	
582	Martha & The	I'm Ready For Love	11.1966
	Vandellas	He Doesn't Love Her	
583	The Elgins	Heaven Must Have Sent You	11.1966
		Stay In My Lonely Arms	
584	The Miracles	(Come Round Here) I'm The	
		One You Need	11.1966
		Save Me	
585	The Supremes	You Keep Me Hanging On	11.1966
		Remove This Doubt	
586	Jr Walker & The	Money (Part 1)	12.1966
	All Stars	Money (Part 2)	
587	The Temptations	(I Know) I'm Losing You	12.1966
		Little Miss Sweetness	
588	Stevie Wonder	A Place In The Sun	12.1966
		Sylvia	
589	Four Tops	Standing In The Shadows of Love	1.1967
		Since You've Been Gone	
590	Marvin Gaye &	It Takes Two	1.1967
	Kim Weston	It's Gotta Be A Miracle (This Thing	
		Called Love)	
591	Chris Clark	Love's Gone Bad	1.1967
		Put Yourself In My Place	
592	The Originals	Goodnight Irene	1.1967
		Need Your Lovin' (Want You Back)	
593	Jimmy Ruffin	I've Passed This Way Before	2.1967
		Tomorrow's Tears	
594	The Marvelettes	The Hunter Gets Captured By	
		The Game	2.1967
		I Think I Can Change You	
595	The Velvelettes	Needle In A Haystack	2.1967
		He Was Really Sayin' Something	
596	Jr Walker & The	Pucker Up Buttercup	2.1967
	All Stars	Any Way You Wanta	
597	The Supremes	Love Is Here And Now	
		You're Gone	2.1967
		There's No Stopping Us Now	
598	Smokey Robinson &	The Love I Saw In You	
	The Miracles	Was Just A Mirage	3.1967
		Swept For You Baby	
599	Martha & The	Jimmy Mack	3.1967
	Vandellas	Third Finger, Left Hand	
600	Shorty Long	Chantilly Lace	3.1967
		Your Love Is Amazing	
601	Four Tops	Bernadette	3.1967
		I Got A Feeling	
602	Stevie Wonder	Travelin' Man	3.1967
		Hey Love	
603	Jimmy Ruffin	Gonna Give Her All The	
		Love I've Got	4.1967
		World So Wide, Nowhere To Hide	
		(From Your Heart)	
604	Gladys Knight &	Take Me In Your Arms	
	The Pips	And Love Me	4.1967
		Do You Love Me Just A Little Honey?	
605	The Contours	It's So Hard Being A Loser	5.1967
		Your Love Grows More Precious Every Day	
606	The Isley Brothers	Got To Have You Back	5.1967
		Just Ain't Enough Love	
607	The Supremes	The Happening	5.1967
		All I Know About You	
608	Brenda Holloway	Just Look What You've Done	5.1967
		Starting The Hurt All Over Again	
609	The Marvelettes	When You're Young And In Love	5.1967
		The Day You Take One (You	
		Have To Take The Other)	

610	The Temptations	All I Need	5.1967
		Sorry Is A Sorry Word	
611	Marvin Gaye &	Ain't No Mountain High Enough	6.1967
	Tammi Terrell	Give A Little Love	
612	Four Tops	Seven Rooms Of Gloom	6.1967
		I'll Turn To Stone	
613	Stevie Wonder	I Was Made To Love Her	6.1967
		Hold Me	
614	Smokey Robinson &	More Love	7.1967
	The Miracles	Come Spy With Me (Orig. 'B.' side	
		Swept For You Baby)	
615	The Elgins	It's Been A Long Long Time	7.1967
		I Understand My Man	
616	Diana Ross & The	Reflections	8.1967
	Supremes	Going Down For The Third Time	
617	Jimmy Ruffin	Don't You Miss Me A Little Bit Baby?	8.1967
		I Want Her Love	
618	Marvin Gaye	Your Unchanging Love	8.1967
		I'll Take Care Of You	
619	Gladys Knight &	Everybody Needs Love	9.1967
	the Pips	Since I've Lost You	
620	The Temptations	You're My Everything	9.1967
		I've Been Good To You	
621	Martha Reeves &	Love Bug Leave My Heart Alone	9.1967
	The Vandellas	One Way Out	
622	Brenda Holloway	You've Made Me So Very Happy	9.1967
		I've Got To End It	
623	Four Tops	You Keep Running Away	10.1967
		If You Don't Want My Love	
624	Chris Clark	From Head To Toe	10.1967
		Beginning Of The End	
625	Marvin Gaye &	Your Precious Love	10.1967
	Tammi Terrell	Hold Me Oh My Darling	
626	Stevie Wonder	I'm Wondering	10.1967
		Every Time I See You I Go Wild	
627	The Spinners	For All We Know	10.1967
		I'll Always Love You	
628	Barbara Randolph	I Got A Feeling	11.1967
		You Got Me Hurtin' All Over	
629	Gladys Knight &	I Heard It Through The Grapevine	11.1967
	The Pips	It's Time To Go Now	
630	Edwin Starr	I Want My Baby Back	11.1967
		Gonna Keep On Trying Till I Win Your Love	
631	Smokey Robinson &	I Second That Emotion	11.1967
	The Miracles	You Must Be Love	
632	Diana Ross & The	In And Out Of Love	11.1967
	Supremes	I Guess I'll Always Love You	
633	The Temptations	(Loneliness Made Me Realise)	12.1967
		It's You That I Need	
		I Want A Love I Can See	
634	Four Tops	Walk Away Renee	12.1967
		Mame	
635	Marvin Gaye &	If I Could Build My Whole	12.1967
	Tammi Terrell	World Around You	
		If This World Were Mine	
636	Martha Reeves &	Honey Chile	1. 1968
	The Vandellas	Show Me The Way	
637	Jr Walker &	Come See About Me	1.1968
	The All Stars	Sweet Soul	
638	Chris Clark	I Want To Go Back There	1.1968
		Again	
639	The Marvelettes	My Baby Must Be A Magician	1.1968
		I Need Someone	
640	Marvin Gaye	You	1.1968
		Change What You Can	
641	The Temptations	I Wish It Would Rain	2.1968
		I Truly Truly Believe	

642	The Elgins	Put Yourself In My Place	2.1968
		Darling Baby	
643	Rita Wright	I Can't Give Back The Love I	2.1968
		Feel For You	
		Something On My Mind	
644	Shorty Long	Night Fo' Last (vocal)	2.1968
		Night Fo' Last (instr.)	
645	Gladys Knight	The End Of Our Road	3.1968
	& The Pips	Don't Let Her Take Your	
		Love From Me	
646	Edwin Starr	I Am The Man For You Baby	2.1968
		My Weakness Is You	
647	Four Tops	If I Were A Carpenter	3.1968
		Your Love Is Wonderful	
648	Smokey Robinson &	If You Can Want	3.1968
	The Miracles	When The Words From Your Heart	
		Get Caught Up In Your Throat	
649	Jimmy Ruffin	I'll Say Forever My Love	3.1968
		Everybody Needs Love	
650	Diana Ross & The	Forever Came Today	4.1698
	Supremes	Time Changes Things	
651	Chuck Jackson	Girls, Girls, Girls	4.1698
		(You Can't Let The Boy	
		Overpower) The Man In You	
652	The Isley Brothers	Take Me In Your Arms (Rock	4.1698
		Me A Little While)	
		Why, When Love Is Gone	
653	Stevie Wonder	Shoo-Be-Doo-Be-Doo-Da-Day	4.1698
		Why Don't You Lead Me To Love ?	
654	Bobby Taylor &	Does Your Mama Know About Me?	5.1968
	The Vancouvers	Fading Away	
655	Marvin Gaye &	Ain't Nothing Like The Real Thing	5.1968
	Tammi Terrell	Little Ole Boy, Little Ole Girl	
656	R. Dean Taylor	Gotta See Jane	5.1968
		Don't Fool Around	
657	Martha Reeves &	I Promise To Wait My Love	5.1968
	the Vandellas	Forget Me Not	
658	The Temptations	I Could Never Love Another	
		(After Loving You)	5.1968
		Gonna Give Her All The Love I've Got	
659	The Marvelettes	Here I Am Baby	6.1968
		Keep Off, No Trespassing	
660	Gladys Knight &	It Should Have Been Me	6.1968
	The Pips	You Don't Love Me No More	
661	Smokey Robinson &	Yesterlove	6.1968
	The Miracles	Much Better	
662	Diana Ross & The	Some Things You Never Get	6.1968
	Supremes	Used To	
		You've Been So Wonderful To Me	
663	Shorty Long	Here Comes The Judge	7.1968
		Sing What You Wanna	
664	Jimmy Ruffin	Don't Let Him Take Your	7.1968
		Love From Me	
		Lonely, Lonely Man Am I	
665	Four Tops	Yesterday's Dreams	8.1968
		For Once In My Life	
667	Stevie Wonder	You Met Your Match	8.1968
		My Girl	
667	Jr. Walker & The	Hip City (Part 1)	9.1968
	All Stars	Hip City (Part 2)	
668	Marvin Gaye &	You're All I Need To Get By	9.1968
	Tammi Terrell	Two Can Have A Party	
669	Martha Reeves	I Can't Dance To That Music	9.1968
	The Vandellas	You're Playin'	
		I Tried	
670	Paul Petersen	A Little Bit For Sandy	9.1968
		Your Love's Got Me Burning Alive	

671	The Temptations	Why Did You Leave Me Darling?	10. 1968
		How Can I Forget?	
672	Edwin Starr	25 Miles	9.1968
		Mighty Good Lovin'	
673	Smokey Robinson &	Special Occasion	10. 1968
	The Miracles	Give Her Up	
674	Gladys Knight &	I Wish It Would Rain	10. 1968
	The Pips	It's Summer	
675	Four Tops	I'm In A Different World	11.1968
		Remember When	
676	Marvin Gaye	Chained	11.1968
		At Last (I Found A Love)	
677	Diana Ross & The	Love Child	11.1968
	Supremes	Will This Be The Day?	
678	The Fantastic Four	I Love You Madly (vocal)	11.1968
		I Love You Madly (instr.)	
679	Stevie Wonder	For Once In My Life	11.1968
		Angie Girl	
680	Marv Johnson	I'll Pick A Rose For My Rose	12.1968
		You Got The Love I Love	
681	Marvin Gaye &	You Ain't Livin' 'Til You're Lovin'	12.1968
	Tammi Terrell	Oh How I'd Miss You	
682	Jr Walker & The	Home Cookin'	1.1969
	All Stars	Mutiny	
683	The Isley Brothers	I Guess I'll Always Love You	1.1969
		It's Out Of The Question	
684	Martha Reeves	Dancing In The Street	1.1969
	The Vandellas	Quicksand	
685	Diana Ross & The	I'm Gonna Make You Love Me	1.1969
	Supremes & The	A Place in The Sun	
	Temptations		
686	Marvin Gaye	I Heard It Through The Grapevine	2.1969
		Need Somebody	
687	Smokey Robinson &	Baby, Baby Don't Cry	2.1969
	The Miracles	Your Mother's Only Daughter	
688	The Temptations	Get Ready	2.1969
		My Girl	
689	David Ruffin	My Whole World Ended (The	3.1969
		Moment You Left Me)	
		I've Got To Find Myself A Brand New Baby	
690	Stevie Wonder	I Don't Know Why	3.1969
		My Cherie Amour	
691	Jr Walker & The	Road Runner	3.1969
	All Stars	Shotgun	
692	Edwin Starr	Way Over There	3.1969
		If My Heart Could Tell The Story	
693	The Isley Brothers	Behind A Painted Smile	4.1969
		One Too Many Heartaches	
694	Martha Reeves &	Nowhere To Run	3.1969
	The Vandellas	Live Wire	
695	Diana Ross & The	I'm Livin' In Shame	4.1969
	Supremes	I'm So Glad I Got Somebody	
		(Like You Around)	
696	Smokey Robinson &	The Tracks of My Tears	4.1969
	The Miracles	Come On Do The Jerk	
697	Marvin Gaye &	Good Lovin' Ain't Easy To	5.1969
	Tammi Terrell	Come By	
		Satisfied Feelin'	5.1969
698	Four Tops	What is A Man?	
		Don't Bring Back Memories	
699	The Temptations	Ain't Too Proud To Beg	5.1969
		Fading Away	
700	Brenda Holloway	Just Look What You've Done	6.1969
		You've Made Me So Very Happy	
701	The Marvelettes	Reachin' For Something I	6.1969
		Can't Have	
		Destination: Anywhere	

702	The Originals	Green Grow The Lilacs	6.1969
		You're The One	
703	Jimmy Ruffin	I've Passed This Way Before	7.1969
		Tomorrow's Tears	
704	Diana Ross & The	No Matter What Sign You Are	7.1969
	Supremes	The Young Folks	
705	Marvin Gaye	Too Busy Thinkin' 'Bout My Baby	7.1969
		Wherever I Lay My Hat (That's My Home)	
706	The Honest Men	Cherie Baby	8.1969
707	The Temptations	Cloud Nine	8.1969
		Why Did She Have To Leave	
		Me (Why Did She Have To Go?)	
708	The Isley Brothers	Put Yourself in My Place	8. 1969
		Little Miss Sweetness	
709	Diana Ross & The	I Second That Emotion	9.1969
	Supremes & The	The Way You Do The Things You Do	
	Temptations		
710	Four Tops	Do What You Gotta Do	9.1969
		Can't Seem To Get You Out Of My Mind	
711	David Ruffin	I've Lost Everything I've Ever	9.1969
		Loved	
		We'll Have A Good Thing Going On	
712	Jr Walker & The	What Does it Take (To Win	
	All Stars	Your Love)	10.1969
		Brainwasher	
713	Marv Johnson	I Miss You Baby {How I Miss	
		You)	10.1969
		Bad Girl	
714	Gladys Knight	The Nitty Gritty	10.1969
	& the Pips	Got Myself A Good Man	
715	Marvin Gaye &	The Onion Song	10.1969
	Tammi Terrell	I Can't Believe You Love Me	
716	The Temptations	Runaway Child, Running Wild	10.1969
		I Need Your Lovin'	
717	Stevie Wonder	Yester-me, Yester-you, Yesterday	11.1969
		I'd Be A Fool Right Now	
718	Marvin Gaye	That's The Way Love Is	11.1969
		Gonna Keep On Tryin' 'Til I	
		Win Your Love	
719	The Isley Brothers	Take Some Time Out For Love	11.1969
		Who Could Ever Doubt My Love	
720	Blinky & Edwin Starr	Oh How Happy	NR
		Ooo Baby Baby	
721	Diana Ross & The	Someday We'll Be Together	11.1969
	Supremes	He's My Sunny Boy	

BRITISH EPs (Extended Play)

LONDON-AMERICAN
RE:

1295	The Miracles	Shop Around	10.1961

STATESIDE: SE

1009	Various	R&B Chartmakers No. 1	1.1964
1014	Little Stevie Wonder	I Call It Pretty Music But The Old	1.1964
		People Call It The Blues	
1018	Various	R&B Chartmakers No.2	4.1964
1022	Various	R&B Chartmakers No.3	6.1964
1025	Various	R&B Chartmakers No.4	9.1964

TAMLA MOTOWN: TME

2001	Various	Hitsville USA No.1	3.1965
2002	The Contours	The Contours	3.1965
2003	The Marvelettes	The Marvelettes	3.1965
2004	The Temptations	The Temptations	3.1965
2005	Kim Weston	Kim Weston	3.1965
2006	Stevie Wonder	Stevie Wonder	3.1965

2007	Mary Wells	Mary Wells	5.1965
2008	The Supremes	The Supremes Hits	5.1965
2009	Martha & The	Martha & the Vandellas	5.1965
	Vandellas		
2010	The Temptations	It's The Temptations	2.1966
2011	The Supremes	Shake	2.1966
2012	Four Tops	The Four Tops	2.1966
2013	Jr Walker & The	Shake and Fingerpop	2.1966
	All Stars		
2014	Various	New Faces From Hitsville	4.1966
2015	Kim Weston	Rock Me A Little While	4.1966
2016	Marvin Gaye	Marvin Gaye	4.1966
2017	Martha & The	Hittin'	10.1966
	Vandellas		
2018	Four Tops	Four Tops Hits	3.1967
2019	Marvin Gaye	Originals From Marvin Gaye	3.1967

STME:

2020	Stevie Wonder	A Something's Extra – bonus	9.1976
		record for Songs In The Key	
		Of Life (7" 33rpm)	

BRITISH ALBUMS

Oriole: PS

40043	The Contours	Do You Love Me	7.1963
40044	The Miracles	Hi! We're The Miracles	7.1963
40045	Mary Wells	Two Lovers	7.1963
40049	Little Stevie Wonder	Tribute To Uncle Ray	8.1963
40050	Little Stevie Wonder	The 12 Year Old Genius	8.1963
40051	Mary Wells	Bye Bye Baby	8.1963
40052	Martha & The	Come And Get These Memories	8.1963
	Vandellas		

STATESIDE: SL

10065	Various	On Stage Live!	3.1964
10077	Various	The Sound Of The R&B Hits	5.1964
10078	Little Stevie Wonder	The Jazz Soul Of Little Stevie	5.1964
10095	Mary Wells	My Guy	9.1964
10097	Marvin Gaye &	Together	10.1964
	Mary Wells		
10099	The Miracles	The Fabulous Miracles	11.1964
10100	Marvin Gaye	Marvin Gaye	11.1964
10108	Stevie Wonder	Hey Harmonica Man	1.1965
10109	The Supremes	Meet The Supremes	12.1964

TAMLA MOTOWN : TML (Mono)/STML (Stereo)

11001	Various	A Collection of 16 Big Tamla	3.1965
		Motown Hits	
11002	The Supremes	With Love (From Us To You)	3.1965
11003	The Miracles	I Like It Like That	3.1965
11004	Marvin Gaye	How Sweet It Is	3.1965
11005	Martha & The	Heatwave	3.1965
	Vandellas		
11006	Mary Wells	My Baby Just Cares For Me	3.1965
11007	Various	The Motortown Revue Live	4.1965
11008	The Marvelettes	The Marvellous Marvelettes	4.1965
11009	The Temptations	Meet The Temptations	4.1965
11010	Four Tops	Four Tops	6.1965
11011	Choker Campbell	Hits Of The Sixties	6.1965
	& His 16-Piece Band		
11012	The Supremes	We Remember Sam Cooke	7.1965
11013	Martha & the	Dance Party	9.1965
	Vandellas		
11014	Earl Van Dyke &	That Motown Sound	9.1965
	The Soul Brothers		

11015	Marvin Gaye	Hello Broadway	9.1965
11016	The Temptations	The Temptations Sing Smokey	10.1965
11017	Jr Walker & The All Stars	Shotgun	10.1965
11018	The Supremes	The Supremes Sing Country & Western & Pop	10.1965
11019	Various	Hitsville USA	12.1965
11020	The Supremes	More Hits By The Supremes	12.1965

STML:

11021	Four Tops	Second Album	3.1966
11022	Marvin Gaye	A Tribute To Great Nat King Cole	2.1966
11023	The Temptations	The Temptin' Temptations	3.1966
11024	Smokey Robinson & The Miracles	Going To A Go-Go	2.1966
11025	Billy Eckstine	The Prime Of My Life	2.1966
11026	The Supremes	The Supremes At The Copa	2.1966
11027 (TML)	Various	Motortown Revue Live In Paris	2.1966
11028	The Supremes	I Hear A Symphony	6.1966
11029	Jr Walker & The All Stars	Soul Session	6.1966
11030 (TML)	Various	Motown Magic	6.1966
11031 (TML)	The Miracles	From The Beginning	7.1966
11032	Mary Wells	Greatest Hits	7.1966
11033	Marvin Gaye	Moods of Marvin Gaye	10.1966
11034	The Isley Brothers	This Old Heart Of Mine	10.1966
11035	The Temptations	Gettin' Ready	10.1966
11036	Stevie Wonder	Uptight	9.1966
11037	Four Tops	On Top	11.1966
11038	Jr Walker & The All Stars	Road Runner	12.1966
11039	The Supremes	Supremes A Go-Go	12.1966
11040	Martha & The Vandellas	Greatest Hits	2.1967
11041	Four Tops	Live!	2.1967
11042	The Temptations	Greatest Hits	2.1967
11043	Various	A Collection Of 16 Original Big Hits Vol. 4	3.1967
11044	Smokey Robinson & The Miracles	Away We A Go Go	3.1967
11045	Stevie Wonder	Down To Earth	4.1967
11046	Billy Eckstine	My Way	4.1967
11047	The Supremes	Supremes Sing Motown	5.1967
11048	Jimmy Ruffin	The Jimmy Ruffin Way	5.1967
11049	Marvin Gaye & Kim Weston	Take Two	5.1967
11050	Various	A Collection Of 16 Original Big Hits Vol. 5	6.1967
11051	Martha & The Vandellas	Watchout!	6.1967
11052	The Marvelettes	The Marvelettes	7.1967
11053	The Temptations	Live!	7.1967
11054	The Supremes	Sing Rogers And Hart	9.1967
11055	Various	British Motown Chartbusters	10.1967
11056	Four Tops	Reach Out	11.1967
11057	The Temptations	With A Lot O' Soul	11.1967
11058	Gladys Knight & The Pips	Everybody Needs Love	1.1968
11059	Stevie Wonder	I Was Made To Love Her	12.1967
11060	The Detroit Spinners	The Detroit Spinners	1.1968
11061	Four Tops	Greatest Hits	1.1968
11062	Marvin Gaye & Tammi Terrell	United	1.1968
11063	Diana Ross & The Supremes	Greatest Hits	1.1968
11064	Various	Motown Memories	1.1968
11065	Marvin Gaye	Greatest Hits	2.1968
11066	The Isley Brothers	Soul On The Rocks	2.1968
11067	Smokey Robinson & The Miracles	Make It Happen	2.1968
11068	The Temptations	In A Mellow Mood	3.1968
11069	Chris Clark	Soul Sounds	2.1968
11070	Diana Ross & The Supremes	Live! At The Talk Of The Town	3.1968
11071	Chuck Jackson	Arrives	6.1968
11072	Smokey Robinson & The Miracles	Greatest Hits	6.1968
11073	Diana Ross & The Supremes	Reflections	7.1968
11074	Various	A Collection Of 16 Original Big Hits Vol. 6	7.1968
11075	Stevie Wonder	Greatest Hits	8.1968
11076 (TML)	Dr Martin Luther King	The Great March To Freedom	7.1968
11077 (TML)	Various	Motown Memories Vol 2	10.1968
11078	Martha Reeves & The Vandellas	Ridin' High	8.1968
11079	The Temptations	Wish It Would Rain	8.1968
11080	Gladys Knight & The Pips	Feelin' Bluesy	9.1968
11081	The Elgins	Darling Baby	9.1968
11082	Various	British Motown Chartbusters Vol.2	11.1968
11083	Brenda Holloway	The Artistry Of Brenda Holloway	10.1968
11084	Marvin Gaye & Tammi Terrell	You're All I Need	10.1968
11085	Stevie Wonder	Someday At Christmas	12.1968
11086	Shorty Long	Here Comes The Judge	12.1968
11087	Four Tops	Yesterday's Dreams	1.1969
11088	Diana Ross & The Supremes	Sing And Perform Funny Girl	2.1969
11089	Smokey Robinson & The Miracles	Special Occasion	1.1969
11090	The Marvelettes	Sophisticated Soul	1.1969
11091	Marvin Gaye	In The Groove	1.1969
11092	Various	The Motown Sound – Collection Of 16 Original Big Hits Vol. 7	5.1969
11093	Bobby Taylor & The Vancouvers	Bobby Taylor & The Vancouvers	2.1969
11094	Edwin Starr	Soul Master	2.1969
11095	Diana Ross & the Supremes	Love Child	1.1969
11096	Diana Ross & the Supremes & The Temptations	Diana Ross & The Supremes Join The Temptations	1.1969
11097	Jr Walker & the All Stars	Home Cookin'	2.1969
11098	Stevie Wonder	For Once In My Life	2.1969
11099	Martha Reeves & The Vandellas	Dancing In The Street	4.1969
11100	Gladys Knight & The Pips	Silk 'N' Soul	4.1969
11101	Billy Eckstine	Gentle On My Mind	7.1969
11102	Mary Wells	Vintage Stock	NR
11103	Tammi Terrell	Irresistible	5.1969
11104	The Temptations	Live At The Copa	5.1969
11105	The Fantastic Four	The Fantastic Four	6.1969
11106	Jimmy Ruffin	Ruff 'N' Ready	5.1969
11107	Smokey Robinson & The Miracles	Live	6.1969
11108	The Monitors	Greetings! We're The Monitors	6.1969
11109	The Temptations	Cloud Nine	9.1969

11110	Diana Ross & The Supremes & The Temptations	TCB	7.1969
11111	Marv Johnson	I'll Pick A Rose For My Rose	8.1969
11112	The Isley Brothers	Behind A Painted Smile	9.1969
11113	Four Tops	Four Tops Now	9.1969
11114	Diana Ross & The Supremes	Let The Sunshine In	9.1969
11115	Edwin Starr	25 Miles	9.1969
11116	The Originals	Green Grow The Lilacs	11.1969
11117	Chuck Jackson	Going Back To...	9.1969
11118	David Ruffin	My Whole World Ended	9.1969
11119	Marvin Gaye	MPG	9.1969
11120	Jr Walker & The All Stars	Greatest Hits	11.1969
11121	Various	Motown Chartbusters Vol. 3	11.1969
11122	Diana Ross & the Supremes & The Temptations	Together	2.1970
11123	Marvin Gaye & His Girls (Mary Wells, Kim Weston, Tammi Terrell)	Marvin Gaye And His Girls	1.1970

11124	Various (TML)	In Loving Memory	11.1969
11125	Bobby Taylor	Taylor Made Soul	1.1970
11126	Various	Merry Christmas From Motown	11.1969
11127	Various	Motortown Revue — Live	1.1970
11128	Stevie Wonder	My Cherie Amour	1.1970
11129	Smokey Robinson & The Miracles	Take Some Time Out For...	1.1970
11130	Various	A Collection Of 16 Big Hits Vol. 8	1.1970
11131	Edwin Starr & Blinky	Just We Two	1.1970
11132	Marvin Gaye & Tammi Terrell	Easy	1.1970
11133	The Temptations	Puzzle People	2.1970
11134	Martha Reeves & The Vandellas	Sugar N' Spice	12.1969
11135	Gladys Knight & The Pips	Nitty Gritty	12.1969

Appendix 2: Bestselling Motown Singles

The Top Ten Selling Singles in the UK on the Tamla Motown label.
1   I Just Called To Say I Loved You – Stevie Wonder, 1984
2   Hello – Lionel Richie, 1984
3   Three Times A Lady – Commodores, 1978
4   I Heard It Through The Grapevine – Marvin Gaye, 1969
5   One Day In Your Life – Michael Jackson, 1981
6   Being With You – Smokey Robinson, 1981
7   All Night Long (All Night) – Lionel Richie, 1983
8   Reach Out, I'll Be There – Four Tops, 1966
9   I'm Still Waiting – Diana Ross, 1971
10 The Tears Of A Clown – Smokey Robinson & The Miracles, 1970

With only two entries from the sixties, this makes interesting reading in the context of a book such as this – weighted as it is towards that decade. Perhaps it shows how on-the-money Berry Gordy's decisions were after the move to LA, sales-wise at least. Perhaps it also shows that real 'smash' hits had to be blander and more easily digestible, than some of the label's artistic highpoints from the sixties. Having said that though, there are some great records here!

Appendix 3: Rare Motown Singles

The 25 Most Valuable Motown UK 45 Single Releases
1	The Valadiers I Found A Girl/You'll Be Sorry Someday	(Oriole CBA 1809, 3/63)	£550
2	Mike & The Modifiers I Found Myself A Brand New Baby/It's Too Bad	(Oriole CBA 1775, 10/62)	£450
3	Eddie Holland If It's Love (It's All Right)/It's Not Too Late	(Oriole CBA 1808, 3/63)	£375
4	The Marvelettes Locking Up My Heart/Forever	(Oriole CBA 1817, 4/63)	£275
5	Martha & The Vandellas I'll Have To Let Him Go/My Baby Won't Come Back	(Oriole CBA 1814, 3/63)	£275
6	Eddie Holland Jamie/Take A Chance On Me	(Fontana H 387, 3/62)	£225
7	Barbara McNair You're Gonna Love My Baby/The Touch Of Time	(Tamla Motown TMG 544, 1/66)	£165
8	The Spinners Sweet Thing/How Can I	(Tamla Motown TMG 514, 5/65)	£165
9	The Spinners That's What Little Girls Are Made For/Heebie Geebies	(Columbia DB 4693, ?/61)	£150
10	Barrett Strong Money (That's What I Want)/Oh I Apologise	(London HLU 9088, 4/60)	£150
11	The Miracles What's So Good About Goodbye/I've Been Good To You	(Fontana H 384, 3/62)	£125
12	Paul Gayton The Hunch/Hot Cross Buns	(London HLM 8998, 11/59)	£125
13	Blinky & Edwin Starr Oh How Happy/Ooo Baby Baby	(Withdrawn Demo TMG 720, 11/69)	£120
14	Carolyn Crawford When Someone's Good To You/My Heart	(Stateside SS 384, 2/65)	£100
15	Martha & The Vandellas Come And Get These Memories/Jealous Lover	(Oriole CBA 1819, 4/63)	£100
16	The Velvelettes Lonely Lonely Girl Am I/I'm The Exception To The Rule	(TMG 521, 7/65)	£100
17	Kim Weston I'm Still Loving You/Just Loving You	(Tamla Motown TMG 511, 4/65)	£80
18	Choker Campbell Mickey's Monkey/Pride And Joy	(Tamla Motown TMG 517, 5/65)	£80
19	Smokey Robinson & The Miracles More Love/Come Spy With Me	(Alternate B-side TMG 614, 7/67)	£80
20	The Marvelettes Beechwood 4-5789/Someday Someway	(Oriole CBA 1764, 9/62)	£80
21	The Miracles You've Really Got A Hold On Me/Happy Landing	(Oriole CBA 1795, 1/63)	£80
22	Marv Johnson Come To Me/Whisper	(London HLT 8856, 5/59)	£75
23	Earl Van Dyke Soul Stomp/Hot'N'Tot	(Stateside SS 357, 11/64)	£75
24	Kim Weston A Little More Love/Go Ahead And Laugh	(Stateside SS 359, 11/64)	£75
25	Marvin Gaye Stubborn Kind Of Fellow/It Hurt Me Too	(Oriole CBA 1803, 2/63)	£75

Notes: No 8 The Spinners – Copies showing as by The Detroit Spinners are worth less
No 12 Paul Gayton – This was also out on 78 rpm and is valued at £120
No 9 The Spinners – This record was included on the Record Collector original listing in 1991, but, whilst it was recorded by Harvey Fuqua with

The Spinners, it predates their Motown contracted period. However the track has been included on subsequent Motown retrospective collections by the group.

Generally demo copies of the above would be worth more, but in a few cases as with No 8 The Spinners are actually worth a bit less. It is also interesting to note that the top values have not changed a great deal from a similar listing published in *Record Collector* in Issue 145 from Sept 1991. Remember also that if US issues were included, Frank Wilson's "Do I Love You" would be way in advance of everything.

UK issue EPs and LPs, especially the former, are also extremely collectible, with values comparable to the above.

(priced according to *Record Collector Rare Record Price Guide 2002*)

Appendix 4: Motorcity Fanclub's Top 100 Motown Tracks

In 1997 Mike Critchley's Motown and Motor City Fan Club ran a members poll to vote for their top singles. Look out for your favourite, and take note of the huge commercial hits that simply don't appear here! Girl groups perform extremely well, as do the softer sounding male group tracks. Go Figure! The results show the U.K.'s love of certain lesser known tracks above certain expected ones, and make fascinating reading:

1 The Temptations – My Girl	52 The Temptations – Just My Imagination
2 The Contours – Just A Little Misunderstanding	53 The Miracles – You Really Got A Hold On Me
3 Martha and The Vandellas – Nowhere To Run	54 Marvin Gaye – What's Going On
4 Mary Wells – My Guy	55 The Supremes – Nothing But Heartaches
5 The Isley Brothers – This Old Heart Of Mine	56 The Temptations – Papa Was A Rolling Stone
6 Martha and the Vandellas – Heatwave	57 Martha and The Vandellas – I'm Ready For Love
7 The Marvelettes – Please Mr Postman	58 The Miracles – Shop Around
8 Kim Weston – Helpless	59 The Temptations – The Way You Do The Things You Do
9 The Marvelettes – When You're Young And In Love	60 Gladys Knight and The Pips – Didn't You Know You Have To Cry Sometime
10 The Elgins – Heaven Must Have Sent You	
11 Martha and The Vandellas – Dancing In The Street	61 Jr. Walker and The All Stars – Shotgun
12 The Supremes – Stop In The Name Of Love	62 The Supremes – Up The Ladder To The Roof
13 The Four Tops – I Can't Help Myself	63 Chris Clark – Love's Gone Bad
14 The Velvelettes – Needle In A Haystack	64 The Four Tops – Bernardette
15 The Four Tops – Baby I Need Your Loving	65 Martha and The Vandellas – Quicksand
16 The Supremes – You Can't Hurry Love	66 Martha and The Vandellas – Lovebug Leave My Heart Alone
17 The Supremes – Where Did Our Love Go	67 The Miracles – Ooo Baby Baby
18 Diana Ross – Ain't No Mountain High Enough	68 Barbara Randolph – I Got A Feeling
19 The Supremes – Come See About Me	69 Bobby Taylor and The Vancouvers – Does Your Mama Know About Me
20 Martha and The Vandellas – Jimmy Mack	70 The Marvelettes – The Hunter Gets Captured By The Game
21 The Supremes – Baby Love	71 The Supremes – My World Is Empty Without You
22 The Four Tops – Ask The Lonely	72 The Temptations – Since I Lost My Baby
23 The Supremes – Back In My Arms Again	73 The Marvelettes – Playboy
24 Brenda Holloway – When I'm Gone	74 Diana Ross – Upside Down
25 Kim Weston – Take Me In Your Arms And Rock Me	75 The Supremes – Touch
26 Mary Wells – Two Lovers	76 Marvin Gaye and Tammi Terrell – Your Precious Love
27 Smokey Robinson and The Miracles – The Tracks Of My Tears	77 Smokey Robinson and The Miracles – The Tears Of A Clown
28 The Marvelettes – Don't Mess With Bill	78 The Supremes – Buttered Popcorn
29 The Supremes – When The Lovelight Starts Shining…	79 Jr, Walker and The All Stars – What Does It Take To Win Your Love
30 Jr. Walker and The All Stars – Road Runner	80 The Temptations – Ain't Too Proud To Beg
31 The Contours – Do You Love Me	81 Martha and The Vandellas – My Baby Loves Me
32 The Supremes – Stoned Love	82 The Marvelettes – Too Many Fish In The Sea
33 The Four Tops – Reach Out I'll Be There	83 The Supremes – You Keep Me Hanging On
34 The Supremes – Reflections	84 The Supremes – Love Is Here And Now You're Gone
35 Diana Ross – Remember Me	85 The Four Tops – Standing In The Shadows Of Love
36 The Marvelettes – I'll Keep On Holding On	86 The Temptations – You're My Everything
37 Gladys Knight and The Pips – If I Were Your Woman	87 Edwin Starr – Twenty Five Miles
38 The Supremes – Love Child	88 The Temptations – I Wish It Would Rain
39 Marvin Gaye and Tammi Terrell – Ain't No Mountain High Enough	89 Brenda Holloway – Hurt A Little Every Day
40 Stevie Wonder – Uptight	90 Stevie Wonder – Signed, Sealed, Delivered I'm Yours
41 Brenda Holloway – Every Little Bit Hurts	91 The Marvelettes – My Baby Must Be A Magician
42 The Temptations – Get Ready	92 The Temptations – It's Growing
43 Thelma Houston – Don't Leave Me This Way	93 The Jackson Five – I'll Be There
44 Jimmy Ruffin – What Becomes Of The Broken Hearted	94 Jr. Walker and The Stars – Walk In The Night
45 The Velvelettes – These Things Will Keep Me Loving You	95 Edwin Starr – Stop Her On Sight (NB. Although Motown musicians, not technically Motown)
46 Frank Wilson – Do I Love You	
47 The Supremes – I Hear A Symphony	96 The Marvelettes – Danger Heartbreak Dead Ahead
48 Barbara McNair – You're Gonna Love My Baby	97 The Miracles – My Girl Has Gone
49 Stevie Wonder – A Place In the Sun	98 Martha and The Vandellas – In And Out Of My Life
50 Barrett Strong – Money	99 The Spinners – It's A Shame
51 Marvin Gaye – Can I Get A Witness	100 Smokey Robinson – Being With You

Appendix 6 – The Motown Museum

The famed building of the golden years, now housing the Motown Museum.

When Berry Gordy upped roots and moved his operation to Los Angeles in 1972, he or someone close to him must have realised the historical worth of the Hitsville building at 2648 West Grand Boulevard in Detroit. The empire had begun there, and there was history in the very fabric of the building that was worth preserving. If you visit there today, you will find The Motown Museum under the overall control of Motown old timer Mrs. Esther Edwards. Visitors can see most of the rooms that have been set up to represent the company in its heyday. The original building at 2648 served as company headquarters and as Berry's home, but as things grew the company offices eventually occupied more than seven houses on W. Grand Blvd. Eventually a ten story building at 2457 Woodward Avenue in downtown Detroit would serve as the world-wide company headquarters until the big move in 1972.

The foyer and reception areas have been restored to how they were circa '61/2, with the 1960s cigarette machine (35c a pack!), candy machine (10c) and the infamous time clock. A partitioned area in the lobby once served as Berry Gordy's office, when Diane Ross was his secretary. It later became the main switchboard area.

Berry Gordy's apartment was on the first floor, and still contains the original master bedroom set and orange couch. With the company growth these rooms became taken over for the shipping department, rehearsal spaces and as a working area for Holland/Dozier/Holland in Berry's old bedroom.

The gallery area contains various photographic exhibits, gold records, early album covers, artefacts and memorabilia. There is a hole in the ceiling through which can be seen the echo chamber built into the attic to create reverb in Studio A. The primitive system routed sound out of the studio, through the chamber and back into a live mike.

Downstairs in the control room, there is the upgraded three track recording machine that followed on from the original two track machine that was used for all the earliest hits. The little room that was once Martha Reeves' office when she was an A&R secretary was changed to become the central tape library for master tape recordings, and is now seen in this guise.

Studio A, known as 'The Snakepit', was opened in 1959. It had previously been an old photographic studio, but in its new persona was in use 24 hours a day, 7 days a week until 1972. Today it is seen pretty well as it was left, with all its original equipment and some instruments of the day. Adjacent to the studio are the three isolation rooms that were built when the studio upgraded to eight track capacity. They were used to isolate different instru-

ments, or groups of instruments, to obtain the purest sound possible. Two of the three rooms are visible today. One contains displays of original studio equipment such as a disc cutting machine, a half-inch tape machine and a patch panel. The other is now used as a video room showing a film of the golden days at the building.

Stylish performance outfits made for Brenda Holloway, The Supremes and the Temptations are also on display at various points, together with a white glove and black fedora hat from Michael Jackson. You can also "Shop Around" at a gift shop that sells expected items like videos, CDs, books (maybe one day this one?), clothing, programmes, photos and novelties.

The Motown Museum is obviously a must for any musical tour of the U.S., or any trip that can take in Detroit. We must be thankful that someone had the foresight to save it!

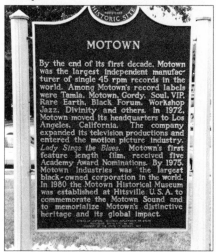

Outside the Museum.

Missing You

So many of the great members of the Motown family are no longer with us. Below is a partial list of those we miss so much.

Benny Benjamin
Florence Ballard
Thomas 'Beans' Bowles
Yvonne Fair
Melvyn Franklin
Marvin Gaye
Ty Hunter
O'Kelly Isley
James Jamerson
Marv Johnson
Eddie Kendricks
Hattie Littles
Shorty Long
Clarence Paul
Laurence Payton
T. Boy Ross
David Ruffin
Tammi Terrell
Georgeanna Tillman
Sandra Tilley
Earl Van Dyke
Junior Walker
Mary Wells
Ronnie White
Paul Williams

R.I.P.

Permissions and acknowledgements

Photo credits

Final Quotes

Berry Gordy – songwriter, talent spotter,
producer, business man.

"We have certain principles and standards of the kind of people that we like to work with. We feel that integrity, respect, loyalty, and just being a good human being is very important." *Berry Gordy*

"People don't realise the personal relationships we have; the same that we had in the ghetto." *Smokey Robinson*

"We came from ghetto areas in Detroit, from basically the same schools. So when Berry organised the company, he had so much talent within the immediate neighbourhood. It was just like a family." *Joe Billingslea of The Contours*

"Everything was very personal. Walking into Motown was like walking into a corner store where you know everybody, instead of walking into a big, cold supermarket. It's like going into a restaurant where the owner works himself. It's personalised." *Diana Ross*

"It was just a bunch of kids together enjoying themselves, like a party. We were getting high off our music." *Mary Wells*

"We called Motown the Motown College. We had the strictest rules, we were very critical and hard on ourselves as writers, producers and entertainers. It was like a school for all these things that have to do with entertainment. You had to be the best. You would work no matter how long it took, you would rehearse and stay at the piano. It was like a campus and it worked." *Lamont Dozier*

"Once a Motowner, always a Motowner." *Smokey Robinson*

"He was a little man with a big dream." *Jackie Wilson on Berry Gordy*

"I earned 367 million dollars in 16 years. I must be doing something right." *Berry Gordy*

About the editor

Kingsley Abbott is a freelance music writer who regularly contributes to *Record Collector*, *Mojo* and other publications. He believes in maintaining breadth in musical taste, and still loves good record shops.

He lives in Norfolk with Elaine, children Rosie and Luke, four cats, and an indeterminate number of visiting young people.

His other books include:
Back To The Beach: A Brian Wilson and The Beach Boys Reader, Helter Skelter, 1997
Fairport Convention: Fairportfolio, SK Productions 1997

U.W.E.L. LEARNING RESOURCES